THE LIVING LIGHT DIALOGUE

Volume 9

THE LIVING LIGHT DIALOGUE

Volume 9

Through the mediumship of
Richard P. Goodwin

Living Light Books

The Living Light Dialogue Volume 9
Copyright © 2017 Serenity Association

Through the mediumship of Richard P. Goodwin.

All rights reserved. Printed in the United States of America. No portion of this book may be reproduced—electronically, mechanically, or via internet transmission—without advance, express written permission of the publisher except in the case of brief quotations embodied in critical articles and reviews. No derivative work—games supplemental material, video—may be created without advance, express written permission of the publisher. For information address Living Light Books, P.O. Box 4187, San Rafael, CA 94913-4187.

Cover design copyright © 2017 by Serenity Association

Cover photograph by Serenity Association, 2017; copyright © 2017 by Serenity Association.

www.livinglight.org

Library of Congress Control Number 2007929762

FIRST EDITION

This volume of teachings is dedicated to the spirit friends who brought to Earth the Living Light philosophy. With eternal gratitude, we pray that we may demonstrate these principles and continue to bring to publication these teachings.

CONTENTS

Acknowledgement xi
Preface xiii
Introduction xvii
CL 1 - Our Spiritual Responsibility 3
CL 2 - The Freedom of Faith 9
CL 3 - Morals and Natural Law 14
CL 4 - The Vital Force of Psychic Phenomena 21
CL 5 - Levels of Awareness 27
CL 6 - Divinity and Direction 34
CL 7 - The Love of Living 38
CL 8 - The Living Demonstration 42
CL 9 - The Living Dead 47
CL 10 - Inner Levels and Outer Limits 52
CL 11 - Evolutionary Incarnation 57
CL 12 - The Meaning of Salvation 62
CL 13 - The Web of Destiny 66
CL 14 - Man's Only Suffering is His Denial of God 69
CL 15 - Man, The Universe 75
CL 16 - Attention and Energy 78
CL 17 - The Wisdom of Tolerance 82
CL 18 - The 125th Anniversary of Modern Spiritualism . . 86
CL 19 - Genuine Mediumship 91
CL 20 - Growing in the Light 97
CL 21 - Psychic Common Sense 100
CL 22 - Man's Magnetic Field 104
CL 23 - Expanding Consciousness 108
CL 24 - Class Excerpts 111
CL 25 - Acceptance, the Divine Will 119
CL 26 - The Journey of the Soul 123

CL 27 - Adventures in Consciousness 128
CL 28 - New Horizons. 132
CL 29 - Respect—The Law of Consideration. 135
CL 30 - The 126th Anniversary of Modern Spiritualism . . 138
CL 31 - Value—Man's True Mirror. 143
CL 32 - Third Anniversary—Serenity Church. 146
CL 33 - Man's Spiritual Search. 150
CL 34 - Mediums and Their Message 154
CL 35 - Leadership and Responsibility. 160
CL 36 - Psychometry (Aura Sensing). 166
CL 37 - Magnetism—The Invisible Power 172
CL 38 - Justice and The Law 177
CL 39 - Self-Control—The Philosophy of Spiritualism . . . 183
CL 40 - Experience, The Mirror of Motive 187
CL 41 - Application—The Law of Supply. 193
CL 42 - Self-Will, The Wheel of Illusion 196
CL 43 - The Love of Living 201
CL 44 - Fourth Anniversary—Serenity Church 207
CL 45 - Destiny—A Spiritual View. 211
CL 46 - Patience—Pain and Pleasure 216
CL 47 - Spirit Lands and Spirit Bands 220
CL 48 - Sailing the Ship of Destiny. 226
CL 49 - The Fountain of Youth 230
CL 50 - The Way We Are 235
CL 51 - Beginning Anew 240
CL 52 - Forgiving, The Path of Freedom. 247
CL 53 - When It Means Enough 254
CL 54 - Our Brother's Keeper 256
CL 55 - The Fifth Anniversary of Serenity 261
CL 56 - Plants, Animals, and People 267
CL 57 - Accepting Our Birthright 273
CL 58 - Dynamic Perspectives 277
CL 59 - Review and Renewal 282
CL 60 - The Lessons of Life. 289

CONTENTS

CL 61 - The Fullness of Life 293
CL 62 - The Awakened Soul 296
CL 63 - Harmony, The Law of Health 300
CL 64 - Promise, The Destiny of Life 304
CL 65 - Six Years of Serenity 309
CL 66 - Inspiration 314
CL 67 - Man's Law 321
CL 68 - The Fullness of Life 326
CL 69 - Harmony, The Law of Health 329
CL 70 - Life's Purpose. 334
CL 71 - The Joy of Teaching 343
CL 72 - The Source 350
CL 73 - New Experiences and New Attitudes 353
CL 74 - The Continuity of Change 359
CL 75 - Our Changing Attachments 364
CL 76 - Attaining Universal Consciousness 369
CL 77 - Seven Years of Serenity 376
CL 78 - Our Invisible Friends. 384
CL 79 - The Power of Acceptance. 392
CL 80 - Survival, The Miracle of Life 396
CL 81 - New Attitudes and New Experiences 405
Special Memorial Service 410
Special Discourse 1—Soul to Soul 416
Appendix. 425

ACKNOWLEDGMENT

Grateful acknowledgement is made to the many friends and associates for invaluable aid in compiling this book, for their helpful suggestions, for their loyal interest and encouragement.

Special acknowledgement is due to those who painstakingly and selflessly transcribed and proofread the text.

PREFACE

It was through the mediumship of the Serenity Association founder, Mr. Richard P. Goodwin, that a philosophy known as the Living Light was given in more than 700 classes over a twenty-five-year period.

To be specific, the philosophy was imparted through Mr. Goodwin by a magistrate who had lived on Earth some 8,000 years ago. The former magistrate is known to Living Light students as "the Wise One," and he narrated the journey of his soul on the other side of life, the experiences—especially the difficulties—he encountered in having to face himself, as well as the teachings he earned to help himself through the realms in which he traveled. It was his decision to share the teachings with souls on both sides of "the curtain."

Prior to the advent of the Wise One, Mr. Goodwin had prayed for a teacher from the realms of light. Mr. Goodwin, since age fourteen, had been the instrument through which spirit was able to communicate with those seeking help. But he saw that his mediumship brought only temporary solace, because the people he was trying to help soon became fascinated with the phenomena and ignored the help that spirit was imparting. He prayed for someone who would bring forth teachings that would benefit any soul seeking a path to a greater awareness of himself and of God.

His prayers were answered in 1964 when the Wise One came through for the first time. Mr. Goodwin, at first apprehensive about what this new teacher would impart, was taken into deep trance and not able to control what was being revealed through him. Upon hearing the recorded classes afterward, however, he became convinced of the goodness of the teacher and of the value of the simple, beautiful teachings. This, then, was the beginning of the Living Light philosophy given to Earth through the mediumship of Richard P. Goodwin.

In carrying out the request of the Wise One and Mr. Goodwin, students of the Serenity Association transcribed from audiotape the classes that had been brought through. Because most are in the form of teacher-student interaction, the classes became known as *The Living Light Dialogue*; and the students were instructed to publish the classes as a multi-volume set of the Living Light philosophy. *Volume 1* was published in the autumn of 2007.

The present book, *Volume 9,* begins the Church Lectures series of classes, which were delivered by Mr. Goodwin on the first Sunday of the month during the devotional services of the Serenity Spiritualist Church. *Volume 9* includes the lectures from CL 1 through CL 81, as well as the lectures entitled, the "Special Memorial Service" and "Soul to Soul," covering the time period of August 7, 1971, through September 3, 1978.

The foundation of the classes—the foundation of the Living Light philosophy itself—is the Law of Personal Responsibility which states, in part, that we are responsible for all our experiences, and that our experiences are the return of the laws that we have established with our thoughts, acts, and deeds. Through greater awareness of our thoughts and by exercising our divine right of choice, we may choose to establish laws of greater harmony and goodness.

The Living Light Dialogue teaches that we have come to Earth to learn the lessons that are necessary to free us from the dictates and limits of our own thoughts and judgments, which are the mental patterns that we follow through our own lack of awareness and are so very potent, forceful, and limiting. These teachings guide us in making the necessary changes in our thinking in order to free ourselves from those patterns and to express our soul consciousness.

The choice of guiding the direction of our life, as stated by the Wise One when he speaks of being with a person, place, or thing, is, in essence, of being in this world and not a part of this world. He further explains that no matter what experiences we encounter, no matter what we do or do not do, we—our spirit—may view the experience in objectivity from a soul level of consciousness where peace reigns supreme.

The teachings of this volume help us to restore harmony or balance in our life by flooding the consciousness with spiritual affirmations and prayers, a few of which can be found in the appendix. When reason is restored, by balancing our sense functions with our soul faculties, we will consciously experience peace. Without annihilating our ego or our sense functions, we will find a pathway of expression for our soul. Where there was once disturbance, now there is acceptance. Where there was disease, now there is poise. And where there was hopelessness and despair, now there is reason, divine neutrality; and peace shows the way.

If you make the effort to apply these laws, such as, "If man is a law unto himself, what are you doing with the law that you are?", and demonstrate the wisdom of patience, the truth of this philosophy will be your living demonstration.

As the teacher states in CC 130, "My journey of many centuries and much experience has brought me here to Earth to share with you these simple teachings that have come as the effect of a long, long, long journey. Let not *your* journey be so long in the realms of illusion. For it is not necessary for you. For in your evolution, you have earned an awakening. But it is up to you to do something that is constructive and worthwhile."

INTRODUCTION

[This introduction was written by Mr. Goodwin and originally appeared in *The Living Light*, which were the first teachings of the Living Light Philosophy published in book form. The entire text of *The Living Light* was republished in *The Living Light Dialogue*, Volume 1.]

> "Think, children. Think more often
> and think more deeply."

The teachings in this book were given as a progressive series of lessons to a group of four students who were sitting for spiritual unfoldment with me beginning in January of 1964. The communications were regular until October of that year, when nearly a seven-year silence ensued, and resumed in 1971 to the present. They were received in three ways by me as a channel. The main text was taped from a direct control of my voice in deep trance at special sittings of our group, during which I had no experience of the voice or what was being transmitted. A few scattered verses were given independently when I was privileged to see and hear our teacher clairvoyantly. I have also been a channel for this communicant when speaking from the podium at church and in answering difficult questions at our public seminars.

Nearly all we know about our teacher is contained in the lectures. He reports that he had tried for sixteen years to break through an interference barrier that the channel had to deep trance. When our conditions were in resonance with his patient wisdom, he came through ready to teach his understanding. I have seen him as an old man dressed in white with long flowing white hair. He has blue eyes, slightly smiling and deeply compassionate. I have always called him the Old Man. The students liked to call him the Wise One. He is surely one of those often called a Teacher of Light. I do not know his country, although he indicated at one time that he was from 6000 B.C., and a form of a judge in his time.

The text is often difficult, but it is complete, having been transcribed word for word from the original tapes recording the trance voice. It is presented with a minimum of punctuation to be freer for the individual interpretation of each reader. The lessons given before the long silence are phrased with many allegories often paradoxical. There are repetitions and renewals of theme, but it is explained that if an understanding is not perceived, compassion dictates that it be said again. Some of the topics have but a simple mention with little development but all are revealed, we are told, according to merit.

The Old Man is a fine teacher. He has in a hundred ways intertwined his allegory, progressive explanations, unfolding exercises, and timely references to reach a multitude of levels of individual understanding. A notable change is his more direct style of presentation beginning in 1971.

There is an endearing intimacy of person that can be felt through his lectures, a meaningful and loving encounter with a wise friend. Like an old man, he makes a mistake and conscientiously corrects himself a few paragraphs later. He listens often and carefully to our earnest discussions of his words. He consults with a group of experts on evolution and cites their learning in his lesson. His use of the direct address "children" or "my children" is not patronizing but infinitely loving and supportive.

A word must be said about the teachings. The Old Man makes clear that his lessons are not dogma, a creed or a narrow way, but simply his own understanding offered to us as a form of instruction to aid us in our own individual progression. When he speaks of Laws, he does not refer to man-made rules or moral traditions but to the cosmic and atomic way-things-are, the natural world of what-is, the universal laws of life, part of the original creative design and through which creation is fulfilled. These laws are beyond the possibility of being changed, suspended, transcended, or destroyed but they are ever a tool of mankind, not his master. First, through our awareness of the universal laws and then slowly through our developed understanding, the powers of creation are accessible to us. Not power over men's minds or circumstances, but power over whatever is selfish and imperfect in ourselves is the way up the eternal ladder of progression. When the Old Man cautions us concerning the Law of Responsibility or gives us a thinking exercise to explore the Law of Identity in a dynamic manner, he prepares us to take another step. And all move in accordance with the Law of What Can Be Borne.

Our teacher shows us how the two worlds are drawn together. In his realm, he describes, there is a great diversity of thought, many schools of understanding; but the Light is always known by the Light. Because of the interdependence of the two realms, listening to our discussions helped to clarify his teaching to others on his side of the curtain. His love and gratitude he humbly equates with ours.

The lessons to be perceived are not new, they are very old, but they are new to certain levels of our being. I would personally advise the reader, after reading this volume of discourses in full, to make a daily habit (or when there is a feeling or need) to sit quietly with the book. Open it at random and be guided to the Light by the passage that is there for the day. This technique is still used by the original students who were given the lessons and by many students after them who have studied in unfolding classes with me through these teachings.

Go beyond the words into feeling, into the immediate meanings for you. Touch into the inspiration that flows into the form of this book. It is from the Divine.

RICHARD P. GOODWIN
San Geronimo, California
June, 1972

CHURCH LECTURES

Church Lecture 1

Our Spiritual Responsibility

The topic that was chosen by the spirit world for this morning's discussion, as our chairman said, is "Our Spiritual Responsibility."

Most of us are aware that we are more than a material substance, that we are composed of atoms, electrons, and molecules, that we are mental, and that we are spirit. We are existing in three dimensions here and now at this very moment. And it is our duty and our responsibility to ourselves, to the Divine that is our only life, to become awakened and aware of these dimensions as a personal demonstration unto ourselves, not only of this eternal life, but of our responsibility to it. We cannot sense responsibility unless we are aware of that that we are responsible to. Therefore, the first step begins in awakening the faculties of our soul that are within us at this moment.

We find in this physical, material world that most of humanity is yet asleep in the cradle of creation. And by that I mean that they are not personally aware, as a personal demonstration to themselves, of these three dimensions in which they are existing.

It has been said that life is but a school, and in schools we learn lessons. And be rest assured, my friends, lessons received in a particular dimension can only be fulfilled in that dimension. We know that dimensions fill the universes and that they are not necessarily places or things.

At the moment of our soul's incarnation into form we were aware of these dimensions, but through education to a mundane, physical world, this awareness gradually, but surely, has been dimmed. Because the child is so often ridiculed for the seeming fantasies that it seems to be experiencing, this Divine Light is clouded over. Therefore, it is our responsibility to reeducate the mind to the truth that is within us. We are inseparably united, through this Divine Love, to all things, at all times, and in all places. For the only thing that sustains us, known as Spirit or God, is everywhere present and never absent or away.

We are indeed our brother's keeper and we are indeed responsible for all creation to the degree that we are aware of that responsibility. In clarifying that last statement, I wish to say that regardless of our thoughts, our acts, and our deeds, we will not escape the purpose of our life. It is and does behoove us to fulfill that purpose here and now rather than to be drawn back to this earth realm to hover and to try to fulfill what we had merited, but did not apply.

It is a known truth in this movement that many spirit people, those who have once lived in this physical clay, are magnetically drawn back to this earth realm to complete the work that they were given to do, according to the laws of merit, but did not do. There are many, many reasons for so-called earth-bound spirits. There are those who are attracted to this realm through their emotional attachments. And there are those who cannot escape this realm because they have not fulfilled the purpose of why their soul was incarnated upon it. And until such time as they do fulfill that purpose, they shall hover in these realms and, in time, gravitate to the higher ones.

I have heard it said at times that those who study Spiritualism and have had some of its class work and understanding will automatically gravitate to a so-called fifth sphere. I assure you, my good friends, if you studied seven days a week for a thousand years and you did not apply the divine laws, there will be no fifth sphere awaiting any of us. It is not what you put into the mind that is so important. It is what you do to change what is already there. And that is not easily done for it takes effort and it is so difficult for us to break the patterns that we have placed ourselves in.

We are born. We are spirit and that spirit is whole, complete, and perfect. But it does not shine with its greatest illumination in a mind that is contradictory and filled with indecision. When we make the daily effort to become aware of ourselves, to go within and find out what it is that sends us forth into so many difficulties and pitfalls, and when we balance our spiritual faculties with the functions of this sense body, then, my friends, and only then shall we be free and shall we know the peace and the joy and the bliss that passeth all understanding.

There is no set way to the so-called ultimate or the Divine, for creation by its very laws of duality guarantees the variety of form. Therefore, there is no philosophy, there is no religion, and there is no set way that will work for everyone at any given time. It is true in evolution—and that is what this world is all about, this world of form—that in time we will all find the way, but there is no particular way for everyone at any one time.

There has been many words written and many words spoken concerning the world of spirit and concerning its various planes and spheres. I wish to state at this time that these planes and these spheres are not something outside of you. They are something within us. They are states of consciousness or awareness. And it is true that we at one time may have gravitated in our consciousness to the third, the fourth, or even the fifth sphere. And at other times we're down in the second or third. That, my good friends, is wherever we are in thought and in motive.

It is the motive that is the germ, that is the seed, that produces the tree and all the effects. A person may say, "I try to do good and all that comes to me is seeming grief and disaster." Then I can only say to that friend, you must go within and find from what level of consciousness that your motive has received its birth. Is your motive a seed from your faculties of being, your soul's expression? Or is your motive given birth in the functions and sense world of creation?

And I assure you if you will look sincerely and honestly within, you will find the cause of all things at all times. For nothing, my good friends, can ever happen to us that is not caused by us. There is no power outside of ourselves that gives us wealth or health, but it is the power that is within us. And therefore, it is our responsibility to awaken to that great, neutral, Divine Love and so express it in our lives.

Thank you.

I said at the opening of this little talk that on the first Sunday of each month we do open the forum to your questions and answers. And to the very best of my ability, I am always grateful whenever I can serve the Spirit. And I will give to you whatever answers are given to me. So if you would just be so kind to please raise your hand, if you have any questions of a spiritual nature, please feel free to speak them. Yes.

Do we all have guides and teachers even though we are not aware of them?

The question is, Do we all have guides and teachers, though we may not be aware of them? It is my understanding over these past thirty-one years, from seeing many people, that everyone has guides and teachers. What level of consciousness or awareness those guides or teachers are on will ever be in harmony with the true spiritual motive of the individual. Thank you.

[*After a short pause, the Teacher continues.*] If you'll just raise your hand. Remember, your question may seem not so important, you think, to others, but if it's important to entertain your thought, then it is important to you. Yes.

If the man in A Wanderer in the Spirit Lands *did not have a place to go, how was it that he found hell and heaven and different spheres?*

The question is, in reference to the book entitled *A Wanderer in the Spirit Lands* by Franchezzo, that if he had no place to go, then how is it that he found various spheres of heaven and hell? Is that your question?

Yes, in . . . [inaudible]

In reference to the lecture this morning—

Heaven within.

Yes. Man experiences ever outside of himself whatever is inside of himself according to the law that like attracts like and becomes the Law of Attachment. Prior to the experiencing of a so-called particular sphere or plane of heaven or its opposite, the particular individual would have to have had gravitated in consciousness to that particular dimension. Once having gravitated to the dimension within himself, he or she would experience its effect outside of themselves. It is ever in harmony and in accord with the law that like attracts like and becomes the Law of Attachment.

And that is why it is a known fact in spiritual communication that there are a multitude of churches in the world of spirit with various denominations and philosophies and teachings. For those who have their need, that's just as long as they will exist. And when the need for them is no longer present, they will disintegrate back to their source. Thank you. Yes.

In respect to unfoldment, I know many students practice unfoldment of a spiritual nature. Can you tell us a little bit about the activities from this point of view: some people study unfoldment and perhaps the condition that they are experiencing isn't beneficial to that unfoldment at this time.

Yes. You wish me to speak on the unfoldment processes?

In respect to individuals, perhaps it didn't happen now or next year.

Yes.

Perhaps spirit is waiting for the right moment to . . .

That's a very good question. And I will be most happy to be the channel to speak on that, whatever is given to me, because it is very important to all of us. And the statement and question was, that there are, seemingly, students who do unfold and do not receive particular beneficial results. Is this your statement?

Of a spiritual nature.

Of a spiritual nature. And the question therefore arises in the mind, Then of course what benefit is spiritual unfoldment, if working and striving to unfold these faculties reaps us not a beneficial effect? Well, my good friends, we're all on various rungs of the ladder of eternal progression. And there are no two flowers identical, even though, like these beautiful flowers this morning—they may be called chrysanthemums—I assure you that there are no two of them, and there are no two petals upon them, that are identical. Therefore, in this unfoldment process it is true, as the Good Book says, that many are called and few are chosen. Because everyone that is called at any particular given time is not necessarily ready. Consequently, they have not yet gravitated to a spiritual motive and purpose for unfoldment. And therefore they would not receive a beneficial effect, but they would receive from the level that they have gravitated to.

This is the great danger of psychic unfoldment. If the psychic awareness or communication with these various dimensions, if it comes prior to the opening of the soul faculties, then it is indeed seemingly most unbeneficial because the awakening and opening of the psychic sense exposes us to what is termed the astral world and the mental world, the mass thinking of the world. And those things, my good friends, are not particularly pleasant.

And this is why you will find that Spiritualism never has or does it recommend these various crutches for unfoldment, such as Ouija boards and crystal balls and tarot cards. Any time an individual depends upon anything exterior to themselves for spiritual unfoldment, they are becoming dependent cripples to the thing that they are depending upon. Remember that nature and creation is designed to be a tool of man and never his master. Therefore, in unfoldment do not rely upon anything outside of the Divine within you, for the Divine within you will impress you and guide you to whatever you may or may not need for study and for application.

It isn't just the studying, my friends. That's not the difficulty. It's the application. We can read a thousand times a thousand books and if we do not apply what they are speaking, then it is of no value and no use to us. When this day of electronics, with the electronic companies producing these so-called bioscopes and all these electronic gadgets for so-called meditation and awareness, when we depend upon devices, we shall become ruled by devices not only in this physical, material world, but in the invisible worlds of spirit.

So whatever you do or take with you this day, take with you the thought that you are whole, complete, and perfect and strive by going into the silence to find that great perfection and neutrality. Thank you.

AUGUST 7, 1971

Church Lecture 2

The Freedom of Faith

Some time ago the spirit teacher chose for his topic for this morning, "The Freedom of Faith."

I know that we all have various thoughts of what faith means, but I am sure that we are all in accord of what freedom means. For freedom to us is to be without bondage, to feel the expression of the Divinity within us. Now faith is usually associated with some particular religious sect or philosophy, but in the way we are presenting it in this short talk, it means to us a conviction, a conviction beyond a shadow of any doubt.

When we become receptive to this free spirit that is within us, this great conviction becomes the predominant factor in our minds. And so it is that we present this topic, "The Freedom of Faith." For when we become receptive to this free spirit we are convinced in all our acts and activities, in all our thoughts and endeavors, that there is a Divine power within us that is guiding, controlling, and forming all things for the greater good of ourselves and all creation. We are beset day-to-day in our workaday world with many obstructions, with many negative experiences. We are beset with those things because that is what our mind is convinced of. And being so convinced our paths are filled with many obstacles and with many obstructions.

Spiritualism in its efforts to bring this light to humanity has for many, many years been gravely misunderstood. It is misunderstood because those who have visited it have not spent the time and the effort to thoroughly study it and then to apply. If they will do that, they will find the greatest faith that they have ever known. It doesn't matter what you call it; it only matters that it works here and now.

We have spoken before that this life-giving energy that flows through us and all creation; that it goes, under our direction, through the power of attention or thought. And so it is, my good friends, whatever your attention is upon that and that alone is what you are creating. For we are indeed creators and we have choice. That is what we were born with. That is our birthright. We may choose to place our attention upon the things we desire to overcome and not upon the things we wish to become, and so be deluded and discouraged at our expression in this old, material and mental world. But the choice is ever up to us. For every experience that we encounter comes to us along the magnetic lines of attraction. Therefore, look wisely at your experiences for they are the reflections, the effects of what our mind is emanating. I know that it is ofttimes difficult to realize and to accept that all of our experiences we have willed into action, but, my good friends, it is indeed a subtle, but demonstrable, law of nature.

The teachings of Spiritualism are very clear: like attracts like and becomes the Law of Attachment. And if we will make the effort in these day-to-day activities to pause before we react, then we will not lose this divine power, we will not give it away to the obstruction. But we will gravitate in that moment of silence to our faculty of reason—the only faculty of our soul that has the power to transfigure us.

The Good Book states be renewed, be transformed by the renewing of your mind. If we will not make the effort to guard our thoughts—and we know that most of us are not even aware of our thoughts—if we will not make those efforts, my good friends, we cannot and we will not change our lives. I know that everyone within the sound of my voice desires to make various changes within their lives, changes for the better. But the desire, my friends, must rise within your consciousness to your faculty of reason. There, that great light of truth will cast over the dark shadows of ignorance and superstition, and you will be so inspired to make the necessary changes within your thoughts to transform your lives.

And when you keep faith or conviction with this reasoning faculty that is within each and every human being, when we do that, we shall find this great freedom. The choice is ever up to ourselves: to either wander in the chains of bondage and the darkness of ignorance and superstition or to go to that faculty of reason and be free.

There is no religion, no philosophy that will give to you that which you are not willing, ready, and able to accept. The Divine Light of Truth flows through all religions in all times. But man has presented it in different ways in different ages in his attempt to understand the Divine neutrality, the Divine love, the Divine indifference.

God we understand to be this Divine wisdom, this Divine love, this Infinite Intelligence. But it cannot express itself in our lives unless we are willing to educate this so-called king brain, this house of the senses, to the realization that there is a divine wisdom that guides the ship of all creation. Learn to be free, my friends, free from the prison house that we have permitted our mind to place us in.

Things have power over us only because we have given power to those things. Our thoughts are our lives and we have that freedom of choice to stay in the slavery or to free ourselves from the self-imposed bondage that ignorance has placed us in.

Faith and conviction, which in truth is faith, must so permeate our conscious and subconscious mind that they are in perfect accord, harmony, and balance, that the divine superconscious, the channel of this great Neutrality, may move through our being and so adjust our lives that we know this great peace, this great happiness, this joy, this love.

Pause each moment. Stop and think. Spiritualism strives to get humanity to think for themselves. It offers no dogma and it offers no creed. It has no book of authority, but it has the divine authority within each and every human being. Whatever you choose, choose wisely. You choose the food you eat, at least to some extent. We choose the clothes we wear, the cars we buy, and the places where we live. But how many of us spend those moments in the course of a day to choose our thoughts. And our thoughts, my friends, are the building blocks that place us on the great Mountain of Aspiration or build the penitentiary in which someday we find ourselves.

We are strongest while we are yet here in the flesh. This is the time to awaken to the truth that is within us. Spiritualism is a religion of daily application for it is a religion of self-culture. It knows beyond a shadow of any doubt and offers to humanity the way to know that eternity is here this moment. There is no heaven or hell that awaits us. It is only a state of consciousness in which we are this moment. Therefore, my friends, free yourselves through faith, through conviction. Learn to be constructive with those blocks you are building. Study and apply. There's time for all the other things that the senses seem to need. Give a few moments to the faculties of your soul.

So many people think that we're going to leave this old, physical body and we're going to be in a beautiful world of spirit where there's only peace and love and joy and harmony. Heaven and hell and purgatory, they are states of consciousness. We are in them this moment. And when the piece of clay goes back to Mother Nature from whence it came, we will find ourselves looking across the land in another dimension and there will be all our own creations and those of like kind, those of like thought. So unless you have found this heaven now, this moment, don't look for it tomorrow. It won't be there. No, not until you make it yours now. For that is the heaven on earth that so many seem to hope for and yet so few seem to strive for.

Thank you.

You are now free to ask whatever questions that you have of a spiritual nature. And I know that there are those amongst you who may not understand or agree with what we have to teach, but we're more than happy to share and exchange our thoughts with you. So would you kindly raise your hands if you have any questions at this time. The gentleman in the back, please.

Yes, I'd like you to give me clarification on the will of man versus the will of God. I get confused.

Yes.

Our own will fighting with the will of God.

Thank you. The question is a clarification on the will of God or the Divine and the will of self or man. Spiritualism understands and teaches that man not only has functions, operating through the mind, but that man is a spirit and has what is known as soul faculties. The teachings of Spiritualism are not to annihilate your functions, but to bring them in to balance with your soul faculties. For when the soul faculties are in perfect balance and harmony with the sense functions, this permits the divine Infinite Intelligence to flow unobstructed through your life and therefore express its great freedom.

We find the divine will in our soul faculties, not in our sense functions. We must understand that in the expression of the functions there are times when it is the expression of divine will. There are times when it is not. But each and every one of us has a conscience, and our conscience is a spiritual sensibility with a dual capacity. It knows right from wrong; it does not have to be told. Therefore, when we are guided by our conscience, whether it is expressing through the functions or faculties, we can be assured that it is the will of a higher nature, call it the Divine, whatever you wish, that is expressing through our lives. There is no one outside yourself [who] can tell you when you're expressing the Divinity within you or when you're expressing these functions of creation. But your conscience will tell you in all your acts and activities. Does that help with your question?

Thank you.

You're welcome. We have a few moments left, if there are any other questions. [*After a short pause, the Teacher continues.*] Did the gentleman in the back row have a question or was it private?

[The person's response is inaudible.]

Being no more questions and the hour is passing late, I thank you all for your kind attention. Thank you.

SEPTEMBER 5, 1971

Church Lecture 3

Morals and Natural Law

The first Sunday of each month has been traditionally set aside for a short talk and questions and answers. It has always been a policy of mine not to expect from another what I am not first willing to do myself. And I do try to stay with that policy as I have asked all of my students, "Please, for your own spiritual growth, do not rely upon notes for they are crutches." And that that we rely upon we become dependent upon.

And in this religion of Spiritualism we are trying to help those who are trying to help themselves to find the one and only power that is within, known by Spiritualists as Spirit, known by others as God. It's the one Infinite Intelligence. And that is the thing that we try to demonstrate, to teach, and to rely upon. Therefore, when a lecture is given to me by my spirit teachers, I receive the title. I do not know from that what they will speak about. But if I am able to be receptive to them—and the title chosen this morning is, "Morals and Natural Law."

We understand from the principles of Spiritualism the statement that the highest morality is contained in the Golden Rule: To do unto others as ye would that others should do unto you. We would like to go just a step further with that statement in our understanding. Morals are considered to be that awareness of what is right and wrong in accordance with one's duty.

We know that our conscience is a spiritual sensibility with a dual capacity. And that dual capacity is right from wrong. In a world of form and variety people have varied awareness of this conscience, this spirit that is within, and therefore, their understanding of what is right or wrong may or may not agree with ours. Usually, it does not. That that we desire for ourselves we must be willing to permit another to desire the same for themselves. So if it be our desire to go beyond liberty and law—and natural law is what I am speaking of—into what is termed license, then we must be willing and ready to accept that in another when it comes back to us. For whatever we choose to express as our right or wrong, by the very natural law that what goes out shall return, we guarantee the experience to befall us. And this is what I mean by morals and natural law.

We have choice and we are free to do what we consider right or wrong to the degree of our awareness and understanding, but we can be rest assured, my good friends, whatever it is that we do or are doing, it shall return to us, for that is the law of the universe.

The tendency of the human mind is to constantly go out and see the effect of things as a cause. But in Spiritualism we learn, step by step, that each and every experience that we encounter we have set into motion; it is a subtle law.

Live, my friends, and let live is the keynote of truth. For when we judge another we guarantee that very judgment to befall us. For we are not the judges. We are the witnesses of our own experiences. It is so easy to see the sawdust in another's eye for we are blinded by the plank that is in our own. And I have said so very many times that energy, your vital life force, follows attention. And if our attention is constantly upon another, seeing the weaknesses instead of the strengths, then we can be rest assured those weaknesses we see in another shall befall us. For as an old saying goes, it takes one to know one. It takes a weakness within ourselves to recognize a weakness in another.

Therefore, for our own salvation let us go within ourselves and let us ask that this light within us may be awakened. Let us concern ourselves with the work that we have to do and let the others do theirs. You cannot, my good friends, live for another, you cannot breathe for another, you cannot think for another, but you can breathe and you can think and you can live for yourselves. And when you garner up these thoughts, these multitude of thoughts that swim in the gray matter of the mind, and you concentrate them upon the fulfillment of your soul's purpose in form, then you shall fulfill the purpose of being. You shall find a great freedom and a great peace.

The mind tends to look about and to constantly criticize and even to condemn, but, my good friends, those experiences outside are the mirrors. They are reflecting back your state of growth. If we do not open our faculties of being there will be no spirit world to enter, but we all, by the laws of nature of having a mind, will enter the mental worlds. For it is through the faculties of being that we are awakened and garner up the spiritual substance necessary to create a form from spirit and, therefore, express in a spiritual body.

Who is so illumined to judge the world? To judge the things around and about them? Who is the Christ incarnate? Yea, he didn't even judge the ones who crucified him for he knew the law: to forgive is to free.

Our understanding of morals is constantly changing because we are looking at morals from a traditional point of view. We are looking at them as what we have been taught and educated to, of the virtuous and the so-called right and wrong, but I tell you that right and wrong is known by your soul. And your conscience will dictate to you as an individualized soul what is right and wrong for you. There are many religions and many philosophies that teach many things and many different paths. And I know in my heart that they are serving those who support them, for our beliefs support us, as long as we support our beliefs.

The actions of today and the so-called morals are not what they were in the Victorian era. They're constantly changing as the soul within our youth today is seeking to break from the bondages of tradition to find themselves. That, my good people, is their inherent right. And it is no one's right to deny them the path that they are choosing to find themselves. Whatever their so-called morals may or may not be, the natural, demonstrable laws of nature will reap her harvest. Vengeance is never ours. As the Good Book says, "Vengeance is mine . . . saith the Lord." It does not belong to man, but it does belong to the law. For those who transgress natural, divine laws shall suffer the consequences of those transgressions without man dictating what those transgressions and effects are to be.

It is our purpose to reveal to mankind these demonstrable spiritual, mental, and physical laws. And we can go to that one, great statement: whatever goes forth from you is guaranteed to return to you. No one can transgress that natural law. So whatever your experiences, whatever your effects, do not seek the answer outside of yourselves, because the truth does not lie there, my friends. The truth lies within you, and your spirit knows; it does not have to be told by your mind or by the mind of another.

I am so grateful to live in this day and age because I am privileged, I feel to some extent, to have revealed from these realms of spirit the great, golden age that was prophesied to enter this world in the '70s. I see around and about me the greatest spiritual renaissance the world has ever known taking place. And you, too, can see that if you will look through another dimension of thinking that is within yourselves.

The prophets of doom have ever been amongst us. And it seems the easiest path [is] to be a pessimist, to be negative, but it takes equal energy, my good people, to be optimistic. A pessimist never sent the rocket to the moon, nor did he ever invent anything worthwhile. Learn to be optimistic, learn to express the positive within you. Each moment, each day we're expressing the level of our faith. Some of us have a little faith and some of us have a little bit more. But stop and think. When we're speaking, that is revealing the degree of faith that we have unfolded.

If I had listened three years ago to the prophets of doom, there would be no spiritual retreat in the mountains of Mendocino. And again, if I had permitted my senses to listen to the prophets of doom, there would not be this day, nor this church. But I have faith in that great, divine Love that permeates all things at all times. And if we are making the effort to serve it, it will serve us.

My God is not a small God. And I pray that each day this God will get greater and greater and greater. Because it will ever be as great as you open up your minds to receive it. Therefore, who shall we be to question the morals of another, the morals of a community, the morals of a world. When we go within ourselves and we question ourselves, then the greater light will shine through us. And truth, my good friends, is taught through indirection, demonstration, and example. Let us, therefore, be concerned with what we are doing and not concerned with what everyone else in this world is doing. Because if we're doing our part, like attracts like and becomes the Law of Attachment. We will become attached to that that is right for us. We need not be concerned with that law.

Thank you.

As I said at the opening of this little talk that you are free, the first Sunday of each month, [to ask questions. So if,] at this time, you raise your hand, I will be happy to serve the Spirit in that respect. Yes.

You said that sometimes when you leave the body and you don't go on to the spiritual realms, but to the mental realms?

The question is—the statement was made that sometimes there are those, when leaving the physical body, they go into a mental world and not into a spiritual world. And in reference to that question, it is absolutely true that we cannot express in a dimension if we do not have a vehicle composed of the elements of that dimension.

Now we all have a mind and we express in a mental and physical body at this time. We all have the potential of garnering up spiritual substance that we may express in a spiritual world upon leaving this physical body. But not everyone has garnered up that spiritual essence. It is garnered up through an awakening and an expression of the faculties of the soul. There are many untold millions who have left this physical world and are expressing at this time in a mental-astral world.

Now I wish to make it very clear that it does not mean that we have to study any particular philosophy or religion in order to express the soul faculties by which the spiritual substance is garnered up to create the spiritual body. There are many very fine and good people who have never heard of religion who have garnered up a very fine spiritual body while yet here in the flesh. It is because they are expressing their soul faculties. Does that help with your question?

Yes. Thank you.

Thank you. Are there any other questions of a spiritual nature? Yes.

Several times you have mentioned, in your lecture, the prayer for spiritual healing, which includes "And I will do my part." It sounds so simple, until you stop to think of what your part is. I mean, for instance, would it particularly include a period of daily meditation and special things that we would have made.

Definitely and positively. The question is in reference to the spiritual prayer, as brought forth by our National Association. And the statement is, "I will do my part." Absolutely and positively. Spiritualism endeavors, and continues to endeavor, to explain to humanity the part that we must do to be receptive to the divine healing powers. It does require a daily silence, for God heals through the silence. When there are thoughts entertained in mind of a controversial nature, that is an obstruction to the divine, neutral power flowing through the atmosphere. Therefore, when we entertain these controversial thoughts, we are not receptive to this healing.

God is the perfect harmony expressed everywhere. We have put our self out of harmony or out of balance physically, mentally, and spiritually. And this effect of an inharmonious state of being is termed by man, "poor health." But he has the power within him to balance himself and, in so doing, express his divine birthright of perfect health.

The question therefore arises that some children are born with certain tendencies and conditions of poor health. That that creates a thing, by the power of creating, is greater than the thing created. The power that sustains all the universes, known and unknown, is certainly far greater than all this form and creation. But we must unfold this great faith within ourselves and we must know beyond a shadow of any doubt. The mind, the intellect serves a purpose. And when we recognize the purpose of mind and intellect and we recognize the purpose and power of the Divine Spirit, and we use the Divine Spirit when it should be used, and we use the mind as we should use the mind, then we shall be free of these many obstructions that we have created and put our self into the bondage of self. Does that help?

Thank you very much, ladies and gentlemen. Our time is up.

OCTOBER 3, 1971

Church Lecture 4
The Vital Force of Psychic Phenomena

The topic chosen for this morning's discussion was "The Vital Force of Psychic Phenomena."

As many of you who visit this center of Light are aware, I am given by my spirit teacher the topic. And my good friends, that's all I'm given. So I do ask that you may be at peace and receptive to whatever the spirit has to say. This church asks you to believe nothing, but to open your minds and to broaden your horizons.

Vital force, by that word I mean what is called, by others, prana, by some, life-giving energy, by that term I mean the divine energy that flows through and sustains all things. This vital force or energy is ever the servant of our direction. So many people interested in the science of Spiritualism attempt, in many ways, to awaken their dormant psychic faculties. And in those attempts they ofttimes become very discouraged. They see many things in other realms that seemingly either do not come to pass or are not in harmony with their preconceived thoughts and attitudes of mind.

This vital force of this phenomena becomes dissipated when we entertain in thought controversies and disturbance in the gray matter of the brain. This vital force is the power and the energy, properly directed and used, [that] gives us perfect health and perfect peace of mind. We can sit and theorize and analyze until we have dissipated this vital energy at the sacrifice of our good health and peace of mind. Many a wise man has said a man without a goal is a ship without a rudder. And that, my friends, is because there is no direction, there is no concentration upon the purpose of Life herself.

No one can tell you how you are to serve. They may share with you what they have found. This energy, this vital force, when it is not flowing through the form, the mind, unobstructed is like water held by a dam. This dam is the mind. And sooner or later this force is going to overflow. It's like electrical current: either we use it or it destroys us by causing a disturbance in the mind.

All spiritual teachers of all times have taught service, selfless service, is the path to spiritual illumination. And if, my friends, we cannot get the self out of the way—it is the self, the so-called little self, that causes us all of these problems.

We know that those with small minds have a small God, because they cannot conceive of anything different. When we truly make the effort through a daily silence, a meditation program, and we start on that great adventure to conquer inner space—for that, my friends, is the only thing we will ever conquer. We may travel to outer space through centuries untold, but it is only inner space that man himself will master. And when we start to go within, we find locked in the deep recesses of our own subconscious all of the animal characteristics from which the form of man has evolved. And when we find those realms and those dimensions within, we shudder. And some, from that experience, begin to believe in a devil, an opposing force to good, only because they are not familiar with the true purpose of Life herself.

I remember years ago, in my unfoldment, experiencing many times what in Spiritualist terminology we call the elementals. And I said to a very fine teacher at that time—because the experience continued for several years—that "it is almost beyond my capacity to bear." And she said to me, "Richard, in time those forces will flit across the base of your brain and you will no longer be disturbed by them." I said to her at that time, "Why, when we're trying to serve a spiritual purpose, must we be tormented by these demons of the deep?" And she said to me, "They are a part of the creation of form within." I recognize that day and I was a bit disturbed: I did not realize that I was quite that bad.

What I'm trying to say, friends, is that these feelings of envy, of greed, of jealousy, of animosity, this desire for so-called power, and all of those things are within all of us. Let us not deceive ourselves by denying the truth. But look at the brighter side. Though we are composed of the elements of nature and we are subject to the laws governing those elements and this form we call human is evolved through eons of time from forms lower than its present stage, there is a great light, a great tranquility, that we may find within when we find our own soul. But we will not find it by shuddering from the experiences necessary to reach it.

You may hear many words and read many books, but none of us can have a spiritual experience without making the effort to find the spirit within ourselves. At the gate of heaven stand the demons of hell. Do not forget that, my friends. You may think that there is a greater way, that you may surround yourself with the great, white light of eternal truth. Oh, yes, but when we surround our self with that light, we best create it from the light that is within us. Because like attracts like and becomes the Law of Attachment. And if we think that we can just mentally surround our self in that great, white light, do we not realize that we are surrounding within it all of these human tendencies that seem to disturb us?

Spiritualism is the only religion, the only philosophy, the only science that I have ever found that leads mankind on the path within. There he has the eternal right, for it is his divine birthright, to find himself. And we cannot find ourselves until we start to go within and we stop to think. So many times in our day-to-day activities we do not like the way someone speaks, the way they dress, or the way they move. My good friends, we have either been there, are there, or going to be there. For that to which we are adverse by the very laws of magnetism we shall become attached to. There is no escape from divine justice. And divine justice flows through our conscience.

You may ask the question, "What does all of this have to do with the vital force of psychic phenomena?" My good friends, it has *everything* to do with the vital force, the divine energy. Because this vital force is the power that holds the planets in space, it is the great energy that attracts the atoms, the electrons, the molecules in an intelligent manner to shape the form. The thoughts that we entertain release this divine energy, this vital force from our very being. And thoughts are more than things; they are the causes of things. A thought of beauty goes out into the atmosphere from the human mind, which is its vehicle, and it creates in other dimensions its kind.

Remember, to think one thing and to manifest its opposite is an absolute guarantee of failure. And this is why the teachers have taught put your house in order before confusion sets in. That that you desire in a material, physical dimension, learn first to create in a spiritual, mental realm. Man is the great creator, sustained by this vital force.

And do not be deceived, my friends, and think that we have reached the gates of heaven because we may see things in other dimensions, that we may have awakened a certain psychic faculty. I assure you in thirty-one years of looking into these dimensions that the psychic realm is not the realm of spirit. And the spirit realm cannot be reached, cannot be communed with, until we have opened to some degree the faculties of our soul. I do not say that psychic phenomena does not serve its purpose, because it does. But I ask you to think and to consider. It is only a dimension through which we all must pass to reach the soul, the heart of God. Therefore, the wise student recognizes the many forms that appear before his psychic vision, but he learns to discern. And in discerning, we grow. Those seeking understanding and the purpose of Life herself, they do not tarry in the psychic realms. They visit them, as we all do, though multitudes are yet to be awakened in their conscious mind to that fact.

Not only does man dream, but all forms dream. The animal kingdom, the plant kingdom, and, yes, the mineral kingdom. Without the release of this psychic energy, this vital force, through the state of mind known as dream, the sanity of the mind, by that I mean its balance, would be disrupted and destroyed. Mankind constantly, consciously desires one thing and subconsciously desires its opposite. There is no harmony, no balance in that type of thinking. Therefore, nature in her divine wisdom, this great Infinite Intelligence, has set into motion certain laws by which this vital force may be released in what is known as the dream state.

In this day and in this age, as prophesied centuries ago, the light of the dawn has come to mankind. We see it in the disturbances and in the revolutions taking place amongst us. That is only the outward expression of the inner disharmony and discord, because man today is indeed spiritually dissatisfied. He knows that there is something better than to be guided by all the theology and the dogmas and the creeds of ancient times. His spirit is awakening. And in its awakening there are great disturbances in the outer world, for the outer world is but the effect of the inner world. Do not misunderstand these revolutions taking place amongst us. They are blessings in disguise for they are revealing that mankind shall no longer be chained to the bondage and the power struggles of superstitious dogmas and creed.

The youth of our day is beginning to think for themselves. They are awakening to their divine birthright. And many amongst us do not understand that, and from lack of understanding we know fear, for fear is born out of the mire of ignorance. So let us stop each day to think and may we not concern ourselves with analyzing and judging those that we do not agree with.

Look at the ants, my friends. I see no difference between them and the angels. Look at them and see how they work, see how they produce. The Infinite Power has given us a body through which we may accomplish and serve the purpose of the soul's incarnation. It is true, perhaps I am a bit partial, because I believe in work. I do not and never have believed that so-called salvation comes through faith alone. Indeed, as the angels have sung, the workers win. It is the soul's expression to serve. We seek joy, we seek bliss, and we seek peace. It does not come, unless we permit this vital force to flow through our beings unobstructed.

In conclusion, I would like to share with you a little story that I was privileged to read the other day. And it's about a lady who had been making regular visits to her physician on a monthly basis. And each month her doctor gave her a prescription. On this one day on her visit he sat down and he wrote out her prescription. And when she picked it up and read it, it said "One trip to Niagara Falls." And she said to her doctor, "Why on earth would I want to go there?" And he said, "Madame, you have been visiting me for many years and I have been hopeful that you would awaken." He said, "The greatest good that I could possibly give to you is to send you somewhere to find something bigger than yourself."

Thank you, friends. Thank you.

Now we do have a few moments left, if there are any amongst you who have any questions concerning the subject discussed this morning, please feel free to ask your questions at this time. [*After a short pause, the Teacher continues.*] If there are no questions, I thank you because then I won't have to work anymore. Thank you very much.

NOVEMBER 7, 1971

Church Lecture 5
Levels of Awareness

On the first Sunday of each month we set aside our devotional services for a short discussion of spiritual matters and a question-and-answer period following it. This morning the topic, chosen by this world of spirit, is "Levels of Awareness."

We understand in Spiritualism that the Divine that flows through us expresses through what is termed "mind," and that the brain is the vehicle in this dimension for the expression of mind. In expressing the spirit that flows through us, this great Energy, this Divine Love is directed by mind using brain as its vehicle. This inner mind is like a great computer and according to the habit patterns that have been established, the Divine expresses through various levels at different times.

It is not easy to change an established pattern; it is not easy for anyone. But unless we consider to make, as a daily exercise, to rise this spirit within us, this divine Energy, to what is known as the faculty of reason, before we permit expression, then we are not going to be free while yet encased in physical form. When this life force, through daily effort, is raised to this faculty known as reason, it expresses on a much higher level than it would otherwise.

And in speaking of these levels of awareness, I should like to give a few examples that I have found and experienced. One of the first levels of awareness is to see everything that happens to us—the good and the so-called opposite—to be caused by influences and forces outside of ourselves. That, my good friends, is a very primitive state of expression. It is the fertile soil in which superstition grows and controls our life. And in religions of the past and, yea, even to this day in various areas, there are untold numbers who still believe that all cause belongs to God, that everything that happens to us is his fault. We praise this Divine Power when we appreciate the effect, and there are those who curse it when they do not. That is one level of awareness.

Then there are those who have evolved to another level, and they attribute all the good that happens to them to be caused by them. And all the so-called bad to be caused by other people and forces outside of themselves. That's the second level of awareness.

And then there are those, my good friends, who have gravitated to the third level of awareness, who recognize, who realize, who know beyond a shadow of any doubt that everything that happens to us is, indeed, caused by us—the good, the bad, and the indifferent.

Man's spirit evolved through many forms and we are at this present state of evolution and we have choice. We may choose to direct this great power through levels of awareness that will serve the divine purpose of the soul's incarnation; but until such a time as we can rise to that third level, we are going to continually and constantly experience this dual creation of which our form is a part. All things indeed stem from one source and one source alone. But man has been given choice to direct this great Divine Love, this neutral Power; but unless we practice as a daily pattern to stop and to think before we speak, we cannot maintain or sustain divine indifference or neutrality.

In the multitude of experiences that we encounter in this life expression, when desire supersedes the faculty of reason, we have many, many experiences and they're not all enjoyable by us. Desire is a function and unless it is fulfilled, it causes great disturbance in the human mind. From desire, unfulfilled, comes anger, comes greed and jealousy and envy—all of those things that none of us enjoy or want. I have said many times never, never suppress desire for it is energy; fulfill it or educate it. Many students have said to me, "Well, how do I educate a desire that my mind is entertaining?" Stop and think, my good children, energy, misdirected, flows through many avenues of expression and one of them is known as desire, but we have the great power of choice. We may redirect the energy that it may flow through our soul faculties, and in so flowing it shall awaken and unfold the only part of us that is eternal.

What, indeed, does it behoove a man to gather all these things of creation at the sake of losing his own soul? By that statement we do not mean that a soul can be eternally lost. Many do not understand when Spiritualism declares it speaks to the living and not to the dead, because it speaks to those who are spiritually awakened to some extent and degree. The dead, we find yet in the flesh. There is no greater so-called death than spiritual death. We may be here for an hour or we may be here for ten years; we do not know the time when the Divine shall call us to other dimensions. If we have not made the effort to awaken our own soul, we may be rest assured there will be no spiritual heaven awaiting any of us.

The only things that we can take into the higher realms of the world of spirit are our soul qualities, our faculties. Therefore, is it not wisdom that dictates to awaken them while yet here? Many religions for untold centuries have spoken of heaven and of hell, and some religions speak of purgatory. But the level of awareness that we have this moment is the one that we'll take into those other dimensions. And therefore, if we do not make the effort today to awaken this soul, then we're going to take with us all of our desires, all of our envies and greeds and jealousies, all of our hates and all of our fears, and all of our superstitions into what is termed an earth-bound realm.

When we awaken ourselves within, we will know that truth is one, expressed through all. We will know that all teachings and all spiritual books are designed by a higher intelligence to guide us, though there are many paths, back to ourselves, back to God. You may search the universes, my good friends, for an eternity, but there is only one place that you will ever find God, and that is inside of yourself. Because, though God expresses through all form in all dimensions, unless we can awaken to the God within ourselves, we cannot see it in another. Because we cannot see anything that we are not aware of. How could we recognize jealousy if we did not have an awareness of it? Does someone teach us what jealousy is? No, my good friends, this old form—this that is garnered up from the elements of nature—evolved from many other kingdoms, known as the animal nature. It has that within us. And when we experience it with another, it is only an awakening of it within ourselves. We have dipped down to that level of awareness.

If it is truth we are desiring, if it is freedom from the bondage of creation, if it is the peace that passeth all understanding that you are seeking, you have within your being this very moment the power and the way to find it. As our little booklet states, "Give the people light and they will find their way."

Spiritualism is not interested in building giant cathedrals. It is not interested in converting humanity to its membership. It is interested and striving to serve the spiritual light of truth. Spiritualists number in the millions, but they do not tag it Spiritualism because they do not know. We can go to church on Sunday and have a wonderful spiritual awareness, but unless we alone make the effort to stay in that level, we are not serving God, the Divine. Man serves God in a multitude of ways, whether it's digging a ditch or preaching a sermon.

This church does not question who comes and who goes because we are not concerned or interested in those things. We are concerned and interested in serving a Power to which all things are possible. And when that Power is truly served, we accept what comes and what goes without any feeling or any concern.

Many times the angels from the realms above have spoken that service is the only path they've ever found to spiritual illumination. Think, my friends, what selfless service does. It frees the energy of the great power of the spirit that is within us. It frees it in a level that is, indeed, freedom itself.

We know what we send out, like the great circle, returns to us whether we like it or not. So whatever our experience is and whatever our needs may be, remember, to God within all things are possible. And you may pray throughout eternity; and until we awaken that truth within us, they cannot—those prayers—be answered, for we and we alone are the obstruction. We and we alone are the obstacle to the divine love that seeks to flow unobstructed through all things, for that is the sustaining power that keeps them, for a time, in form.

There has been, I know, many things spoken on incarnation and reincarnation. And each one, we must realize, has the divine birthright to express through that level if that is their choice.

As we said this morning to our new members, this church imposes no heavy task upon anyone. Think of the freedom of that statement. My good friends, what we impose we guarantee upon ourselves. And if we want love, then we must express love. And if we want fulfillment, we must become fulfillment in our level of awareness.

All things that we experience are but the effects of the level we are expressing through at that moment. It isn't our neighbor's fault, our husband's or our wife's, but do not feel defeated, for we will attract that. We have the divine right to make a change in ourselves. And we have the choice this morning to think about that and truly make the daily effort. These patterns, these habits of mind are not easily changed. And, indeed, a slow growth is a healthy growth, because if you force change upon yourself, it will not be beneficial. We must grow to the things we wish to change to. We cannot sit and say, "I now have freedom. I now have spiritual light," or "I have learned selfless service," or "I have controlled self-will." The very statement in itself guarantees a continuity of the experience. When we have learned the lesson, my friends, it no longer entertains our mind. When we have truly perceived it, when we have learned tolerance, we express it but we do not entertain it in thought.

Thank you.

If there are any questions at this time, please feel free to raise your hands. Yes.

Could you, please, maybe, elaborate a little bit more on redirecting desires or directing that energy?

Yes. The question by the lady is, Could we expand on our understanding of redirecting the energy through the vehicle of expression known as mind and brain? Is that your question? Yes.

This energy that flows through us, my good friends, must be expressed. It must be or it becomes like a dam and it is blocked. And instead of leaving our universe so that it may flow unobstructed—if we block it, if we do not free it, then it causes a discord and so-called disease in the human mind and body. If we will pause before we act, if we will pause the moment the mind entertains a thought and ask that we may be guided to our faculty of reason, that we have as our divine birthright, which is a faculty of our soul, if we will do that as a daily practice, we will find, in time, that we no longer express through intolerance and through these varying functions. But we must stop to think. And we must try every day in every way to pull this energy, so to speak, to the faculties of our soul.

Now it has been stated to keep faith with reason for she will transfigure thee. But the faculty of reason is not reached just by calling upon it because there are many faculties that precede it.

And the first faculty of being is duty, gratitude, and tolerance. The second faculty of being is faith, poise, and humility.

In all thy getting, get understanding. When understanding floods our universe, we express through the faculty known as reason. When understanding awakens within us, we express tolerance, for understanding precedes tolerance. When we express intolerance, we may be rest assured that we have not, in truth, perceived understanding. To understand a thing, be it a person, dog or cat or tree, is to know the thing, the essence of it. And when you know the essence of a thing, you know yourself because the true self is the spirit that is everywhere present, never absent or away.

We are indeed our brother's keeper in the spiritual sense. We are responsible to ourselves and to all our creations. And that that comes to us is attracted to us like a great magnet from something within ourselves. We cannot transgress natural, divine law. And therefore think, my good friends, each and every experience in our lives we and we alone have called forth. And if we will truly strive and pray and work for understanding, we will know that as an absolute truth.

The conscious mind knows one thing, while the subconscious or so-called inner mind is doing something else. There is no freedom, there is no love without wisdom. And it is within our power to awaken it. No one can do it for us. No one here in flesh and no one hereafter in spirit. Not even God transgresses God's law. Because if the Power did that, it would no longer be the Power to which all things are possible according to the law. And man is a law unto himself, because, you see, we alone choose the level of awareness through which we are going to express. And that level is a set law by the laws of nature and divine law. But we and we alone may rise to the different levels. We may choose to listen and we may choose to see. Or we may choose to block the things that are in our very best interest.

It's like the man that prays for something. And God, working through man, never to man, brings it to him through a person he cannot tolerate. God has answered the prayer. Man has not passed the test. Thank you.

Are there any other questions? [*After a short pause, the Teacher continues.*] If not, the hour is getting late. Thank you kindly.

DECEMBER 5, 1971

Church Lecture 6
Divinity and Direction

The topic that was selected for this morning for discussion is "Divinity and Direction."

I am sure that most of us present have some degree of awareness that we are not here in this earth expression by chance, that we are aware that we are something and that indeed something cannot come out of nothing. Therefore, we look about us and we see such a variety of expression in this earth realm in this world of creation and the question arises within our minds, at times, "Why am I here? Where am I going?" And also does the question arise in that line of thinking, "Where have I been?" Because we know, as I said, that something cannot come from nothing. And we understand, some of us perhaps, that that is form is creation. Therefore, that part of us that is the vehicle of the divine expression, or so-called Spirit, the formless, had beginning and is coming to an ending.

The teachings of Spiritualism are eternal progression. And from that teaching we do not accept that Spirit, God, can progress, because if it could progress, then it would no longer be God or Infinite Intelligence. So from the statement of Modern Spiritualism—eternal progression—we understand that those teachers from the realms on high, who brought forth that statement, are referring to form, to the vehicle of the divine expression. And so, my good friends, we are not in form what we were a year ago or ten or twenty or forty. And we are not going to be what we are today this moment, for that would be contrary to eternal progression of form.

So what is it we ask is free, unchanging, and limitless that is beyond creation? And we come inside of ourselves and we find a great peace, a great light. And when that light dawns on our horizon and when we have truly found it, if it is only a fleeting glimpse of it, we know that we have ever been and that we shall ever be. And by that statement, my good friends, I am not speaking of this individuality, of this so-called vehicle of this moment that is constantly changing.

Is there any security in change? No, my friends. Therefore, the wise man soon considers, "What shall I attune myself to? If it is truth, security, and foundation that I am seeking, then I will not attune myself to form, for form comes and form shall go. But that power that never changes—for it is the power that sustains all things—that is the only thing that never faileth."

Things will come and things will go, but when our faith is truly divinely directed, it sends us inside ourselves. There is where—and the only where—that we will truly perceive truth. And this is why the teachers have taught that truth is individually perceived. We see a portion of it as we evolve through the levels of understanding and therefore, our horizons become broader, our so-called God becomes greater as we and we alone open our sight and begin to see.

If we are attuned to this Divine Love, this neutral Power, then we become directed by it and we no longer are disturbed or moved by the passing changes of this panorama of earth expression. We are in it, indeed, but we no longer become a part of it. Whatever the problem or disturbance of the moment, it came to us by a law that we set into motion, as man is a law unto himself. And as it came, it shall go as we start to express through a greater level of awareness.

This Infinite Intelligence, being intelligent and infinite, knows and does not have to be told.

This vehicle of mind, this so-called brain, serves a purpose in this dimension. This brain is composed from the elements of nature of this planet. It comes from it and it returns to it. What does it behoove us, my good friends, to put reliance upon it, to have faith in it? It is not our salvation. It is not designed to be so. Think of the great eternity that you are. Not that you are going to become, but what we are this moment. For in this moment are we in eternity. We are, in truth, spirit. We are not going to become spirit, but we *are* spirit. And we have that wonderful opportunity to make the choice of truly becoming aware of our divinity this moment and acting accordingly.

As long as we permit this mind, this brain, to govern, to guide, and to control our lives, we shall not find and experience this peace that passeth all understanding. The mind has established patterns and those patterns are not easy to change. When these patterns begin to disturb us, it takes great effort to recognize it in the sense that it is all within ourselves. No one, my good friends, brings us joy and no one brings us grief, but we and we alone accept or reject it by becoming mentally in rapport with it. As long as we need the experiences of doubt, of fear, of lack, and of limitation, as long as we ourselves need so-called poor health and loneliness and all those things, as long as we need them, we indeed shall experience them. As long as we need attention drawn to us—the self—then we will continue to see the cause of all experiences outside of ourselves. But when we withdraw from this multitude of expressions and we sincerely seek to find our true being, then, my good friends, we will gravitate to a level of wisdom.

Many people can show you a way, but your way is your right. And all ways are right ways for the individual, because no matter where we wander, no matter what we do, or where we go, we cannot in truth separate that which is divine. For that that comes from the thing, by the Law of Coming, is destined to return.

Think, my good friends, you have the opportunity and the choice to be free this very moment. The path is not easy, but it is possible. It is demonstrable. It can be done. But the patterns of false gods must be dethroned. For that that we give power to in our thought becomes our master, our god, and we become its slave. If we are disturbed by the fluctuations of this material world, if we are disturbed because someone we are attached to does not do, think, and act the way that we desire, we have become the slave and they the master.

This world or any world is not designed by divine plan for just one person. The world does not cease to revolve in space because we decide that we're dizzy. All of these things we have the wonderful opportunity to use. It's when we abuse them that we become destroyed by them. Ofttimes man seeks and prays for understanding. His prayers become answered as the divine Infinite Intelligence brings understanding to him, but not in the way that he has decided that he should receive it.

When we truly awaken to the divinity within us, our lives will become divinely directed. God does not give us health or its opposite. God does not give us wealth or its opposite. God *is*. We and we alone make the choice whether we want to accept it or to reject it. Remember, that that we define we limit. How can we define, in truth, Infinite Intelligence? We limit it in expression. But surely in this new year, this new cycle, the beginning of the cycle of nine years, the journey begins with the first step. You have the power to set into motion a new life, a new being. That power is ever within us. That that we believe, we become. Think of that great power as energy, the Divine, follows attention.

We, my children, are ever becoming in form as the spirit of truth is striving to express itself. Truth is not readily accepted at any time in so-called history, because the mind does not wish, nor desire, to change or leave that which it is familiar with, to go onward to other levels which it is not yet familiar or secure with. But unless we are ever ready and willing to change, we will stay where we are because we are who we are.

Thank you.

On this, the first service of the month, it is set aside for your questions and answers. We have a few moments left. If you have any questions concerning the discussion of this morning or spiritual matters, please feel free to raise your hand. [*After a pause, the Teacher continues.*] If there are no questions, it not only means I won't have to work those minutes, but it also means that whatever was said has registered, somehow, in your spirit, your soul, and you are not prompted, evidently, to question. But before I leave I'd like to speak forth what our father of our philosophy gave in the 1860's when he said the power of the mind to question presupposes and guarantees no less its power to answer.

Thank you.

JANUARY 2, 1972

Church Lecture 7

The Love of Living

On the first Sunday of each month, it is my privilege to serve as the channel for the world of spirit to bring to you the lecture, the discussion for the morning. To those of you who are familiar with our devotional services here, I know that you're aware that our lectures or sermons we try to keep to fifteen to twenty minutes. Because it has been the feelings of the spirit people that if we cannot get the message to an individual in that length of a lecture time, then it is doubtful that the message will reach them.

I do hope that I may be, once again, receptive to this spirit teacher that has been with me for so many years. He chose as his topic for this morning's discussion, "The Love of Living."

We all have varying understandings of the word *love*. And the understanding that has been given to me over these years is love is like a great magnet. It is a magnetic force within the individual that attracts unto ourselves the thing we love the most. Now, we love many things in this world of creation. We may love another person, an animal, a plant, an automobile, or a house. We have this divine choice to choose what it is that we desire to love, for that that we love, my friends, indeed it does befall us. But it is not the love that so many think about in their conscious mind. It is a feeling that rises from the depths of our soul. And those who choose to use this great power, known as love, wisely will attract unto themselves beneficial results.

At one of the morning discussions entitled, "Levels of Awareness," the spirit explained the various levels that we are expressing through. So many people think that they love someone else and there's no response. When we encounter that type of experience, my friends, let us consider: Is this a selfless love? Is it an unobstructed flow of this power that is within us or is it a selfish love that we are expressing? For that that is a pure love is a love that goes out, has no consideration or want or desire for return. And when love flows through our being on that level of awareness, it goes forth into the universe and according to the law upon which it is sent out, it does indeed return to us.

Much has been spoken in this church and at our various classes and seminars on what is termed selfless service. When we do something because it is right to do it, then we are not concerned with the effect, we are not concerned with the harvest.

And so it is with love, when we express love for the sake of love, we will indeed experience what so many teachers through the ages have called God or Divine Energy.

So many of us ask for happiness and for joy or we ask for supply. We constantly seem to be in the asking vibration. My good friends, we are emanating, in that respect, an attitude of lack of the thing that we desire. As long as we maintain that attitude of mind, that rate of vibration—like attracts like and becomes the Law of Attachment. If we believe that we have need, then indeed need shall we experience. But if we rise to our faculties of being and there become awakened that this so-called God, this Infinite Intelligence *is* love, and on that level we express this power, then there is no experience of need or of lack.

It has been said that God, Love, Divine Energy—call it what you wish—is either first in our life or has no place at all. And so it is, for the only thing that is eternal is not the form—it's not this created vehicle—it is the divine Spirit that we are expressing this very moment. So if you are not satisfied or pleased with your present state and condition, stop a few moments; pause and think. You have at your disposal the greatest power in all the universes. It doesn't matter what you call it; we understand it to be Love. But that type of love, my friends, cannot be expressed until *we* get what is termed the self out of the way.

Let us think each day, each moment, before we speak. Because the spoken word is life-giving energy. And if we will only pause and go to the level where the power expresses itself unobstructed, then we can say in truth, "I speak my word forth into the universe knowing that it shall not come back to me void, but accomplish that which I send it to do." That, my friends, is what love in truth does. And so in our day-to-day acts and activities when we are disturbed with either our business or domestic affairs, stop and think. There is no greater power than what is this moment, this instant, at your disposal. If we decide to use it wisely, if we use it instead of abuse it, indeed, shall we experience a heaven upon this earth.

I should like to mention a bit of the class study that is given to the students of this association. And in that respect I want to mention this faculty of reason. We understand that reason flows through consideration, for 'less we consider a thing we cannot have any light of reason concerning it. So if we will take the time to consider why certain experiences come into our lives, if we will think about that, we will be able to reason and to understand. As wise men have said before, in all your getting get understanding.

We all want a better world, but wanting it is not getting it. We cannot experience this better world that we're all seeking unless we're willing to become it. We know that truth is taught through indirection, demonstration, and example. When we become the living example, then this world will be a world of love, a world of heaven here and now.

Thank you.

The first Sunday of each month is set aside for a short question-and-answer period concerning either the morning talk or anything of a spiritual nature. If any of you feel moved or prompted to ask a question at this time, I will be more than happy to serve, to the best of my ability, as the channel for your answer. So please feel free to raise your hands, if you have a question. Yes.

I'd like to know—it seems to be my understanding that the path to spiritual illumination is selfless service. Would that also be the path to be able to use the correct expression of divine love?

Yes, the question is, the gentleman understands the path to illumination is selfless service and would that be the path and the expression of divine love? In reference to your question, I would say absolutely and positively so. If we understand Infinite Intelligence or God to be love, then we see all around and about us this great expression in all forms in creation. We understand that God or Love is the great source of all things. We also understand that nothing is impossible to this great power, if we, the channels, become receptive to it. Remember, my friends, that man is his own best friend and his own worst enemy.

But we don't have to remain an enemy to ourselves, unless we are enjoying the experiences that it brings us. We indeed are never left without choice. And so it is through selfless service this great power is expressed through a clear channel. And in so being expressed, this great energy is released and the good comes about and returns to us. Thank you.

Did someone else have a question? [*After a pause, the Teacher continues.*] Did you have a question? If not, I thank you. I guess according to the laws of merit I won't have to work so long this morning. Thank you very much.

FEBRUARY 6, 1972

Church Lecture 8

The Living Demonstration

I will try to the best of my abilities to still my mind that whatever may come may serve the purpose for which the Spirit has intended it. To those of you who are familiar with Spiritualism, its science, philosophy, and religion, you are aware that Spiritualist mediums and students do not prepare lectures or what they are to say when they are serving the Spirit. If we permit ourselves to prepare lectures and prepare ourselves in the normal sense of study, what happens to us, when we go to speak for the Spirit, the mind gets in the way and we give to you only what the mind has garnered up.

The purpose of Spiritualism is not to serve the mind, the intellect, but it is to serve what we term the Living Light. That is not possible if we cannot still our own mind and let the power of the Spirit flow. This morning the Spirit gave to us, when the programs were printed, [the title of] "The Living Demonstration."

This day, called Easter, [is] traditionally set aside as the day of resurrection of the spirit from its house of clay. Millions and millions of people believe in that great event, but so many seem to fail in applying that to themselves. The mind does not desire to entertain the possibility of so-called death. That which the mind cannot understand, it does not desire to entertain in thought. And so it has been for centuries a multitude of superstitions have grown causing fear, wars, and disturbances.

The living demonstration is the demonstration of this moment, this great eternity. We all know that we are not the flesh for we see this clay body return to the elements from whence it has come. We know in our own inner being that we have always been. When we are at peace with ourselves, this soft voice that speaks in a whisper within us, it tells us, "You are here to serve a purpose and that purpose is to share the divinity which you are in truth."

How many times have religionists spoke of faith? And how many times and in how many ways can the message be given? We have faith in so many things. But it seems at times we lack this great faith when it comes to the things of which the mind is not familiar. We have faith when we sit in a chair that it won't collapse. And we have faith when we turn the key in our car that the motor will start. We have that faith because of a multitude of experiences.

Now the time has come for us to make the effort to experience things of the spirit. We know that things of the spirit are discerned by the spirit. And the question is: How do we find that spirit inside of ourselves? If we will be sincere with our investigations and with our applications, we will find this living spirit that is the real self. We are not the suit of clothes that we wear. This great eternity, this great creation, it wears many suits of clothes in many planes of consciousness.

Think of the great power that is within our being. Think of this great so-called magic of believing. We believe that we're here this moment and, to us, we are experiencing this church service. My good friends, I know there are some who will say that is an absolute fact. But let us ask the question: What is fact to one is, indeed, fiction to another. It becomes a fact to us when we believe it. It is a fact that man has sent his rocket ships out into outer space and landed on the moon. But to many, it is not a fact; it is a fiction. Do you not understand that it is the magic of believing? We have the choice to believe as we desire.

God, the divine, neutral, infinite power, sustains us. Man and man alone is the one who guides his ship of destiny. How many times have I heard, "I'm experiencing these difficulties because that is my karma." Let us pause for a moment and ask ourselves who caused our karma or effect. God and no influence outside of ourselves has caused that. We and we alone are doing those things to ourselves, but we indeed have the power to make the change.

The teachings are very simple in Spiritualism: whatever you believe you indeed shall become. For this is a becoming world caused by our own beliefs. If you believe in a divine, limitless power that knows no lack or limitation, then indeed shall we experience this great, limitless flow. But if we believe in limitation and lack, if we believe in illness and all those so-called negative things, then, my good friends, that's all we can experience. For the mind cannot experience what it first does not accept in thought.

When we make the sincere effort every day in every way to guard our thoughts, we will indeed change our lives for the better.

How many times it has been spoken that the children inherit this so-called heaven. Let us analyze that statement. What does it mean? Does it mean children in physical age or children in mental acceptance? We believe so many things because we have computed that they are facts. But man and man alone has made them facts. God didn't do it and neither did anyone else. If we accept that things are difficult for us, when we go to do them, my good friends, they cannot be any other way, for we have created that and that is what we will experience. If we accept in our minds that it's difficult to tolerate people because they're not the way that we are, be rest assured it will indeed be difficult for us to tolerate them.

We are composed of the elements of nature and this form that we are wearing, that we are using at this moment, is composed of all those things. Whatever we see in another indeed, in truth, is within our self. We may have seen it many years ago and suppressed it in the depths of our subconscious. And then at a later time, we see another human being expressing what we have suppressed. It calls forth from within our self that feeling, that emotion, and we become intolerant.

We are spiritually one in truth. God cannot be separated and still be God. And when we find that oneness within our self, we will indeed find it outside of ourselves. Why, we must ask the question, do we make this beautiful life that we have the great privilege of enjoying so difficult for ourselves?

Spiritualism teaches and demonstrates the Law of Personal Responsibility. If we wish to remain in the delusion and illusion of our own creations, then we're going to continue to blame everyone and everything outside of our self for our experiences. Then we're going to be miserable or happy depending who we meet and where we go. Sooner or later, my good friends, we will become weary of a day of sadness and a day of joy. Sooner or later, we'll turn within ourselves and then we'll start to grow.

All of our experiences we indeed have willed into action; it is a subtle law. But the old mind, the brain, desires so many things. It desires more than it is willing to work for. All things are possible to what we call Infinite Intelligence or God, and we are all a part of this great God. So whatever it is you sincerely desire, it is right where we are. All that we need or could ever want is inside of our self. The illusion of time and space—and indeed it is an illusion of the mind—says that it's over the mountaintop: "I cannot reach it until so-and-so and so-and-so change their way." That is not the way we find it in truth. If we wish to continue to make false gods, to give people, places, and things power over us, then we're going to be destroyed, sooner or later—this old form—by the gods that we have created.

We cannot be free as long as we entertain fear. We cannot be free until we demonstrate what is known as faith. We unfortunately have made ourselves the slaves of our creations. My good friends, we will find in time that that is not the purpose of our soul's incarnation into this form.

How many millions of spirits leave this earth dimension to find themselves with the same problems, the same grief, the same misery that they had while yet in flesh. We cannot be free until we have freed our self. Leaving the physical body does not, in any sense of the word, guarantee freedom for we have a mind that goes with us. And whatever we are attached to, it stays with us. Our joys, our sadness, all of those things.

Think how much time we spend in thought concerning this material world. It comes and it goes. It serves a purpose if we do not permit it to become our god. The living demonstration is the demonstration of the moment. You have the right to express through a level of awareness that frees us. That is the divine birthright of every human soul. And it is the living demonstration.

Thank you.

APRIL 2, 1972

Church Lecture 9
The Living Dead

Thank you, Mr. Chairman, platform workers, members, and friends. As our chairman said, it has been the policy here on the first Sunday of each month to present a subject of discussion and a question-and-answer period following.

Those of you who are familiar with our church are well aware that the workers in this church are requested not to prepare any subject matter for what they're going to speak on because in so doing they only obstruct the flow of the spirit of spontaneity. And so it was a few months ago that this topic was given to us entitled, "The Living Dead."

Now many will understand just from that title that we're going to speak on those who have left the flesh, but that is not fully what this discussion is about. We understand the dead, one who is dead, is unaware. We may be dead to the knowledge that man has landed on the moon or that there is a new invention for the betterment of mankind. That that we are unaware of, we are dead to. And so it is that we're speaking this morning on the living dead. The dead, good friends, are not all in the so-called world of spirit. So many of the dead are here yet in the flesh.

It is beyond a shadow of any doubt our divine birthright to be aware of the dimensions in which we truly live. So many people are unaware or dead to the demonstrable truth that telepathy is an absolute science. So many times in the course of our day we have thoughts of things. We have impulses and disturbances within our mind. How many amongst us question, From whence cometh this thought? No, we usually take it for granted that we are the originators of that thought. Little realizing that the thought may have come from another, for to mind communication distance is of no import.

In conducting the first classes to be given publicly on spiritual awareness techniques in this church last Thursday evening, it was indeed pleasing to note the sincere students who became, from personal demonstration, aware of thoughts in their minds that were being sent by other groups of students. This is happening to us all of the time. Whether or not we are consciously aware of these influences does not change the absolute demonstrable fact that these influences have an effect upon our lives.

I have heard some people say, "I'm not influenced by anything outside of myself. I put a divine protection around and about me!" My good friends, we are but receiving sets and receiving all types of transmissions, because we have yet to find ourselves. Why have the philosophers said, "O man, know thyself and ye shall know the truth and the truth shall set you free"? How much time are we spending in our day-to-day activities to know ourselves? Our minds are so cluttered and entertained with what everyone else is doing because it does not meet, ofttimes, with our petty approval. How can we be free, my good friends, as long as we're concerned with what everyone else is doing? Have we reached such a stage of spiritual illumination that we can become the judge of another's acts and activities? Have we become so great while yet in flesh?

Does not that type of thought of prejudgment, of knowing what is right for everyone but ourselves, is that not a demonstration indeed of the living dead? Dead to understanding. Dead to consideration. Dead to reason. Dead to logic. And even dead, ofttimes, to hope. We do not, in this church, in any way mean to judge or to be concerned with what those souls who enter these doors do or do not with what they have received. There is a divine Power that holds all things in space. And when one makes the effort to touch that divinity, then they know that God, Infinite Intelligence—call it what you will—is over all things at all times.

A wise man once said, "Manifest the divinity within yourself and all things will be harmoniously arranged around you." How, good friends, can we have peace and joy when we spend so much of our time in concern with what others are doing or not doing? When we and we alone become the living light, when we express that divinity within ourselves, thought of what others are doing will no longer entertain our mind.

We're all here to serve a purpose, to be free, to share the light that we have received. But he who shares the light, be it a true light, does not dictate what another must do with it. When we give what we have to give and we care less what the people we have given it to do with it, then we shall be free. Free from the fruits of action.

What is it, we must ask ourselves, that attaches our mind to our actions? What is it that's concerned with what someone does with the efforts that we have given? If we have made our efforts from the dimension known as brain, self, or ego, then indeed are we concerned with what another is going to do with it. But if we have become the channels for the light to flow, then we will be the servants of the light and we will not be concerned with what comes out of it. What is it within us that thinks it knows more than the infinite intelligent Power known as God or Spirit? What is it within us that thinks we know more than the Power itself? Think, my good children, and be free. But we cannot be free, we cannot awaken, we cannot be alive until we find the spark within ourselves.

Surely we know that we are not here to suffer, we are not here to struggle, we are not here to experience grief and sorrow and lack and limitation. Who or what is it that does that to us? Surely it is not a God of love. It is not an infinite intelligent Power. But indeed if we think, we will know. We do it to ourselves. Man and man alone is his own best friend, and man and man alone is his own worst enemy. So let us be a good friend to ourselves. Let us look at our own light. And in so doing then we can walk in the light.

When we seek what another has, we are turning the back—our back—on what God has given to us. Not everyone in this world is meant to be a musician or a mathematician or a medium. But we're all meant to be what the Divine has given to us. So let us be about what *we're* meant to be. Let us find that within ourselves. He who seeks to save the world shall lose himself because he has not sought to save himself.

Thank you, friends.

If there are any questions on this morning's discussion, you may feel free to raise your hand and ask them. If there are not, then I'm free to sit down and rest. And that means, surely, I would have merited that. So if you have any questions, please raise your hand. Yes, please.

Is there any time when one has to sit in judgment for the courage of their convictions? I mean, if they are—have a conviction and it does not meet with others, does not one have to judge what is right in the situation, not only for themselves, but those around them?

That is a very interesting question in regards to judgment, in order to sustain or maintain the courage of one's convictions. And in reference to your question, I should like to say the understanding of this church and Spiritualism is the laws of merit: that whatever happens to us is caused by us; that as water reaches its own level by its own weight, that like attracts like and becomes the Law of Attachment. It is also the teachings: to be in the world and not a part of the world; to be with a thing and not a part of the thing. That way, through that demonstration, we are ever free wherever we are under any condition or circumstance.

It is when we entertain the thought that we know by the principles that we have established for our self what is right or wrong for another (or group of people) that we become these great judges. Now it is stated that he who judges shall be judged. And how just such a law indeed is. If we entertain that we have a principle that is right for us, and being right for us, it is right for the rest of the world, especially for our friends and our relatives, especially for the religion we have adopted, especially for the schools which we send our children to, then indeed we are treading on very deep, deep water.

Man is responsible to himself and to all his creations. But when man permits his principle or principles to become the law of the land for everyone to abide by, then we are no longer being true to the Law of Spiritual Responsibility—responsible to the light that we have received. The only way that I have found that we're ever going to be free is to live in accordance with the highest light that we are able to receive and to leave each and every individual free to follow the light that they have received.

Now unsolicited help is ever to no avail. And so it is, those who are seeking and thirsty shall go to the river of water to drink. It is not our responsibility to take the water to them and try to pour it down their mouth. If we have found the river, our responsibility, obviously, is to share our awareness of where it is. It is not our responsibility to tell everyone we meet, that "You must drink of this river because it has done so much for me." Because what is pleasure to one at any given moment is pain to another. The form is evolving. The soul is expressing itself through a multitude of forms and a multitude of dimensions. We cannot be free, in flesh or out of flesh, if we dictate what is right for another. Thank you. Did that help with your question?

Yes.

Are there any other questions before we finish? [*After a short pause, the Teacher continues.*] Thank you, friends. Thank you kindly.

MAY 7, 1972

Church Lecture 10
Inner Levels and Outer Limits

Friends, most of you are familiar with the teachings of this association, in that our workers are requested not to prepare themselves for any lectures at any time. When we prepare ourselves mentally to speak on a topic, what happens to us is we get into a mental level, then we are not receptive to the spirit or the vibration of the moment in which we are to speak. And in preparing lectures and things of that nature, we find that we're speaking over the heads of the listener—or under them—but it is not being received. And that is not the purpose of this association. A few months ago my spirit teacher who has been with me for a number of years, who requests the topics that are placed on the program, asked to speak on "Inner Levels and Outer Limits." I do not know what he's going to talk about, but if I am able to be receptive, through my clairaudience or clairsentience, that I may receive these thoughts and give them forth to you, I will indeed be most grateful.

Most of us are aware, to some extent, of the world around and about us, of this physical world. We're aware, to some extent, of the house we live in, the car we drive, and the clothes that we wear. We're aware of the things that we don't like, as well as aware of the things that we do like. But indeed are few of us aware of the reasons why we like or we dislike a person, place, or thing. We know that we like it or dislike it, but in all honesty we don't know why. It has often been said that there is no cure for our illnesses—and that's what our dislikes are, and also our likes—unless we can find the cause.

And in speaking on inner levels and outer limits, we're going to try to broaden, to some extent perhaps, the horizons of the listening ear. The mind can be likened unto a tape recorder. It plays certain tapes under certain circumstances and conditions according to what has been recorded over a lifetime of experiences.

We look about the world we live in and we see that some people are born with certain talents and some, seemingly, are born without them. That some seem to be in a state of joyousness and happiness, while others appear to be born in conditions that are miserable and surely grieving. Then the question arises within our being: If there is a Divine Power and all things are brought into balance in time, why are some souls incarnated into different bodies with different experiences? But if we look a little deeper, we'll find that the experiences of yesterday, to some of us anyway, are not the experiences of this present moment or of today.

It has been said, "Hold not to form for form shall pass." And yet this old brain, known as the great computer, the recording machine, holds steadfast to that which it is familiar with. Why, we ask ourselves, do we hold to patterns that are not benefiting our soul, our spirit, or even our mind? What is it within us that insists upon holding to disturbances, to worry, to lack, to limitation, to all these negative things? And when we search deeply, we find in ourselves that we are so familiar with that particular tape or recording that it's difficult to change it.

Some time ago a lecture was given in a seminar on poverty, and I'd like to express a little bit about that lecture. The understanding of this teacher is that poverty—physical, mental, or spiritual—is nothing more or less than a weakness in our character, a deformity of our personality. For there is something within us that needs attention. And if that is the way that we're finding of gaining this attention, which is energy, to be drawn to us, then that is what we're going to continue to use.

It has also been stated: faith is that which moves the mountain. When we rise to another level of awareness within ourselves we find that faith and fear is one and the same thing. We fear and do not place our hand in the flame because it will burn. We have absolute faith that that is what will happen and we experience what we term fear. We have fear that if we jump off a two-story building, we will have damaging effects upon our body. Don't you see, my good friends, that fear is nothing more than absolute faith, and that that we have faith in, we in truth *are*. God does not do it to us. We and we alone do it to ourselves. I am not suggesting or recommending that you try jumping off the bridge and swim in the ocean after, because the fear is so deep-rooted in the depths of our own mind, which is absolute faith that's what will happen.

As man continues to direct his faith, the greatest power in all the universes, to these negative, disturbing things, then that is what man will ever continue to experience. Our outer limits are narrowed by ourselves. We have faith that certain people will act a certain way under certain conditions. Therefore, that's the only way we can ever see them act under those conditions, because, my good friends, that is what we have faith in.

It is more than helpful to spend a few moments of each hour to think where our thoughts are. Are they limited or are they limitless? For they indeed go out like the great circle and return unto us some day. If our minds continue to entertain the thoughts of worry and disturbance, we indeed continue to experience what the mind directs.

So many times we think that we're thinking and what we're really doing is permitting the gray matter to go and whirl by itself without any direction in any way, shape, or form. We must come, someday, to the question of, "Why am I here, how did I get here, and where am I going?"

Someday we will have to face not what we think we are, but what we really are. There's only one judge that I've ever found and that is the so-called judge known as conscience. Conscience, in my understanding, is a spiritual sensibility with a dual capacity; it knows right from wrong; it doesn't have to be told. That's the thing, my friends, that we face someday.

No one has to tell you what will save you. You already know what will save you from yourself. You don't need to read a book or attend a church or to pray each day to find God, because you already are God. As soon as the self, the self-interest, the self-concern, the self-preservation, all these self-orientated thoughts that swim in the mind, as soon as those are freed from our soul, the light of our spirit shines forth and then we know where we came from, why we're here, and where we're going. That, my good friends, is the divine birthright of each and every soul encased in flesh. And it is possible not tomorrow, but this moment, this day, to find our eternal spirit. And once we find it within ourselves, we will see it in everything no matter where we wander.

The Light is only known by the Light. Be not concerned with what others are doing or not doing. Be not concerned for what has gone yesterday. It has left you and you cannot do a thing about it. Be not concerned about the years ahead. Be thoughtful of this moment that you may be free, free from the bondage of self.

Thank you.

Now, if you have any questions concerning the discussion of this evening, please feel free to raise your hand. I will be most happy if I am able to tune into these dimensions again and answer any questions that you may have. Are there any questions, please? Yes.

Did you not indicate that fear is conditioned by what we learned and, if so, isn't the conscious also conditioned then?

That's an excellent question. And the lady has said, Did not the lecture indicate that fear is a condition and—a conditioning—and if so, is not the conscious mind also conditioned? To the best of my understanding, this so-called fear is nothing more than the power known as faith. That fear and faith is one and the same thing. It has been stated that that we fear befalls us, because fear is faith. It can be stated that it is the negative part of faith and that faith is the positive part of faith. But when it comes right down to it, it is this divine power, and we and we alone are directing it.

And it is true, to the best of my awareness, that we are conditioned or programmed to these so-called fears. We're programmed by the environmental conditioning of our mind. We are programmed, to some extent, by the hereditary processes of mind. And we are programmed by those whom we associate with.

Now the reason that we are programmed this way deals with the law that states like attracts like and becomes the Law of Attachment; that we are known by the company that we keep simply because like attracts like. Now, if a person is striving to awaken or free themselves from various conditions and circumstances, then it behooves that individual to associate with people who are not in harmony or rapport with their programmed patterns of mind. That is not easy because when a person is programmed to self-orientated thoughts and they try to associate with people who are programmed to selfless service and not programmed to self-orientation, there is not a rapport. And the person must make great effort to free themselves of all their self-concerns.

We are indeed conditioned through these experiences, but our spirit, which is the Divine flowing through us, is greater than creation for that that sustains and maintains creation is greater than the created thing, as the father is greater than the son. So we can, through daily spiritual exercises, reprogram our minds to a more free expression of our spirit. Does that help with your question? Thank you.

Are there any other questions before we finish? If there are, please raise your hands. [*After a short pause, the Teacher continues.*] Thank you. Thank you very much.

JUNE 4, 1972

Church Lecture 11
Evolutionary Incarnation

On the first Sunday of each month we have this discussion that I've been privileged to give way to the spirit, and hopefully, be that in order, I may be able to still my own mind that whatever comes through may in some way be instrumental in helping you to help yourselves. For we know that the healer must first make the effort to heal themselves before it can be given to another. So first we seek within our own being the way to the light, to higher ground. And once having found it, we do not impose it upon another, for they have their rights to find their way and in their way.

The [topic] that was brought forth a few months ago by the spirit for this morning's discussion is entitled "Evolutionary Incarnation." And before speaking on that, I should like to say, to those who are new to the understanding of Spiritualism, the basic principle of the modern movement of National Spiritualism. It states in our manual that a Spiritualist is one who believes in communication with the world of spirit by means of mediumship and who endeavors to mold his or her character in accordance to the highest teachings derived from such communication. With that type of a basic principle for a foundation, we cannot expect that a Spiritualist is going to fit into a particular mold. We're not going to be able to tell whether they're a Spiritualist or some other religion because they are in communication with the highest levels of intelligence that they are able to communicate with at any given moment.

We know that like attracts like and becomes the Law of Attachment. And so it is as we attempt to be more receptive to these so-called invisible dimensions that are around and about us. We find, in Spiritualism, a similarity in the sense of the basic principles and the nine declarations. But we also find a great individuality, an expression of the freedom of one's own spirit.

This morning's discussion is entitled, "Evolutionary Incarnation."

Some time ago it was given to me an understanding from the world of spirit concerning the purpose of the soul's incarnation into form. I am sure that we will all agree that something cannot and does not come out of nothing. We understand that Spirit is the formless, the free, the Infinite Intelligence expressed in form. We also understand that soul is individual. Being individual it has form or shape, because that that is individualized [is] put into form. Therefore, individualized soul is the form or covering of the divine spark known as Spirit.

We look around and about us and we see so much variety of expression of this so-called God or Divine Power. We ask ourselves the question, "Why am I here? What is it that has placed my feet here at this moment? Why was I born into a certain family at a certain time? Why was I not born before, or even later?"

We look about and see that all of our experiences here and now are but effects of causes set into motion by ourselves. If we understand that law for this moment and if it is a divine law, which means eternal, then we must consider and question the reason why we are here in this physical, earthly form in this year of 1972.

It is my understanding, at this present stage of awareness, that the soul is evolving through form and forms unlimited, that it has entered this Earth planet, this physical form, at the moment of conception according to laws that it has set into motion at another time, in another place, in another age.

In speaking on evolutionary incarnation, I ask that you not be confused with what the common theory of return or reincarnation is. I am not speaking of life before in physical form on this planet, but I ask that you consider the reasons and to question why you entered the form that you have. Why wasn't it some other and why was it now?

We look about this earth realm and we see that Life herself is a school and an education. It doesn't just happen. It's caused by laws that we and we alone set into motion. We have come to this planet in this time to serve, which is the only true purpose of our soul, our spirit. For there is no greater servant than the Divine Power, known as God.

We have come here according to those laws established. And the mind says, "If that be true, then why am I not aware of the times before?" Things of the mind are known by the mind and things of the spirit are discerned by the spirit. Man has the golden opportunity to find his soul inside himself. No one can tell you the way to find it. They can only share with you the way that they have found it.

When we awaken to that great truth within our being, we will no longer ask the purpose of our being, we will no longer stumble in the darkness of the night. We will know that we have lessons to learn, that we have a divine birthright to express the freedom of our own soul. Freedom of the soul, my friends, is something within us, not without. Freedom of the soul does not mean free to act in any way that we choose without concern or consideration for another's right. Freedom of our soul is an awakening that illumines our mind and knows that we are indeed eternally free.

Wherever we wander, whatever we do we cannot and we will not escape the laws that we and we alone have set into motion. It behooves us, my good friends, to ponder and to think. If there are things in our lives that we are not happy with, only we and we alone have placed them there. There is no power, no God outside that does it to us. Let us think and be honest with ourselves.

It can be thought a sadness to witness souls along the path who reach a level of awareness known as spiritual arrogance, but that is their right. Sometimes the light dawns within a person and when it happens, they are so enthusiastic, so grateful. But we must stop to think. There is no one that I have ever found that knows the right way for you to awaken your own divine birthright. As I said earlier, they can only share their understanding. There are so many religions in this world today. There is so much diversity of thought, and yet they are all seeking the same thing. They're all climbing up the Mountain of Aspiration. They're all trying to get back home. Home, which is ever inside of ourselves.

Thank you.

If there are any questions concerning the discussion, you may feel free to raise your hand. Yes.

As students, how do we go about finding this path to our own soul?

The question has been asked by the lady, as a student, how do we go about finding this path to our own soul? There are many, many paths to the one and only truth. Each soul is here in form expressing itself according to the laws it has set into motion. To some, in their state of awareness, finding that path may be harmonious or in rapport with the way another has found their path. There is no guarantee that that will be for you. I can only say that when the time is spent each and every day to still the mind, to tap that power, which is Peace or God within the self, that Divine Spirit will show the way that is right for you. Each one has the divine right to find their way.

Think, my friends. Thought is the vehicle through which energy expresses itself. Mind knows things of the mind and spirit discerns the spirit. If we are truly attempting to find our self, the purpose of our being, then we must consider making the daily effort to still our mind. Because it is our spirit and our spirit alone that knows the way for us. Does that help with your question?

Yes. Thank you.

Thank you. Are there any other questions? Yes.

You said this morning in the lecture that in this dawning of spiritual understanding there is sometimes a layer of arrogance.

And then would it follow, by nature, that as that understanding grows, we then find, rather than arrogance, a very harmonious, reasonably humble attitude towards God and the environment?

Thank you very much. The question is stated in reference to a part of the talk that spoke of the level of spiritual arrogance. Spiritual arrogance, which expresses itself in knowing what is right for everyone else, comes to the mind if the power moves in our being prior to the opening of our soul faculties. Now there are many soul faculties: duty, gratitude, and tolerance; and faith, poise, and humility. The opening of these centers, called many names, is critically important before the student becomes receptive to this great power, known as God. When this power, called by the Hindus kundalini or the serpentine power, when this prana, this energy, is released and begins to move through our being, unless our soul faculties are awakened to some extent, it magnifies whatever the mind habitually entertains. For example, if we have a bit of temper, it becomes a big bit if this power is released within us.

Now all religions and all philosophies are trying to teach mankind to harmonize his thoughts, to recognize, to realize that we, in truth, are one and one alone; that there is no power outside of our self that isn't first within our self.

And so in regards to those levels known as spiritual arrogance, I can only say that it is obviously an error of ignorance, a lack of tolerance or understanding. Thank you.

Does someone else have a question before we finish? Yes.

You often speak of cause and effect. And I was wondering, how did this cycle begin? Is it like a beginning of one's life or does it go back to the beginning of mankind?

The lady has asked a question in reference to the mentioning of the Law of Cause and Effect. If we understand that God, the Divine Spirit, is formless, is free, then we understand that the Divinity is beyond cause and effect; that God *is* peace; and peace is the power. Cause and effect have to do with form. It has to do with creation. Whatever is form is under the Law of Cause and the Law of Effect. There is no escape from cause and effect in what is known as creation. But man is not creation. Truth is not creation. Creation is under the Law of Change. It *is* change and it is constantly changing. It begins and it ends.

And this is one of the purposes of Spiritualism: to reveal to mankind that he *is* eternal; that he is not cause and effect; that he is simply using the vehicle of cause and effect. And this is why the teaching is: Be with a thing and never be a part of the thing. Be in the world; do not be a part of the world. When that dawns in your conscious mind, you will be free while yet in form.

Thank you. I see our time is up. Thank you kindly, friends.

AUGUST 6, 1972

Church Lecture 12

The Meaning of Salvation

The topic that was selected for this morning's talk has been entitled, "The Meaning of Salvation." That title in the movement of Spiritualism, to many, perhaps, is indeed controversial. For the Spiritualists firmly believe that salvation, if one can believe in it, is something that is within oneself, that there is nothing outside of us anywhere that can save us. So when that title was placed on our programs, a couple of months ago, there were many thoughts concerning it. For it is the first time, to my knowledge, that that has been used in the movement of modern Spiritualism.

There is so much concern about religion and science. There is so much thought and investigation in this day and age whether or not there is a practical, applicable philosophy for everyday living. Many think that Spiritualism and Spiritualists are concerned primarily with the so-called afterlife. There is no question that we are concerned with life itself, whether here or hereafter is no import for life is life and eternity is eternity.

Should we leave this physical dimension this moment, we're not going to find anything any different than the moment before we left. We have a mind and a mental body; that is something that is not composed of the physical elements of nature. It is something that is composed of mind stuff, and that is not a physical thing. We have a brain through which this power, this mind, functions and expresses itself. It is activated by what the Spiritualists call mind stuff. And that, my good friends, doesn't change because it leaves the vehicle through which it is presently expressing itself.

What does this meaning of salvation truly mean? To one person it means to save, to preserve, to continue to exist. If we understand the tenets of spirituality, then we know that that that is, cannot be lost and cannot be changed. Truth is truth. It needs no defense. It just is. To others, salvation may mean to save from the destruction of oneself. What is it, my friends, that we're concerned with saving? Is it our thought patterns? Is it our attitudes of mind? Is it our personality?

Let us be thoughtful of life in its fullness. When we pause to think, we know in truth that this moment, this life, is but one expression of an untold number; that Spirit, being God or Infinite Intelligence, cannot have a beginning, for that that has beginning indeed guarantees its own ending. What salvation, then, is there in holding to form and to change? Each moment and each day we are thinking, bit by bit, new thoughts and we're doing new acts. Here this moment there are those who have come for the first time to this church, to this center; that, to them, is new.

So what is it that we are seeking? What is this true meaning of salvation? Does it mean to clear the mind from all of the thoughts that it has entertained, from the errors that it has stepped into, to find its true self? For the true self, the Divinity, the spark within us, cannot be saved. For it already is; it always has been; it always will be. There's nothing to save it from.

When we, as individualized souls of truth, make the daily, moment-to-moment effort to be at peace with ourselves, then indeed we shall find this so-called true salvation. For we shall find ourselves and having done so, we will experience the peace, the freedom, and the joy of eternity. For eternity, my friends, is ever the moment that you are aware of. It is not yesterday. It is not tomorrow. But it is the moment that you have conscious awareness of.

Material science has gone a long ways and, yea, shall go even further. But the power that moves substance or matter, its cause of movement is not in matter itself. It is a power that man cannot touch, he cannot take apart, and he cannot analyze. He can only see the effects of this power, but not the power itself. That that is spiritual is only known by spirit. But we *are* spirit. And we can know it with our spiritual being. But when we go to express it, we put it, once again, into form and doing so, we guarantee its opposite. We guarantee the duality, which is the Law of Form.

So let us ponder and let us think. We are ever free in the moment that we choose to be so. We can, at any given time, rise our awareness, our state of consciousness, to a level where this peace passeth beyond understanding. We have the power. We always have had the power. For in truth, my good friends, the part of us that is the real being, that and that alone is the power. And that and that alone is true so-called salvation.

Thank you.

If there are any questions, you may feel free to raise your hands at this time, and I will be happy to share with you my understanding. [*After a pause, the Teacher continues.*] If there are—Yes?

Good morning, sir. You said that we chose to become a soul. And soul did not exist before we were incarnated? Or we chose to become a soul and we were incarnated?

Thank you very much. The gentleman has stated that I said that we chose to become a soul. I don't recall having made that exact statement, but I will try to share with you my understanding of what you have stated.

The power that is, is what we understand to be truth. We also understand that soul is not spirit, but it is the covering of spirit. And that that is covering is form and therefore it must respond to the laws of form, which are duality or choice. We understand that God—call it what you will—Infinite Intelligence does not choose. That it just *is*. That it always has been. That it always will be. That choice exists in what we understand to be form. For God is one, not two, and, therefore, is beyond choice. Choice exists in soul. Choice exists in body. Choice exists in creation, for choice is the Law of Creation. It has been often stated that God's manifestation is variety, and look at nature. And indeed it is.

So in reference to your question, Did we choose soul? I can only say that that which is beyond soul, known as Spirit, is not choice. It just *is*. Our soul chooses, in a sense, its incarnation. It chooses it like we choose anything. We make a decision, which is a choice, but once having made that decision, we cannot escape the laws governing the decision that we have made.

There is not, to my understanding, a haphazard choosing of incarnation on the evolutionary scale. It is a matter of moment-to-moment choosing. And once making that choice, we are guaranteed, our soul, to incarnate into certain bodies, certain circumstances, at certain times. But man is never left without his choice. He must fulfill what he chose yesterday, but he has this moment of eternity to set into motion new choices, new sets of circumstances, new laws. But he is ever governed by the laws that he set into motion yesterday and the day before. Thank you. Does that help with your question?

Yes. Thank you.

Thank you kindly. Are there any other questions concerning the morning talk? If not, thank you very much. Thank you.

OCTOBER 1, 1972

Church Lecture 13
The Web of Destiny

So in speaking this morning on the web of destiny, we're speaking of the things that we are weaving that bind us to certain patterns and to certain expressions. Many teachers have spoken on desire and the so-called pleasure ground of the senses. Many philosophies have taught the annihilation of desire, its suppression. This association has attempted to bring to mankind a bit different understanding concerning desire.

What is it that we mean by that word? Do we mean by the word *desire,* God expressing in a certain way that is satisfactory to our mind and to our brain? If we mean by that word *desire* that, then to annihilate or to suppress it is to deny the divinity, the birthright, of our own soul and our own spirit.

We have tried to teach in this association liberty under law and not license. When we attempt to educate desire, we are simply directing it through another level of awareness, another channel. When we attempt to suppress or to annihilate it, what we're doing in truth is denying our own divinity.

Remember, my good friends, when the love of the formless becomes the love of the form, we are lost in a sea of creation. We have, at every moment, a divine choice. We may choose to fulfill the desires that entertain our thoughts and become bound by them. Or we may choose to entertain the desires of our mind and be freed by them. It is when we recognize and realize that God and God alone is in back of every thought, every act, and every deed, that so-called evil and so-called bad is nothing more or less than undeveloped good. When we realize that, we will pause to think. And in that pausing, in that moment, we will know beyond a shadow of any doubt that we in truth are free.

When we accept with our mind that the fulfillment of desire is God's fulfillment and not our brain's, then we will be free and we will not experience the turmoil, the upset of the so-called brain. Balance is the teachings from on high, not imprisonment into either the so-called pleasure ground of the senses or imprisonment into false security. When desire expresses itself, it is energy, it is love, it is God. But when our mind thinks that we and we alone are dependent upon its fulfillment, that we and we alone must have what we want, when we want, and how we want it—that thinking, my good friends, is what binds us to the shackles of creation.

The topic chosen was entitled, "The Web of Destiny." And we, my good friends, are the spiders that are weaving those webs. Remember that a spider can only traverse the web that it has woven; the soul can only express on the patterns of thought that man has chosen to express upon. Broaden your horizons and you will see a new life, a new way, a greater freedom, a greater expression of your own divinity. It is when, through error of thought, we give power to people, to places, to things—that, my dear friends, is when the web that we have woven is limited and blinding.

It has been stated to our students before that when desire is the predominant thought in the mind reason cannot see. Why is that so? It all has to do with energy. It has to do with our energy flowing along one particular thought pattern. No matter what our thought may be, if it is thought of creation or form, it can and does ofttimes blind us. When these thoughts of creation, of our mind, when they are balanced with what is known as our soul faculties, with reason, with duty, with gratitude, with patience, with knowledge, and assurance, when those senses or functions are brought into balance with those soul faculties, man indeed is freed. Man indeed finds before his very eyes his own divinity.

Who is so illumined to know what thoughts are right for you? Who is so illumined to tell a man what thoughts are right for him? Right and wrong is ever relative to our understanding. God is not a judge. And God does not bind or enslave the souls. Our soul, our divinity, may have wandered from its home, from its source. But that that wanders from a thing, in its very wandering, is already on its way back home. Because one may be a little greater distance from his home than another may be, does not grant to anyone the right to judge the distance.

It is the tendency of the mind to judge, to declare. The reason that it does those things is because of its own insecurity. So many of us in this world of expression are so insecure. We can garner all of the wealth the world has to offer, but it does not grant us security. Because by the very nature of creation, which is duality, which is positive and negative, which is loss and gain, again and again on the wheel of delusion of form, there is no security. As long as our minds look without to find security, that's just as long as we are ever going to be insecure.

Security, my good friends, is when we find God. And that we find inside ourselves. When we find this thing they call God, when we find it, we shall know it. We won't have to believe it, because we will know it. Then, no matter what happens in the world of creation, you will move through time and be not moved by it. For having found your true birthright, you will become what you have found for you have always been it and have only wandered from it.

Thank you.

If there are any questions of a spiritual nature, you may feel free to raise your hand and ask them at this time. [*After a pause, the Teacher continues.*] If there are no questions, as I said once, months ago, that means I've had a merit system that's not too bad for I will pause to rest.

Thank you.

NOVEMBER 12, 1972

Church Lecture 14
Man's Only Suffering is His Denial of God

As the chairman has stated, the subject chosen for this morning's discussion is, "Man's Only Suffering is His Denial of God."

I am sure that most of us are in accord in the statement that man's God is ever equal to his understanding. In this association we do not understand God to be a judge or a power that makes choices for man. But we do understand this great Infinite Intelligence to be just that: infinite and intelligent. A Divine Power that sustains all creation. Choice is not something that God has unto himself. It is something that form or man has. So it is that man and man alone chooses what he wishes to do with this great power known as God. Now the question arises in the mind when we say that man is the one who has choice, not God, then the question arises, "What's going to make me a good person and a godly person? To do what's right because it's right to do right."

There are natural laws governing form or creation. When those laws of nature are transgressed, then man suffers, if you wish to call it that, the consequence. When we learn about these laws governing nature, we abide with them and flow with their immutableness because it is foolish to do otherwise. For example, we know that our being, our body, requires a certain amount of sleep, of rest, of food, of water, because that is what we have chosen for it to do. Some people require twelve hours of sleep and some people require two or less. Some people require three meals a day and some require one meal in two days. That is entirely dependent upon what we have accepted in mind, not this moment, but in all those moments and years before.

If we have accepted limitation, if we have accepted the need for eight hours of sleep—because that is what most people have accepted—then when we don't have it, we don't feel like we think we should. And the reason for that is because man is a law unto himself. And so the wise man, recognizing and realizing that man is a law unto himself, asks himself the question: "Then, God, what am I doing with the law that I am?"

Who is it, that has any common sense, that enjoys suffering? God does not give it to us, nor does God take it away. Only man can do that, for man is the one that has made the choice. He chooses to be happy and he chooses to be sad. He chooses to suffer or he chooses to be free. When man makes the latter decision and chooses to be free, then he must pay the price for the freedom that he has chosen. And then the question arises, "Why should freedom have a price tag?" My good friends, *we* have made freedom a price tag, because of our cherished opinions, because of our cherished thought patterns, because of what we have accepted in our mind as the right way in any given situation. That is the price tag that we must pay for freedom. *We* have done that to ourselves.

Now I know there are many students who would prefer to put that blame on their parents, you know, that last generation. But let us go beyond creation and let us go to the inner meaning of the soul's true purpose. A soul enters form according to the divine laws of merit. If that soul has entered in a family which is difficult for the child, then that's the lesson, one of many, that the child has to learn. God didn't do it to the soul. The soul did it to itself.

There is no power that I have ever found, outside of the divine power within man, that causes him joy or sadness. Man and man alone may choose to be receptive to what we call Infinite

Intelligence, to this Divine Power, this Great Neutrality, but *he* must make that decision in any given moment.

It is not, I am sure, for many, including myself, easy to change a thought pattern that has been long entertained in mind. The reason, my good friends, that it is not easy for most of us is because thought is a vehicle through which energy expresses itself and it literally makes a groove in the gray matter of the brain, a groove like on a record. And our conscious mind may be likened to the needle that plays on that record of our own brain. If we have played a tune for years, what I mean by that, if we have thought a certain way in a given situation for a long time or used a great deal of energy in entertaining a thought, then when the conscious mind, that needle, slips to that groove, to that part of the record, it repeats itself. And it is indeed most difficult to move the mind, the conscious awareness, to another groove. But it is not impossible at any given moment. Remember, my good friends, the longer you entertain a thought, the more difficult it is to change it.

It is the very nature of the mind to attach. It must attach to something or it loses its balance. Recognizing and realizing that it must attach to something, a wise man attaches it to that that is formless, to that that is free. And that we understand to be God. For if we permit it to attach to creation, we will guarantee joy and we will guarantee suffering, because creation by her very nature is the poles of opposites. There is nothing in form that is not dual. The only thing that is oneness—and oneness is freedom—is called God or peace. So what is it that we should waste our life-giving energies in permitting this mind to attach to things that are dual?

It has been stated that concentration is the key to all power, and we understand that concentration is one, never two. It means to put the mind pointedly and fixedly upon the object of your choice until only the essence remains. For the essence of a thing is the truth of the thing. So let us become aware of the essence of divinity. After all, it is awaiting our recognition this very moment.

Remember that no one can help us to change the grooves that we and we alone have created. Someone may share with us the way that they have found to make those changes that you may be seeking, hopefully. But they cannot do it for us, for that is contrary to the very laws of nature.

We see in this era of 1972 many changes. It's not—today's generation—what it was even in my day. And that hasn't been that many years. Why was it, and is it, so difficult for the generations to accept the changes? Well, it's very simple, my friends. We, in our ignorance through pride, have denied our own divinity, known as God. We have decided what is right and what is wrong. And everyone in all the universes in creation has made their decisions. Why is it that we are so ignorant to judge another, to judge the world, when even God himself doesn't even judge us? What is it within our form that thinks it's such a king that it may rule all of God's creation, that it may dictate and declare what is right for the world?

Is that the God you understand? If it is, think and ponder. It's such a limited one. Let us consider broadening our horizons and in so doing, be free. Man cannot be free—it is contrary to natural law—until he can in truth broaden his horizons, that his consciousness may expand and encompass the universes. For where, may I ask, can you not find God? It was said to me once that God is like a flea. You never know where you're going to find him. And so it is. Let us be humble.

God, the great power that is, is the greatest servant there ever was or there ever will be. He permits the rain to flow on all his trees and flowers and people. He doesn't know partiality, because he's not partial. He doesn't know choice, because he came before choice. He's greater than all things, because, my friends, he is the sustainer of all things.

If God doesn't choose hell for us, why does a sane man choose it for himself? That's known as denying your own divinity. What good is it worth being in an earth realm where there's nothing but apparent chaos, because everyone is deciding what's good for everyone else? What is it, this great brain, known as ego, this great pride? That's what forgets our divinity. It's only the brain. It got that way through ignorance, through forgetting its source. My friends, this thing called brain or gray matter is composed from the elements of nature. It has no eternity. It has no continuity. It comes from Mother Nature and to Mother Nature it shall return. For that that comes from a thing, by the law of coming from it, is destined to return to it.

You want to be free? Then pause and think. Don't plead with God and beg him for change when you're not willing to change yourselves. God is not going to do anything that we are not receptive to. Think about it.

It is not my purpose to decide what's right for anyone. But it is my purpose to share whatever light I may have received. How can you teach a student to be free when they're not even free to be taught? How can we have joy when we deny joy to the rest of the world? How can we have peace when we deny peace to another? How can we live in harmony through denial? How is that possible—to have heaven on earth—when we decide what that heaven is, when it shall appear, and how long it's going to exist?

When man is grounded in self, he sees like a horse with blinders: one direction and one only. He sees God in what he chooses to see God in and cannot see God in anything else. The teachings are to love all life and know the Light. But as long as we insist upon the false gods that we have created—these gods known as choice, these gods known as what's right or wrong for us; those, my dear friends, are the false gods of creation—they will ever fail us, no matter how well we serve them, because they are the created gods of mind stuff. And being created, they have dual expression. They will ever fail you. It is their very nature.

But, be of hope, for hope's eternal and truth is inevitable. We can make the change in eternity, and eternity is this moment, this very instant. The students have been given an exercise to help them to become aware of the false gods of their own creations. And I'll be happy to share that simple exercise with the congregation this morning. I am well aware that many people do not like to hear the thing that may help them the most. After all, who likes a shot of penicillin, when they're diseased, when it's the thing that's going to heal them? So I understand, I hope. Remember that irritation wakes the soul. It is satisfaction that lets it sleep. So let us awaken, if that's what we desire. The exercise that was given is that the student may sit in peace and think of a person, a place, or a thing that they truly love, that they have a strong feeling for. You know, some people say, "I never loved. I don't know what it is." Perhaps they always have and never recognized that that's the name for it. However, to someone or something or a place that they're very fond of and I assure you there is no one in this church that isn't fond of something or someone or someplace. To choose wisely and to entertain that in thought until they have the full experience of that great power of love or of fondness. Having the full awareness of it, they're now to change their thought and yet maintain the feeling. Now they choose someone that they dislike, or something or some place. And there is no one that doesn't dislike something. That would be contrary to the laws of creation. And whether we like it or not, we are in creation and we're attached to it until we decide to make the change. If the student is able to maintain and to sustain this great feeling of love to the person, place, or thing that they dislike, they are on the path to freedom. If they are not able to do so, that means that false god of decision is greater than the true God of freedom. It's a simple exercise. I highly recommend it as a daily use before your silence or meditation time.

Now I know to some, from the movement in the congregation, that perhaps the lecture has been a bit strong. But tell me, friends, would you rather have something strong and be free, or would you prefer something weak and stay a cripple?

Thank you.

DECEMBER 3, 1972

Church Lecture 15

Man, The Universe

And so it is this morning, I believe I am scheduled to lecture on, "Man, The Universe."

For many years these friends from the world of spirit have repeatedly asked that we broaden our horizons, that we expand our consciousness, that we be more receptive to the possibilities and to the probabilities that life is not only eternal, but that life is everywhere. My good friends, again and again it is spoken that God is everywhere present and never absent or away. We understand God to be this great Infinite Intelligence. If it is, in truth, everywhere present, never absent or away, that simply would mean that there is no place in all the universes that life does not exist.

Indeed, we must ask ourselves the question, "What inside of us could possibly entertain the thought that we and we alone are the only evolved, intelligent beings in all of God's universes?" In this age we are going to see great things throughout the universes. There will be a great need for spiritually-awakened people to help the masses that they do not stumble and fall along the way.

We in truth know that we are indeed one. There is no separation in truth. The power that moves our body, that causes us to think, is one and the same power. We are a universe in and of itself. Everything that we see and everything that we hear, wherever we go and wherever we be, is ever, my good friends, inside of our self. It is the illusion caused by our mind, through error and through ignorance, that causes us to think the things that we need or desire to attain are in some far-off, distant place. As long as we choose to limit our universe in that way, that's just as long as it's going to be that we remain these so-called little men.

God, the Divine, is a kind power. It *is*. It doesn't have to be told. It is the eternity. The moment that it expresses through form—form, being the dual expression of creation, makes choices. And we can choose at any given moment to be happy or to be sad, to be limited or to be limitless. My good friends, it is totally dependent upon our self.

For centuries man has cried to what he has called God for help. We can never receive help until we become receptive to it. But the brain, the mind, the ego decides what help is for oneself, where it's to come from, when it is to come, and how it is to come. When that happens man and man alone becomes the great obstruction to his own freedom, to his own peace, and to his own joy.

And so the question rises, "How can I be receptive to the things that I feel that I need or desire?" When man becomes in harmony with the thing desired, he becomes it in mind, in thought, and in being. When that happens he experiences it in a physical, material world. My good friends, this is a thinking world. Everything that you see is nothing more than the effect of the power known as thought. And as was stated during our healing services, thought is the vehicle through which God—the greatest power there'll ever be, there is, or ever has been—it is the vehicle through which that power moves.

There are many teachings on the new thought age of how to be positive. We can indeed be positive with what is known as our conscious mind. But if our conscious thoughts are not in rapport or in harmony with our subconscious ones, then we have failure. And so it is the students are taught to know yourself, through daily, silent meditation. For when man knows himself, he will free himself. For he is his only obstruction and he is in truth his only way.

What is a godly man? We understand that to be good. And what is good? Some say what is good to them is indeed bad to another. When we express the divinity within ourselves, we cannot help but awaken to the great truth that the one and only God there really is, is a God of power, of humbleness. It knows. It doesn't have to be told. It has total consideration. It does not give to one and deny to another. For when the rains fall, they fall on everything.

Choice, my friends, is made by man. And therefore, he chooses to be healthy and he chooses to be sick. He chooses to be wealthy and he chooses to be poor. How does man make those choices and yet be ignorant, consciously, of what he has done? It depends, my friends, on what you are entertaining in thought in the depths of your own inner mind. It depends on what you have been brainwashed to from childhood up to your present moment.

How does man find out what his mental obstructions are, when he does not make the effort to know himself? So many in these works of spirituality and in communication have asked, many a student has asked, "How can you contact this other dimension?" My good friends, it's very simple. It is the mind that communicates with mind. And it is the body that communicates with the body. And it is the spirit that communicates with the spirit. And so indeed is it simple. Awaken our own spirit. And when our own spirit awakens it will contact all the spirits around in the atmosphere that it is in rapport with.

If we are attracting things to us that are distasteful, it is so simple to stop, to pause, to think, to recognize, and to realize that our soul is expressing through a level of awareness and we are experiencing something that is distasteful to us. All we have to do is to think and think more deeply. And we will rise from that level of awareness and in so doing the experience that we are experiencing will disappear as it came to us from within our own being.

Remember that no one saves us but ourselves. No one can and no one may. We alone must walk the path. Teachers only show the way. We have the right at any moment, my friends, to awaken to our birthright. There is no reason, no reason whatsoever that we should be sad or miserable or sick or disturbed. Peace and peace alone is the only power, for peace is God. And we have the right to choose that peace this moment here and now. But in so choosing it, we must also guard and protect it. For we go out into a world where there is seeming much disturbance. And if we become in harmony with those disturbances, we are robbing ourselves of the great peace that passeth all understanding.

I have, for many years, made it a practice to take a few moments each day and talk to myself, for man, in truth, is three, not one. Most of humanity is aware of their conscious mind. A few, a very few of their subconscious. And, yea, even fewer of their superconscious. And so it is, if you choose to do so, make a practice of talking to those other two. They are part of our self. If you do so, you can free yourself and truly serve the purpose for which we have been sent here.

Thank you.

JANUARY 7, 1973

Church Lecture 16

Attention and Energy

I'm sure it is of interest to all of us, not part of the time, but all of the time. For we understand that this mind of ours is a vehicle which directs the power or the energy known as

Infinite Intelligence or God. And so we see in all of our acts and our activities that our attention goes in a multitude of different areas at different moments through the course of a day. When we realize and awaken to the great truth that we are giving forth this life-giving energy to whatever we are entertaining in thought at any given moment, we can see the great value of what the new thought school calls positive thinking or constructive thinking.

Everything in this universe that we see around and about us is nothing more than the effect of directed energy. If we find in our lives that we are entertaining the thought of need, the thought of lack, or the thought of limitation, what we are in truth doing is directing energy into that level of consciousness. And in so doing we are guaranteeing beyond a shadow of any doubt the very thing to govern our lives. They say that it pays to be positive. Well, it does more than that, my good friends. It frees us from the limitation that we have set into motion. If it is true—and Nature herself demonstrates that truth—that everything is the effect of directed energy, then it behooves man to choose wisely what he is directing his thought to.

Many people have stated that they have tried this new thought school and tried for many months, or even years, to think positively and constructively without any beneficial results. Well, it is very evident, my good friends, that we may have tried, but only with this conscious mind. Remember that the conscious mind is the electrical mind, the directing mind. And the so-called subconscious is the magnetic, the attracting mind, the receiver. We have spent a lifetime in directing thought into negative avenues. We do not change that in the course of a minute, unless we have truly awakened to ourselves and, in so doing, know the truth and are able to demonstrate it wholly, fully, and completely. It is a matter of retraining. It is not a matter of what you must push into the mind to free it, but it is indeed a matter of what must be taken out of it in order to free it.

We are all here this morning according to directed energy, to laws that we and we alone have set into motion. We made the choice and we made that choice according to many variables that are set in motion inside of our own mind. We could be someplace else, we can say to ourselves. But we're not. We are here for a purpose. If we are not here for a purpose, then we are no longer thinking people with any sense of reason or light. I am sure we are not here because there was no place better to go in the multitude of places there is in this universe and in this city. But we're here because there is something inside of us that is seeking something.

We may decide that we know what that something is. Or we may decide that we're not quite sure. Well, whatever it is that we will decide, that and that alone is what we will receive. If we decide that we're not sure and we're filled with doubt and uncertainty, then that is the only thing that we can receive, because it is the only thing that we're sending out.

No one anywhere asks us to believe in anything. We have a reasoning faculty that we are born with in this universe. And that reasoning faculty is very clear. It says, "Man, think, and think more deeply. " Think for yourself. Look deep within your own being and see what it is that is influencing your thought, your acts, and your activities. Are we influenced by our friends or associates and those in authority? Or are we influenced by our own soul in the fulfillment of its own destiny? Let us ask ourselves that question a bit more often. Let us not be the leaf upon the water that's constantly tossed from shore to shore. Never finding its true home, because its true home it is not seeking. We cannot find, my good friends, what we're not seeking. So let us first ask ourselves, "What is it in truth, in this life, that I am really seeking?" So that we may use this divine energy in a practical, logical, and reasonable way.

Ofttimes a person will expose themselves to a teaching with preconceived thoughts and ideas of what they should be receiving from it. And, of course, if they do not receive what they have set into motion, then they are disappointed. Because man is a law unto himself, he sets into motion that disappointment. When we go to school to learn any subject we don't tell the teacher how to teach us and we don't tell the teacher how much we are to learn. We go to receive and to be receptive, not to accept blindly, without thought, but at least to have an open mind, which is a clear mind.

And so it is in our daily life when we encounter so many different things, what is it that we and we alone are setting into motion? Life herself is like a great mirror. She reflects back to us every moment of every hour what we and we alone are sending out into the atmosphere. Now that is not such a pleasant thing to some of us some of the time, but at other times, it is indeed a most pleasing thing to be aware of. But the law herself is totally impartial. If all of the experiences are reflections of levels of awareness that we are entertaining at any given moment, then the law is totally impartial. It works at all times and in all ways.

Remember, friends, no one does it to us and no one does it for us. We may be guided by our own spirit to seek help in a multitude of different areas, but when it comes right down to it, we and we alone will use what we receive wisely or foolishly. That is entirely up to ourselves. We are never left without choice in this world or in any world, because choice is the Law of Creation. We have the day and we have the night. And so it is wherever you find form or creation, this constant choice, these decisions that must be reached. Most people think, "Well, I'm fortunate. I only have to make a few decisions in the course of a week." How sad and untrue that is. We are making decisions every instant of every moment; that is the very nature and characteristic of the mind. Because it is dual. We are choosing, at this instant, to listen or not to listen, to accept or to reject. And this process of the mind is going on constantly at all times.

So let us think more deeply, my good friends. And let us be free here and now. Why wait and seek some heaven off in somewhere that we know not? Why not seek it this instant? Because if we don't find it this instant, it is certainly indicative that we are never going to find it at any time.

This moment and this moment is your moment. Ask yourself what you're going to do with it. Yesterday has gone with all of its joy and all of its sorrow. If man directs this great energy back there, he is only dissipating it, for nothing can be done with that that has already happened. To this moment, he can do everything, for he is this great power itself. So let us work with the moments in which we can do something. Usually a person worries about what's going to happen tomorrow, next week, next year, and etc. Of what import is that if you are thinking in this moment and utilizing every bit of that energy to fulfill the true purpose of your soul's incarnation?

It is stated, at least in this Serenity understanding, that joy is the inside job, that God is a God of joy. So let us be more godly in all our thoughts and activities. And let us be joy *this* moment. Let us express the right of our own divinity here and now.

Thank you.

FEBRUARY 4, 1973

Church Lecture 17

The Wisdom of Tolerance

The topic, as the chairman has said, has been entitled, "The Wisdom of Tolerance."

Now in the understanding that we have at this time tolerance is one of the triune soul faculties; that it is inseparable from duty and gratitude. We do know that without tolerance, there is no gaining of understanding, for one cannot understand what they do not express tolerance to.

Indeed, it is seemingly difficult to express tolerance when one encounters in their daily activities those who, for some reason or another, do not face their personal responsibilities. But if we will make the great effort to express a little tolerance, we will indeed gain a bit of wisdom and see that no matter what it is and no matter who it is, they are simply expressing a certain level, a state of consciousness, at that particular time.

Each time that we express intolerance, we give, from our very being, power to the thing we're not able to tolerate. For that that disturbs us, my good friends, is that which controls us. So a wise man stops and ponders and thinks. Who is it, or what is it, that you wish to control and enslave your soul? If it is true—and it is our belief and understanding that it is true—that our soul is inseparable from the Divine, that it is one and the same thing, that it is only logical and practical that if we're going to give any power to anything, we give it to that which is giving power to us. So stop and think, my friends, whenever you feel a need to express intolerance, you are being indeed controlled by that very thing.

We look around [and] about us in this world of creation and we see so many different things. We will guarantee that which we cannot tolerate to befall us. The reason that we will guarantee it is because it is only through tolerance that we will gain understanding. And whether or not we think that we wish understanding, it is the divine purpose of the soul's incarnation to gain understanding.

And so it is, the Bible prophets have spoken so many times, In all your getting, get understanding. For the moment that you get understanding, you awaken your soul from its sleep, from its slumber of satisfaction. Indeed it is difficult, seemingly, for many people to awaken from their slumber, to make changes within themselves. Why is it difficult to change? Why, it's very simple. We become satisfied with that with which we're familiar and we feel a strange, but false, security. That is why it is seemingly difficult to make changes, because we have permitted ourselves to be governed by fear.

And what is fear? Nothing more, my friends, than the direction of energy into the negative or creation. The same energy, of course, directed through the soul faculties or through our spiritual being is known as faith. But it is indeed one and the same thing. That is the reason that we find it's such a struggle to go out into the world and to tolerate.

It's not a matter of tolerating. It is a matter of tolerance. And I understand a great difference between those two words. One means, to me, to put up with someone because it's in your best interest. Then they say that that's to tolerate someone. Tolerance is to awaken that you are indeed in creation, that you are indeed a part of all things, that whatever you may like or dislike in another human being is inside of our self. Of course the mind says, "Well, I've never acted that way." That is no guarantee, my friends, that its potential *to* act that way is not inside of ourselves. So tolerance is something that's inside of us. It's a recognition. It's a realization that we are indeed all things, and therefore, it is not wise for us to judge. For he who judges only judges himself and in so doing guarantees the very judgment to befall him, that he may gain more understanding and to become aware of why a person acts this way or that way.

Indeed is it true that in all your getting, get understanding. For with understanding, there is no such thing as war. With understanding, there's no such thing as discord and disharmony. There's only peace, the peace that passeth all understanding. But it is fear and fear alone that causes the ignorance that makes us what they call intolerant in things and people and in circumstances and conditions.

When we stop and our mind is entertained with thoughts about what everyone else in this world should be doing, what the politicians shouldn't be doing, and what the religionists should be doing and that's all we can do—is entertain that type, that attitude of mind—then indeed are we intolerant and indeed are we in turmoil.

They say that joy is an inside job. How many of us express joy in the course of a week or even a year? Why is it so few people are joyous in this world? Why? Only from lack of understanding themselves. Joy is an attitude of mind. It comes when we open the soul faculties and when we remember that indeed we are (our soul) divine, that indeed does it have a purpose to serve. When we're about our Father's business—and our Father is inside us, ourselves—then we're going to know why we are here. And when we know why we're here, we will have an indication of where we're going and where we came from. For something, my good people, cannot come out of nothing. So we came here from somewhere, from something, and by that very law we're going somewhere to something.

It was said once that man is never born; he only becomes aware of the dimension in which he is expressing. So if man is never born, of course, man never dies. And so how long will it take us to awaken to the great truth that we *are* this great eternity? Not these few years that we have a conscious awareness of. You cannot count the centuries that your soul has expressed in time. They cannot be counted by the human mind.

Think, my good friends. What are you doing with the life that you are? What is it that you are seeking and have not yet found? If you have difficulty in your search, the obstacle and the obstruction is the intolerance that is within us. That's the only reason that we do not find the light of truth is because so often we become opinionated. We have our opinions and they don't agree with everyone else's opinions. Of course not. That's creation. No man ever found anything in form that was identically the same. Not even a spoon made identical is identical, because that would be contrary to the Law of Creation.

And so it is, if there is something that you do not have, that you desire, that you feel is needed for you, recognize the great truth that it is right where you are. It is inside of your very being. And when you express the first soul faculty, known as duty to your soul, gratitude for its expression, and tolerance for the other souls that are an inseparable part of yourself, then you will find the Light that will free you while yet in flesh.

Thank you.

MARCH 4, 1973

Church Lecture 18

The 125th Anniversary of Modern Spiritualism

As our chairman has already stated, we are celebrating on this the last Sunday of the month of March the beginning of the era of modern Spiritualism.

There are so many who are new to this understanding that we like to speak forth our beginnings, as they are not known by many people. Indeed it was in the year of 1848 on the 31st day of March that the now known spirit rappings were brought into being in Hydesville, New York, through the mediumship of three little children, known as the Fox sisters.

What meaning does this beginning have to us, this day, 125 years later? As we look over the history of the religions in the past 100 years, we find that a great change took place in the 1860s and again in the 1890s. We see from the beginnings, known as the spirit rappings, that a whole new concept of spiritual awakening came to the world. Out of this new era, birth was given to many new philosophies. A teaching that we were no longer eternally damned, that we and we alone were responsible for all of our acts and all of our activities, that indeed there was no savior waiting for us, that the salvation that the world had spoken of for so many centuries was inside of us, the only place that we will ever find truth, my friends.

So many seek truth or freedom outside of themselves, but that is not possible when man has yet to find it inside. It has been stated before that the world around us, of course, is nothing but a mirror reflecting back to us exactly where we are.

What do these new teachings brought to the world, known as Spiritualism, mean to us this moment in our daily acts and activities and in our mundane jobs? Why, it's very simple, my friends. Spiritualism is concerned about this moment. *This* is our eternity. So many think we're concerned about the dead. I don't know of any Spiritualist that ever talked to the dead, for the dead, to us, are those who are asleep and in lethargy in the error of ignorance. Who would waste their time speaking to those who are not awake?

And so it is, my friends, that we stop to think now, this moment. Where are we going in this world? Look and see where have we been, for that is indicative of where we are heading, unless we are willing to awaken the Divine Spirit that is within us, that Infinite Intelligence, that we may know beyond a shadow of any doubt that where we are this moment is what we and we alone have set into motion.

There will be no changes in our lives, unless we are willing to make those changes. There is no power, my good friends, no power in any universe anywhere, that can free us until we and we alone are willing to take the step inside of our self that leads to freedom.

How often the mind deludes us and dictates to us that all the causes and all of the bad and seeming good is outside of us. How often do we give this life-giving power to things that are of no import? This, indeed, is the message that Spiritualism is striving to bring to the world, not just the possibility of communion with another dimension. The true purpose of Spiritualism is to help us awaken to the great truth that we and we alone are responsible for all our thoughts, acts, and activities. It is not the fault of our parents, nor is it the fault of society, our friends, or our relatives. There is no fault, except the level of awareness, the attitude of mind, that we choose to entertain at any given moment.

Many times the voices from on high have spoken. The changes that you see that are necessary, do them now and do them quickly, for it is not easy to change patterns that we have become habituated to. It is not easy for anyone. It takes strength of character, a strong will, and great determination to serve the Divine. Not because the Divine is a hard task-maker—we don't believe that way—but because *we* have made the things that will free us difficult to attain.

It is the tendency of the mind to garner, to gather, and to possess. It does those things—and it is its natural tendency—because of its error of ignorance. If we will but pause and think a bit more deeply and a bit more clearly, there is nothing in the universes to possess. We have already been given everything. The reason that we feel a need for things is simply because we have denied our own divinity and in so denying that divinity, we have lost the awareness that the Divine is expressing through us at every moment, that according to our attitude of mind and according to our receptivity to it, shall we be aware that all things indeed are ours. For how can they be otherwise, my good friends, when we, in truth, are all things?

Spirit is either a universal, infinite intelligence or it is not. If we believe in that divine Infinite Intelligence, then we no longer entertain in thought need for anything. That is one of the many messages that Spiritualism has to bring to this world. Why do we want to continue to entertain obstructions, disturbances, seeming poor health, and the like? What is it inside of us that seems to enjoy suffering? Surely there is no one, while expressing reason, that would entertain the thought that we have come to this world to suffer and to be limited. That exists only in our own error. But the Divine, indeed, has granted the soul what is known as free will. We may choose at any given moment to be free or to remain bound in our own limitations.

The Serenity Association is very grateful for what has been brought to it. Let us say, in other words, for what it has been and is trying to be receptive to. For we do not teach, nor believe in, a God that is a giver. We simply believe in a divine Infinite Intelligence that is totally neutral, that has not denied you of your free will by choosing that it will give to one and take away from another. Having accepted that teaching, we find, through a receptivity to that limitless flow, that we are awakened to a greater understanding, perhaps. And in awakening, we sense and feel and experience this peace that passeth all understanding.

We are trying to share with you, my good friends, the understanding that God is a divine, neutral power that sustains all things, always has and always will, that when we pray what we do in truth is get our self out of the way. Through a new attitude of mind, we have a different level of awareness. And in so doing, we become receptive to the Divine Power that flows totally unobstructed.

So many people say they've prayed and they're such a good soul and yet God seems to deny the things they need the most. Well, my dear friends, as long as we entertain that type of thinking, that is just as long as we're going to be denied from the things that we think that we need. Let us come to a greater understanding. Let us rise our soul to a level of light where we will know beyond a shadow of any doubt what life in truth is all about. So the question arises in the mind, Well, how do we rise our self, our awareness, to this greater level where all things flow unobstructed? It is a simple word that takes us there. And man has called it faith. But what indeed is faith? Is it not when the mind is wholly and completely convinced of the perfect outcome of any situation and has no question whatsoever concerning it? That we understand to be faith. And when it is demonstrated, there is no obstruction because we, our brains, our beings, are no longer in the way.

Many people find that the teachings of Spiritualism are similar to many of the new-thought religions. My good friends, we are indeed very grateful that humanity finds that similarity, for it is Spiritualism, in its birth 125 years ago, that gave birth to the so-called new-thought religions. And if we will study the history of religion, we will find these new-thought religions, though a bit different from Spiritualism, were given birth from that humble movement.

Today we have the science of parapsychology and we have the societies of psychical research. Why did they come to the world? They came to the world to investigate a new religion. To investigate a religion that was striving to demonstrate that there was no death and that there are no dead.

And so it is that in this day and age Spiritualism stands humble in the world knowing in truth that it is indeed the parent of all your new-thought religions.

My good friends, the modern movement of Spiritualism did not come to this world to build cathedrals. It came to this world to awaken the souls that are lying sleeping, that are, through error, giving the divine power to things, to this great illusion, known as creation.

Remember that anything that you feel or touch, sense or see has been created by the power known as mind. And so it is, if something troubles you, my friends, recognize and realize the great truth: it is a creation that exists in the gray matter of your brain. It does not exist in truth; that you can, through a change of thought, remove the obstruction in the sense that you will rise to a different level of awareness, a different attitude of mind and no longer be aware of that particular illusion and delusion.

So let us be at peace with ourselves, for the true self is the God self. And when we pause, there, in that garden of beauty and eternity, we sometimes wonder why we have slept so long. Thank you.

MARCH 25, 1973

Church Lecture 19
Genuine Mediumship

The topic chosen for this morning's discussion was "Genuine mediumship." For so many people, it seems, do not understand what the word *medium* or *mediumship* truly means. Our national association has defined the word *medium* as a person who is sensitive to vibrations from other dimensions and through whom intelligences from those dimensions are able to convey messages and produce the phenomena of Spiritualism.

There is indeed much more to Spiritualism and to mediumship than conveying messages. The very nature and purpose of mediumship is to bring awareness to the world, for man is responsible for all his acts, thoughts, and activities and indeed is it sad to be responsible for effects from causes that we have set into motion through so-called unawareness. Some will say that it does not seem just that man should be responsible for the things of which he is not aware of doing. That, my good friends, is no excuse or exemption from the divine laws. Because man has chosen, at some time along his evolutionary path, to no longer be aware of the dimensions of which he is indeed a part, has no blame outside of our self. If we choose to sleep when there is work to be done, that choice is our divine birthright. But if we choose to awaken ourselves to what this world is really all about, then that, too, is our birthright.

So what in truth is genuine mediumship? To my understanding, friends, it's becoming aware of the world that we in truth live in.

So many people think that we're going to leave this physical piece of clay and we're going to go off there to some world of spirit. Well, my good friends, if we have awakened to a world of spirit within our self, then we will be able to go to that world of spirit because it does not exist outside of us, for us, if it does not exist inside of us this moment. We're in heaven now. We're not going to it. And we're in that so-called opposite place, if that is what we choose. But we and we alone are making this choice.

Many times the students, over the years, have thought that they're doing their part by doing a daily meditation and going to church on Sunday, when they feel so inclined. For it is the nature of Spiritualism not to impose upon the individual souls and, therefore, by its very nature we do not require its membership or its friends or students to attend any church or this church. Friends, we indeed will get out of anything, be it mathematics or playing golf, whatever it is that we are putting into it.

Mediumship is not just spirit communication. It is not just standing on a podium giving messages. It is not having people come to you and ask about their stocks. It is not about solving marital problems and the like. That is a very minute part of mediumship. Mediumship is an awareness of why a person is experiencing certain effects in their life. It is a revealing, a revelation, of the causes that the individual soul has set into motion. Without mediumship in the world, there is no awareness of the dimensions we truly live in.

So many people think that mediumship is some special gift that a few have and that the Divine, so-called God, has denied the rest of the world. My friends, everyone is a medium. And everyone is demonstrating to some extent, whether they like it or not, a phase of mediumship. For we are all governed and controlled by the levels of awareness, the so-called invisible influences, that we choose to be in rapport with. Because we do not see those causes does not in any sense of the word deny us of their effects.

Where cometh our thought? Ask yourself the question. If it cometh from within yourself, from your own being, then if you will ponder and truly think, I am sure you will agree that it's quite a mixed-up being we have come to be. For one moment we decide on one thing, only in the next moment to decide on something else. My friends, it is what we are in rapport with. It is what level of consciousness that we have chosen, at any moment, to express.

In the unfoldment of mediumship, we must remove the obstructions that we and we alone have created. It is not a matter of belief. It is a matter of awakening.

Mediumship is a communication with many dimensions. They are not all the world of spirit. There is the dimension known as the mental world and ofttimes, if a medium is in rapport within himself with that level, then that is what is expressed. There is a dimension known as a desire world. If that is what the medium's own soul consciousness is expressing, then that is what he will be (or she will be) in communion with.

And so it is, friends, that the first step in genuine mediumship is becoming aware of oneself. How can we possibly help another soul up the eternal ladder of progression if we are not willing or able to help our self? And this is our understanding of the meaning, when they said in that book, "O physician, heal thyself." What kind of logic or reason is it to think that we can serve the Divine and help another, when in that very serving we are not capable of helping our self?

This association has no such teaching. We do teach and try to demonstrate that whatever, in this universe, happens to us is indeed caused by us. There are no forces or influences, my friends, anywhere, anytime, in any universe that has power over you unless *you* choose in your thinking to give power to it.

Remember, not everyone lives, thinks, or speaks the way that we would like to have them do. But let us ask our self the question, What is it inside of our self that desires that another human soul should think, should act, should speak or do what we want them to do? Let us think about that before we even attempt to unfold mediumship. Because, my friends, it is indicative, if we want the world to be a certain way, it is indicative that our world, our universe, is small and narrow and it will not open up to encompass God's divine variety of expression.

In unfolding on this spiritual path, there's a soul faculty known as duty, gratitude, and tolerance. Duty to what? the question rises in the mind. And tolerance for what? And gratitude to whom or to what? It is very clear. Duty to the only part of us that is eternal, not the form and not the flesh, and not the thought, for it comes and goes. Duty to that eternal spirit that is the true self. Gratitude for the opportunity of its expression. And tolerance for the levels within our self that are so difficult to grow through.

What does it benefit us, my good friends, to speak a thousand words unless there's a single act? If the words cannot stimulate within our mind the interest, the drive, the motive to move within our being to a greater light inside of our self, then the words, no matter how many they may be, have gone in vain.

Think where you are. Think what you're doing to yourselves. Because if you will think about what you're doing to yourselves, then I know you will think about what it is doing to another. My friends, it is a very selfless thing to take the time each day and stop and think about yourself. Think a little deeper. Because if you will take that time, you will, in time, broaden your horizons.

I have never met an individual that has been completely satisfied and I hope I never do, because there is nothing more detrimental to the soul's awakening than the sleep known as satisfaction. The moment we permit ourselves to be satisfied, we stop striving to do something better. And so it is, the divine discontent, that we are ever striving for perfection. And what is it within us that strives for perfection? Why, my good friends, it is the one and only thing that is perfect, the divine Infinite Intelligence, ever seeking to express itself, and the mind experiences that as a drive to be perfect in all it acts and in all its endeavors.

Mediumship has a great purpose to serve for everyone. For everyone in truth is a medium, for they are to some extent in communication with some dimension. And who is so illumined to judge whether it's the dark one or the light one? The individual themselves, from their own experiences, they and they alone will know which dimension they are communing with.

We are never alone, no matter who we are and no matter where we are. There are those entities around and about us that we have attracted from our thoughts, our acts, and our deeds. And if we will be at peace, we will see them and we will hear them. If we are in negative vibrations, you can be rest assured we have a multitude of friends on this side and the other side to help us stay in our negative lethargy. But if we are willing to use some strength of character, to stand up and know that we have the divine right to express joy, happiness, divine supply, and all the good that comes from those levels, if we have the will power expressing through our being, then we will indeed find this heaven that so many have sought for so very, very long.

Sometimes in the unfoldment of the students I'm called because of certain experiences that they have encountered, that they feel are detrimental to themselves. Well, my friends, the experience encountered and the feeling of its being detrimental is nothing more than what is inside of our self. No person can experience a psychic or so-called spiritual experience that is detrimental to them if they are not entertaining in thought on some level, conscious or subconscious, the very thing that they are experiencing. Because man is a law unto himself.

If the friends that you have attracted from the other dimension are not serving their purpose the way you think that they *should be*, you can be rest assured, my friend, you are looking in a mirror and those spirits are revealing to you exactly where we are. Not where we *think* we are, but where we are in truth. And so it is with all of this foolishness and paraphernalia of spirit possession and all these things that you read so much about, check the so-called medium or the individual that is having the experience, because, my friends, they are in communication and in rapport with that level of awareness and, therefore, are in dire need of seeking, within themselves, a way out of the prison house they have created.

I tell you that from personal experience, not from reading a book or having someone tell me. I had to grow through my own levels and I'm still in the process. And I am very grateful. In Spiritualism, we call those levels the elementals. Some people call it ventilating. They're going through what is known as the emotional realm. Friends, whether we like it or not, we all have an emotional realm. We're the creators of it; God isn't. And we've all got to face it someday. So let us face it now. Let us face our jealousies, our angers, our greeds, and our envies. Let us face those things. Who are we to be so awakened that we don't have those things existing within our very being? My friends, we're all a part of the human race. Look at the human race and tell me that there is a soul that doesn't have those functions. Because if you do, we're blinding ourselves. We're in the human race. We are a part of the human race. And those functions are a part of creation. I agree, indeed, it is only an error of ignorance. But who amongst us is free, totally, wholly, and completely, of the error of ignorance? Let us awaken within ourselves.

This association is not here to judge. It strives to help those who are seeking. We have a little bit of awareness not to bother with those who are not seeking. For indeed, unsolicited help is only to no avail.

So what is it that we want in life and what is it that we understand about spirit or spirituality? Think, my good friends, think more deeply and think more broadly. Where are we and where are we going? We already know where we've been. If we don't, something's radically wrong upstairs. So let us think where we are *this* moment. And in thinking where we are this moment, we will have an indication of where we're going. And let us forget about where we've been. Because as long as we entertain that back there, that is just as long as we will stay on that level of awareness and not see the light that we are facing this moment, the only moment that is our eternity.

Thank you.

APRIL 1, 1973

Church Lecture 20
Growing in the Light

The topic chosen for this morning's discussion by my spiritual teacher was, "Growing in the Light." We understand in our use of the word *Light*, we use that as a meaning or an expression of truth. For wherever there is light, darkness disappears. And so it is throughout the ages that man has looked upon darkness as error and ignorance and upon light as the path and the truth.

This association presents Spiritualism ever in accord with its own understanding. And that is the great blessing of the philosophy, the religion, and the science of Spiritualism. It recognizes and it accepts that each individual has a divine right to their level of awareness, to their expression at any given moment. And so it is that you will find in the movement of Spiritualism indeed a wide variety of thought and of understanding. But there is a common ground upon which we all stand, and that common ground is very simple: to respect and grant the right to investigate spiritual matters as we spend so much time investigating mundane matters.

Growing in the light, my friends, is something that takes place inside of yourself. It is not something that you go here or there for. Whatever we receive from any philosophy or any religion is ever in harmony with what we are giving to it. If we give it an open mind, then we're going to receive in accord with that vibration. And so it is with Spiritualism and growing in the light.

We're here, my friends, for such a short time and it is not often that we care to think about it. There is no set time that we're going into this other dimension. And the sadness is that so many think it's such a great change. That, my good friends, does not even stand the test of logic, let alone reason. If we are happy this moment, and that is the way we usually are, then, of course, that's the way we're going to be in a so-called world of spirit in another dimension because we take with us what we are. We take with us what we are that we may view what we have done.

And so it is in the teachings that our conscience is what guides our ship. It knows what's right or wrong for us according to the grade of school that we have placed ourselves in.

No one knows in truth what is the best path for you. They may speak and try to guide or to help you, but you and you alone in the depths of your very soul know what you have done with your life. You and you alone have set the laws into motion that guide your ship throughout this great eternity of this very moment. It was said by this teacher once before that if you don't find the awareness of eternity this moment it's indicative that you will have difficulty finding that eternity in the next moment.

This, my good friends, is a thinking world. And it's for the thinkers. Again and again the teachings are given to us that whatever happens to us, we and we alone have caused it. There is no power outside our being that says we're going to do this or we're going to do that. God, the Divine, the Infinite Intelligence—matters not what you call it; it's the one, divine, neutral Power or Energy—is inside of us. And if we cannot find this Divine Power inside of us, we are not going to find it outside of us. Because, my friends, like attracts like and if we don't have that inside, it cannot exist for us outside.

And so in growing in the light, let us pause more often in our activities. Let us ask ourselves why we have the experiences that we do. Do not look to others for the cause; that is only the delusion of the so-called uneducated ego that says that cause is outside of our self. It's not our neighbors to blame. And it's not our husbands, our wives, our brothers, our sisters, our teachers, or our friends or so-called enemies. We stand where we are because we are who we are.

And so how great is the understanding that at any given moment we may choose to change. If there is something that we do not like, it is a very simple process, my good friends, to change your view. And how does man change his view? Simply by changing his thought. We can think things that bring beauty into our lives or we can think the opposite.

How many centuries and how many times must the Divine Spirit express in form for the form to awaken to the greatest truth of all truths? That we are free when we're free in thought. Thought is what is governing our ship. It is the captain. Our destiny is the effect, my good children, of our thought. Let us ponder more often what we are doing to ourselves, for we and we alone are the only doer. The Divine Spirit called God is that great power that sustains what we do. And so it is that good and bad is simply varying degrees of the one and only neutral Power.

When man conceives God in his thoughts, he has created God. And that God will ever be subject to change. It is the God that's in our hearts, that does not begin or end, but sustains us in all things. It's an inner feeling and an inner knowing. To define the Infinite Intelligence or God limits it into form and creation. And so it is that battles go on throughout time, for people, not understanding that they in truth are free, that their bondage, lack, and limitation is only a delusion created by so-called mind stuff.

Whatever it is that you want, choose it wisely. Stay with it long enough and it shall appear in your universe. How sad, there is so much contradiction with our desires. For one minute we desire one thing, only to deny it in the desire of tomorrow. It has been stated that One is God or Infinite Intelligence, that One is the power itself, that One is concentration. And so, my friends, the greatest power you will ever know, the Divine Spirit itself, is waiting inside your being this moment and all moments for you to recognize and to accept there are no impossibilities to the awakened mind. Impossibilities are only the illusion created by a lack of understanding. Guide your ship to brighter shores through the direction of your own thought.

Thank you.

MAY 6, 1973

Church Lecture 21
Psychic Common Sense

The topic that has been chosen for this evening's service was, "Psychic Common Sense."

In this day there appears to be such a great interest in these realms unseen, so to speak. So much is written in these days concerning what is called sensitives, mediums, psychics, clairvoyants, and so forth. But what is psychic and where does the common sense of it fit into our daily acts and activities?

It has been stated many times, from those from this other dimension, that every soul impulsed into this earth realm, being spirit covered with a form, known as soul, has the innate potential of viewing and hearing these so-called spiritual dimensions. Every human being is psychic to some extent. But of what benefit would being psychic be to anyone, unless they know the laws governing the phenomena, the science, so that they may ever remain in control of the things that they view, that they receive, and that they hear?

Many people with an interest in the psychic sciences start their investigations with a variety of books, teachings, and understanding. We accept and realize that whatever we attract is indeed within us and experienced without.

Now, my good friends, if utilizing this so-called psychic power brings a greater understanding to you, brings a greater awakening of the true purpose of your soul's incarnation and, in so doing, helps you to live a better life, to be a better person, to enjoy the true freedom of your own spirit, then obviously there is some sense, common or otherwise, in your interest and in your unfoldment. If using this psychic sense does not bring you peace, harmony, joy, and fulfillment of purpose then, my good friends, it is no benefit to you. It would be much wiser to sit at home and to view the variety of programs that are telecast over your television set. For the psychic dimensions are not there for people with common sense to view them like a movie.

Everyone experiences some type of psychic phenomena. For example, man goes to sleep at night, usually. He loses or sets aside a conscious awareness of the things around and about him. However, he often recalls certain dreams. We agree and are in accord that most dreams are nothing more than the expression of suppressed desires, but there are dreams that are seemingly prophetic. Now one could say that that is simply a self-prophecy. And indeed that may be true, if the prophecy is for the individual. But when it is a prophecy concerning someone that they know and they do not tell that person and that prophecy comes to pass, then, seemingly, it is prophetic. And it is a living demonstration, to the individual, of another dimension, which is commonly known as psychic.

People experience certain feelings and intuitions, they call them. They know they should go here or they shouldn't go there. Some people even know which horse to bet on at the races and they call that some kind of impulse or impression that they receive. Where do they receive it from, my friends? Not from the physical, material dimension. Not from the mind, for the mind is not capable of knowing forthcoming events. The mind itself is only a vehicle through which this divine Spirit is expressing itself. It gathers up information. It knows whatever facts are fed into it. It is the soul that knows what has been, what truly is, and what is yet to be. For the only part of us (this so-called body) that is eternal is this divine Spirit that expresses through what is known as individualized soul. And that, and that part of us alone, is the only part that knows what has been, what is, and what is going to be.

So let us pause to think with our interest in psychic phenomena. Let us ask ourselves the question, "What laws are governing these experiences and why is it that I cannot have these experiences when I, myself, choose to have them?" So many people have these spontaneous psychic experiences, but they have no control over them. They cannot sit down in a chair and prepare themselves that they may be receptive to certain dimensions in an organized, systematized way. My friends, if we cannot control that that we are interested in, that that we are interested in will soon control us.

Spiritualism is a philosophy, religion, and science that strives to help mankind to awaken himself to his own divinity. It has no creed to offer the interested seeker and it has no dogma, because it knows beyond a shadow of any doubt that each and every individual has the divine birthright to express their own soul, to find what man calls God, and the Spiritualists call Infinite Intelligence, in his or her own way.

We try to share in this association the understanding of the divine laws that we have become receptive to and have and are able, to some extent, to demonstrate, for no teaching in no time is valuable to any person who is not able to demonstrate it. If we are not able to apply, in our daily lives, the things that we learn, then why bother to waste the time to learn them?

Let us use this mind, this soul faculty of reason that we have. Let us weigh all things and accept what is good for us, always remembering that in our mind yesterday's good is not always tomorrow's. If it were, man would not progress, man would not be changing. And when we don't change and progress, we stagnate and fall behind.

When the sciences known as the psychic are properly used and demonstrated, they bring not only to mankind, but to he or she who uses them a greater awakening of their own soul.

Spiritualism uses the public demonstration of spiritual communication for the sole purpose of interesting people who are seeking something greater than the material world that we are in. The purpose of the science of Spiritualism is to show mankind that he is affected and controlled by laws and things that he cannot see with his physical vision, that he cannot hear with his physical ears. My good friends, if you are truly interested, you will demonstrate the law unto yourself. You will find what it's really all about. You will not be satisfied with the surface of things. You will have the wisdom of patience, the perseverance, the determination to look and to think more deeply.

Many times it has been said from this podium that man is a law unto himself; that whatever man sets into motion, he experiences, and how true that is. We live in an age when the scientists have finally accepted that man *is* an electromagnetic energy. Spiritualism has taught for 125 years that no thought ever goes in vain; that man himself views the world from varying states of awareness; that those levels of mind or states of awareness are changing moment by moment; that man has within his being the power to set into motion anything that his mind chooses to do; that all things are possible to the one who truly awakens.

Now regardless of your religious affiliations, if you are serving them with sincerity, then they will serve you in kind. But if you are serving them with the thought of how much you're going to receive, then it will be, my friends, so very, very little.

There is no religion known to man today or yesterday or any day that is not founded upon so-called invisible dimensions. And these so-called invisible dimensions are known by man today to be the psychic and the spiritual worlds. So any religion in the world today or yesterday that denies the existence of a spirit world, of so-called dimensions that are invisible to the physical sight cannot, in truth, be a religion, for religion means to bind back to the source—to the nuclei—to God.

How does man see God? How does man know God? When man awakens to a state of consciousness within himself, he may call that great joy, that great peace that passeth all understanding, an awareness of God. And so it is, once man has found God inside, man will know God outside.

Thank you.

JUNE 3, 1973

Church Lecture 22

Man's Magnetic Field

On the first Sunday of each month I am scheduled to give a short talk on a subject that is given to me by my guides and teachers from the world of spirit. This morning the topic that was chosen for me was, "Man's Magnetic Field." A subject that,

I am sure, is not only of great interest, but great import to all people and in all places.

What do we mean when we speak about magnetic fields? In this day and age the scientists have come to the understanding, through their investigation and thorough analysis of the subject of the psychical sciences, that man in truth is an electromagnetic being.

We know, as the Bible has spoken and so have many philosophers of ancient time, that in all our getting, to get understanding. We also know that there is no greater power known to man than the power of love. But as we look into this subject of magnetic fields and the power of love, because of our varied programmed experiences in a lifetime, we have our own conceptions of what is meant by that word known as *love*. In this association, its teachings and understanding of love is the expression of the divine energy. It is in truth man's magnetic field.

Again and again it is spoken that all of our experiences, we have willed into action. And yet it seems that the mind insists upon putting the cause of our experiences out into the universe to conditions, to other people, and to other things. Why is it that the mind insists upon blaming things and circumstances outside of its own sphere and zone of action? It is simply, my good friends, an error in our thought.

Man's need to express this divine energy, which we call love, cannot be suppressed for long. For the lack of expressing this divine power is the true cause of all of our problems. Now man may choose to direct this energy in two or three various areas. If he does not receive a fulfillment from this direction and expression of this divine love, then he has problems. For example, it is a known fact, as we examine man and nature, that all form requires attention, which is nothing more than energy or love. We look at the plants and the flowers of the garden; we see that they receive their energy, or attention, from the sun and from the rains that fall. When man does not receive energy or attention, he becomes disturbed and feels alone. And so it is so just, the divine laws, that repeatedly try to teach us that in truth we are one, separated only by an error in our thought because we cannot yet, perhaps, rise to a state of consciousness where we can see, experience, and know beyond a shadow of any doubt that we are in truth this divine life, that this is not the first expression of it, nor will it indeed be the last.

When we awaken to the great truth that we must express more fully this magnetic power known as love, when we awaken our minds and stop limiting the divine flow, then we will receive a more abundant influx of this so-called energy, known as God.

Again and again our choices in where we're going to direct this energy or power is limited. Man goes into business and as long as the business is successful to his thinking, then he receives some degree of fulfillment. A person chooses a hobby in which to spend some of their time. As long as that hobby is pleasing to the mind, as long as there is some degree of encouragement from within and without, then it will fulfill its purpose.

All things in creation demand to be loved. If they are not loved, or receive energy or attention, then they wither and die. So let us recognize, friends, the laws that govern the universe and the laws that govern creation herself. We are sending and receiving sets. We are receiving ever equal to what we have sent forth into the universe. But this is a new moment in our consciousness, if we choose to make it a new moment.

Again and again the teachings have spoken of how man is controlled by the things that disturb him. Whatever disturbs us and robs us of our peace of mind controls our very soul.

And so it is as we look out into God's manifestation of creation, there are many things that we seem to be in rapport or in harmony with. And there are some things that it seems to be difficult for us to tolerate. My good friends, the things that are difficult to tolerate are the masters that we have created in our thinking. Whoever or whatever disturbs us is controlling our very soul. And we and we alone have given this divine power, this energy, to the thing that disturbs us. We have made them, or it, a god, to rob us of the joy of living. It's in our thinking, friends. It doesn't exist anyplace else.

Some people awaken in the morning and they see the sun shining and they're filled with the spirit of joy and love. They know that it's going to be a great day for them. That is what they entertain in thought and consequently that is what they experience in life. But not all of us awaken in that way. Some of us awaken with problems of the past. Some of us awaken with things that are not going well in our universe. But we have the divine right of freedom of choice. We can choose at any moment, through the power of directed thought, which is the vehicle of God's divine love and energy, to direct it to the things that we wish to become.

Again and again it is taught, that that you place your attention upon indeed you become. Whatever is felt in the depths of the heart is experienced in our lives over and over and over. If in this moment you feel the need for change, if in this moment you feel the need for the joy of living, I ask that you pause in your thinking, that you call forth from within your own being your divine right to choose whatever you desire to choose.

God is not a judge, as we all know, that sits on a throne and tells us of our errors and of our omissions and transmissions. That is not the God that is understood by the Serenity Association. But we do understand a Divine Power, a Divine Love, that is without lack, that is without limit, that is ever available to us, that the only obstacle to its full expression is the limitation our of own thought. So let us, friends, expand our consciousness, broaden our horizon, and fulfill the true purpose of our being.

Thank you.

JULY 1, 1973

Church Lecture 23
Expanding Consciousness

On the first of the month it is my duty, responsibility, and pleasure to serve as the lecturer for the discussion, the topic of the morning. And this morning the topic that was chosen by my teacher in the world of spirit is "Expanding Consciousness."

What is meant in those words *expanding consciousness*? We understand, in this association, that the word *consciousness* means God, the Divine, the Infinite Intelligence. And so it is while we are here encased in flesh that we are striving to expand our awareness of this Divine, this God, that is everywhere present. In what way, we ask the question, may we best expand or broaden our horizon or understanding of the Divine Presence, this Infinite Intelligence? We know that man, our mind, is, perhaps, likened unto a great computer that records all things and loses, in truth, nothing. We know that we have been programmed in our minds to accept or to reject certain things that we experience in life. And so it is that by our own volition, our own choice, and our own will we have established within ourselves a limitation, for we have established that we will accept certain thoughts and ideas and experiences and we will reject others.

How is it possible, we ask, to expand or to broaden our understanding, when we are already conditioned, from childhood on, in what to accept and in what to reject? When we consider accepting in our mind, in our thought, that good exists and expresses in all things, at all times, and in all experiences and all places, then we will become in tune, in rapport, with the good that exists in all things. For if God is God, then there is no experience, there is no place, there is no thought in which God, the Divine Intelligence, is not expressing itself.

Through a lack of understanding of the divine principle, known as creation, man has decided, within himself, what is beneficial to him and what is detrimental. With each person, those decisions, those values, change according to the experiences of each person. What we are trying to share with you this morning is the possibility of entertaining in thought what is known as good, for its opposite is nothing more than undeveloped. When we seek a greater understanding than we have so far awakened to, we will broaden our horizons, expand our consciousness, and our God will become, in our being, a universal God, a God of freedom, and a God of peace, a God that does not reject and a God that does not deny. My good friends, it is our rejections and our denials that cause us all of our problems.

Whatever we are seeking, again and again it has been stated, is also seeking us. And like the hands of the clock of time, every so often they meet. But because of our limited expression of the divine understanding, we reject so many things that come to our lives. We reject them because we do not understand them.

We entertain in thought a mass vibration of constant fear and negation. Fear of so-called shortages. Fear of governments. Fear of people. Fear of our job. Fear of money. Fear of so-called death. And yea, what is it all, my friends, but fear of Life herself. What is it that causes this fear and causes us to express such negation into the world? It is simply a lack of understanding that there is one Power, there is one God, there is one Divine Intelligence that does not deny any good that you seek in your life. The only reason that we do not ofttimes experience what we desire to experience is because we reject the channels, or the people, through which this experience may be made possible in our lives. When we ask God for so many things and then we deny the people through which the Divine Intelligence expresses the good that we're seeking, then, my friends, we're in a constant state of contradiction.

Wise is the man who chooses to understand himself and stops entertaining the thought that he must understand his wife, husband, children, society, the governments, and everyone else. The reason, my friends, we can't understand the people that we seem to be so attached or close to is because we don't understand ourselves. And in not understanding ourselves, the people we look at become the mirrors, reflecting, of course, our own state of consciousness.

When we spend a little more time looking for God inside, we will know God outside. But, my friends, you can travel across the universes seeking for what you call God and peace that passeth all understanding, you won't find it out there. The universe is kind of like a Christmas tree to a five-year-old at Christmas time. There are so many things to choose from: you don't know, really, what to choose.

Let us grow up mentally, my friends, and emotionally. Let us become the adults that our physical beings are. Let us recognize and realize that this life is the one, eternal life, that it is ever as we make it, that it's always as we take it, that there is nothing ever outside of us that has not been caused inside of us. Let us look more deeply within ourselves and let us experience this great joy of living. There is no reason, in any universe, with any person to be without the good that they desire. That good awaits our recognition and our acceptance by a reeducating of our own thoughts. Any rejections or denials, my friends, are within our self.

We believe so much in the material dimension because we have so much energy directed to it. We have, in truth, denied the God of gods, the One that lies within, that has given us everything our hearts could possibly desire. We have denied this God because we have given that power to man and to this material dimension. We have given that great power to our bank accounts, to our houses, to our television sets, to our automobiles, and to politics and all of those things. I simply want to share with you the way to take that power back from things and give it to the Divine that is in yourself.

The things of this dimension, this physical world, are placed here for use. The attainment of them is ever subject to your acceptance of them in thought. If you want a new car and you cannot accept the possibility of driving it, if you cannot accept that possibility and you entertain in thought that you have X limited amount of dollars and cents, that you'll have to work so many years to get it, then you, my friends, establish that law. God doesn't. But if you have the faith and the belief in your heart, not just your head, but in your heart, then, my good friends, you will experience the very thing that you accept. Let us awaken to the truth and to the freedom that waits for our experience and our expression within ourselves.

It's just like in the building of this church, which is in process. I know it because it is in my heart and in my soul. I don't tell God it's going to take so many dollars and we're going to have to do this or that to get it, because then, my friends, we'll get it from man and not from God. And man is lack and limitation.

Recognize when you receive that you are receiving from God. You are not receiving from man and you are not indebted to man. God works through man, not to man. And so when you attune yourself to that great Divinity, to that so-called God, do not reject the people that he expresses through, for the very thing you are seeking is waiting for your acceptance.

Thank you.

AUGUST 5, 1973

Church Lecture 24

Class Excerpts

[*No audio recording of Church Lecture 24 exists. The excerpts below from other spiritual awareness classes were selected by Mr. Goodwin as a replacement for that lecture.*]

[*The excerpt below is from CC 20.*]

When the soul enters form at the moment of conception, this brain that is created, this human intellect, is affected by the human intellect and its expression of both the mother and the father and the grandparents. In other words, the soul enters a mold, a part of which is known as the brain or the human intellect. Now the soul has merited that particular mold or that particular brain. Consequently, we find that some people have a stronger tendency towards intellectualizing things than other people. We find that some people are able to accept by an inner feeling, just an inner feeling that they have, different things without a constant questioning process.

Now it does not mean that the human intellect, which is designed to question, which is designed to store up information, which is designed to doubt—because by being designed to question, it's designed to do the opposite, you understand, and to doubt. Now that does not mean that we do not use the human intellect, because we all do, to some extent. But it does mean that in finding truth and spiritual awareness that we use the spirit. For it is the spirit, you understand, that is the awareness: it is not the mind. Now you can go on and on and on and on and on with the human intellect and the moment you try to mix the human intellect into spiritual awareness, you're going to find, sooner or later, that you have problems. Because, you see, the human intellect is going to accept one thing as truth one moment, only to reject it in the next moment. Because it cannot and is not designed to express truth. It is designed, my friends, to express facts. But facts are not truth.

[*The excerpt below is from CC 15.*]

I'd like a little bit of an explanation on the difference between the conscious mind and the subconscious mind, and also the collective mind.

Yes, you would like a discussion on the conscious mind, the subconscious mind, and the mass mind. Is that correct?

Yes.

The reason we don't call it the collective mind is because the mass mind does not collect; therefore, it is not termed a collective mind in these particular teachings. The conscious mind is an instrument of electrical impulses; the subconscious mind is an instrument of magnetic impulses. The mass mind is a fluctuating combination of electromagnetic impulses. The soul faculties reach the conscious mind direct; however, the subconscious mind expresses them. Communication with the world of spirit or with the spiritual energies is through the conscious mind and the subconscious is what expresses. Now I know a lot of people will say, "How's that possible? When people go off into trance, they're no longer consciously aware." The truth of the matter is they're consciously aware, but not on the dimension of which the masses are consciously aware. Do you understand?

That I understand. What I don't understand is how the subconscious expresses.

It is the reactor. It is the reactor. The conscious mind is the mind that thinks. The conscious mind is the only mind that has the ability to express what is known as choice or free will. The subconscious mind is the reactor of what is fed into it. The subconscious mind is the patterned mind: it has no choice; it has no free will. It simply reacts to what is fed in with the electrical impulses of the conscious mind.

So it is like a receptacle?

Yes, it could be termed that. It's like a vast computer, you see, and it simply reacts. Now there have been many, many teachings and many different ways tried to reprogram the so-called magnetic field of the individual or the subconscious mind. The subconscious mind, which is the magnetic, reacts to feelings. You could sit down throughout eternity and tell yourself positive, positive thoughts; the subconscious can continually reject them. Because you have to learn to put feeling into the subconscious because feeling is what it reacts to. It's the child.

The conscious mind you can educate; the subconscious mind you cannot. You can only repattern or reprogram it; you cannot educate the subconscious mind.

[*The excerpt below is from CC 18.*]

Now before we get to your questions, friends, several students have spoken to me in reference to the seeming difficulties they seem to be having in getting through to their so-called subconscious mind. And I know that you all know that when we entertain a thought, we direct the life-giving power, the energy to it. So if we entertain the thought of difficulty, we guarantee to increase the difficulty. And that is why we try to teach in these classes to direct your thought, which is the vehicle of your divine energy that's expressing to you, on what you want to become. Keep your attention off of the obstruction, because by permitting the mind to entertain the thoughts of the obstruction, the obstruction increases in size and density, and sooner or later, the mountain will fall on top of us.

So when you have an experience that your brain insists upon computing as difficult, change the thought immediately; and in changing the thought, you will change the experience. All experience, as we have spoken again, again, and again, is nothing more and nothing less than the effect of directed energy through the vehicle of thought.

Now, if there is something that you desire to accomplish, then see the accomplishment in its fulfillment and do not tell it how it's to take place, when it's to take place, and all things involved in its fulfillment. Now that takes faith, friends, because if there's something that you want to do or to have, the mind insists that it knows the way. The Intelligence that brings it into being works by very natural, normal law and when we become receptive to the law through which it works, we will not have to be concerned with when it's to come or how it's to come. But that takes faith and that faith is something that we unfold inside of our self. It is not something that we garner up. So if a person is willing to release their desires and their fulfillments to the Infinite Intelligence that moves and holds all things in space, if they're really willing to do that, and they do it, then it shall come to pass. Otherwise, they will go through the other processes.

[*The excerpt below is from CC 15.*]

Well, how do you go about programming yourself?

. . . one of the easiest things to do is to establish, as you're going off to sleep at night, that you will awaken at a definite time. You see, that's a little open door and a good, practical one. You know, I believe in being practical. To me, Spiritualism is a religion of practicality, common sense, down-to-earth, and reason, here and now. We're not just interested in all those eternal hereafters; we're interested in what we can do this moment. So once you have become successful, over a period of at least nine or ten weeks of repeatedly awakening yourself at a set time—and vary the timing—then that means you've got a little open door to the magnetic field. Then, the next step is you start programming certain feelings, like you're going to awaken in the morning, you're going to feel a certain way, and then you awaken in the morning and you do feel a certain way.

All right, that's the next step. You're beginning to open the doors to your other self. Then, you start on a programming of talking to the other person. You see, friends, it just seems so difficult to get through the cement to get the world to recognize and to accept the truth that we are not one person: we are three people. Whether we like that or not, the truth of the matter is that's what we are. So why ignore the very person inside of us that's bringing to us all of these experiences that we consider consciously (electrically) so distasteful to us? So you start making the effort to talk to the other person. Don't worry, you'll get some answers back and they usually will not agree with you.

Now, that's a very sane, normal, natural thing to do, because that other you is running so much of your life, just like everybody else's life. And therefore, when you start using reason and you start talking to that other person inside of you, it'll get all emotional because emotion is its nature. It is the magnetic attracting field. And it will not agree on many things that are reasonable in your conscious mind. But if you treat it as you would treat a little three- or five-year-old child, then you've got a good chance of getting it reprogrammed. If you try ordering it around, that other you, then you're going to get some very serious reactions from it and experiences, you see.

Now, whenever you have a thought, "I don't like the way that person is doing that," and you don't express that thought, that triggers the magnetic field inside the subconscious and you start sending energy down there. Do you understand? Fortunately, the Divine Wisdom, in its Infinite Intelligence, has caused us to have what is known as a state of sleep so that we can dream and release those hostilities that we keep putting down there, don't you see?

But if you will learn to recognize that you are a conscious being, that you are a subconscious being, and that you are this divine neutrality, this superconscious being, then you will bring the poles of opposites into balance and you will express through the trinity of truth, and you will know your freedom. And you will no longer be bound and enslaved by the disharmony, the discord, and the imbalance between the conscious and the subconscious being, which we truly are.

[*The excerpt below is from CC 20.*]

Well, the thing is that the mind is designed to serve the purpose of the mental world. And the spirit is designed to serve the purpose of the spiritual world. And so when we mix the two, we sometimes, ofttimes, get a hodgepodge, you see. It takes a mind to know the mind; it takes a spirit to know the spirit. So if it is the spirit that we are seeking, and I am sure that's what we are all seeking, then let us place our attention upon that spirit, that it may express itself and that we may have that feeling. Now, naturally, in our searching, we use the vehicle with which we are most familiar. And obviously, most of us are most familiar with the mental body, because we have not spent the time to become familiar with the spirit and with the soul body and the spiritual body. But as we spend more time and more attention, which is more energy, on the spiritual, then we will be in a position to use the spiritual to guide our ship.

[*The excerpt below is from CC 18.*]

Well, now, first of all, the only minds to bring into balance are the conscious and the subconscious, because when they're brought into balance, the superconscious flows through the three bodies of which we are presently aware. Now in reference to the multitude of computations in that computer that is within all of us, if the person, the student that is sincerely trying to find the truth that lies waiting within themselves to be expressed and that Light and freedom, if they make the day-to-day conscious effort through kindness to talk with this other person—you see, it seems to take students so long just to entertain the thought and the possibility that they're being controlled by another individual. Now the truth of the matter is we're all controlled by this other individual that is within us. Now different religions and different philosophies teach different things. They say it's the animal nature. They say it's this, they say it's that, and etc. The simple truth of the whole matter is this: spend some time each day in talking with it, because it *is* there. It is the magnetic field that attracts things into our lives and if we are not pleased with the things that we are attracting in our lives, then we must work with the magnetic field.

Now the faculty in which kindness is expressed is the bridge between the electric and the magnetic fields. And therefore, by using what is kindness—you may use whatever words that you choose—as long as you use firmness and kindness, because if man uses what he calls kindness, it may come from his emotional realm. You want the kindness of reason, and the kindness of reason is a firm kindness. And I'm sure, through that application, that you will have a freedom from the patterns that you are seeking to be free from.

[The excerpt below is from CC 14.]

I wanted to ask you, if you would, please, to expand on the understanding of awakening the mind to the spirit. You just said to recognize that you are not the doer, but that the spirit is. Could you give us an exercise that we could use to awaken our minds?

Yes, thank you very much . . . And in reference to your question on an exercise that would help us to awaken our minds to the Divine Spirit that flows through us, I think the best possible exercise that any student could use was anything that they found that would help them to educate what is known as the ego. Now the end justifies the means when the end is an eternal thing, such as the spirit, and the piece of clay is coming and going.

Our greatest obstruction, the biggest stumbling block in our path to awakening is what is known as the ego. We do not teach an annihilation of it, but we do teach an education of it. You see, we spend so much energy while we wake and while we sleep on telling ourselves how great we are. We don't necessarily use those particular words, but we use a multitude of expressions to kind of fatten us up and make us look better or make us at least think that we are better.

Now any exercise that comes to your mind that would help you to educate this three-letter wall that we all have would be of great benefit in awakening the mind and permitting your soul and your spirit to express itself. However, I know you would like something specific—that's the way the mind works—and so if you would consider, before you express, to ask yourself in all honesty, "From what level cometh my thoughts?" Before you express. And you'll start to look objectively. Ask yourself, "Why am I thinking this and why am I doing this? Is it something that I want or is it something that my inner being knows would be for the best of all concerned?" That's a simple exercise that I've used for a number of years. It cannot help but benefit, because that that benefits one has the potential of benefitting everyone.

SEPTEMBER 2, 1973

Church Lecture 25
Acceptance, The Divine Will

As our chairman has stated, on the first Sunday of each month it is my privilege to share with you the understanding of this association. And the topic that has been selected, as our chairman stated, is "Acceptance, The Divine Will."

Perhaps it would be of benefit to share with you our understanding, first, of the meaning of divine will. By that statement we do not mean to imply some authority or some divinity outside of our self that has decided or is deciding what is in our best interest. We do mean, however, a state of consciousness within our self—the highest state of consciousness possible—where divine will manifests itself and knows beyond a shadow of any doubt what is best for our own soul.

Acceptance *is* the divine will, for without acceptance, there is no experience. And without experience, there is no growth, there is no progression, there is no evolution. And it is the divine purpose, plan, and will that the soul, encased in form, is in a constant state of expansion, growth, and progression. Now the question comes to mind, what is it that we accept and what is it that we reject? And how are our decisions reached? We all know or at least we have read, heard, or been told that we do have free will. We have the right to accept a certain experience or thought and we also have the right to reject it. Whenever we reject a thought in our mind, what we are in truth doing is accepting an alternate thought.

Depending on what level of consciousness, what state of mind, what rate of vibration that we are in at the moment of acceptance depends entirely upon the experience that we will live or grow through.

One of the seeming great difficulties for the human mind, in acceptance, is when it expresses through what is known as the lazy-man's level of acceptance, and that is called presumption. For example, we may be driving down the highway and a car is coming up beside us and at a glance we, perhaps, may see the front fender. We see that it's yellow; it seems to be a similar color yellow to the taxicabs. So without thought, we *presume* that it is a taxi that's pulling alongside. That is the lazy-man's level of acceptance. Lazy because we do not make the effort, nor do we express the soul faculties of patience and investigation to see whether or not it is a taxi or it is a car that is painted a similar color. So in acceptance we find that we must make the effort to become aware of what level of acceptance we are expressing.

We reject many things in this life. We reject them because they do not fit into our limited program of acceptance. For many centuries, man rejected a flight to the moon. He even rejected the possibility of flying at all. But some men, in those centuries, entertained that possibility and as the entertainment of that thought began to permeate the atmosphere, other minds gradually, slowly but surely, began to accept the possibility that man could fly. Once the possibility of a thing is accepted within the human mind, then we are on the path to its attainment.

When we accept the limitations of our own opinions of what has taken place in the past, when we accept that our happiness comes to us in a certain way, when we accept that our supply, spiritually, mentally, and materially, is through certain avenues, then we are limited by those acceptances. Consequently, we and we alone, as has been said again and again, make our own destiny.

When this acceptance is broadened within our mind, when we make more effort to accept the great truth that to the Divine Intelligence, which is expressing through us, all things are possible—but, you see, my friends, it takes a little bit of faith to accept the possibility of all things because we are governed and controlled by the acceptances that we have established in the past—when we make the conscious, moment-by-moment effort to become aware of the areas in which we have limited our own divine expression, the avenues in which we have limited our divine freedom, then we will broaden our horizons, we will expand our consciousness, and we will no longer recognize—for it will no longer exist—a lack, a limit, or a disturbance.

Man has the divine right to perfect health. He has the divine right to perfect peace and he has the divine right to perfect harmonious abundance. But we must learn to broaden our acceptance, which is the divine will. We must learn to think when we are asked a question. We must learn to think before we speak a word. Then, we have the opportunity to be free and to enjoy the great wonder of life itself.

It is a simple process, if one will choose it, to make a conscious effort, upon awakening in the morning, to put their house in order; that is, to arrange their mind in such a way that confusion will not take control of their soul. If one, upon awakening each day, will make the conscious effort of where they have limited themselves through what is known as rejection or acceptance of an alternate path, if one will write down each day, every day, what it is that they truly want in life and then write down how they expect what they want to manifest itself in their life, they will begin to think why they have not already experienced what they're seeking. They will see within their own mind that they have limited, because of prior experiences, they have created an obstacle, an obstruction to what it is they truly desire.

It is a fact in creation that attainment comes from payment. There is a payment for the air that we breathe: the payment is the working of our lungs and other parts of our body. The effort must be made. And so it is, in all of your seeking and desiring—for it is the nature of the carnal mind to desire—in all of that seeking, recognize what you have accepted, not this moment, but what laws you have set into motion through your acceptances of moments, of days, of months, of years that are past. Then go to work on broadening those channels.

For example, a man may decide that he no longer wishes to fulfill a particular desire that has been entertained for a number of years. But to accept not to fulfill a desire, the acceptance is not on the level of where the desire truly exists. And so we must broaden our understanding and we must ask our self the question, "Why have I now accepted to make this change? Is it because my experiences of a lifetime, instead of bringing me peace and fulfillment, have brought me bondage and disturbance?" If that is true, it simply reveals, my good friends, that we have not been thinking or demonstrating the natural Law of Balance. Balance in all things frees us from the bondage of one thing.

So we are seeking in life to express the Divine Spirit which we truly are. And we and we alone have limited it to certain avenues of expression, and in so doing—which is an imbalance in the mind—and in so doing, we have and we are paying the price of our own lack of awareness.

Some time ago it was brought forth that presumption is the Law of Descent. And so, my friends, do we not see, in the course of our daily acts and activities, how many times we presume this or we presume that? What is it within us that presumes we know what such and such is like? Is it because we have had certain experiences and by those experiences, we have established within our self judgment concerning certain levels of consciousness? If that is what we have done then, of course, we have given our freedom, our peace, and our happiness to those particular things.

Acceptance, the divine will, is indeed a state of consciousness where freedom flows unobstructed. But freedom, my friends, is not license to do what we want to do, when we want to do it, and how we want to do it. Freedom is control. Freedom is control of ignorance and control of error and control of imbalance of our own mind. There is no reason why each and every soul expressing in form should not and cannot be free. There is no reason why we do not enjoy this world in which we have merited our sojourn, to enjoy the peace and the joy and the wonder of Life herself. But we have accepted a limited expression of God. And by accepting a limited expression of the Divine, the Divine is not fulfilling its true purpose through our being because *we* have become the obstruction.

Thank you.

OCTOBER 7, 1973

Church Lecture 26

The Journey of the Soul

The topic that was selected for this morning is "The Journey of the Soul."

There are many theories concerning the soul's incarnation into this realm that we call the earth. And for a few moments, I would like to spend a little thought on the theories that are prevailing in our world today and have been for many, many centuries.

One of the most popular theories in the Christian world, the Western world, is the theory that our soul comes new, direct from God or Allsoul, whatever you may choose to call it. If that theory were to be correct and true, our soul, being composed of what would be called soul substance, of course, would all be the same. And the soul, the mind, the mental body being an effect of that soul, we would all think alike. And the physical body, being an effect of our mental body, then we would all look alike.

So we go on to one of the other ancient theories and that is the theory of the Eastern world that was popular, and is even to this day with thousands of people, that our soul evolves through the lower kingdoms and evolving into the form known as the human. If it transgresses certain laws, then it returns to the lower animal kingdom. And that is the theory of the soul of transmigration.

Then we go on into the Eastern world, again, to another theory concerning the soul's incarnation on earth, and that is commonly referred to as re—or return—incarnation. And in the theory of return or reincarnation, there are varying thoughts of how long a person stays in another dimension before the return to the earth dimension in human form. There is, also, a great question concerning where this soul has come from in the first place.

Now we all give some thought, at some time in our lives, to the question of why we are here, where have we come from, if any place, and where are we going. The teachings offered in the Serenity understanding of Spiritualism—which is that our soul is the form of the Divine Spirit—as this power expresses in creation, we have what is known as a covering, and that covering we call soul. We understand that our soul does not differ in its quality, but it differs greatly in its quantity. It is like the mind. Mind is composed of mind stuff, and what has a mind is all from the same source, but it does vary and differ greatly with its expression or its quantity. And so we have this understanding that our soul, impulsed into being, varies from person to person; that it is constantly, moment-by-moment expanding itself, though we cannot physically see what is taking place.

Now the soul enters this physical world according to the established laws that it alone has set into motion through the experiences that it has encountered in its evolutionary process. In other words, the teachings of Serenity are not that your soul has come direct from God, as a new expression, but that it has and is evolving, not just through what is known as the earth realm or the earth planet, but that it is evolving through the solar system.

I know there has been much talk, especially of late, concerning the possibility of intelligent life on other planets in this particular solar system. Well, my friends, it takes a very limited view of life not to accept the possibility that there is intelligence someplace, in all of God's universes, outside of the earth realm.

As our soul evolves, expressing itself through the varying forms, known as creation, it makes its choice, each moment, on whether or not it will spend fifty years or a hundred or a thousand to learn the lessons that must be learned in order that it may fully express itself. These choices and decisions, my friends, are not within the hands or the power of anything outside of ourselves.

We look around into this world and we see souls entering form, some of them in perfect health and some of them not. We look back through our own life and we see that we had different opportunities and different experiences than either our own brother or sister, our mother or our father. Why are these experiences and these opportunities so varied to each human being? Well, it's very simple. Because when we entered this particular form, *this* life, we had, and do have, certain tendencies that we have already brought with us. These tendencies within our soul to certain things will go on with us into the next expression. And so it is, my friends, that it is a constant process of thought and consideration.

I know that it does seem at times, to some, that a great deal of time is spent in trying to understand and work with their own spirit, their own soul. And it is indeed most understandable, for it is rare in this world that many of us have spent any time at all concerning our own eternity. And so it is that when we step on the spiritual path to help our own soul, it does seem that we're spending a great deal of time, because, you see, my friends, we spent a lifetime spending no time at all on our own godhood within ourselves.

So let us ponder and think, and let us be honest with ourselves. We are not here by chance. We are not going to leave this earth realm by chance. We are going to leave this earth realm when we have fulfilled the purpose for which we have come here. That purpose, that moment, that day and its fulfillment is known in a level of consciousness within ourselves. Before our soul entered earth, at the moment of conception, it reviewed all of its experiences that it was yet to encounter. And so it is within the realm of possibility and probability for us to go deep within ourselves and make the right decision in all things at all times. But that place, my friends, is known as the silent sanctorium, where perfect peace reigns supreme within our own being.

Again and again it has been stated in this church that peace and peace alone is the power of God. Well, friends, what does peace really mean? It means a perfect balance or harmony between the electric and magnetic field of which we in truth are. Without the electric and magnetic field, there would be no creation, there would be no form for the divine, formless Intelligence, known as God, to express itself.

And so it is, in all our getting, we seek to get understanding. Not understanding of people and things in a world of experience, but understanding of our own divinity. But that understanding is not something that you're going to gain from reading a book or talking to another person. It is something that you are going to awaken to when you make the effort to find God.

I know that the word *God* is not readily accepted in the materialistic age in which we are living. And it is indeed, at least to me, understandable why, in this world today, the word *God* seems to repulse so many. My friends, it is very simple. Too many words and too much writing has been given to the world in the name of God. Consequently, we see around the land a great division in the thinking of the human being. But let us try, at least, and consider that there is something inside of us that has always been; there is something inside of us that will always be, that the Spiritualists call Infinite Intelligence. If we do not, at least, consider in our life at some time the possibility of eternal expression of consciousness, then there is no reason for us to struggle another day. Why bother to go through the trials and tribulations that beset us in creation, if there is not something better that we can attain? And if that something better that we seek to attain is not eternal, then why bother, my friends, to seek it in the first place? That is known, to me, as God.

We are not here, nor are we going from here, until we have fulfilled the laws that we and we alone have established for our self. We ofttimes question why a soul enters life here; perhaps it stays a day, a week, a year, or even ten. We question, then, What kind of a God would take a beautiful child? We question because we do not know. If we knew, we would not ask the question. If we sought to understand the divine, natural laws of life, we would not have to question why a week-old babe is taken from the earth realm, because we would know that that soul, having set the laws into motion, was destined to express in this earth realm for a day, a week, or even a year. There is no power, my friends, outside of us that dictates what is best for us.

But there is, within us, what is known as our conscience. Our conscience is not something that we care to face often. The reason we do not care to face it is quite simple: it dictates reason to our mind, for it is a spiritual sensibility with a dual capacity. It knows right from wrong within our own soul. And no one has to tell us what to do. We know what to do. But it takes character, it takes courage, it takes strength to face ourselves.

Why does it take so much strength and courage and character to face ourselves? It takes that, my friends, because we have permitted our self to be so very many different things. We're happy, then we're sad. We're joyous and we're glad. We're miserable and we're free. But we can be all the things we want to be, if we are willing to demonstrate a little bit of discipline with ourselves.

The Divine Intelligence, known as God, infinite, eternal Love, is not responsible for what man has done and is doing with his own divinity. If God were responsible, then we would no longer have free will or choice in anything.

When we look within ourselves on our journey of our own soul, let us not look with discouragement and despair. Let us not look with blame and frustration, because that, my good friends, is not going to help you. But let us try to be objective. Let us realize and recognize that we can be the peace, the joy, and the love that is in truth our moment-to-moment divine right.

Thank you.

NOVEMBER 4, 1973

Church Lecture 27

Adventures in Consciousness

This morning we will be speaking on "Adventures in Consciousness."

So many people wonder why they experience so many different things in life. And the wondering is, of course, because we have not yet found the cause of these experiences, which in this understanding is known as effects.

It has been stated in our teachings that imagination is an indispensable part of the creative principle, the principle law that governs creation or form. If man does not imagine, he cannot believe, for man cannot believe anything that he cannot imagine. And so it is in speaking on adventures in consciousness that we would like to share with you our understanding of imagination.

We imagine a house or a car or a painting, and then we create it. But we cannot create anything until we have first imagined it and then believed it. And so it is, my friends, with all of our experiences, we first must imagine them. We must believe them in order for us to experience them. And so it is in life that man has, and is, imagining many types of gods, many types of beliefs. But without that process of belief or imagining, he cannot experience, because he cannot experience what the mind cannot first accept.

We are not stating that God is imagination, because God is formless and free and that that is formless and free the mind has great difficulty in imagining. For the mind is an instrument that places things into form through its own beliefs. And we must get through the mental or mind realms before we can be in true rapport with that divine, formless free Spirit, known as God.

There are many ways, or adventures in consciousness, to find that God that we are seeking. And well the question may be asked, Why are we seeking this God or this Divine Source? It's really quite clear, my friends. We have wandered from our true source, which is known as Freedom, Peace, or God. And in that wandering, it's like a thirsty person on a desert. It seeks to return home.

And so in these adventures of consciousness in all of these beliefs, in all of these imaginings, let us remember one thing: that that survives all creation, that that sustains it, that is before it and goes beyond it, is known as our spirit. That is the only thing, my friends, that is enduring. For all other things that are brought into form return to the source from whence they came. So it behooves us to consider more often what we are doing with what we are aware of, for knowledge to anyone is indeed worthless without the effort of application.

Many times it has been spoken about the soul faculties, and especially the one on faith and patience. Sometimes we seek for years for something. And when we see it, we lack the patience, the wisdom, to endure, if it means enduring, the time necessary for its true fulfillment or attainment. There is no fast growth that is lasting or stable. Many times students will come to the spiritual light, blink their eyes in amazement, and rush off into the world to express what they have found. My good friends, unless we take the time and make the effort to make it our own first, and that means making it our own—gaining the understanding necessary and [making] the effort to apply the understanding in our day-to-day acts and activities. Man cannot be the instrument of granting understanding to another, nor can man be the instrument for the healing of another until he has first demonstrated the healing and the understanding in his own life each day in every way. How is it possible to teach another if it is not first within our realm of consciousness to teach ourselves? And the Good Book says, "O physician, heal thyself."

I am not one of those people who feel that I may be instrumental in helping another human soul if I cannot make the effort and apply the teachings or understanding that I have to myself. I believe there is a word that man has coined to best express that level of consciousness and I believe that word is known as *hypocrisy*. Of what benefit, my good friends, is it to speak of spirituality, to speak of God's love, to speak of God's guidance, to speak of God's power, to speak of God's light and understanding, if we our self are not experiencing it first for ourselves?

And so in speaking on adventures of consciousness, I can assure you from personal effort of many years that it is my understanding that all things that come into our universe are a direct effect of laws, mental and spiritual, that we and we alone are setting into motion. Because we may not be aware of those laws is no exemption from their effects.

So we first consider working with the vehicle with which we are most familiar, and that vehicle, my friends, is known as our mind or mental body. When we are truly at peace, this mind and mental body, these so-called emotions, they come into a perfect balance, into a harmony within ourselves. Our body then expresses that harmony and that is known as perfect health. We begin to see in the wonder of Life herself that we are indeed an inseparable part of the whole, that we have come to earth to serve a purpose, to fulfill our own being.

The purpose for which each soul enters this earth realm is known within the consciousness of each and every individual. It is not necessary to seek out into the universe what your true purpose in life is, for it is known to you and it is available for the asking. How does one find his purpose in that simple asking? If one is truly seeking the Divine Intelligence, the Eternal Good, of which they are an inseparable part, then one will find that goodness within themselves and that goodness will reveal in the quiet of their own mind the true purpose of their life.

Where indeed, my friends, are we going, if we don't have some review, consciously, of where we have been? Each day we step out into the world with so many levels of consciousness and we experience a great variety of adventures. And so it is you are here today, this moment, and you are experiencing an adventure which is the effect of a law that you have set into motion. And you will leave this church this day and experience another adventure. But what does it behoove the traveler if he does not have some direction of where he is going? There comes a time in life when the traveling and the adventures have indeed served their purpose. And when they serve their purpose, man pauses to rest. And when he pauses to rest, he begins to think on other levels of consciousness. And in that thinking, he awakens to himself and knows the work that he has to do. It is known within our own soul. And none of us will escape the inevitable, eternal adventure of returning to God.

Thank you.

DECEMBER 2, 1973

Church Lecture 28

New Horizons

This morning's topic, entitled, "New Horizons," encompasses much more than a so-called New Year resolution. New horizons, my friends, is something that is taking place with us each day, every day, for we are constantly in a process of accepting new thoughts and ideas and removing the ones that we find no longer have value for us. In this understanding, there has been much discussion on the value and the importance of our own mind, our thoughts, for they are indeed the universe that we ourselves experience.

We all, in this world, are seeking something. That something to us means our success, whatever the endeavor may be. We understand that success is ever in proportion to our expression of the soul faculty of duty, gratitude, and tolerance. If we look throughout our lives, we will see that we express what is known as tolerance in varying degree. It is indeed, perhaps, to some, a wonder and an amazement of how much tolerance people are able to express when they have a desire of attaining something, but that is ever the revelation of the divine natural Law of Creation. Man's desire, then, is in proportion with his expression of tolerance. And so we find whatever we truly desire in life, we have all of the tolerance necessary for its attainment, depending, of course, upon the extent or degree of our own desire for any particular thing.

There is no man here or hereafter that is what could be called a complete failure. We are successful in something and it is the very nature of form to constantly change, to progress, to refine itself.

Many of us, perhaps, are not aware that this is not our first conscious awareness, this physical realm, called earth. And, indeed, it will not be our last. We have come here on different grades of evolution. Our spirit being one and the same; our soul varying, of course, in its quantity or its expansion.

What is it that man seeks in life itself that has any lasting value? What is it, the question may rise in the mind, that we really do take with us when we leave this physical dimension? My friends, all of the thoughts that you entertain, all of your emotion, and all of your attitudes are what go with us into these other dimensions. For that that is known as death is only a change, a returning of the physical form to the physical elements of which it has been composed. But the mind that brought it into being goes on with us. So let us look as we face this new year. This day let us ask ourselves honestly the question, "What has true value to my life?" And if we will, in retrospect, look for a moment backwards to those days that have gone, we can but very quickly see the values of yesterday are no longer the values that we hold today. Is there anything that we thought of value a year ago or even ten that has consistently remained with us, that is serving a purpose to help us to have peace of mind, to have the joy and the wonder of living itself?

There are few in this world today that are prepared to make the eternal journey, the inevitable journey, that we're all going to make. And because we may be young or old matters not, for that day, my friends, is coming. It is guaranteed for all of us. And there is none of us that know the exact moment that that so-called spirit of death will visit and knock at our door. Does a man with common sense give it some thought? Surely we must at least consider a journey that we're all destined to make, because if we do not give it some consideration, you may be rest assured, my friends, we will not, in any way, be prepared for it. Many people have many different views of what it's going to be like when they leave this earth realm, but they don't really give it a sensible, a logical study and investigation.

If it is true—and from these thirty-some years of communicating with these dimensions it is true to me—that we do take it with us, then let us find out today what it is that we truly have. If it is true—and it is true, I assure you—that we take our emotions, our feelings, and our attitudes with us, that those are the realms, the dimensions in which we shall live and express ourselves, then let us weigh within our minds what attitudes we have, what things we are mentally, emotionally attached to, because that's where we're going to find ourselves, friends. And there will be no dense, gross physical body to blind our view. We're living in those dimensions this moment, but most of us see them not because our minds are so attached to physical substance.

In these worlds known as worlds of spirit—and many dimensions there are—our thought becomes the most important asset that we have, for things in those dimensions are created from the substance of mind-stuff. If we are not able to keep our mind, for some period of time, on one thing, then we will not be able to create the better things in those so-called other dimensions. The same principle is operating this moment, today. The experiences that we encounter, we are so prone to blame another.

Because God's manifestation is variety, we have a tendency not to approve or care to associate with things that are different from ourselves. It does not mean, my friends, that we must be where we desire not to be, but it does mean that we have the ability and we make the effort to be the person that we truly are without trying to be someone else. We are all individualized souls and, therefore, we all have something to offer to ourselves and to the world. Find out, my good friends, what you are, then you will know who you are.

Thank you.

JANUARY 6, 1974

Church Lecture 29
Respect—The Law of Consideration

This morning's topic for discussion [is] entitled, "Respect—The Law of Consideration."

In giving thought to that statement, one must ask the question, "If respect is an expression or demonstration of the Law of Consideration, does man in truth respect all things that he considers?" And in giving thought to that, we find that is not necessarily true. For there is another part of that faculty of respect and consideration, and it's known as value.

We find, as we go on in life, whatever we have a value for, we have a desire to attain. And the degree and the extent of that value and desire prompts us to a greater consideration. And as we demonstrate that Law of Consideration, we express some degree of respect. Now what is it in life that man finds of greatest value? It is really very clear, my friends. All we have to do is to ask our self, "To what do I give my greatest amount of respect? Do I respect this material world in which I live and move and have my being? If I do, then it is obvious and it is evident that I have some value for it."

What is it that causes man to experience within himself what he calls value? My friends, we cannot have value for anything until we accept within our self in our own mind that it is something that we desire because we believe that it has been beneficial to someone else. And so as we go along in life with our so-called respect and consideration and value, we find that they all stem from what is known as belief and desire. Therefore, man is governed and controlled by his own beliefs, whatever he in truth accepts within himself.

If man believes that the government is not doing what is valuable to him as an individual or the way that he thinks is the right way, then soon he loses what we call respect and no longer demonstrates the Law of Consideration. Remember, friends, without consideration, there is no understanding. And without understanding, there is no light. Therefore, we stumble in what they call the darkness, which is our own blindness and ignorance.

How can man best help himself to that that he desires to attain? If we will consider, as many times has been spoken from this rostrum, if we will consider that we and we alone are the true cause of all of our experiences in this life and the ones yet to be, if we will truly accept that great truth and no longer depend upon the whims and fancies of creation, no longer depend upon people, places, and things, then we will find what is known as true value. True value is something that is ever with you. It is not something that comes and goes.

And until such time as we give more consideration to the dimensions that are not seen by our physical sight, but by the very Law of Evolution we are destined to awaken to, until such time as we give things of the unseen an equal balance with things seen by the physical senses, then we are not going to be freed from the invisible influences around and about us, because we are not considering them, and in not considering them, we cannot understand them, let alone, believe in them. Again and again it has been spoken that man believes what appeals to himself at any given moment. And indeed that is true; once again demonstrating the individualization of the soul, the covering of the formless, divine Spirit.

And so in speaking on respect, so many of us think, perhaps, that we must demand respect. Well, that is true in a sense, if we demand it of ourselves. But if we fall into the misunderstanding that we must demand respect and consideration from others, if we believe that we are not receiving that, then we can be rest assured, my friends, that we are not giving it. We cannot receive anything in life that we do not first give.

Now a person may say, "Well, I desire to receive a substantial income in this life and be financially solvent. How is it possible for me to first give that, when I do not yet have it?" And that is the problem that man has created. As you believeth, so you becometh. If man will first *believe* that he has what he is desiring, then he will come to a level of consciousness within himself where what he desires is expressing itself. And like the great magnet of the universe, where like attracts like and becomes the Law of Attachment, man will experience what he truly believes. But that takes more than a thought, my friends, it takes the sustaining power of the Divine. And how does man become receptive, to a greater degree, to that sustaining power? Well, they've called it many words, my friends, and one of those is *faith*. Faith is an absolute conviction within our own mind that we already have what we have been seeking.

Now many times with these new-thought movements and positive thinking and self-improvement teachings in the world, man tries to demonstrate that law, but he doesn't try very long. He might try for a month, a week, some, perhaps, even for a year. So we find that it takes not only the faith, but it takes patience.

We look about and we see that some people are able to demonstrate what is known as a positive attitude and to experience the so-called good things in life. And perhaps they've been able to do that with some effort in a week or a month. And so we go along six or eight months or, perhaps, a year or two and we're still not able to demonstrate it. It doesn't mean that the principle of that law is not working, because what works for one, by the very law and its own principle, works for everyone. But we're all a little different, like the blades of grass in the meadow.

And so for some of us, it's going to take a little bit longer than for the rest of us.

We have all accepted, through the laws of belief, different thoughts in our mind, and we have also rejected other thoughts in our mind. And so we cannot look at another and try to become a carbon copy, my friends, for in so doing we will deny our own divinity, our own individuality. Let us accept what we believe we are *this* moment. And in accepting that, if we are not satisfied or pleased, then let us have the wisdom, the courage, and the strength to begin to change.

Thank you, friends. Thank you.

FEBRUARY 3, 1974

Church Lecture 30

The 126th Anniversary of Modern Spiritualism

This morning, we are speaking on the 126 years of the Modern Spiritualist movement.

It was during this month on the thirty-first day of March in the year of 1848, that the now, world-renown Fox sisters—those three little children—had their psychic and spiritual experiences with one who had passed on. I will not spend a great deal of time on the physical history of Spiritualism, for the libraries of our world are filled with its history.

When we look at Modern Spiritualism, if we look to see the cathedrals that it may have built, the physical institutions that it may have opened, then we are looking at something that we will sadly be disappointed with. Spiritualism did not come to this world to build physical cathedrals of stone and mortar. It came to this world to build cathedrals of the soul. And so it is with the Spiritualist movement, there are few indeed, very few, physical structures. However, if you will pause and look deeper, you will find that its philosophy, its science of communication, its religion has spread across the land in ways that have renewed the minds of men and has indeed transformed their lives.

Spiritualism is not a religion that has a great promotional program, a drive to convert the souls of this world. It is a philosophy which is demonstrable by its own science. And being a personally-demonstrable religion, man does not need to identify himself as this or that because he knows, when he truly understands this philosophy, that he is indeed a part of the great, united whole.

In transforming the lives of humanity, from a very humble beginning in that year of 1848, from those scientific demonstrations many new, so-called, philosophies, religions, and teachings have come to our world. For it was from the Spiritualist movement that the religion of Christian Science was given its birth by that wonderful founder, Mary Baker Eddy. A woman who spent her years as a Spiritualist medium and was inspired to found her own organization. From the Spiritualist movement came what we know today as Unity, the Church of Christianity. For it was the Fillmores [Charles and Myrtle Fillmore], serving in the Spiritualist movement, who by their spiritual teachers and guides were inspired to found that movement. And of rather recent date, we find another religion doing great work in this world and that is known as the Church of Religious Science, founded by a psychic, a medium, and, truly, an inspired man, the late Ernest Holmes. In France of the last century, we found another movement given birth, and that is known in our world as Theosophy. The late Madame Blavatsky was another medium in the Spiritualist movement.

We could go on and on and on listing the many schools of learning, the many, seeming varied, philosophies, churches, and religions that have been founded in this last 126 years from the efforts of an organization known as Spiritualism. Today we have in our universities what is known as parapsychology. From what did it grow? It grew out of the seance rooms of England

and America to enter into the halls of learning that man may become more awakened: to know and to demonstrate to himself that he is not the flesh and not the body; that he is an eternal spirit, once having shed this physical clay, can demonstrate to the satisfaction of any honest skeptic that there is no death, that there are no dead.

When we truly understand the work that is being done and has been done by the pioneers and workers of the Spiritualist movement, when we open our eyes to see the untold multitudes who cross the veil into what we, by error, call death, when we see their eyes awakened from the work that is done by the selfless workers, who, day upon day, speak with those on the other side to help them to adjust to their new experiences, when we see and demonstrate that whatever in this life or the next life that happens to us has indeed been caused by us, we will not wallow in the dimensions of what are called self-pity. We will be grateful for what we have, and in that gratitude we will open doors to a greater abundance and supply of good in our lives.

One of the very basic teachings of this movement is that like attracts like and becomes the Law of Attachment. It is so important, my friends, not just what you think, but how you think. For it is how you think, when you think with feeling, when you think with emotion, that you set these laws into motion. Life herself is a great mirror that reflects back to us what we are thinking into it. For all outward manifestations are in truth revelations of inner attitudes of mind. Now when we pause in our day-to-day activities and we sincerely and honestly give that some thought, we will begin to renew our minds and to transform our lives.

It is stated that every knock is a boost and to the man who has the slightest bit of light, it can be. For 126 years, a world that was not ready to accept change in its religious attitude repeatedly knocked what they did not understand. But the degree and amount of energy that has gone into knocking what we don't understand guarantees, by the very law that energy follows attention, to rise it to its heights. And this is why we know, from many years of experience, that anything new that comes to the world does not come to the world by the thinking of the masses. History repeatedly proves that to us. Change, my friends, is the divine law that governs all creation. And we are expressing—our soul, our spirit—through creation. So the teaching of Spiritualism is: Be ever ready and willing to change. The stone the builder rejects becomes the cornerstone.

My friends, our mind, our intellect is designed to serve a purpose, and designed, indeed, it is. It is not the whole. It is not complete; it cannot and never will be, for it is a vehicle of expression. And all vehicles are limited by the Law of Form. So let it—our mind, our intellect—let it serve its purpose, but let it accept and realize and recognize that the formless and the free cannot be confined in so-called space. Without acceptance of something greater than the intellect can seemingly comprehend, man limits himself and obstructs the freedom of his own divine, formless spirit.

What purpose have we come to this world for? How many of us have truly found that purpose? Be assured, my friends, when you find it, you will not be able to speak it, for the mind itself cannot comprehend it.

And so in this year of 1974, let us give thought—perhaps a bit more—to what we're doing today with what we have. Let us not dream in wishful thinking of the things we want, because in that type of thinking, my friends, we cannot see the things we already have. A wise man, surely, takes stock of the assets that he has merited in his soul's journey through these universes. And when he takes [stock of his] assets, he thinks about those things, then he begins to do something with them.

Remember, my friends, you can change yourself, you can transform your life, but you will never change another. You may be instrumental in sharing with them something that you think you have, but you, as an individualized soul, will not change another human soul here or hereafter. The change in our life must come from within our self. And how does this come about, my friends? By the Law of Acceptance. Man cannot demonstrate, nor experience, what he has not first accepted.

And so we all move in this old earth realm and we move in the blocks here in our heads that we have created. Remember, a wise man said long ago that condemnation prior to thorough investigation is the true mark of a ignorant man. Let us not be ignorant with our lives.

We are all seeking something in this world. We are seeking what we call, in Spiritualism, as soul fulfillment: a fulfillment of the purpose of our being. We did not come here, surely, just to eat and sleep and to move like robots. We have a mind to think. We have a spirit that uses that mind. We cannot find cures in anything unless we can find their cause. And we cannot find their causes, if we have not already found them, unless we're willing to accept something that we have not yet accepted.

So when you are seeking in this universe, think about that. Think about your life as it is this moment. And think about what you, as an individualized soul expressing your divine right, what *you* want to do about it.

If you are not ready to make changes in your life, then it is obvious that you will not make them. But, you know, this duality of creation serves a wonderful purpose. Sooner or later we either become bored, tired, disgusted, discouraged, or just plain miserable with something. Of course, the something is our own attitude of mind, but that does not help us when we're in that level of consciousness. What does help us, friends, when we're in those levels of consciousness? And I never met a human soul in my lifetime that wasn't in one of those levels at sometime. So what is it that frees us from it? It's known, my friends, as awareness. To be aware that we are going into that level of consciousness, to be aware at the very beginning. And when we are aware of that at the beginning, those who have studied spiritual laws know the way to get out before we get trapped.

Now, my friends, our time for lecturing is usually, approximately, eighteen to twenty minutes. We might say that we put a limit on things. Well, when you live in a world of illusion—and that is what this world is—filled with limitation that man has created, then you are sensible enough, hopefully, to be guided by it. However, before finishing with this morning's talk, I would like to say this. Those who do not see, or will not at least accept the possibility of these other dimensions that are influencing our life, are indeed suffering the great misery of what is known as ignorance or darkness. Who in their right mind wants to go out into this world blindly, not know where they're going, but to be pushed from shore to shore by the waves of creation, known as time?

Let us think on this day of the great effort that has gone into bringing this philosophy to this world. Let us give some kind thought and consideration to the pioneers of the Spiritualist movement, who were repeatedly persecuted and prosecuted, that this understanding may be kept in this world to free those souls who are ready, willing, and able to make the effort.

Thank you.

MARCH 24, 1974

Church Lecture 31

Value—Man's True Mirror

Speaking this morning on the topic that has been chosen, "Value—Man's True Mirror," we liken this mirror in which is, in truth, of course, a reflection of our self, of our levels of awareness, and our levels of consciousness to the experiences that we encounter in our day-to-day acts and activities. For we all know, I am sure, that experience, in truth, is the mirror of our own thoughts, attitudes, and acts. When looking into this mirror of life, known as experience, we gradually, slowly but surely, awaken within ourselves a greater understanding of what it is, in truth, that we value.

Now man's values may be likened unto the sun: there has never been, nor will ever be, a day in eternity in which the sun shines exactly in the same way. And so it is with all creation, there is never a moment in which our thought, our attitude, is exactly, precisely the same. The question then arises, "What is it that would be in my best interests to value? If what I see in this world and within myself is never exactly the same, then that indeed is indicative that it is not reliable." And so it is, my friends, we do not find reliability in what we call creation or form, for it is never the same. And therefore it is not reliable.

What then is in man's best interest to direct his reliance to? It is called, my friends, by many names. In this understanding we call it Infinite Intelligence or God or Spirit. That is the only thing that can be relied upon, for it is the only thing that is ever the same in all eternity. Though it expresses through forms—and many there are—and that's where all these changes take place, not in the Divine Intelligence, for that is a oneness. It is a security upon which all souls, in time, will see is the only reliance they truly have.

And so, my friends, let us pause to think and let us see what it is in life that we truly have value for. Look over the short span of this earth time and the time you have been aware of it, and see how many times in those short years your value has changed. Ask yourself the question, my friends, "If a wise decision had been made in the beginning of my thought, would my values go through the changes that I have already experienced with them?" Of course, the answer is indeed simple and clear. No, there would be no such thing as a change of our value. For we would have chosen in the very beginning the only thing in truth that is valuable.

Now each day, each week, each year that we express in this life, we go through many, many changes. We are always seeking something, and yet it ever seems to escape us. We seek this and we seek that. Sometimes we meet it, sooner or later, but when we meet it, we no longer want it because our values, in the process of waiting, have already changed. So isn't it, my good friends, such a waste of time, such a waste of energy, and such a waste of effort to seek and to chase a rainbow that either you cannot catch or, having caught it, you no longer want? Surely that is not reason. It isn't even logic.

And so we ask ourselves the question, "If that is what life is truly all about, then what am I doing here? And what indeed is the true purpose of my being?" There is a state of consciousness within all of us that knows why we have come to earth, what we have to learn, and where we are going. But it takes a little bit of effort to find that state of consciousness within our self. The reason that it takes a little bit of effort is quite simple. The mind, the so-called brain, which is the vehicle of its expression, has decided what is best for it. And when man decides what's best for himself, he becomes the living demonstration and the obstruction of the Divine Intelligence, known as God, in directing his life.

Now isn't it only, truly, common sense that we would pause for a few moments each day, that we may become receptive and rely upon the only thing in eternity that is reliable. But we have that choice and that decision to make.

As long as we permit our mind to decide what is best for ourselves, then we will guarantee our mind to decide what is best for everyone else. And when our soul expresses on that level of consciousness, we guarantee to be robbed of the peace that passeth all understanding. For the law which is demonstrable—that like attracts like and becomes the Law of Attachment—reveals to us where our values truly are.

You see, my friends, we don't need anyone to tell us where we're going, because we already know where we're going.

When we accept the truth inside of our self, then we will know where we are, and knowing where we are, dictates where we're going. Knowing where we are also reveals where we have been.

I know that all people do try to value what they call their divine right to think for themselves. But the sadness of that statement is, as man thinks he is thinking for himself, not truly knowing himself, he is only the effect of attitudes of mind, of patterns of thought, that he has been programmed to by his environment and by his upbringing. Therefore, what we value so much—the right to think for ourselves—is the very thing, my good friends, that we are not doing, until we, in truth, know ourselves. Not the way we think we are, but the way we truly are is what is truth, and that, my friends, is freedom.

Thank you.

APRIL 7, 1974

Church Lecture 32
Third Anniversary — Serenity Church

This morning on the third anniversary of this church, the topic is in keeping with that occasion. And so we are speaking on this third anniversary of Serenity Church. In thinking on that topic these past few days, many experiences and memories, of course, are brought to mind in the founding of this center, in its service to the community, and, of course, in its growth and its pains of growth. An organization of any type is merely an effect of the efforts that its membership and its friends put into it. It cannot be any lesser or any greater than the parts that compose the whole, known as a church or an association. And so it is with Serenity. It offers to this community, and to whatever part of the world that it may reach, a philosophy of self-awareness and improvement.

Now, all of us see things in life from our own vantage point and so it is with this little church. It is combined of a number of people who see things in various ways; who see its purpose, perhaps, a little different than the next person. However, there is one principle that is common to all its membership and to all of its friends. And that principle is the principle of awakening to our own true purpose in this life.

Many people in these short three years have passed through the doors of this church. Some have returned and some have stayed. It is not important to me, at least, as the founder of this church, whether those who pass through these doors stay or go. What is important is that the purpose for which the association was founded is being served. And that purpose, my friends, is to serve God to the best of our ability, to recognize and to realize that each and every human soul is serving God in the way that they have found best for them at any given moment.

We are here to share with you a philosophy, a science, a religion that we have found of benefit to ourselves. It is not our purpose to decide whether or not it is beneficial for you, for when we permit our minds to decide what is best for another, then we are becoming the judge and the jury of what is best for things outside of ourselves. The business of living, my friends, is an all-consuming process. The business of living one's own life—it is a full-time job, if we want to live it correctly for ourselves.

So let us give it some thought this morning, on this special day for Serenity, not for individuals and personalities, but for the principle for which this church is here today. The question may be asked, "What is it really doing and what isn't it doing?" If you look in a physical world, then you're not going to see a church structure of its own. That has not yet come to pass. But to us here at Serenity, it will come at the right time and in the right way. The most important thing to us is that the teachings that have helped us so much to this point in life may be shared with those who are truly seeking them.

And so it is that all of us have a responsibility. We have a responsibility to what is known as divine justice, for that that benefits us is not what we try to push down another's throat, but it is our responsibility to share with those who are seeking that which already has proven to help ourselves.

Many times people come to the light and they view it and having viewed it, they feel so much better. And then there are those who come to the light and find it too blinding for them at that moment. And so they go, to come another day at another time. Then there are those who come to the light and having viewed it for a time, wish to view something else. And so it is in a world of creation. And so it is justly so, for man truly values that which he has to make great effort to attain. And having attained what he first valued, value starts to diminish when there is no longer great effort made to keep the attainment. It's like a man that's on a desert. He doesn't miss the water until he can't find a well. And when he can't find the well, his thirst becomes unbearable. And so it is, my friends, in our seeking to find God. Let us not take for granted what we already have, for when we take for granted what we have, we only guarantee to lose it. Let us adjust, my good friends, our perspective. Let us be honest with ourselves.

Truly, the motives are varied for those who seek the Eternal Light of peace and freedom. And although those motives are varied, in time they grow to one—to one motivation, to one purpose, to one principle. Remember, we have wandered far—many of us—from home, but that only guarantees that we will wander back to our home, the home of our soul. My good friends, the home of our soul is not a physical structure. It is not a physical organization or church. A church is simply an effect of our seeking the home of our own soul. If we feel more comfortable in one church than in another, then, my good friends, wisdom herself dictates that is where we should be.

In this month's issue of our magazine, the *Serenity Sentinel*, there is a beautiful poem by an unknown author. When I first read it, it touched the very depths of my soul. That poem is entitled, "It's Not Your Church, It's You." Truly, the author of that great poem was inspired from the realms of illumination because he saw clearly that the disturbances and dissension that we sometimes view in what we call a church is not the church itself; it is our own pains of growth. It is our own attitude of mind. [*Please see the appendix for the complete poem.*] Remember, friends, if we cannot be happy with ourselves, inside of ourselves, then we cannot possibly be happy with the world and with people around and about us. So let us be about our Father's business and let us work on ourselves. Let us look more clearly at our soul. Let us find the meaning of life and let us wander back home to God, where we are all trying to be, in our own way.

I would like, before closing, to share with you the humble beginnings of this association, to those who are not familiar with it. Six years ago this year, we founded what is known as the Serenity Spiritualist Camp Association or Camp Serenity, in the mountains of Mendocino. It had been a vision of mine for a number of years and it finally came to pass. Three years ago this month, we opened the Serenity Church. I had, for a number of years, entertained the thought that if there was anything in life that I didn't want, it was a church. My reason for entertaining such a thought, I would like to share with you. On my level of consciousness, a number of years ago, I saw what I thought was so much dissension and disturbance in what is called an organized church or religious body. I could not understand at that time how people seeking the peace of God, the harmony and the unity of the Divine, could possibly express such discord and dissension. The years passed. And the thing that we are adverse to, we guarantee. I had not thought, at least myself, that I had, in my entertaining of not ever having a church of my own, created an adversity. But obviously my presence here reveals it.

At the request of a group of people from the realms of spirit, known to us as the Spirit Council, these doors were opened in order that these teachings and this philosophy and religion may be shared in this community. They were opened for that sole purpose. They were not opened to build a building of stone and mortar, though that may come to pass. But they were opened to help those souls who were seeking an understanding of Life herself. When they were opened, I had received one promise from the world of spirit: the one thing that changed my attitude and permitted me to move in the direction of founding a church. And that one promise I would like to share with you. The angels who brought this center into being said to me, "If you will open for us a spiritual center, we promise you that those who enter its doors and become a membership to support it will grow or go, but harmony and unity and the purpose for which we are bringing it to the world shall carry on."

And so, I am indeed grateful this day, though many have come and many have gone, a few have stayed. And the process of harmony and unity and serving God continues on.

Thank you.

MAY 5, 1974

Church Lecture 33

Man's Spiritual Search

The topic that was selected for this evening's discussion, "Man's Spiritual Search," may also be stated as man's surrender and acceptance. It seems in this world that we are constantly searching for something. And it seems in that searching that we have great difficulty with staying with anything long enough to find out whether or not that is what we are truly searching [for].

What is it within us that causes us to go from one thing to another, on a constant seeming eternal treadmill? What is it within us that is dissatisfied with the things we find without? My good friends, as we have often spoken, the things without—satisfaction or dissatisfaction—are merely a revelation of the discontent that stirs within our own soul, within our own being. The obvious reason why we are not able, seemingly so, to stay with any particular study or endeavor is because of our unwillingness to surrender. Until we reach a state of consciousness within our own being where we are willing, ready, and able to surrender what we consider is our knowledge, what we consider is right—until we reach that state of consciousness and we're willing to surrender to a Divine Wisdom, to a Divine Intelligence, we are not going to find the things that we are truly seeking.

You see, my good friends, man, being a part (his form) of this world of creation, has what is known as choice or free will. And so it is that man repeatedly decides moment to moment and year to year what is best for himself. And because we use this vehicle known as brain to make those decisions, we guarantee the continuous change for our own lives. When we surrender what we consider so important (our decision-making by our own mind and brain) when we reach that point, we become receptive to the divine will of acceptance. Then, my good friends, we are on the path to freedom.

A man may well ask the question, "If acceptance in truth is the divine will, then why is it that man has what is known as choice, a vehicle by which he may decide which is best for himself?" If we did not have the mind to make decisions, then, my friends, we would not have the opportunity to grow, to evolve, to unfold. However, there is a way in which we may become aware of which is the Divine Spirit that is motivating us and which is the created brain. Whenever you have a thought concerning your acts and activities or those of another, when you have that thought and you are able to release it from the bondage of your mind, being not concerned whether the answer returns to you in a moment, a day, a year, or ever, when you are truly able to do that, then, my good friends, you will never again need be concerned on making decisions.

The law is very, very clear. What goes out from our being, from our mind, goes around in a circle and returns to us. Man is not only the living demonstration of his own thoughts, he is the living mirror of himself. All we need to do, my good friends, is to look at life's experiences, to look at our friends and our associates, to look at our involvements, to look at our responsibilities, to look at our own desires and we will see how far we are on the eternal path of progression. It is not necessary, nor is it advisable, for someone to tell us where we are, because, my friends, we do indeed know where we are. But ofttimes we don't want to look at that. We don't want to look at the people around and about us. We don't want to look at the circumstances and conditions and face the great truth that that indeed is where we have put ourselves.

Now, my friends, if we look at life and we become discouraged, then we guarantee a continuity of discouragement, for man and man alone is the law unto himself. But if we look at life with hope and with a spiritual search to return home to that great peace, that heaven that is within our own consciousness, if we look at life as a challenge unto our self, to bow in humility to a greater power than our own brain, if we look at life that way, then indeed will we find life's true purpose.

We all have come to the earth realm with different motives and different thoughts. We have entered the human race in varied circumstances and conditions. We did that according to the law that we set into motion. But having done it, my friends, we're not left without the ability, without the awareness to do something about it, if we are not pleased or satisfied with what life seems to be offering to us. Remember, the offering of life is the revelation of our level of consciousness. So let us look at life more cheerfully and make a greater effort to do what we came to this earth realm to do.

So many, I hear, say they don't know why they came to earth. They can't remember what they did before in this evolutionary path of incarnation and, therefore, they don't know what their purpose in life is. My good friends, anyone who makes the effort to set aside the so-called brain or ego long enough to be peaceful, to be receptive to the Divine itself, will know in their own soul and their own heart why they came to this earth realm, the job that they have to do, and how far along the path they are. We don't have to be told that, my friends. We already know it.

There is an inner urge within us that constantly, repeatedly prompts us to do what is right for our own soul. We all have those promptings, but it seems we do not often listen to them, let alone apply them. Let us take a few moments more often in the course of a day. Let us think what we're doing with the opportunity that we have merited. What are we doing with the life that we have, not what are we going to do, but what we're doing now, this moment?

Many times a person will say, "Well, I can't do this because of that and I can't do something else I want to do because of the circumstances and conditions that I am presently in." My friends, we all do what we really want to do. That may not seem to be true on certain levels of consciousness, but the truth is we all do what we really want to do. So if it is that we want to go somewhere, if we really and truly want to do that, we will go there. And if there is some work that we want to do, if we truly want to do it, all of the excuses and all of the devices will disappear into the nothingness and we will do what we truly want to do.

Now, I know that many, perhaps, may disagree with that understanding, but be considerate with yourself and give it some thought. Because I know if you will give it some thought, you will find that it is true. How many times do we say to a person, "I wish I could do that but because of something, I can't." And we know in our own consciousness that that is a device. It's not a method; it's a device. You see, my friends, there's a difference between devices and methods. Devices are self-motivated for self-interest, but a method is legal when the motive is pure. And therefore, there is indeed a vast difference.

How does man find his home, the one he has wandered from? He finds it when he removes all those layers that cover his own light and his own soul. How do we remove those layers of so-called intelligence and so-called knowledge? How do we remove them? My friends, they're not removed until we bow in humility to an infinite Divine Intelligence that holds the stars in space. No, my friends, look at the world herself. Look at all of creation. What mind, what individual mind could possibly entertain the thought that it knows completely what is best for itself when it can't even hold one single star in the solar system? Think, my friends. Accept the greatness of God. Call the Intelligence what you will. At least, accept it in your life and be free.

Thank you.

JUNE 2, 1974

Church Lecture 34

Mediums and Their Message

And this morning we're speaking on a subject that is indeed not only important to the movement of Spiritualism, but it is important to our world today. And that subject is, "Mediums and Their Message." Our National Association defines medium or mediumship as one who is sensitive to vibrations from the spiritual world and through whom intelligences from that world are able to convey messages and produce the phenomena of Spiritualism. We look at that definition, yea, with even a broader aspect for mediums are not only sensitive to spiritual emanations from a spiritual world, but they are sensitive to vibrations from a mental world, from an astral world and also, of course, from this physical world.

Now the true purpose of mediumship is to establish communication intelligently, logically, and reasonably with other dimensions and to know what those dimensions truly are. And so it is, my friends, before anyone can unfold what is known as genuine mediumship, they must first start on the path of self-awareness. For how is it that an individual can know beyond the shadow of any doubt what is from a mental realm, what is from the depths of our own subconscious, or what is from, indeed, a realm of spirit? We can know what dimension we are expressing through by being on that plane of expression. And so it is, my friends, if the message of the medium is from a spiritual world, then the medium at that time is on a spiritual world in their own soul consciousness. If they are not, then, obviously and evidently, the message is not from a world of spirit. And so it is, my friends, that all people everywhere have the potential of communication with other dimensions, including the so-called world of spirit. For what is possible for one is, of course, possible for all. And so it is that we are speaking today on mediums and their message.

So many times people newly exposed to the philosophy, science, and religion of Spiritualism seem to misunderstand its true purpose. My friends, its purpose is not to serve as fortunetellers for a material world; its purpose is not to glorify the so-called egos of the unfolding mediums; its purpose is not to solve all of your problems that so many seem to desire to continue to create. That is not the purpose, to my understanding, of genuine mediumship. The purpose of mediumship is to reveal the cause of the experiences that you are experiencing, to help you to see that there is a better way to live in life, that there is a purpose to the moment in which your soul is expressing.

There are many avenues through which those who have left this realm will strive and try to help you to change your thinking. For in changing your thinking, my good friends, you indeed will change your life for the better.

And so it is that mediumship and its purpose serves the world in which we live. We are not just interested in a dimension over there that someday in 20, 50, or 60 years you are going to experience. The spiritual world, my friends, is the spirit within your own being here and now. If you awaken your own spirit, your own soul—that is, if you awaken your mind to it—you will experience this so-called world of spirit. And having experienced it, you will remove from your conscious thought forever the superstition and delusion known as death. My friends, if for no other reason, Spiritualism and communication serves a great purpose if it only removes from your thought the delusion of death. For there is no death, my friends. There's only a change, a change of form.

Does it not behoove us to give some thought to dimensions in life that are influencing our very being? Who amongst us chooses to be blind to reality, to be blind to truth? Mediumship and Spiritualism is not concerned with your so-called tomorrows. It is concerned, my friends, with your today. For we know if you truly apply the philosophy of Spiritualism, if you make the effort to apply it, you will transform your life, for you will have transformed your thinking. We teach in this understanding that all experiences are the direct effect of a level of consciousness or an attitude of mind of each and every individual. My friends, that teaching must be repeated endlessly, for it is the repetition of error that has placed us where we are today. And so through the same Law of Repetition do we make a slight change in our thinking.

I have heard many say that they go to a Spiritualist church and either the message is correct or the message is not correct. Are we using, truly, total consideration when we make the decision and the judgment that the message is either correct for us or it is not correct? Do we in truth know the various dimensions that are influencing our life or have we entered a church of this nature with the preconceived thought and opinion that we want to hear a certain thing to a certain question that we are entertaining in mind? That is not the way that spiritual communication works. It is indeed the way that mind reading and telepathy work. That does not mean to say that you will or will not receive an answer to your question when you go to a church of this nature. That, my friends, depends upon the laws that you and you alone have set into motion. If it is true—and it is demonstrable—that all experience is indeed a mirror reflecting back to us our own attitude of mind, then that law is not exempt from the experience of communion and communication. No, my friends, whatever you are seeking is indeed also seeking you. And like the hands of the clock, opportunity every so often shall meet.

And so it is that we are here this moment. There are a multitude of motives. But be rest assured, my friends, if those who have gone before us to another dimension, hopefully, from the realms of light, are able to reach your consciousness to help you to make a change in thought, to bring about a more peaceful, a more fulfilling, a more abundant life here and now, then indeed the purpose of mediumship has been served. But remember, my friends, we can never experience in life, here or hereafter, anything that we are not willing, ready, and able to accept. If you can't accept the possibility of eternal life this moment, this day, then it's indeed indicative that you will not accept it tomorrow.

So let us think for a moment. Let us think about where we are, here and now, because we have this awareness of this moment. Then let us ask the question, "How did we get to this point in evolution today? Where have we been?" Because looking at where we have been may serve a purpose of helping us in deciding where we want to go. So few people want to think about that so-called day when it's our time to leave this physical body. But, friends, look at it this way: that so-called day is *this* day; it's *this* moment. Our thoughts are in a constant process of change. And so it is as we accept new thinking, new ways of living, the yesterdays die and leave our universe.

With so much interest in this age in so-called psychic phenomena, with so much interest in telepathy and mind reading and psychokinesis and the moving of physical objects by the power of mind, with so much interest in our world today, let us use reason, my good friends. I assure you the psychic is not where it is. It serves a purpose, if it is used wisely. It is not the thing to seek. Neither is mediumship and communication with other dimensions. That is not the thing to seek and that is not what the students and members of this church, I hope, are seeking. We seek what we call God, the Divine, the Eternal Light and Truth. By seeking that, all things that are in your best interest for your own soul evolution shall be added unto you. But woe to the man or woman who seeks the glory of so-called psychic phenomena and mediumship. For indeed it is sad what they do to their own lives. You don't seek so-called spiritual gifts, my friends, like you seek to be carpenters or musicians. That is not how it works at all.

We all have what is known as a soul talent. Now isn't it wisdom that dictates that we should permit the thing that we are most able to do in life to unfold itself? How do we find what our natural soul talent really is? We find it, my good friends, when we find God. Because when we find that light within, all things within our universe are revealed to us. So often in life man does not care to accept the humble jobs and the menial tasks, for he is above those things according to his own thinking. But, don't you see, my good friends, the menial tasks and the humble jobs—that's God's greatest work, if we put God into it.

Think for a moment, think of what you are doing to yourselves. For one moment still your mind and ask yourself honestly that question, "Where am I going? I know where I've been, but where am I really going? Am I so entertained by what this mundane material world and its merry-go-round has to offer that I have lost perspective, that I can no longer think for myself, because I'm brainwashed with either a television set, a radio, or a newspaper?" Is that where we have put our soul at this point in our evolution?

My friends, don't think for a moment that you're some brand new soul, descended direct from God. That is not the understanding or the philosophy of this association. Our soul is an evolving process. It has expressed through untold centuries and will continue to express through untold centuries.

And so let us ask our self how many times must we learn the same lesson? Please do not confuse this philosophy with so-called reincarnation. We understand our soul evolves through the universes and does not necessarily return to this planet to learn its lessons. Think, think how many centuries your soul has been striving to get where you are today. Are you satisfied? Are you in truth pleased with yourself this moment? Are you getting from life all that you indeed are desiring? Have you found the purpose for which your soul has entered this earth realm? Or is it necessary, my friends, to keep the mind so active in so-called creation so that you won't have to think anymore?

I assure you there is more to life than raising a family or building a business or even a church. There's more to life, my friends, than things. All things come and all things go, but your soul goes on forever and ever. That is what you have to live with.

I've heard many people say, oh, they can't be alone, they can't be alone. What does that really mean when we think we can't be alone? Does it mean that we must have someone near us or by us that we can talk with, that we can communicate with? And if so, what is the need? Why? Does it mean that we are not willing to face our own thoughts, our own emotions, and our own attitudes? Does it mean that we cannot be still by our self and God and look at our self honestly and objectively? Does it mean that we are so miserable in the depths of our own being that we must constantly have our mind entertained with people and things? If that is what it means, friends, do yourself a favor and start to think where you're going.

May we in this moment and in this day take the message that is given to heart. Let us not judge another's life, that we may not be judged our self. But let us be receptive and let us think. At least, my friends, you have the divine right to think and you have the divine right to a life of happiness, to a life of abundance, to a life of joy, and to a life of purpose.

Thank you.

JULY 7, 1974

Church Lecture 35
Leadership and Responsibility

In speaking this morning on the topic of "Leadership and Responsibility," we are in truth speaking about one and the same thing. For man does not lead without desire and man is not responsible without desire. And so we see that whatever in truth we desire we are responsible for and are in truth leading.

Man is filled with so many desires in the course of a day. We must ask our self the question, "How is it possible, when the mind is filled with so much desire, that it is able to function at all in this world in which we live?" And we see that there is, controlling desire, what man calls value. For whatever it is that we make an effort to attain, we have some degree of value for. And so in the course of a moment or a day we are in a constant process of making choices. Think, my good friends, wherever we are this moment in time is a revelation of the decisions that we have made of our own choices, an effect of our own desires. Now that is rather a positive and definite statement, but let us think for a few moments. Once man desires, he sets a law into motion to fulfill the desire that he is expressing. And so man is led along the path of his own desires and that path is known as the law, the law that man has established. Now the question may arise in our minds that we are not experiencing in life what we truly are desiring. The reason, my friends, that we think that way is because we so easily have forgotten the desires of yesterday. And so it is that man indeed is a law unto himself.

Now we all are leaders and we all are responsible to the things that we lead. We are responsible to ourselves for where we are this moment on the evolutionary path of evolutionary incarnation. We did not come to this world haphazardly, by chance, and we will not leave this world by chance. For the universe is governed by immutable law and man is the microcosm of that great universe, the macrocosm. When we awaken within ourselves to the truth that frees us, which is a recognition and an acceptance that whatever in life happens to us is indeed caused by us, then, my good friends, we will become the captain of our ship and indeed the master of our destiny. So often in life we seek to blame influences, circumstances, and conditions outside of our self for the effects and the experiences that we are having. Well, as long as we seek to blame, to find the cause outside, then we're never going to get to the root of any problem. For the cause, my good friends, ever lies within our self.

We look across the land and we see so many things that we desire. But it has been stated many times that desire has no light. And indeed it has no light, for when the mind desires something, it does not at that moment use the faculty of reason. It does not use the function of logic. All it knows is that it desires. Once the desire is fulfilled, it no longer has value to man. And that is why a wise man seeks a goal that is unattainable. For once you attain any goal in life, you no longer make the effort to continue on and to progress and to broaden your horizons and to expand your consciousness. And so, my friends, what is it that is worthwhile in life to lead? What is it within us that has an eternal, lasting value? What is it that will weather every storm and every change, which is the Law of Creation? That something that is above and beyond, and yet expressing through creation, is called by many names. It's called God. It's called Infinite Intelligence.

And let us think for a moment, is there anyone in all of the universes who does not believe in God? I question that there is anyone, or has there ever been, who does not believe in God. They may not believe in the concepts that the world has created and named God. But there is no man of reason, there is no man of logic or common sense that does not realize, recognize, and accept that there is an Intelligence in the universe that holds the stars in space, that there is an Intelligence that can create life—something that man has never done; something that man will never do. Man may bring together the necessary negative and positive poles of nature, but he will never create life. Because that takes an Intelligence greater than his own brain. That Intelligence, my friends, the Spiritualists call Infinite Intelligence. We do not find a God of form, but we find an Infinite Intelligence that sustains all form everywhere, from the pebble on the beach to the crown of man himself. This, my good friends, is something you can value, for it is something that has always been, that expresses by divine law, that is immutable, that will always be.

All things, my friends, that are form have a beginning and by the Law of Beginning, they indeed have an ending. And thought, my friends, is form, for it is something the mind has created. And so when man seeks God, the Infinite Intelligence, with his mental body, with his thought, then God will become a concept, a created form. And this is why it has been stated, "When of thy mind thou seekest to know the truth, on the wheel of delusion thou shalt traverse." [Discourse 1, which is published in *The Living Light* and *The Living Light Dialogue,* Volume 1] It is also stated that God, the Divine Intelligence, is equal at any moment to our understanding. Well, of course, the Infinite Intelligence is equal to our understanding, for man is the one who either expands or narrows his understanding. That is not something that the Divine Intelligence does, but it is something within the free will of man himself.

And so I ask you, "What is worthwhile in this life, or any life, to lead or to be responsible to?" Your children are born; they grow and go, and so do your husbands and wives, your brothers and your sisters. Governments rise, to fall again, to rise again. Money comes into your pocket and disappears again. What is the security that man has in Life herself? We all, I am sure, will agree: it is not our jobs; it is not our professions; it is not our bank accounts; it is not our wives, our husbands, our sons, or our daughters, our governments, or even our religions. It is the Divine Intelligence that you are able to be receptive to at any given moment. It is the only thing in life itself that will not fail you because it is not dependent upon the fickle mind of man.

And so does it not behoove us to give some thought to the true purpose of Life herself? Of what benefit is it, my good friends, to slave and to strive for this or that, when it will be such a temporary experience to us? What is fifty or a hundred years or even a hundred and fifty, when you are speaking about an eternal journey? One that you have always been on, one that you will ever continue to be on. Anyone who stops to think, knows that there is no death, that there are no dead. All they have to do is study Nature herself. And they can see that that comes from this earth realm, by the law of coming from it, shall return to it.

Man knows deep within his own being that he is an inseparable part of the whole, known as Infinite Intelligence. Man also knows what he does to himself has an effect upon *all* the rest of the universes. Not just your close associates, but an effect upon *all* of nature. So man can say, "Well, that must be such a microscopic effect that I have." But when that microscopic effect becomes the mass thinking of the world of the human race, then we see the changes take place in our lives.

Let us make a little effort, my friends, to find the peace that passeth all understanding within our self, because a moment never goes by when it would not be of benefit to use. Without peace within our being, my friends, we have no self-control. We have a constant and continuous battle between what we call the sense functions and the soul faculties. Let us awaken the peace within our own being that we may have a perspective in life, bring a balance into this world, and truly enjoy what it has to offer to us. There is no need for anyone to experience the disturbances, the miseries, and the griefs that they insist, so often, upon experiencing.

My friends, everyone and everything in creation needs attention. The blade of grass needs the attention of the sun and the rain and the nutrients of the soil or it dies and does not serve its purpose. And so does every creature in all the universes have this insatiable need for attention, which we call energy. Now, my friends, there are many ways of gaining attention, which, of course, energy follows. But let us think of a way of gaining and receiving this energy or attention without the need of having people do certain things to satisfy our own desires. I assure you this energy, this attention is available to all of God's creatures. All you need to do, my friends, is for a moment be at peace. For when you're truly at peace, you will have all of the so-called love, attention, or energy that you could possibly utilize at any given moment.

What has placed us in the condition and the circumstances of having to seek other human beings fulfilling our desires to gain this energy or love or attention? It is from the error of ignorance itself. Man says, "I can only experience love when I have a companion." As long as man says that, man will establish that law and that is the only time he will ever experience love, is when he has a companion. But a wiser man says, "I see God everywhere in all things. I am an inseparable part of that so-called God. It's smiling in the leaf of the tree and in the sun itself." And man can experience that great so-called divine love or energy and be free from the fluctuations and the power control of other human beings. Don't you see, my friends, we sell our soul to the things that we *think* we need. What could we possibly need when the Divine Intelligence has given us everything? What could we need, but the error within our own mind, the error within our own thinking, that we feel this way or we feel that way when we have or have not what we desire.

Let us look at things perhaps a little differently. Let us accept that everything we already have, because in truth, my friends, that is the fact. We can within the power of our own created mind have all the things that we think that we need. But it's the mind that says we do not have it in the physical substance. The mind says that because the mind is limited and the mind does not know the eternal law, the truth of how things come into being.

All things are the effect of directed energy through the power of thought. It is known as image. And so when man believes in his heart, in the depths of his being, that he has the image that he has created, then man will experience it in this physical world. But they say, my friends, that that takes what is known as faith. Well, we understand faith to be an absolute conviction. We are convinced that we don't have something and so we are using the Law of Faith to keep from experiencing it. We can use that same law and experience it. When so-called faith or conviction is expressed through a negative level of consciousness, we experience what is known as fear. When that same energy is expressed through a positive level of consciousness, we experience what is known as faith. And so how true the law the prophets expressed in that book, "As a man believeth in his heart, so he becometh."

So let us believe in prosperity. Let us believe in peace. Let us believe in success. And let us see the good everywhere, for the goodness within and without is what the religionists call God.

Thank you.

AUGUST 4, 1974

Church Lecture 36
Psychometry (Aura Sensing)

It is indeed with great pleasure that I speak this morning on the topic, as our chairman stated, "Psychometry (Aura Sensing)," for there is such a great interest these days on things of the psychic and the spiritual nature. It is very little understood—this word and its meaning of *psychometry*. Psychometry can be stated simply as soul knowing or aura sensing. Now wherever we are and whatever we do, we are constantly exposed to vibrations that we cannot see, hear, or sense with our physical senses. But that does not mean, my good friends, that we are not influenced by these vibrations that permeate the atmosphere. Whenever we touch anything with a physical contact, we deposit from our very being electro-magnetic energy, which in turn permeates the object which we have touched. Now this energy, which is emanating from our aura, can, by proper sensing, be interpreted for what is truly taking place within our mind at the time that we touched this so-called object. So often people think that if they ask a question on a piece of paper that that is the answer they will receive. And my friends, that would indeed be true if psychometry were the only phase of communication or mediumship. But it is not true, my friends, because there are other phases that are blended in with psychometry, such as clairsentience (or sensing clearly) and clairvoyance and clairaudience.

Now if it is true—and it is demonstrably true—that all objects emanate a certain vibration, depending upon the vibration of the people who have touched it, then it stands to reason that when we go certain places and we touch certain things, that we are, depending, of course, upon our receptivity, we are affected and influenced to some degree. The more sensitive we become, the more we are affected by these vibrations that permeate the atmosphere. And so the teaching is to balance our sensitivity with what is known as our sensibility, to use our reason and our logic.

So many people interested in the psychic fields do not seem to understand the many phases involved with communication. There is such a thing as telepathy, a conscious awareness of another person's conscious thoughts. There is, of course, such a thing as mind reading, which is a conscious awareness of another person's subconscious thoughts at the time. Then there is what we are discussing here this morning, known as psychometry. Psychometry is revealing what your basic attitude of mind and pattern really is. You may or may not be consciously aware at that time of those patterns which are influencing your life.

And so it is, my friends, that we go through the course of a day with many varied feelings and emotions. We are all transmitters and receivers. We are receiving the broadcast of anyone that we are on that level of consciousness and in rapport with. For example, you may receive a feeling within your being and not know why you feel the way that you do. My friends, it can and does reveal that you are receptive to another individual who is at that time broadcasting that feeling and that emanation. And so the question must arise, "If it is true we are transmitters and receivers, then how does one protect themselves to maintain their so-called individuality when they are exposed to such a multitude of vibrations in the atmosphere?" My friends, it has been stated by all teachers of all times. Man, know thyself and ye shall know the truth and it is the truth that will set you free.

And so it is that we go on the inward journey to know our own mind. To know the things that we have long forgotten. To know the desires of yesterday, for they are the laws, my friends, that are controlling your today. If you do not awaken to that truth, then you will continue to be the effect of long forgotten desires that have never been fulfilled, that were suppressed into the depths of our own subconscious. Those, my friends, are what you are experiencing today, this moment, unless you have become aware of your true self and you know the law and apply it. So many people in this understanding study and know the law extremely well, but when it comes to application, they seem to stumble and to fall. And why is that so, my friends? Does it not reveal to us our true values? Is that not a revelation? When we do not have the strength of character to demonstrate the laws that we know, is that not a revelation that it does not yet mean enough to us?

And so it is, my friends, in speaking on psychometry, aura sensing, let us become aware of our own aura, the emanation from our own mind and body. And when we truly become aware of that aura, that is the one that we can do something about. We cannot do something about someone else's vibration, but we certainly can do something about our own.

So let us become aware of our true feelings and motivation; then we will know at any given moment why we are experiencing what we are experiencing. We will not have to ask someone else why we are the way we are when we are, because we will know why we are the way we are when we are. Because, my friends, that is truth and that truth is freedom. It is freedom from the controls and influences that are governing our lives. It is freedom from the discord and the disturbance within our own mind.

It has been often said that man really gets what he truly wants. And how true a statement that is. We always experience in life what we really want to experience. Many, I know, will disagree with me, because they have forgotten what desire they had of yesterday and what law they set into motion. And today it is being fulfilled in a time when it is no longer desirable. Think, my good friends, it's ever and for always inside of our self. It's never out there. When will we ever get it into our consciousness and apply that great truth? God is not outside, my friends, until God is inside. And so that's where the work must begin. It must begin inside of our own mind. It must begin in our daily acts and activities. God, peace, freedom, abundance, call it what you will, must mean enough to us to make the daily, conscious, constant effort. Again and again and again. Century after century after century, if that's what it takes to awaken our soul and to free us.

You hear so much about so-called psychic protection. Well, the psychic, mental, spiritual, or emotional protection, my friends, is not a great white light that you can circle around your being. It is the white light of pure thought, a sincere heart, and a true purpose. If you wish to call that the great Christ light, then that is fine. But it is only made manifest within our own being and it comes from our own efforts. It doesn't come from reading this or that. It doesn't come from a great education. But it does come from application. Applying the law. Fulfilling the purpose of our soul's incarnation.

My friends, we have evolved to this point in time and we are continuing to evolve to other points in so-called time. We came here with many lessons to learn. The lessons we have to learn this time are the ones we flunked last time, as our soul continues to evolve through time and space. And I would like to clarify, especially to those who are new to our understanding, that does not imply a return to this Earth planet, for that is not the teachings of Serenity. It is our understanding and demonstration that our soul is evolving throughout eternity. That this is one of the stepping stones and one of the planets on which it is expressing.

So think, my friends, that which is difficult for you this time, master it so you will not have to go through it the next time. If it is temper that is your weakness, then work on it today. If it is tolerance, then do something about it. For the continued experience, my friends, becomes more and more difficult. If it is continuity, then demonstrate it. Because if you keep postponing it—that's why we are where we are today! We put it aside yesterday. We put it aside in those other lives. We didn't want to face it. Face it, my friends, that's the only way it's going to get better. If you turn your back on the things that are difficult today, you will face them throughout eternity, until you have mastered them. For your soul is in a form that is the crown of creation on this planet. You are indeed the captain of your ship and the master of your destiny. But unless you make that decision now, my friends, not tomorrow, then you cannot and you will not free your soul from the difficulties that you may be experiencing.

It is said that all souls carry their cross, that in time they reach their crown. And how very true that is. But what is a cross? Symbolic of a struggle and suffering. But whose suffering and struggle? Man's suffering and struggle! And why has man made it a struggle and a suffering? Because man would not face the truth and the truth says clearly and simply, "It's all inside my own head. It doesn't exist in somebody else's. It exists in mine. I set that law into motion. And I and I alone, with God's help, which is within me, can change that law."

How does man change the laws that he has set into motion? Simply, my friends, by setting new laws into motion. And what is it within us that sets a law into motion? My friends, think, for it is thought. The universe is the law's meditation and man is an idea of it. As mind is ever one in substance with the idea and the whole idea, so man and the law and the universe are one and the same. So become aware of your thoughts, my friends, your attitudes, and your feelings, for those are the laws that you are setting into motion. And do not be discouraged for the laws that you set into motion yesterday, for you, too, can change those.

Remember, when you express thought, you are releasing from your very being electro-magnetic energy. That is scientifically demonstrable. It goes out into the universe, attracts its kind and returns to you tenfold. If you are disturbed or ill at ease, do not entertain it in thought, my friends, for you guarantee its own continuity. If you think you are in lack and limitation, do not entertain it in thought or feeling, you guarantee its own increase. If you are having difficulty with getting along with people because you can't have your own way, don't entertain it in thought, you will guarantee the avalanche. Don't you see, my friends, it is indeed in our mind.

What is worthwhile and peaceful to entertain in thought? Well, my friends, it's peace itself. Peace, that great peace which brings balance in our life, that is the power known as God. And when you demonstrate the divine will known as acceptance, then you will indeed change your thinking and transform your life.

Now, what does all of this have to do with psychometry and aura sensing? It has a great deal to do [with it], my friends. Prophecy is nothing more nor less than the revelation of the laws that you and you alone have set into motion. And therefore, it cannot and will not be ever more than 90 percent accurate, because man has that 10 percent free will to change his mind, to change the laws that he and he alone has set into motion.

And so, think. What are we doing with what we have? Everyone within the sound of my voice has a talent that is useful to this world. Perhaps they like the talent they have and perhaps they don't. But that is not what's important. What *is* important, my friends, is that is what we have earned; that is what we have merited by the laws that we and we alone have set into motion. So let us learn a little about our self, for that's what religion should be all about. Not about some far distant time of where you may be going, but what are you doing today and how can you be better at it. That, friends, is religion, back to the divine source within ourselves.

Thank you.

SEPTEMBER 1, 1974

Church Lecture 37
Magnetism — The Invisible Power

As our chairman has stated, this morning's topic is "Magnetism — The Invisible Power."

Now those of you who are familiar with the philosophy presented here at Serenity are well aware of the law that clearly states that like attracts like and becomes the Law of Attachment. Now the question must be asked, By what process does this like attract like and become this Law of Attachment? We understand that the conscious mind releases electrical impulses from the human brain; that the subconscious mind releases magnetic impulses from the human brain; that man in truth is an electromagnetic being. We have also stated that one experience in life calls forth another of like kind, unless the essence from that experience is taken, which is the indispensable ingredient for the reeducation of the senses. Well, my friends, when we look at life and experience, we can clearly see that all experience is the effect of magnetism, for it is our own subconscious, emanating magnetic impulses into the atmosphere, once having an experience, continues to attract the continuity of those experiences in our life.

Many of my students have stated how difficult they find the struggle, the struggle of making changes in their thoughts and feelings. And, of course, when we understand how the law truly works, then we surely can understand why it is indeed so seemingly difficult for man to make the slightest change in his life. Now we all are seeking, of course, a change to something. Some of us think, perhaps, what that change is going to be. However, my friends, when that thought of change is entertained in your conscious mind, it must get into your own magnetic field. It must be accepted there in order to bring forth the experience or change that you are truly seeking. How can we get a new pattern into our magnetic field, or subconscious, unless we first, through the power and the process of visualization and feeling, establish that new pattern so that it may attract what we in truth are seeking. And how does that take place, my friends? It takes place simply by the Law of Believing.

When we truly believe anything, we create it in our consciousness. We create it not only electrically, but we create it magnetically. And when that takes place—if, for example, we have created something in our conscious mind and we equally create it in our subconscious (and that is 50 percent in balance) then it will manifest itself. For when our conscious and subconscious mind is in harmony this so-called Divine Intelligence, known as God, moves through an unobstructed vehicle, called man. It moves through what is known as the channel of our own superconscious. Now this superconscious energy, this channel known as the superconscious, through which the divine energy flows, is totally neutral, completely impartial. And we call that energy God or Divine Love.

So whatever it is that you are seeking in life, remember it is within your power to attain it, dependent, of course, upon the effort that you make—and you alone make—to bring balance into your life.

My good friends, there is much talk in the world about positive thinking. Well, be rest assured, you may have all the positive thinking that you could possibly experience and unless you have an equal amount of love and feeling, the positive thinking is not going to get you anywhere. Because it only is in your electrical, conscious mind. It hasn't entered your heart and your soul, where the power that moves the universes, through *your* efforts, can be directed to bring into your life whatever it is that you want.

There is another statement in this philosophy that says man always gets what he really wants. And so few people seem to want to agree with it. They don't want to agree with that statement because they don't want to take the time and the effort to investigate it. Of course, my friends, we always get what we really want, whether we like it when we get it or not. We and we alone have set the law into motion. Now if we have forgotten the law that we set into motion ten years ago, that's not God's fault. That's man's fault for not having a better memory. So let us think. Today's manifestation in life is the effect of the various laws that we set into motion by our acceptance, by our belief, by our thought of yesterday. But let us not delude our self and say, "I'm having a terrible experience. That is my karma from twenty lifetimes ago." It doesn't work that way, my friends. It's a good cop-out, but it doesn't really work that way.

When our soul enters this life, it enters into a body and into a family, a town, a vibration that it has merited. Now that's where it begins and ends at that point. From that moment we have a vehicle through which our soul may express itself and the vehicle that we have merited is the one that we have got. We can do something with that vehicle. We can't blame it on those experiences of evolution. We can only blame it on the moment of the now. This is the only moment over which you have any power to do anything. Think about that, my friends. Yesterday's gone; tomorrow has not yet come. This is the moment that you are in God. Give that more thought. For this is the only moment of which you are consciously aware. And your conscious mind is the electrical power which is necessary to be balanced with the magnetic energies to bring you your life's experiences. So man and man alone must give more thought to his own mind, give more thought to his own feelings.

You know, it's so easily demonstrated in our lives each day and each moment. What we really have a liking to or feeling for, we make sure that we experience it. We just attract it right out of the atmosphere. What we really and truly, in the depths of our heart and soul, really want in life, believe me, it waves a red flag in the atmosphere and it just pulls everything right unto us. Think about that. If you want bacon and eggs for breakfast, you be rest assured, you get bacon and eggs for breakfast. And if you don't want them for breakfast, you be rest assured, you get something else. Believe me, that's how it really works. Now, think, my friends. Think about the life of this moment, so you won't have to think in regret those moments yet to be.

Now, you know, so few people want to think about what they call death or transition. I'm trying to help my people and my students to give it a little more thought. They're dying every moment to be born again. We teach that each moment, *each moment* is a new day and a new beginning, if you choose to make it so. But you see, my friends, that's going to take some effort on your part. It's going to take a little bit of what they call self-control, to control your mind, to control your feelings, so you don't have to be the victim in this life that is meant to be enjoyed.

We're not, in this philosophy, teaching that, you know, you have all of your heaven and everything over there. Maybe three or four centuries after you get out of this physical world, everything is beautiful. Why should we teach that when it's the farthest thing from the truth? My friends, if life for you is not beautiful this moment, well, that's only indicative that it's not going to be beautiful the next moment. But you can change that. You can change that if you really want to. And remember now, we always do what we really, in truth, want to do. We can look back at life, if we want to, and say, "Well, I didn't get my way there or there or there. But the days and the years passed and I have my way today concerning the things of yesterday. But now

I'm concerned; I'm not having my way about this moment." Well, where's patience, friends? We teach that wisdom lives in patience. Well, none of us want to be called stupid. So let's think and let's be a little bit wise. Be a little wise about today and tomorrow will be plenty wise enough for you. You won't have to worry about it.

You know, what does worry do to our mind? What in truth is worry? Well, we understand that worry is absolute faith in a negative outcome. You see, if we were thinking about a positive outcome, if we had some belief about the situation, there wouldn't be any worry. But you see, whenever you let your mind worry and you let your mind be concerned about things, including our self, of course, what happens is you direct this Divine Energy, known as God, to that very situation. So you say, "Well, it's very questionable that the economy of the country is going to improve." Then *you* become the instrument through which the question becomes greater. And you and I are a part of the country; we're a part of the human race; we're a part of the world. But if *you* think and *you* believe that things are better, then things will become better.

You see, this wonderful world experienced what they called a depression many years ago. Because that's what the people believed and when you believe something, you become the something. And when the people of a country believe in problems, then problems are guaranteed in a country and in our own personal life. So, let's not worry about running the universe when God is doing such a fine job with it, don't you see? That's not our responsibility, to worry whether or not the sun's going to continue to revolve in space and the stars are going to stay up there in the sky. Someone greater than you and I sustains those things. This is what I'm talking about, friends. Where is our energy directed?

By some great law that man can yet not duplicate, and nor will he ever be able to duplicate, a divine spark entered physical form and we call it a soul. And that is our real being. Now, man may bring together the positive and negative poles of creation in such a way that the divine spark, which is impartial, will enter into form. But man will never in truth create the life force herself. No.

And so think, if something is bothering your mind, if you are not satisfied with the way that your life is going, why not give something greater than the human brain a chance to go to work? The reason that things are going the way they are is because we have a limited understanding. And our understanding is limited because we don't have full acceptance in our life. So when we broaden our horizons, we demonstrate the divine will known as acceptance, and our understanding will expand. And, of course, God, the Divine Intelligence, is equal to our understanding. So let's have a big God in our life. Let's get rid of those meagerly, stingy, false gods of our creations, known as beliefs. And let's open up our soul, our heart, and our mind to a God that can really do something. And then we will know in truth the joy of living.

Thank you.

OCTOBER 6, 1974

Church Lecture 38
Justice and The Law

This morning's topic for discussion is entitled, "Justice and The Law." Now many of us, I am sure, have different understandings on what justice is and on what law is. We understand in this philosophy that all experiences in life are simply the effect of a level of consciousness that we have chosen to express upon. Now so often man says that he did not choose the experience that is so distasteful to him. But, my friends, that choice is made within our own mind, within our own consciousness.

We stated earlier in this philosophy, many, many months ago, that acceptance is the divine will; that this Divine Infinite Intelligence expresses itself through form. And so expression indeed is God's manifestation. However, my friends, we and we alone, consciously or subconsciously, choose all of the experiences in life that we encounter.

Now what does that have to do with justice and the law? It has a great deal to do with that title, for we understand, whereas man does indeed have choice, that man, in truth, is a law unto himself. He sets the laws of life into motion by his own attitude with any experience that he encounters in life. Many of us may say that we are not aware that we chose to enter this earth realm as part of our evolutionary process of our own soul, but remember, friends, that decision is the mother of destiny. And once we have made a choice, we set a law into motion. And that law must be fulfilled to the degree and to the extent of our own acceptance. And so, indeed, does it behoove us, if we are seeking divine justice and an understanding and application of divine law, to respect the divine right of expression of all form everywhere.

Whether or not we agree with the expression of another depends on what type of law that we and we alone set into motion. For example, if we encounter an individual who we find is difficult for us to tolerate, then what we have done, in truth, is given the power of our own consciousness to that individual that we cannot tolerate. That is a demonstrable teaching, for whenever we think of people that are difficult to tolerate, we immediately experience a lack of the peace that passeth all understanding.

In speaking of these laws, we must have clarification and discernment of the laws of society, of a government, of a country, and of a people. The laws of any country and any society, anywhere, are enforced by what is known as negative faith. And negative faith is known as fear. For example, if you cross the street against the red light or you transgress any of society's laws, you have already accepted in your consciousness that a payment from you will be extracted. And it is that fear or negative faith, which we have accepted, that helps us to survive harmoniously in a society and in a country.

So often, my friends, we enter different paths of understanding of the purpose of life and we forget, so easily, that a multitude of other sincere people are on, in truth, the same path, but it looks a little different to us because it is not exactly the path that we ourselves have chosen. That does not deny the truth that the other soul is reaching the light of eternal truth as well as we are, but it does mean that in all the getting in the universes, only the getting of understanding is of any benefit or of any lasting value. For when man gets understanding, he then is in a position to apply the divine laws that he now understands.

And so it is as the mind seeks a multitude of things through what is known as desire, we wouldn't have to go on this merry-go-round of searching and seeking and struggle if we would simply pause to think, to be at peace that understanding may rise in consciousness. For when it does, all things that you could possibly desire shall manifest in your life according to the divine law and application of understanding. This philosophy teaches that God, the Divine Intelligence, is ever equal to our understanding. And how true and demonstrable that is. Man cannot truly apply what he does not first understand. The teaching is, also, that understanding is the very foundation of all our soul faculties. And man's understanding is ever in accord with his expression, his application of what we call the soul faculties. The first of those being duty, gratitude, and tolerance; faith, poise, and humility. If it is truly understanding that you are seeking, then remember to express through at least those first two soul faculties. And in the years of teaching students I have found one of the most difficult of the soul faculties to express through is known as tolerance.

You see, my friends, we are the effect of the accepted patterns of mind of yesterday and this is what we judge life with, unless we have understanding. And we cannot have understanding until we open our soul faculties. And so it is that we are in a constant process of judgment and we are in a constant process of what we think justice is. And so we have in our world one person deciding what justice is; another deciding what justice is, and the two cannot agree. Of course, we cannot agree, until we recognize and accept in our own consciousness that our decision, that we call just or justice, is based upon the acceptance and programming of our own subconscious mind. How can we be free from the programming of a lifetime? Well, we cannot free anything that we cannot first find. And we cannot find anything that we do not first have some idea where to look for it. And so that is our teaching and our understanding: that our subconscious is controlling so much of our life, that's where we had best start. And how does man do that? He's found many different ways. You have psychology in your world. You have psychiatry. You also have peace and meditation.

When a person starts upon a meditation process, a daily meditation, they go through a multitude of experiences. And so often in what they call meditation the experiences that they encounter have nothing whatsoever to do with the so-called world of spirit. There are times when it does. But until we first understand what is in the depths of our own mind, then how are we going to discern what is a spirit of the departed and what is a manufacture of our own subconscious? What is the form of desire, if we do not understand it? How do we know which it is? So in the process of spiritual unfoldment, let us give some thought and some effort in the Spiritualist movement, at least, to what is spiritual and what is mental. Let us be honest with ourselves and let us set the example and let us recognize that man is more than one being. Man is a physical being, which is the effect of a mental body. And man is a mental body, which is the effect of a soul body, and that is the expression of what we call the Divine or God.

So let us think, my good friends, about justice and the law. Let us be just with ourselves, with our efforts, and with our endeavors. Then we will be in a position to demonstrate the divinity of the law itself.

Now what is law? You hear so much about laws everywhere. What is a spiritual law and what is a mental law? Man decides how he wishes to direct energy; that energy we call the Divine. When man makes that choice of how he wants to direct the divine energy—and he makes that choice by the mental process of thought. When he makes that decision, he directs the divine energy through what is known as the vehicle of thought and that becomes a mental law. Now what's the difference between those types of laws, which man is doing all the time, and the divine law? The divine law, which is the energy itself, its sole purpose is expression. That *is* the divine law. And it is the divine right of the form to make the choice and have whatever experiences that it decides upon by directing that energy into whatever expression that he so chooses.

This philosophy teaches liberty, not license. And when does man lose liberty? Man loses liberty when he goes into license. And how does man go into license? By transgressing the law. Now what do we mean by license? By license, we mean to do what you want, when you want, and how you want, to who you want. That is not the teachings of Serenity or of Spiritualism, but you can do that, if you choose. But it is the negative faith or fear that keeps us in some degree of balance in the world and in society.

Faith serves a wonderful purpose. We have faith when we turn the key in the car, it starts. And so we have faith when we flip the switch, the light goes on. We also have faith, if we put our hand into the fire that it will burn. Now where did we get that faith? We do not believe in a God that's a giver; that gives to one and takes from another. And this is why I, personally, do not believe in what they call "spiritual gifts." I believe in the teachings of National Spiritualism and its Declaration of Principles that clearly states personal responsibility. Well, if I'm personally responsible, then, of course, there's not some God giving me something that I haven't already earned through my own efforts in an evolutionary process, known as the soul's evolving through space. That does not mean we do not have gratitude, for we are not the ones that can make the stars move in space. But, let us think, my friends, who gave us that faith that if we put our hand in the fire, it will burn? Did we receive it the moment our soul was impulsed into being on this earth plane? Is that when we received it? No, I'm sure you'll all agree; we received it either from our parents or guardians who were teaching us to stay away from the stove or we would get burned.

And what is so interesting, my friends, you know, so much is talked about the human ego and its tenacity. Well, don't think it comes with old age. It comes right with us at the moment of birth. You can take a three-year-old child and tell him not to touch the fire and be rest assured, sooner or later, some day they're going to touch it. Now, why are they going to do that? Does it mean that they don't believe us? What does it really mean? Well, it means that they choose to have their own experience, burn or no burn. So, you see, a super-ego doesn't come with old age; it's with us right in the beginning. It serves a good purpose. You get burned once and if you have a strong enough ego, it says, "I don't want that experience again." And so, when it is tempted by the temptation of putting its hand in the fire again, its little ego says, "No, I didn't enjoy that experience." And therefore, *that* desire is stronger than the other one.

Now, we know in our world today that there are people who are able to walk upon hot coals and fire and, yet, not be burned. Well, does that mean that those people have received some kind of a special gift in life? Why, it certainly does not. It simply means that they have a greater understanding concerning the laws of life than the rest of us have.

So, friends, let's pause in our life a little more often. And if there's something that you are seeking and desire, and it seems to continually escape you, don't look outside for the cause. You can change that. Whatever you are seeking is also seeking you. The only obstruction, my good friends, is the lack of expressing through the soul faculties of faith, poise, and humility; duty, gratitude, and tolerance and the soul faculty of patience, acceptance, and total consideration. So remember, do not be frustrated when you do not receive what you think you should be receiving. Ofttimes, according to the law that you and you alone have set into motion, it is the best thing that ever happened to you. So let us pray for more understanding.

Thank you very much.

NOVEMBER 3, 1974

Church Lecture 39

Self-Control — The Philosophy of Spiritualism

Our lecture is entitled, "Self-Control—The Philosophy of Spiritualism." So often in life we think we are in control of our experiences, of the things that we encounter, but, unfortunately, that is rarely true. We think on a conscious level that we are doing what we have chosen to do, and yet on an inner level, a deeper level of consciousness, we are only the victims of past experiences. Let us look clearly at life, our life. For it does us no good and is of no benefit to look at another's life when we cannot yet see our own clearly. So let us look at our life. Let us ask ourselves the question, "Am I truly in control of my emotions, of my attitudes, of my feelings?" For without self-control, there is no order in our life. And without order, there is no system.

Without a system, there is no success. And without success, life has no purpose. And without purpose, there is no hope. And without hope, who could call that life? So let us think, my good friends, a little more deeply at what we call the philosophy of Spiritualism.

When we go to our daily activities, to our work or to our churches, or we meet a friend or an acquaintance on the street, what is it that controls our smile or our frown? Is it the moment, that moment of meeting the individual? Or is it through a law of association that experiences of past events are triggered, so to speak, in our mind, in our subconscious and we frown or we smile? Without awareness, there is no control. And without control, there is no freedom. So what are we doing with the eternal moment of now? The moment, which we have often said, is the only moment that you have, that you have any power over.

So often we feel, perhaps, that life is not going our way. Well, of course it's not going our way because we don't yet know our way. And we have to know a thing before we can see the thing. So if you are not happy with your experiences this moment, remember where the cause is. Remember that it is the mirror reflecting *you*, as an individual, at that moment. If you are depressed and feel you are not succeeding, then look deep inside. It isn't the people out there. It never was and it never will be.

We teach a great deal about the mind in this association. We also teach about the spirit, which is indeed a higher level of consciousness. But we teach about the mind first, because the mind is something that we are a bit familiar with. Let us become more familiar with our intent and our motivation in life, then we will not be guided today by all of yesterday. Without self-control, my friends, whatever thought your consciousness is exposed to controls your life. Whether or not you are consciously aware of it does not change the law itself. And so it is if we do not gain this self-control in the here and the now, then, when we leave this physical body, we leave the same way. So if you are depressed today, if you are discouraged, if you are not satisfied with events in your life, then remember, they're not going to change until you choose—*you*, as an individualized soul, having the divine right of expression—until you choose to control the levels of consciousness that you find distasteful.

So often in life a person will say, "Well, I was in such a good mood. I was feeling great until I met this other person. And every time I meet this other person, then I'm miserable because they are so miserable." Let us analyze that type of thinking for a moment. Our teaching and philosophy is that like attracts like and becomes the Law of Attachment. So if you keep meeting people that are miserable and unhappy, it is because on a level of consciousness that you are not yet aware of, you are miserable and unhappy. But because of the lack of self-control, the conscious mind cannot grasp, nor see, what is taking place in the emotional body and in the subconscious mind.

And so it is in life, the only thing worth seeking, the only thing that has any power to change your life, to transform you, to bring you the fulfillment your soul is seeking, the only thing is called peace. But man does not attain peace without control, for he must first control the war of his own emotions. He must control those feelings and attitudes of mind that express through him and rob him of the peace that passeth all understanding. Peace, which we understand to be God, the divine, neutral, intelligent Energy expressing through all form, that great Peace we experience through self-control. You can be in this world and not a part of this world. You can be with a thing and not a part of the thing, if and only if you practice, you demonstrate, and you apply what is called self-control. Control your feelings. Control your emotions. And then, my friends, you won't have to blame God or some other cop-out in life for the way you are experiencing life. There is no greater God, there is no greater power than that which is attained from self-control.

Think, my friends, if that word doesn't yet mean enough to you, then look at it from a different level of consciousness. Think! What a victim we have become. The victim of circumstances and conditions. The victim of people's emotions and attitudes. The victim of propaganda that floods our consciousness. Who in his right mind wants to be the victim, the slave of an attitude of mind, of an experience in life that is not enjoyable, that is not beneficial, and that is not progressive for his own soul? Now who is to decide what is progressive for oneself? Who is to decide what is beneficial or enjoyable? Only the individual himself. And what level of consciousness is capable of making that decision for us within us? They call it the conscience. It's known as a spiritual sensibility with a dual capacity. It knows right from wrong in a world of creation and no one has to tell it.

So all we need to do, my friends, through a little bit of self-control, is to listen to the still, small voice within. It knows what we're doing and it knows what we're not doing. And it speaks to us in the silence. And if we will listen to it, we may have to use a bit more control with some of our desires, but it doesn't mean that we will be without them completely.

Let us think, truly think. You know, they say that gratitude is applied appreciation. So let us be grateful for the opportunity that our soul, in its evolution, has merited. Let us be grateful by applying the appreciation that we feel.

My good friends, the here and the now is Spiritualism's main interest. This is our first interest because it does not behoove mankind to be interested in twenty centuries from now when he doesn't have enough interest yet in this moment, because this is the moment that is telling us what twenty centuries from now is really going to be like. Often we have spoken that heaven is not a place you're going to go to, but it's a state of consciousness that you're growing to this moment in the here and in the now.

Who, with any common sense and reason, wants to give away so freely his divinity? To give to other people, to circumstances and to conditions, the peace that passeth all understanding, which is, indeed, our divine birthright.

If the lecture of this morning, though short, has reached your consciousness, you will have different feelings. Some will not appreciate it, for they will have taken it very personal. Others will think it is beautiful and drift along in the same level of consciousness that they have been in for a lifetime. Remember, my friends, irritation wakes the soul. 'Tis satisfaction that lets it sleep. So let us not be satisfied with this moment. Let us strive to be a bit better. Let us strive for a little more awareness, a little more freedom.

And let us not look at the governments and politics because we're not getting what we want. Let us look in the place where the only change can ever be made. Let us not blame the educational system of the country and let us not blame our neighbors, our employers, and our landlords. But let us look clearly where we can make the only transformation that's going to be worthwhile.

This philosophy does not teach you what is right or wrong. It teaches you the divinity of your own soul. You already know what is right or wrong. No one has to teach you that, my friends. All we need is a bonfire lit under us so we can move forward in time and get something done. So often in this world you hear all this theorizing and nowadays they call it "rapping." Well, let's stop trying to do something in life and let's just get it done!

Thank you very much.

DECEMBER 1, 1974

Church Lecture 40

Experience, The Mirror of Motive

It is ofttimes seemingly difficult in having the experiences in this mundane world to associate those experiences with an attitude of mind, with a law that we as individuals have set into motion. The seeming difficulty in tracing the effect or the experiences of life back to the causes, which lie within our own consciousness, the seeming difficulty and obstruction is our own so-called self-will.

All souls in form are striving to express their own divinity. It is because we have limited the fullness of God's love that we suffer in this so-called world of creation. Now the question may well arise, "How do we, as individualized souls, obstruct and limit the fullness and freedom of the Infinite Intelligence, known as God?" Because of our limited understanding of our own brain, we state in our mind that this way or that way is the only way for us to have a certain feeling or experience. Because we have been granted in our evolution what is known as self-will, because we have been granted what is known as choice, we, therefore, have become a law unto our self. We may choose the left path or the right path, for we have earned in our evolution that right. However, that divine right, known as choice, does not come to us without its own responsibility. When we are honest with the part of us that is the only eternal part, known as our spirit, our soul, our true self, then and then only will we see, truthfully and objectively, the cause of all experience that we encounter. Because the inward journey back to God, which is within us, is a relative new journey to most of us here on earth, it is not such an easy path to find the causes of our present experiences.

And so we have a teaching in this philosophy and that is that energy follows attention through the vehicle of thought. And that that man directs this divine energy to increases, multiples, and grows. And so our teaching follows to put your attention, your Godhood, upon that which you desire to become; remove this attention, this great Infinite Intelligence, called God, from that which you desire to overcome. Now, we may hear that great truth and then find such a struggle and difficulty in application.

The only struggle or difficulty in applying the truth that frees us is our unwillingness to control our own mind.

Whenever we are having an experience that is distasteful to us, that continues to repeat itself in our life, it reveals to us the degree and extent of self-control—that is, the control of our own mind—that we have, in truth, in this life been expressing. No one in any world consciously chooses to suffer. Suffering is no more or less than the effect of divine, natural laws that have been, or are being, transgressed. And so the first question arises in our mind, "What are the laws that have been transgressed in my life by myself that I may free my soul from this so-called miserable experience?" My friends, that is not the way. It does not behoove us to look at transgressions until we have risen to the level of consciousness where we can control them. And so the first thing to do is to control the energy, your energy, which continues to create the experience that you do not choose to have consciously in your life.

Our teaching is that forgiveness frees our soul from the bondage of self. And so the first step is forgive yourself, that you may be forgiven. For we cannot be forgiven until *we* have set the law into motion by forgiving our self, by forgiving the levels of consciousness within us that are so intolerant, lacking understanding of the path of another human soul.

Sometimes in going into a spiritual understanding, we seem to become, at least we think, so illumined. And we look out at the world and we think that everyone else seems to be in darkness. Beware, my friends, that is known as the lower light of illusion, created by mind stuff. So let us ever look inward. Let us truly and sincerely pray for forgiveness, for there is none of us in the universe that is not in need of forgiving the transgressions that we seem to continue to make through error of ignorance.

When we pause in our thought and we accept in our consciousness the great eternal truth that we and we alone are a law unto our self, that Life herself is the way that we alone make it, that Life herself is ever the way that we take it, we then will stop giving away to people and things our divine right, our own divinity. Our soul has journeyed to this earth realm to serve a purpose. And if in the transgressions that we seem to continually make, the suffering in life becomes so intense that we cry like a voice in the wilderness for something better, if that is the way we've set the law into motion, we will still arrive in the light of eternal freedom. But let us do it, let us do it this moment. Let us do it now. Yesterday has gone. You cannot change yesterday; it is a thing of the past. You cannot change a moment ago, but you can change your attitude, your acceptance this moment. This is the great moment, my good friends, the great moment of your life, for it is the only moment of which you are consciously aware.

For many centuries there has been what people call New Year's resolutions. Let us have moment-by-moment resolutions. Let us resolve within our mind to be freed from the bondage and the chains that have bound us to the past.

When we are feeling good and we are happy, we want to capture that moment; we want it to continue. The way that it continues, my friends, is dependent on your own acceptance. You have the power, as all children of God do, you have the power within your mind to choose heaven, which is a state of consciousness. But you also have the power within your mind to choose its opposite, known as hell. When we rely upon any thing, person, or place outside of us, we deny our God. And when that takes place, we pay the price and we pay it dearly, to such a point that in time we'll walk upon the inward journey and we will find ourselves. Remember that all things outside of you are simply instruments of one Divinity. It is expressed through a vast variety of forms. But when you find the God inside of yourself, then you will find that great God outside of yourselves.

If you are having difficulty in finding God, then think, my friends, God is ever equal to our understanding. And so as we expand our understanding, our God becomes more full in our lives.

Some of my students over the years have asked how to find God. They find God so thin and so distant from them. When we ask that question, we open a door in our consciousness to start upon the path where we may find that eternal Light. But there are many stumbling blocks on that path. They are the stumbling blocks of man and his own self-will. If God is thin in our consciousness, then it means we are fat in our consciousness. It means that our thought, our decision, our judgment, our intolerance is bigger than our acceptance of an authority that holds all things in space. I assure you, my good friends, there is no way that I have ever found of finding the fullness of God without expressing through the soul faculties of duty, gratitude, and tolerance, of faith, poise, and humility, of acceptance, which is, in truth, the divine will. When we as individualized souls become less important, God, for us, will become more important. Then we will not have to worry about how thick or thin this great Divine Intelligence truly is because we will be permeated with its light, with its love, and with its truth.

Everyone, I know, wants to do the job that they have come to earth to do. But let us not tell a Divine Intelligence how hard it is, because by doing that it becomes a lot harder than we think this moment. When these experiences in life become such a struggle, remember the divine, demonstrable law: direct your divinity to something else.

Everyone, it is said, has a cross to bear. But the cross is only the stepping stone to the crown of freedom. Only through a lack understanding is man intolerant to the rest of God's creation. Let us not be so important in life that we know which path another human soul must walk. Let us not think in limited view.

Let us encompass all of the children of God, and that includes the animals and Nature herself.

Let us not worry what our brother is doing, for that energy that we use for that level of consciousness is depriving that energy to heal our own mind, to heal our own body. Let us, rather, accept that we are an inseparable part of what is called a human race. And let us accept that what one soul does, all souls are capable of doing. And we never know the moment or the hour when another soul will do what we think is such a sin. Let us remember, as we look in this world, whatever experience we encounter, whatever we see another human soul doing, that we are an inseparable part of this human race and the potential of doing identically the same thing is ever at our fingertips. And we never know, because when we set the Law of Intolerance into motion, we guarantee that experience that we are intolerant of to come to us someday, that we may be granted understanding for that level of consciousness because it exists within our own mind. I assure you, my friends, our adversities not only become our attachments, they are the chains which bind us to hell itself.

So let us consider opening a new consciousness. Let us have the courage of our convictions. Let us commit ourselves to our own God within our own consciousness, because only through commitment to that which is our only life can we truly be free. This body has come from nature and it shall return to nature. And when it starts in its process of returning back to the ground from whence it came, if you have not committed your mind, your soul, and your spirit to what we call God, the Divine Intelligence, then you will have that great struggle and suffering to face, for that has been your divine right of choice.

Thank you.

JANUARY 5, 1975

Church Lecture 41
Application—The Law of Supply

This morning's topic for discussion, our morning lecture, is entitled, "Application—The Law of Supply." Now, a topic for discussion of this type is, indeed, one of the most sensitive that can publicly be discussed. Let us think for a few moments what happens in our mind when we mention the word *supply*. If we believe that we are enjoying supply in the things that we believe that we need, then there is a good feeling, a good emotion, that comes over our being. If we believe that we are short in what we consider is the supply of our needs, then a different feeling, a different emotion comes over our mind. What does this, in truth, mean to us? Does it mean that we are, in truth, the instruments for the divine, limitless, abundant flow called God or Infinite Intelligence? Or does it mean that through an error of ignorance we have become the obstruction of this divine, limitless, abundant flow of energy?

Most of us, I am sure, are aware that supply of anything, be it material, mental, or spiritual, is nothing more nor less than the effect of directed energy. Now man has what is known as free will. Man and man alone has the choice, within his being, of how he wants to direct this divine intelligence or energy. If we permit the experiences of yesterday to be the guidance for our eternal moment of now, then the emotions and the feelings of yesterday will continue to control our lives. If, in looking backward, we see that we have accepted what the masses of people have chosen to accept, commonly referred to as lack and limitation, then we and we alone have chosen to give our divine birthright to the masses, to those who choose to suffer in self-created lack and limitation.

All forms are an inseparable, eternal part of One. Our affirmation in this philosophy is truly quite simple. It says, "I am spirit, formless and free. Whatever I think—*Whatever I think*, that will I be." And so it is, my good friends, that we have not only the golden opportunity to choose what we think, but we have the divine right to apply what we think.

Our lecture topic is "Application—The Law of Supply." It does not benefit mankind to learn the divine, natural laws of life and not move them into physical, material, mundane application. We know that man, in truth, is spirit, mind, and body. The spirit is not limited. God, the Divine Intelligence, does not choose to withhold from you, or anyone, anything that you are seeking. It is the lack of applying the divine, natural laws that cause us to accept this or that is not for me. The rain falls on all of God's creations, the humans and the plants alike, and so does the sun shine.

When we feel emotional concerning our seeming temporary inability to attain what our minds are seeking, it simply means that the divine law is not being applied in what is known as the electrical field of your own being. It does mean that it is imbalanced (the understanding of God's natural law) in the magnetic field. We know that our magnetic field, our subconscious, is that which attracts things to us. We also know that it is our electrical field that sets the law into motion, that puts it into application that we may speak our word forth into the universe, knowing that it shall not come back to us void, but accomplish that which we are sending it to do.

So often in life, it seems, there is misunderstanding of what spiritual laws or spiritual vibrations truly are. So often in life, it seems, that we choose to separate God, the Divine Intelligence, our spirit, from what we call the material, mundane, and mental worlds. When we do that, we become a house divided. There has never been a time in recorded history that so-called lack or poverty guaranteed spirituality. Spirituality is inseparable from our mental body and our physical, mundane body. We have the divine birthright to enjoy the fullness of the world in which we are expressing. To enjoy the fullness of our spirit does not in any way, shape, or form guarantee the necessity of the limitation and starvation of our physical and mental worlds. It does mean, my good friends, an effort, an application of the natural laws that we may enjoy the fullness of the life that we have a right to enjoy.

When our mind looks out at the world, it says, "This is all I have. And being all that I have, I must keep it. Because if I do not keep it, then tomorrow I will be without it." Our philosophy teaches and demonstrates that man and man alone is a law unto himself. If we believe, if we accept that what we have this moment is all that we have, then we transgress God's divine, natural law and we become the obstruction for the eternal, limitless flow. We deny, in fact and in application, our own divinity. It is taught to seek ye first the kingdom of heaven and all things shall be harmoniously arranged about you. When we free our mind and our emotions to giving to the only source, the *only* source that is qualified to give back to us in times of so-called need, then we are becoming in harmony with a source of supply that will never, ever fail us. That does not mean, my good friends, that we sit in a rocking chair and dream about prosperity, for in the process of so doing, we transgress the very Law of Prosperity.

What does the word *prosperity* mean? It means to prosper, to multiply, to increase. Are we multiplying and increasing when we do not apply the laws that govern the increase? Think, my good friends, because we have yet to accept the freedom of our own spirit, from an error in truly understanding our own spirit, then we look at a world that is filled with chaos, that is constantly promoting one shortage after another. The shortage, my friends, does not exist in truth. It exists in the delusion and the illusion of our own mind. However, if we believe that that is the way to live, then that, too, is our divine right. But let us, in desiring our divine right to think, let us respect the divine rights of others. Let us respect the divine right of the souls on earth who have chosen to fulfill God's divine, natural laws, who are experiencing prosperity from laws that they personally have set into motion. Let us not look at another and desire what he or she has. For in so doing, my good friends, you deny what God has waiting for you. Whoever looks upon another with the desire for what they have attained guarantees the limitation until such time as the suffering increases to the point where they may understand the reason why they do not have what someone else seems to have.

Let us go directly to the source, which is our right. Let us declare the eternal truth. No one, sincerely, in their heart wants to live in illusion and delusion. No one wants to constantly be in frustration from what the world has called shortages. Let us declare the truth in our lives, my friends, so that whatever you are seeking, you may know is like the hands of a clock (opportunity), it meets every so often. It meets every so often, when you and you alone have fulfilled the natural, divine law. Remember, when we say, "God, that's all I've got," then God, the Divine Intelligence, looks at us and says, so simply, "If you're so smart, then that's all you'll get." Let us be humble, my friends. Let us accept the world the way that it truly is: filled with love and beauty, filled with prosperity and purpose. Let us not become so great in our bloated nothingness, called the human ego, that we deny the good that is waiting for us to take.

Thank you.

FEBRUARY 2, 1975

Church Lecture 42

Self-Will, The Wheel of Illusion

The topic that was chosen for this morning's discussion, I am sure, is of great import to all of us and of great interest.

The question must rise in discussing self-will, the wheel of illusion, what we mean by self-will, perhaps in comparison to what is called in philosophical and religious circles as divine will. It is our understanding, here in Serenity, that God is a divine, impartial, neutral intelligent energy; that this energy, all form, all creation is receptive to; that it is the power that sustains us; that man, as the most evolved form on this earth plane, has what is known as conscious choice. When man exercises what is known as his conscious choice, we understand that to be an expression of his will. However, we must look deeply within our minds that we may see, perhaps clearly, and understand what it is that prompts a feeling within us that causes us to make a choice, to express this so-called self-will.

The experiences of our life, of times that have already past, are the motivating forces within us that make decisions for us in our life, when we are expressing self-will. For example, our mind records all experiences in the recesses and depths of what is known as the subconscious mind. Unless man makes the effort to understand what his subconscious mind really and truly is, then he is going to be, and continues to be, guided and controlled and act by the experiences of yesterday. Our choices and decisions are based upon those experiences, although most of us are not consciously aware of that truth.

Let us think for a few moments and ask ourselves in honesty, "Of what benefit is a decision based upon an experience of the past that is not applicable in my experiences of today?" So how does man become freed from the control of self-will, which is the effect of those experiences? How does man in truth free himself? The Bible prophets stated it very clearly when they said, "O man, know thyself and ye shall know the truth. And the truth shall set you free." Until such time as we make a greater effort to know about our own mind, to know how it controls our life and guarantees all experiences that we encounter, then we, as individualized souls, will not be free.

It is evident that change is not something that the mind is easily accepting at any moment. It may think that it is changing, but the truth of the matter is it is only expressing the same experiences in a little different way. Patterns of many years of use are not easily changed by anyone. And so we look back at our lives and we see that indeed our own history continues to repeat itself over and over and over and over again. We may say that we have changed, that we are no longer intolerant of a certain place or a certain circumstance or a certain person. We may say that and that may be true, but intolerance is still expressed by us. So the pattern of intolerance has not changed at all. It's only expressed in another direction.

When man makes the daily effort to find his true self, when he does that in all honesty and in all sincerity, then he will be able to look at this great computer of his, known as the human mind, and he will be able to let go of those experiences from his emotional, magnetic field and accept an Intelligence that controls the universes—an Intelligence so intelligent that it doesn't need to be told how to guide our lives, for it is the very Intelligence that sustains our lives. But what does it take for man to accept a greater authority in his life than his own microscopic, personal experiences of the past? We must ask ourselves that question. First, we must know what controls us and once knowing what controls us, let go of it, my good friends, for it is not bringing any benefit into your life, unless it is something that you can see by your hindsight, that it has, indeed, been benefiting you as an individualized soul. We have a statement in this philosophy that clearly says "When our hindsight becomes our foresight, we will indeed gain insight." And it's insight that we are seeking in life: insight inside of ourselves.

We ask our self the question—usually it's a statement instead of a question, "I am not successful." But do we truly know what success is? If we have made a declaration in our life from past experiences and are controlled by those experiences and we decide having a great deal of money or material supply represents the degree and extent of our success, then only when we have money and material supply will we experience in our consciousness what is success. For, my friends, *we* have decided what success is. Now the question must arise, Did we in truth decide what success is? No, we didn't decide what success is. Our soul did not enter this earth realm already with the decision that such-and-such represents success. No, my friends, we accepted that from the mass thinking. We accepted it when we were very young, that this is what represents success and that is what represents failure. Can we, in all honesty and truth, say that we are free, that we are truly individuals, when we continue to permit ourselves to be controlled by the thinking, the acts, and the doing of other people?

Think, my good friends, and think more deeply. Where are you in consciousness this moment? How did you get there? And if you are not happy where you are, how can you get out of there? I know of no other way to free the soul, besides a daily, honest soul searching to find out what you have accepted in your lives as truth. For whatever you have accepted, you are the living demonstration today, as we all are that living demonstration of our own acceptance.

Many philosophers have taught that joy is an inside job. My good friends, Spiritualism teaches that all of life is an inside job. For what in truth is life, but the limit of man's own experiences? They did not begin here and they will not end here. No one need to make the effort to try to convince any human soul that life is eternal, for the eternity of life is a living demonstration to the minds who wish to be free to accept the divine truth that is ever presented to them every moment of their life.

Our teachings are quite simple. We teach that acceptance is the divine will. So let us remember, we cannot accept in truth for another what we have not yet accepted for ourselves. You cannot experience health, wealth, and happiness, you cannot be the instrument of a Divine Intelligent Power for someone else to experience health, wealth, and happiness, until *you* have first accepted it in your own mind. For untold ages the philosophers have taught, "O man, heal thyself." Well, let us be about the business of healing ourselves by working on the only thing that can do the job: by working on our own mind, controlling the fluctuations of thoughts and feelings that we continue to experience, to bring peace to our lives, for peace, my good friends, is the power that never faileth.

I am well aware that there are teachings in the world that teach if you don't feel like doing something, don't do it; if you feel like doing something, do it. My friends, liberty without law is nothing more nor less than license. And if you have a feeling that you don't want to do something, ask yourself the question, "What is this feeling that I have based upon? Am I truly aware that this is my own feeling? Or is this some thought that I have become receptive to?" For when you find truth in your own soul, you will not have to be told; you will know that you are an inseparable part of one Divine Intelligence, that you are a receiving station, that you are a transmitter, and that when you get on to certain levels of consciousness in your own mind, you receive a bombardment of that level of consciousness from every human being that is expressing it. How can we protect ourselves? By praying for some divine, white light to encompass us, when we are not in a level of consciousness to receive some divine, white light of protection? No, my friends. When you have a thought, think more deeply, for that thought has placed you on a level of consciousness and you are now the receiving set for every thought transmission, not only in a physical world, my friends, but in other dimensions and other worlds.

And so I know we all have experienced what a thought does to us. We all have experienced a certain feeling that was not tasteful to us, that we could not rid it from our mind. Because, my friends, it was multiplied, it increases, and it grows according to very natural law. Like attracts like and becomes the Law of Attachment is a demonstrable truth.

Serenity Spiritualism does not ask you to accept what is truth, for you already have truth. Truth is individually perceived. If you think that you do not have truth, it simply means that you have no self-control. For freedom is the direct effect of self-control and truth, my friends, is freedom.

Thank you very much.

MARCH 2, 1975

Church Lecture 43

The Love of Living

This morning we'd like to speak on "The Love of Living." We all, I am sure, agree that what is known as Love or God or the Divine or Light is all energy. Without love, nothing survives. Without love, nothing grows. And so it is that love and the love of living is one and the same thing. Without love, there is no life and without life, there is no light; there is no awareness. And so it behooves us to consider what laws, if any, govern this so-called love of living, what natural, divine laws govern Life herself.

The teachings of this philosophy are founded and based upon the divine, demonstrable, natural Law of Personal Responsibility. And so it is when we accept that demonstrable, divine truth of personal responsibility for all experiences that we encounter in life, when we truly accept that law, then we will demonstrate what is known as divine will. Our understanding is that divine will is total consideration, total acceptance. When we go out into this world and have these multitude of experiences—some of them pleasant and some of them not so pleasant—if we will pause to think, if we will gain control of our own thoughts and our own emotions and we will strive to look objectively at the experience—and by objective I mean without emotion, without personal self-involvement as we view the experience itself—then, my friends, in demonstrating the divine will of total acceptance of the total and full responsibility of the experience that you have encountered, you will be free. For the laws of nature, the divine, natural laws themselves, will balance whatever it is to be balanced in your life.

Now this teaching is not a new teaching to the world. It is the oldest of all teachings. It has been presented in a multitude of ways. It has been taught by the ancient philosophers: if only you have the faith of a grain of mustard seed. But how does man gain faith? How does man have faith? Without acceptance, my friends, there is no faith. And so we are demonstrating each day of our lives, hopefully, some positive faith, and surely from the living demonstrations a great deal of negative faith. And what do we mean by negative faith? We simply mean what is known to man as fear. It is so easy for us to react to fear or negative faith and seemingly so difficult to act to positive faith.

All of life's experiences are a revelation to each of us what level of consciousness we and we alone are choosing to entertain in thought. And so, my friends, no matter what the seeming obstruction, no matter what the seeming problem may be in your life today, remember, you and you alone are the only obstruction.

All of us are controlled, to a great extent, by what is referred to in this philosophy as the tapes of past experiences. When man does not accept full responsibility for all experience in his life, he becomes controlled by taped experiences of the past. Consequently, we are accepting, but we are accepting a limited experience of our own past life. That, my friends, is not progression; it isn't even evolution. But it is stagnation. So if you find in your lives that you are happy the way everything is going, then you are doing something that you have accepted. And having accepted it, of course, you are the living demonstration of it. What does that have to do with living? My friends, *that is living*.

What does it have to do with love? Love is the great magnet that calls all things to us. When we as individualized souls rise in our consciousness to become the gods of the universes, then we transgress those natural, divine laws and we demonstrate the limited laws of self.

Man, indeed, is a law unto himself, because man has made himself a law unto himself. He has decided and chosen what he will accept in life and what he will not accept. And the things that he has decided that he will not accept, when he experiences them, he is not happy. Because there is a power, there is an energy, there is an intelligence that is greater than the human mind. It is the intelligence that has created the human mind.

So let us think, my friends, we have come a long, long ways to get to this point in time. Do not deceive yourselves and think that you are a new creation of 10 or 20 or 30 or 50 years or more. Our soul has evolved through untold eons of time. How long must we wait to awaken?

All teachers know that through struggle and suffering man starts to change. But is struggling and suffering necessary for man to make the changes that will benefit his own life? Struggling and suffering is necessary to any soul that is grounded in what is commonly referred to as self-will. There is no God of the Spiritualists that we ever have viewed that demands that his children suffer, that his children be in poverty, lack, and limitation, that they live in misery, sorrow, and grief. Those kind of gods are the false gods of our own mental creations. That is not the Infinite Divine Love that cares for the sparrow and the blade of grass in the meadow.

So think, my good friends, where are you this moment and where have you chosen to go? There is no reason in any mind to suffer and experience a life of grief and misery. It is only our absolute refusal to accept a higher power, a Divine Intelligence, that holds the stars in space, to which all things are possible. But man cannot experience what he refuses to accept. And refusing to accept is the revelation of where we are by our own lives this moment.

And so we may well say, "I am not so sure if this God, this Divine Intelligence, will take care of my needs. I have prayed and prayed and prayed and I do not see the results as yet." My friends, there's more to prayer than a spoken word. There's more to life than what we have yet seen. Prayer is something that is a living demonstration of service. If you pray to God to heal you, if you pray to God for supply, what you have done is denied that he has already given it to you. And when you deny the Divine, the Divine cannot serve you.

So think, my friends, we teach a life of service in this church, service to the Divine Intelligence that is the only thing you can ever rely upon with any degree of satisfaction. And until we rise to that level, until we grow in our own evolution of our own soul to see that the Divine Intelligence is the greatest servant of all—and we want to become the divinity, which is in truth our right—then we must demonstrate the natural laws of Life herself. We cannot sit home and pray or go to church and pray and expect results when we are the obstruction to the power that flows, that heals, that is Life herself. So let us think more deeply and let us go deep within the recesses of our own mind.

It seems so often, in religions and philosophies, that the children of this planet seek them out when things are not going well in their lives. And once making some changes in their thinking, they go on about their old patterns of yesterday, the patterns that put them where they were before they came to religion or to philosophy. What kind of sense is that, my friends? If you have not yet been satisfied with life and you're looking for something better, or the struggle that you are experiencing is too much for you to bear and you seek a better way, once having found it, isn't it reasonable that you would serve it—if not for another, at least for yourself? Let us ask ourselves what our motive in life truly is. For the motive of a thing is the principle of a thing. And

God's universes are governed and controlled by principle. So if we will search in our own mind for our own motivation, then we will know what we're going to get, for we will know what we have given.

The law, the love of life, is totally impartial. Each moment in each day of your life is a revelation of what is going out. So we all want something good in our life, then let us send out like kind. For like attracts like and becomes the Law of Attachment. Let us accept the demonstrable, divine truth of personal responsibility. Let us not look at life, at our employer, our husbands, and our wives and use them for the bat. Let us not do that to ourselves. Let us not blame the church of which we are affiliated for our frailties and our weaknesses. Let us look inside of ourselves when we want to do something and the way is obstructed. Let us not look out at the obstruction; the cause of the obstruction is inside of ourselves. But it takes a little strength of character, my friends, to look in the mirror of life, because so often, when we do that, we do not like what we see. But remember that that is only a passing thing. Look deeper and find your own soul. Declare your own divinity in the spirit of humility and the spirit of selfless service. Because I assure you, my good friends, that is the only thing that is reliable. It is the only thing that will ever free you, for it is the universal law of life.

So often, we think, we hear so much about service, and all of us, of course, are serving something, but let us at least gain enough self-control to wisely choose what it is we're going to serve. Are we serving the importance of our own pride and ego? Are we serving the tapes of past experiences? Who and what are we serving? For we are serving every moment of every hour, every day of every century. Who have we, as individualized souls, who have we made our master? Who has become the captain of our own ship? If we are not able to control our emotions, we are not able to control our own fears, our own motives, our own drives, then someone else is driving us. Ask yourself who that someone else is. Don't look outside for a person. Look inside for a tape that refuses to stop playing in the depths of your own subconscious. That's where to look, my friends.

If you say you're not feeling well, look at the entity of not feeling well that you have created. If you say that you are poor, in lack and limitation, that you have X number of dollars, then look at that entity in your own subconscious mind that is controlling your lives. If you are addicted to pills and medications, look at that entity in your head that's controlling your soul and your own body. Whatever man relies upon becomes his master. Let us not forget that. And once you rely upon a person, place, or thing—be it your own thought—you become the victim and the servant of that pattern of mind.

So let us not be discouraged. But let us become aware of who it is that is guiding our ship of destiny. Is it truly ourselves? Or is it what we have accepted from the world?

Think, my friends, and think more deeply. Our soul came to earth on its evolutionary path not to eat and sleep, nor to be an animal in its present evolution, but to awaken to its own rights, to be free, to consider *all of life* and not just a limited level of consciousness accepted in our early, formative years. You can be what you want to be. It is the law, for we already are. If you say, "I want to be something else," and you're not yet that, then you are not demonstrating the Law of Patience. For all of us, this moment, are what we have desired and chosen to be. If man says, "I did not choose suffering," then man has not yet awakened to his own tapes of his own mind. We are what we have chosen to be by the divine laws themselves. And if we are not happy with what we are this moment, then we can change and establish new laws in our life. But we cannot change until we demonstrate the divine will known as total acceptance.

Thank you very much.

APRIL 6, 1975

Church Lecture 44

Fourth Anniversary—Serenity Church

In commemoration of the fourth anniversary of this church I feel it fitting and proper to discuss, for a short time this morning, the soul faculty of organization. It is the inherent nature of all people, of all form, of all creatures to strive to organize themselves in order that they may fulfill their chosen desires. And so it is in life, when through a lack of control of our own mind we find ourselves in what is known as chaos and disorganization, for it is when the mind, losing control of its own chosen desires, no longer is able to express organization. It is also the nature of all form to desire, for all form expresses, and expression is, in itself, the divine desire. So our teaching in this philosophy is an education, a balance of our functions of desire and our soul faculties of aspiration.

Let us think for a moment how often the thought enters our mind that we are not able to accomplish the multitudes of things that we are desiring to accomplish and we ofttimes use as an excuse the lack of time. We all know that time is nothing more nor less than a conscious awareness of passing events. If we find that we have trapped our self into the illusion and delusion of a so-called lack of time, it simply means that we have not organized our own values, our own priorities.

How does man attempt to express his true divinity, when, in so attempting, his mind is in conflict with what he truly wants to do and what he truly wishes to become? Our minds so often see in life the obstructions. And the law of nature is very clear: to he who sees the obstruction, that soul shall not find the way. And so it is that a wise man will place his attention on what he wants to become in life, not place his attention upon what he is desiring to overcome. For this divine, neutral Energy, known as God, is directed by man's own choosing. And if he and he alone chooses to direct this godhood of his, this great, divine power, on the obstructions in his universe, then only the obstructions shall he view and shall he experience.

We all know what happens to time when we are in the process of fulfilling our own desire. Time passes as of naught. We have no concern nor interest in it, dependent, of course, upon the desirability of our own desire of the moment. And so, my friends, in organization if we look out into the world and we view that it is chaotic, that it is not organized, then we can be rest assured that we, on that level of consciousness, are not organized ourselves. For organization is an effect. It is an effect of a balanced mind; it is an effect of understanding.

And so, my good friends, look within your moment-to-moment life. Look inside your own universe and think what is valuable to you. Was it valuable yesterday? Will it have value tomorrow? If things in this world of creation had lasting value, business would not boom as it does. But we all know that desires of the moment are fleeting. They are not lasting. And so what in life, in this life, in this moment, has any true, lasting, eternal value? What is there when we need it? What is it that sustains us and gives us life itself? What is it that never faileth if we never fail to be receptive to it? The religions have many names for it. Most people call it God. And now they're concerned with whether God should be called "He" or God should be called "She." The Spiritualists for over 127 years have referred to this Divine Intelligence as the Infinite Intelligence, but as long as man views form instead of the formless, then he will have a need to call it "She" or call it "He," because we cannot express in our consciousness what we have not yet accepted.

Society as a whole is an effect of the acceptance of the mass mind of what the religionists and the philosophers have brought to the world. Our teaching is that you cannot experience in life what your mind has not yet accepted. And so, my friends, let us express our divine will and our divine freedom through the soul faculties of consideration and of duty, of humility, of poise and of peace. Let us respect for another in this life what we respect in truth for ourselves. Don't chase the eternal rainbow called organization. It doesn't exist out in the sky, unless you call your own mind the sky. For that's where it is, my friends. That's where God truly is. That's where your peace and your love and your power lie, the godhood that is in your own consciousness. If we don't find God there, we're not going to find him somewhere else hereafter. We're going to be the same person tomorrow in consciousness that we are today, unless we make great effort, great effort to make the change.

One of my students, the other day, informed me that they have finally decided that no one ever changes. The reason that they felt that is because they had made great effort over this past six months to change the thinking and attitude of someone that they are in rapport with. It is contrary to the demonstrable law of creation and evolution that people, along with other forms, do not change, for we all change. But we don't necessarily change the way someone else wants us to change. And so if we're looking at another person and we desire them to change and our desire is truly great, then we cannot see the changes that they are making, because desire, my friends, is the descent into the womb of satisfaction and there it's rather dark. That is where the lesser light is. But remember, expression is the divine desire. So let us choose wisely what we want to desire. Let us look at it clearly before we desire it. And let us accept in our consciousness that we don't get in life something for nothing. Even the air that we breath, the lungs, they work and they pay the price. So let us not go out into the world, let us not turn our eyes and our sight to God and say, "God, here I am. Take care of me," for there is a law of divine justice and balance and all of life gets out of a thing whatever we put into the thing. So if you're not getting something out of life, don't blame life. It simply means you're not putting into life what you thought you were, and life is revealing to you what you have been doing to yourselves.

So, my good friends, in commemoration of the fourth year of this little organization, known as Serenity, my heart is filled with gratitude for the opportunity that somehow in life I have merited or earned to expand, hopefully, my first soul faculty. I am not concerned about the fortieth one. Duty, gratitude, and tolerance takes a lifetime to express.

So, I look over this congregation this day not concerned in my consciousness with how many of you are carrying a Serenity card, for this church was not founded to have people come and go with cards or membership. For God is at the helm of this center of light and whoever is needed to keep God's work going in this world will come. They will stay and they will go according to their own growth. On the opening of this church, four years ago, the first Sunday of May in '71, I stated at that time that this was built on a foundation of truth, that it was open to all souls who were seeking the light. And they would be granted the opportunity to grow or to go. And in four years I have seen many go, but I have also seen a few who grow. That is their right, my friends.

Remember, when we're not organized inside, we have a multitude of suggestions for organizations to organize themselves the way that we desire. But let us first become the living demonstration of organization, before we decide to suggest and demand how another organization should organize itself. Let us organize our personal life. Let us so organize our priorities and our values that a day in our life never goes by that we don't make a conscious effort to serve God. If you don't want to think about God so often, remember, you'll guarantee the day, my good friends, when you'll cry like a voice in the wilderness, because only God can heal you. Only God can give you the peace that passeth all understanding. Only God can fulfill your needs and your desires. But remember that God is equal to our understanding. And so if you express a greater understanding, you will be receptive to a greater God. And a greater God can do more for you than a smaller God.

Think about the needs of others and you will be freed from the suffering and the living hell of grounding in your own self. Think about the work that needs to be done, not only in this physical world, but in all these other universes that so few people seem to consider.

We all know that we are where we are; we all know where we are because in truth we know what we are. So let us make a little greater effort to find a greater way to serve the true purpose of our life. There is no separation in truth, my friends. And remember, when we descend down through self-will, when we hit the bottom of that will, we will begin to ascend in divine will. Self-will considers its own accepted patterns, but divine will has the total consideration of the untold centuries of your own soul evolution. You didn't start in this earth, my friends. That's why you won't end here, because you didn't begin here, and neither did I. You've traveled for many centuries on your journey to get to this point in consciousness and there are untold eons of time yet to go. And when you open your vision and you look in retrospect backwards through the ages, when you truly look inside yourself and see how long it took to get where you are, I know you will give more thought to God's work in your daily lives.

Thank you very much.

MAY 4, 1975

Church Lecture 45

Destiny—A Spiritual View

As our chairman has stated, this morning's discussion is, "Destiny—A Spiritual View." Now all philosophies and religions of our world have taught and continue to teach that God is love, that the truth will set us free. And so we are all seeking not only what we call God, Love, but we are also seeking truth, the very thing that will free our soul. The understanding of God, the Divine Intelligence, in this philosophy, here at Serenity, is that God is a divine, neutral, intelligent energy, expressing through all forms of life; that man, in his limited understanding, is receptive to this energy, this feeling, this goodness or godliness in particular areas of his own choosing. In keeping with our understanding that acceptance is the divine will, that rejection is the self-will, man can view his own destiny.

Some time ago a lecture was given in this church entitled, "Man's Only Suffering is His Denial of God." When man denies the divine right of expression of any form, then man is denying his own divinity. For we understand that all form and all expression is in truth the divine, neutral, intelligent Energy called God. Spiritualism does not understand this so-called God and an opposing force called Satan. We do understand that a seeming bad experience is nothing more nor less than seeming undeveloped good. We understand that there is one God and one Energy and one Intelligence, that when man feels good, he is experiencing that godliness in the ways of his own limited acceptances. And so it is that by our own self-will, by our own acceptance, by our own rejections, we in truth are declaring and have declared our own destiny. The question may well arise, "I entered earth in a certain condition and under certain experiences." We teach an evolutionary incarnation of the soul. As the soul evolves through this great eternity, it establishes laws and boundaries for its own expression.

Now we live in a physical world, governed by physical laws. We understand that we have soul faculties and sense functions. We also understand that creation is a dual expression and that that guarantees pleasure is destined to guarantee pain. Now the reason that that is a demonstrable truth is quite simple: when man experiences what he calls joy and he limits that experience to a particular chosen area of expression, then he has limited his receptivity of God. In time that so-called joyous experience will become your greatest sadness. Life already has revealed that divine, natural law to all of God's children.

We are in the constant wheel, the karmic wheel, of illusion and delusion, chasing from one rainbow to another rainbow and never, ever really finding our own divine home. We cannot find home when we have limited in our consciousness how we will accept our own divinity. Man has health and guarantees his sickness. He has joy and guarantees his sadness. He has wealth and guarantees his poverty. Why do we do that to our self? It's known as an error of ignorance, for that that we rely upon becomes our god. And he who relies upon man for his joy, his supply, his health, his prosperity comes under the control of man's law, not God's law. And in so doing he binds his soul and makes a god out of whatever brings him joy.

When we broaden our horizons, when we open our consciousness and we declare the divine truth, that God, this so-called Love, is expressing through all form, that the experiencing of this love is possible by an awakening of our own consciousness, then, my friends, you will not have to rely upon things, nor people, to express, to feel the goodness, the godliness, which is in truth your divine right. Only a fool would consciously choose to rely upon anyone or anything that will, in time, guarantee the bondage of his own soul.

So let us look at life with a little clearer review. When man suffers—which is the direct effect of his denial of God. Man suffers when he says in consciousness, "I have a need. And this, my God, is the way that it can be fulfilled." Then man suffers. For God, though fulfilling need through form, is not limited by form. And so people grow in this physical world, attach themselves to people and to things to have the joy and the guaranteed sadness someday in some way. If that were not true, our world, our physical world, would not be filled with so many divorces. It would not be filled with so much pain and suffering. It is filled with that, my friends, because we limited, in our consciousness, our God.

And so as we look at life, reviewing it each moment of each day, we view our own destiny. It is not difficult to find where we are in evolution. All we have to do is to be honest with ourselves and ask ourselves what we are. And when we do that and when we are truly honest—for it is only the truth that will set us free. It is not the images that we present to man that sets us free. Those images are governed and controlled by our own limited patterns of mind; that will never be freedom, my friends. If you cannot be honest with yourself, you cannot be honest with your God. And if you are not honest, you will not be free, for freedom does not come to any soul that cannot look at themselves and say to God, "This is me. Am I such a rejected soul in your universe?" Think, my friends, the image is the illusion: what you present to one person, you do not present to another. It is totally and entirely dependent upon your motivation of self-desire. Have you yet found freedom with the image you present? Have you not yet seen that it is in a constant process of change?

When the light dawns in our consciousness, there is only one thing that matters. That one thing, by man, is called God. And when that dawns, you declare your right to your soul. You therefore will free yourself from the duality of creation, from the pain and pleasure of experience. You will not be left void of experience, but you will not become the experience. You will know in your heart and soul that that is God, expressing itself in this or that particular way. You will no longer be trapped in the "bloated nothingness," as Emerson said, of the human ego, because it will not matter any more.

A wise philosopher once said, "Manifest the divinity within yourself and all things shall become harmoniously arranged around you." But the manifestation of divinity is whole, total, and complete acceptance in consciousness. If we believed by studying

Life herself that God does not deny one of his children—be it an animal, a human, or a blade of grass—and if we believe that that is God the Divine, then we must become, as the Bible says, like little children. Well, what are little children like? They are not filled with this pomposity of what is good and what is bad. They are not filled with all of those limitations in consciousness. Their hearts are open and so their souls are free.

Liberty in life is not license in life. Liberty comes through law. And divine law is total consideration. A teaching in this philosophy is that satisfaction permits our soul to sleep, but irritation wakes the soul. And ofttimes it is the things we do not want to hear that are needed to bring us where we want to be in consciousness. So let us think about what we're doing to our self. Let us think about that, my friends. And let us remember that total consideration is God's divine love and that limited consideration is what is called man's love. It is the same energy. There is no difference except the ways in which man has limited the Divine's expression.

Look at the world and look at it clearly. One moment you're filled with the spirit of joy and happiness, the next moment, guaranteeing the very opposite. When that happens to you— and it happens all the time—ask yourself the honest question, "In what way have I decided to experience my joy, my goodliness? Upon what person or thing do I truly rely?"

This philosophy teaches that which you give thought to, you give power to. And when you look at creation and the human race, if you cannot look through it and find God no matter where you look, then you are destined to who knows how many eons of bondage. No one likes to entertain the thought that they are the victim and the slave of their own limited patterns of mind, but our lives reveal that truth. We are simply trying to share with you a spiritual view of man's own destiny. We sang, at the opening of these services, a very old hymn and it was entitled, "Destiny at My Command." So, my friends, look at how, when, and why you receive your goodness and you will know your bondage and you will know your eternal destiny.

Thank you very much.

JUNE 6, 1975

Church Lecture 46
Patience—Pain and Pleasure

As our chairman has announced, the topic for this morning [is], "Patience—Pain and Pleasure."

In this philosophy we teach the soul faculties of being (soul attributes), which correspond to all of our sense functions. And patience is a soul faculty. Now the soul faculties are triune in expression and inseparable. And patience, perseverance, and promise is a soul faculty. The question must arise in our consciousness, "Why does patience bring us pain and why does patience bring us pleasure, if it is, indeed, a soul faculty?" which it is. However, we find, as our soul expresses through and in creation, as that expression is experienced by what is known as our mind—and our mind being a part of creation, governed by the dual laws, the Law of Duality, the light and the night, the right and the wrong—we find as that soul expresses through mind stuff, through the gray matter, we experience what is called pain and pleasure.

How does man escape, if escape could be the proper word used, from this duality, from this karmic wheel of creation, from this great illusion created by our own minds? My friends, it has been long taught in this philosophy that the mind cannot and will not know truth. We all know that it is the truth which sets us free. And if we will pause in consciousness we will find that truth cannot and does not exist in a dual expression called mind.

We find, as we go within our own consciousness, that sooner or later our soul is taken to its true home and that is called our heart. Now all philosophies teach that God is love and so we must ask our self the question, "If that is true"—and it is demonstrably true—"then where does God within us truly reside?" Can he reside in a part of our being that by its very nature knows the opposite of God? No, my friends. God only exists in what is called our heart. And when we try to analyze and to define what is called Love or God, what happens to us? We go into what is called the function of pain and pleasure.

In creation, the illusion created by mind stuff brings us fleeting moments of pleasure, but each fleeting moment is guaranteed by the laws of creation to bring us equal pain. And so we find ourselves in this illusion constantly chasing an eternal rainbow called promise. My friends, sooner or later in eternity the mind becomes very, very weary. Sooner or later it finally accepts that it *is* a part of creation and being a part (our mind) of creation, it is guaranteed to suffer.

We have taught, in this philosophy here, that man's only suffering is his denial of God. We have also taught that man's denial of God is the limitation of his own mind, and that we call, in this philosophy, self-will. And so when we suffer, we may be rest assured we're not in our heart; we are in our limited mind. That's where bondage is, my good friends. Bondage is not where God is and God is in your heart. Bondage is in the head. It's where we have decided what is right and what is wrong. It is where *we* have decided what will bring us joy and happiness. And when we make those kind of decisions—and it is the nature of the mind (the self-will) to do just that—when we make those decisions, we and we alone experience the illusion of creation called pain. And so, isn't it better to finally awaken within, to accept the eternal, divine truth that frees our soul? For you see, my friends, until we learn to separate truth from creation, we will never have the divine freedom that is our eternal right.

And so as we work in this world of creation, when we make the effort to be in it and not to be a part of it, to be with any thing or any person and never to be a part of the person, then we're going to experience what is known as God, the Divine Love. If you are expressing your soul, your consciousness through your heart, you will never experience loss, for you will never experience gain. You will be the perfect balance called neutrality, the Divinity itself. And all things will be within you, for that's the only place they ever existed at all. That awakening is called many things. It's called illumination. It is called cosmic consciousness. It does not matter what we call truth, love, and freedom. It only matters that we permit ourselves to experience it. For once we permit the experience, the fullness of God, when we do that, we won't have to study all the books of the universe to find it. But it takes self-control to reach your heart. It takes control of your own attitudes of mind. It takes control of your emotions and your feelings. And when you control them, your mind will be stilled. And when your mind is stilled, you will be freed from self-concern, which is the epitome of the activity of mind stuff. When man permits his mind to be concerned with himself, then he guarantees all the disasters in life that are necessary to free him from his own illusion and delusion.

Now the truth is not readily received when we're in the mind, because the mind registers that it must surrender, that it must give up. But be of good cheer, my children, for when it registers what it must do, we start our soul to descend in that self-will. And there's a bottom to self-will because there was a beginning to self-will. And when we hit the bottom, we start to rise in divine will. And when we rise in divine will, we have the fullness, the goodness, which is known as God. Then and then only, do we experience the true joy of living. Then and then only, are we freed from want, need, and desire, for man cannot desire what man already has.

And so, my friends, learn to bow the head in humility, for God, the Divine, is the greatest, humble servant there has ever been or will ever be. And surely as you look at creation, you can understand it takes great humbleness and great humility to sustain all of creation, and especially mankind, when the Divine Light views what man does with his God's eternal love and joy.

Remember that so-called desire is the divine expression, that total acceptance is in truth the divine will, that total consideration is the divine love. And when man, when man, having desire, permits the desire, which is the Divine's expression, to be the servant, then he will be freed from being the slave. For desire, the divine expression, is the Divinity and it is a servant. It was never intended to make you a slave, bound in the dungeons and prison houses of hell itself. That is not the will of God. But that has indeed become the will of man. For whatever desire man entertains in thought is only his soul's eternal quest to go home to God. And so what we in truth are seeking is to go back home. But because of our so-called self-will we have so restricted God's eternal, divine right of expression that we suffer because we cannot experience the goodness, which is our birthright, unless we do this or do that. There's only one thing we need to do to have the joy of living, to be freed from the illusion of pain and pleasure. There's only one thing we need to do: is bow our tenacious so-called ego. Bow it in the depths of humiliation that our soul may rise in the heights of humility. There we will be with God and being with God, all goodness and all joy, our true right, will indeed be ours.

But that takes not a thought on Sunday morning, once a week. That takes an effort of our will to control the so-called insanity of our own mind. And if we don't think it's a discordant insanity, then take a closer look at your life and see what you are doing with it. And once you see in truth what you are doing to your own life with all your fears and all your frustrations and all your chasing from here to there—there is no animal on earth that would act so wild and so ridiculous. There is no insect put on God's green earth that does not function in harmony and love.

But man has risen so great in his mind that he thinks he is the king, that he can control whatever he chooses to control. But that which man chooses to control, for a moment, he lives in that illusion. But that moment passes; then man becomes aware that he is now the victim of his own games. And that victimization, sooner or later, will descend in total humiliation, for the soul rising of humility is recorded by the ego as humiliation. And when that happens, he will know beyond a shadow of any doubt that God, in truth, is the most humble servant of all.

Thank you, friends.

JULY 6, 1975

Church Lecture 47
Spirit Lands and Spirit Bands

The discussion for this morning, as our chairman has stated, "Spirit Lands and Spirit Bands," is a subject that is in truth of great import to all mankind, for we are this moment spirit in the here and now. Spirit is not something that we are going to, necessarily, after so-called physical death or transition, for unless we awaken in consciousness within ourselves this moment, there is no spirit land to go to when we leave the physical body. We understand in this philosophy that this divine, formless, free spirit expresses through what is called the individualized soul. This soul, in turn, expresses through other bodies, such as the mental body and the vital body and the physical body in the here and now. The only moment that man knows truth is in the eternal moment of the now. Yesterday is a past review and tomorrow, the future, is a preview. Now let us think in truth, my good friends, about spirit lands and spirit bands, about communication in the here and now. The Living Light Philosophy is a philosophy of everyday living, for the only day that is of any importance is the day of which we are in truth consciously aware.

In the movement of Modern Spiritualism, in its foundation and in its conception, this communication brought to millions of people the awareness in consciousness that they were in truth something besides a mental and physical body; that the possibility of awakening that truth within our consciousness was in the eternal moment of the here and the now. Now in communion with these other dimensions that must first exist within our consciousness or they cannot exist outside, we must awaken ourselves. For example, in communication with dimensions, the mind knows the mind, the body knows the body, the soul knows the soul, and the spirit is the truth. If we in our efforts to awaken within ourselves to the truth—which, once applied, sets us free. My friends, truth does not set us free until we demonstrate the Law of Application.

And so it is when in our unfolding within we entertain in thought, which is a mental body, which is a created body, and we discuss with the life-giving energy of the spoken word these ethereal, spiritual dimensions, what happens, in truth, is this: the mental activity, in truth, being composed of mind stuff, drops a veil, a curtain, between our soul and the divine, eternal Spirit. Because of the abuses for untold centuries of communion with higher dimensions of consciousness, religions of the world have declared that it is not good nor beneficial because of the abuses of the minds of men. We have a little teaching in this philosophy that states, "When of thy mind thou seekest to know the truth, on the wheel of delusion thou shalt traverse."

So let us pause to think perhaps a little more deeply about spirit lands and spirit bands. If the spirit is not expressing in its fullness within our own consciousness, then these so-called departed are not expressing from realms of light or, let alone reason, for they are not the entities which our minds conceive them to be. We know that outward experiences are direct revelations of inner attitudes of mind. We also know that an attitude of mind is dictated and controlled by a level of consciousness. And so it is that when our lips speak—that's the life-giving energy of God—as our heart feels, our words then, indeed, become the savior of the wise, for the instrument within the human anatomy, through which the divine, eternal Spirit, known as God, speaks in clarity and fullness is from the soul through the heart.

It is stated here, in this philosophy, that truth is like a river; it continuously flows. And so it is our philosophy to love all life and know the Light. For the river of life, my good friends, is the stream of consciousness. And when it is permitted to flow in its fullness from what we understand is the divine pulsation, known as the heart of God, then you not only know truth, you apply it. And its application is your freedom. Freedom is the eternal moment of the now, my good friends. It is not something that you're going to get. It is something you already have. But the mind, the mental activity expressing through a physical vehicle called brain, does not know it, for that brain is a dual creation, for that is the Law of Form, the Law of Duality.

And so it is in the religion of Spiritualism, from the untold abuses within it and within the world, because of a lack of understanding its true purpose. Spiritualism did not come to the world to entertain the senses and the functions of man. It came to the world to free the human soul. Because man in his present state of evolution is so grounded in a material world and so active in a mental world, there is little, if any, of the great stream of consciousness called the river of life for his spiritual world. And so it is that truth is taught through indirection, demonstration, and example. And so these angels, who are merely souls who have discarded their physical suit and gone to various planes of consciousness, return to this mundane world in consciousness to demonstrate that there is something, that the Spiritualist call Infinite Intelligence, that is beyond what the physical senses can view.

Now, my good friends, let us think about spirit bands or guides and teachers and helpers. What man grants unto himself he may then grant to another. And so the law dictates, "O physician, heal thyself," for that is the only place that healing truly takes place. God consciousness exists within all form. It is the only healer, the only savior. Whatever method awakens the God consciousness within the human being will heal the human being. Now the methods vary in your world because people in mind stuff or mental activity are filled with rejections and express a few acceptances. So what works for us one moment does not necessarily work for us the next moment. That is dependent upon us. That is dependent upon our ability to control the dream of life, the illusion in which the consciousness called God is expressing itself.

Our teaching, "I am spirit formless and free. Whatever I think that will I be," is a living demonstration of the Law of Identity. And so man, the true man, becomes whatever he identifies with through the divine energy expressing through what we call the thought processes, expressing through the spoken word. So man in truth is his own savior, his own god, his own joy, his own happiness, his own eternal truth. However, what man does with that great freedom is dependent on what man alone chooses to do. We understand that God is a divine, neutral, intelligent Love, Light, and Life. Man has the choice [of] what he wants to do with it. And how do the minds of men, seeming so knowledgeable with all of their learning, perceive the truth and apply it to set them free? Well, the mind calls it suffering. And when the mind has suffered enough, it will pause and it will become still. And when the mind is stilled, the heart will move. The divine pulsation called God in the perfect river of life of rhythm and harmony and peace and truth will express itself.

So we say in this, the Living Light Philosophy, what in truth is the purpose of the science of Spiritualism if first mankind does not receive, accept, demonstrate, and apply the laws revealed in its philosophy? And one of the basic laws revealed in the philosophy of the Living Light is: Like attracts like and becomes the Law of Attachment; that in every attachment is a built-in adversity so that man may not attach to form and sell his soul to creation.

So let us think, again, about guides and teachers, about spirit bands and spirit lands. Whatever we are doing with our effort to free our soul, that's the type of guides and teachers, that's the type of spirit band that surrounds our consciousness. These angels from the realms of light are from the realms of light if we are in the realms of light. And what are the realms of light? But the eternal truth to love all life, for that is the only way that man will ever become a light in the world.

And so, my friends, remember, the spoken word is life-giving energy. And the more energy you feed through mental activity called thought, the less you receive from the realms of beauty, of truth and freedom. So let us be, to the best of our ability, as clear and as free a channel as possible. Let us not be concerned with what mankind does with truth, for if we, as channels, become concerned with what man does with it or thinks about it, then we become the obstruction to the light within, and the beauty and freedom and joy and truth cannot flow in the stream of consciousness to rise the souls of man to the light and to freedom.

And so because of the abuses of the science of Spiritualism, you now have in your world what is referred to as spiritism. And spiritism is nothing more and nothing less than an ignorant and haphazard communication with entities from astral dimensions because the minds of men have gloried in the joy, so-called, and fascination of communication for the sole motivation and purpose of selfish gain. That is what has degenerated the modern-day movement of Spiritualism. But there is the divine, eternal law and that law is: that which descends in self-will shall rise again in divine will. And so truth crushed to earth shall rise again. It is already rising.

And so, my good friends, when you visit a Spiritualist church take thought and pause of your true motivation. The science reveals the possibility of something beyond your mind. The philosophy reveals the eternal truth and when you apply the true philosophy of Spiritualism, you will not have want, need, and desire, for you will be in the flow of divine, eternal truth.

And remember, the mind serves its purpose, and its purpose is to conceive the things composed of mind stuff. And that is its true and only purpose. So lest we become as little children, we shall not enter the kingdom of God. For it is the little children who do not yet have the great mental activity that has caused us, as adults, to be known in the realms of spirit as the children of king brain. Look at life and see what the king brain has brought you. Take an honest view, my friends, and you will know where it is leading you this moment in truth. If our brain, the physical effect of our mind, is so great, then why have we stumbled in the dark so very long?

I hope and pray that it may be in the divine will of Infinite Consciousness the souls present here today may learn the soul faculties of duty, gratitude, and tolerance; to know that that faculty of gratitude (to be grateful for the crumb) is the infinite, divine law of eternal increase; that you may know in your soul faculty of reason that God *is*—it is not a mental gymnastic; that you may not be concerned about how many spirit guides and teachers you have; that you may not be so concerned about spirit lands that you are not making the effort to awaken in your consciousness this moment; that you may permit your faith to be directed to reason, the perfect balance, for only your faith in reason will ever transfigure you and free your eternal, divine soul.

Thank you.

AUGUST 3, 1975

Church Lecture 48
Sailing the Ship of Destiny

The topic, as was stated by our chairman, "Sailing the Ship of Destiny," is in truth the ship of destiny, our own eternal soul. Sailing that ship is the mind of man. And it is the mind of man that chooses in any given moment to chart the course of his own destiny, of his own eternal soul.

And so it is in this philosophy that we have taught over these years that divine will is the total acceptance in consciousness of God's eternal, infinite right to all expression and that self-will, the will of man, is the direct effect of the limited acceptances and rejections of his own mind. And so it is that man is granted the opportunity, in any moment that he chooses to declare it, the divine, eternal right to chart his ship (his eternal soul) on the stream of consciousness to God or to chart it along the shores and to linger for whatever time he chooses in the dreams, the experiences, the illusions, and delusions of his own mind. For God has granted unto man, a God so kind and so humble, the right—think, my children—the *right* to deny him.

And so it is that we spend much of our days and many of our own hours in denying our own eternal right to freedom, to joy, to peace, and to happiness. The God of our understanding of the Living Light Philosophy is a God that has no denials. It is not a God that has been created by man. It is a God of divine, infinite, intelligent, neutral love that supports and sustains all things in all universes, that grants unto man this 10 percent free will. Now why is it that man has such a small percent of free will to choose to chart his own course and his destiny? Because whenever man makes a choice, he establishes a law. And when he establishes that law, he is destined by the very law that he has established to follow it to its own fulfillment and to its own completion.

And so here we are in a world of many experiences, experiences which are mirrors of our own levels of consciousness, of our own soul growth. Now what do we mean by soul growth? Surely, that that is does not grow. We mean by soul growth a control of the mind through which the soul is expressing. And the more we control the mind, the more we express our divinity, the more we express our own godhood. That is what is meant, in our understanding, by soul growth. It's not the growing of the soul; it is the controlling of the mind.

The world is filled with a multitude of religions and philosophies telling to the earth realm which way to go to find God. My good friends, it is not what you need to know to find God; it is what you need not to know to find God. Knowledge knows much, but wisdom knows better, because knowledge is only the reflection of understanding. Man cannot understand what man cannot conceive. Understanding is a soul perception that is awakened within the heart of man. It is a practical and living demonstration of eternal truth. It is not a theory. The world is filled with many theories and that confusion, called theory, man calls fact. It is not facts that you need. It is not knowledge that man needs. It is understanding.

And so the Bible prophets have taught for centuries and prophets, yea, before them, in all your getting, get understanding. But what does a man do with understanding once he has got it? The lack of use is abuse. And does it behoove man to get all this understanding and do nothing with it? That is not the law that is demonstrable. The law dictates in all your getting, get understanding, and in all your giving, give wisdom. And remember that the conscience of wisdom is the love of understanding.

And so, my good friends, where are we this moment in eternity, where are we in consciousness? Is our soul awakened or is our soul sleeping? It is such a simple thing to know for ourselves where we are. All we have to do is look around and about us, for that which is around and about us is the direct reflection of our own soul awakening. If we see, hear, sense, and feel discord, disturbance, and the constant cry for money, which the world seems to be so polluted with, then we can be rest assured that we haven't risen very far in consciousness. The mirror, called experience, is reflecting that great truth to us. So if we must cry, and cry, it seems to be the nature of the mind, then let us cry for God, and we will not be so concerned about this material world in which we are, our physical bodies, a part. However, remember, the physical body is only a direct effect of your own mental body and your mental body is only an effect of the efforts that you alone have made in evolution to permit your eternal soul to express itself.

So man's limitations, his own prison bars, are his own refusal, his *own* refusal to surrender his own thought to the infinite, divine Intelligence, called God, that supports his thought in the first place. For were it not for this Divine Intelligence, your thought could not be sustained.

God does not tell you how to think, for you are an eternal soul, an inseparable part of God and you know how to express your divinity. But only you can make that choice. You can wallow in the depths of self-pity and self-concern, if that is your choice. God will not interfere with your right, the right that he granted to you, to spend the life-giving energy, which in truth is God's, to entertain in thought how miserable you might be or how miserable you have been or how miserable you fear of becoming. God did not do that to us. Man seems to enjoy the suffering that he insists upon entertaining in his own mind. And because we are not yet men enough and do not yet have the strength of character to stand up and face the eternal truth that we and we alone have chosen our suffering and that we and we alone have chosen our joy, when we suffer and are miserable, we insist upon blaming it on the world. Now because so many people insist, from lack of character, to blame their frailties upon another, the world, this day, is in a bit of discord or disharmony. When we stop blaming, we will start living. When we insist upon creating the false gods of attachment to form, the false gods of attachment to things, when we stop creating those false gods—for our attachments have power over us and those things, my children, are false gods. They are the false gods that all prophets for all time have spoken about.

You cannot be free, no soul, until it accepts the eternal truth in consciousness that, "I am Spirit, formless and free; Whatever I think, that will I be." The Divine Intelligence does not interfere with the right that he has granted you to do otherwise. So it is, indeed, within our power to have a life that is meaningful, a life that is purposeful, a life that is fulfilled.

If we accept the delusion of man, then we fear that we're growing old and what will we do in our old age. This is the illusion that man has accepted and because he has accepted that illusion, he experiences the delusion thereof. Age is not a process of your eternal soul or the spirit. Who could call God young or call God old? You would not call truth aged, for truth and God just *is*. Now if you accept that and you do your part, then you will experience the divine right of the eternal fountain of youth, for it is not outside of you. Diets won't bring it to you and not will all of the beauty parlors existing on the earth realm. That will not bring you youth and joy and the spark of life itself. What will bring youth back to you—if you think you're losing it or have lost it—there's one word that will rejuvenate your spirit: it's called enthusiasm, to be in God. And when you become that, you won't have to be concerned in counting the numbers of your life, you won't have to be concerned with doctors and hospitals and sanatoriums, you won't have to be concerned with lack and limitation, you won't have to be concerned with where the next bite of food is coming from or

if you're going to have a roof over your head. You don't need all those things, my friends. All you need is the spark of enthusiasm.
Thank you.

SEPTEMBER 7, 1975

Church Lecture 49
The Fountain of Youth

As was stated, the topic for this morning is entitled, "The Fountain of Youth." It would, of course, behoove us to understand what the fountain of youth truly is. In this philosophy we know that all forms, whether they be mineral, plant, animal, or human, are the direct effect of what is called divine Energy. This energy is not something that comes and goes in the universe. It is a constant, rhythmic flow of energy. The obstruction to this harmonious and rhythmic flow of divine Energy is created by the thought or attitude of man himself. The fountain of youth, from which springeth this eternal, divine Energy, ceaselessly, without beginning or ending, is ever flowing in the universes. However, when man, from his self-concern, from his refusal to surrender disturbing and negative thoughts created by his own mind, he redirects this energy and creates an obstruction in his universe, in his consciousness to the very freedom, the peace, and the joy that he is now seeking.

It is not the easiest thing, of course, for man, it seems, to accept this Divine Intelligence that never faileth. Yet, without this divine, intelligent Energy, the thought of man could not be sustained. It is when man in his evolution relies upon accepted thoughts and experiences, recorded indelibly in his consciousness, that man becomes the obstruction to this divine Energy that grants him the fountain of youth.

This so-called aging process that man says is a natural phenomena of nature is one of the greatest fallacies ever entertained by the human mind. We look over the world and we see that some people in their forties are very old. They're old, depressed, discouraged, and ofttime entertain the thoughts of what a failure they have been in life. Another person in their eighties is alert, awake, alive in perfect health. Now it is not the divine Energy Intelligence, called God, that has done this to anyone. It is those souls in their evolution who have obstructed this divine flow. It is, in truth, a lack of acceptance, a refusal to surrender to the Intelligence that sustains all universes, for man in his evolution has become so important that he dictates to divine, natural law how things shall be. When man does that, as he does so often, he transgresses (by doing that) immutable, natural laws and the effect of those transgressions is poor health and age.

This philosophy, this understanding has been given many times to many people, but in the final analysis when someone is suffering and you explain this eternal truth to them, if they are not ready and willing to make the change in consciousness, then they will continue to suffer. One of the first things the mind does, when things are not pleasant or harmonious with it, is to blame God. And in a way this is a very good sign, because in that blaming of the Divine Intelligence there is a recognition that there is a power greater than their self-will and their self-concern. And so in that sense the blaming of God for all of our weaknesses and frailties can, and ofttimes does, lead us on the eternal path to light and freedom. For that recognition of a supreme authority, greater than our human mind, is destined in time, in eternity, to be recognized by the creatures of earth that are sustained by that power.

Why is it, we ask, that if life is so simple, so beautiful, so wonderful, and so true, then why is it that we have such great difficulty in accepting life the way it really is? That difficulty is the magnetic field of our universe that holds all things to us. Now not all things that come to us are pleasing or pleasant because we, as electrical transmitters in the universe, do not always send out thoughts and feelings that are pleasing and pleasant. And so we see in a world so often filled with disturbance and personality—that's what we seem to enjoy seeing—that is the revelation that that is where we are. We cannot see disturbance in the universe until we become the disturbance that [we] may view it and know it inside of our self.

We have spoken in this philosophy on what is called negative energy. We all know that all things must receive energy in order to survive. Man, unfortunately, has chosen to receive that energy by negative projections from his own mind. He has convinced himself that the squeaky wheel gets all the grease. And if he cries and complains long enough, loud enough, and hard enough, he will get all the attention that he knows is energy. And he knows he needs that energy in order that he may feel good. And so we go through life constantly griping and complaining and projecting how sick we are and how difficult things are and how poor we are. Each time we do that, we get someone's attention and if we don't get their attention, which is their energy, which is God's energy, then we're very, very upset. No one likes to be in the midst of a conversation crying about how they're suffering and have the person that is listening to them tell them they've heard enough. They do not appreciate the auric pollution they are being subjected to and they walk away, hopefully in peace and harmony.

My friends, we cannot live without energy, which, in truth, is God. It is time, if we have any interest in our health, our wealth, in our youth, it is certainly time to consider more frequently how we are going to permit ourselves to receive the sustenance, known as Intelligent Energy, for our own good. Surely the patterns that we have permitted ourselves to be addicted to, known as personality or personal interest and constant self-concern, though feeding us some energy to survive, is never fulfilling. Look around the world and see what happens with a person that has a thought in their mind. The thought that they have been treated unjustly, totally disregarding the divine, demonstrable law that like attracts like and becomes the Law of Attachment, totally disregarding that demonstrable truth. And they entertain the thought of how unjustly they have been treated. Take a good look when that happens to anyone, that you may be objective, that you may see clearly what is taking place, so that when it begins to happen to you, you will be able to free yourself from being the victim of that level of consciousness.

Whenever the mind feels that it has been unjustly treated, it goes out into the universe seeking sympathy. Now our philosophy teaches that sympathy is a sense function; that compassion is a soul faculty; that compassion has the light of reason and understanding; that sympathy is guided and controlled by self-interest. And so we see what happens with a person as they go out into the world to seek sympathy and support for their so-called feelings of injustice. Those who support them become the victims of that self-interest inside of themselves. They become bound and limited and the obstruction to divine, eternal principle, which is the essence of truth.

We don't need to be so interested and concerned with ourselves. When we become less concerned with ourselves, God will consider us more than we could possibly imagine. But God, the great healer, the great sustainer, cannot get into any area where man has risen supreme in his denials, has risen supreme to dictate to the Divine the way life will be.

It is true that man has been granted this 10 percent free will. What are we going to do with the will, that 10 percent, that was intended by the Divine to be free? If we continue to use it for bondage and enslavement of our eternal soul, then there's not even a half of 1 percent to be used to free ourselves.

It was stated at one of our classes that it would be of great benefit to the human race if they would carry with them a little pocket tape recorder and tape record their conversations. How often they speak of themselves and how often, in speaking of themselves, how negative, how limited, and how concerned they truly are. You cannot be free, my friends, that way. If freedom is the effect of truth, which it is, and truth is God, the Divine, then you cannot have what you absolutely, tenaciously refuse to permit to enter your consciousness. And I know that the students of this philosophy know in truth that those souls who are constantly entertaining their own thoughts and their own self-concern, who are constantly projecting negative complaints into the universe are in dire need, for their souls are in the very depths and pits of the universes.

This philosophy teaches that selfless service is the only path to spiritual illumination. That's not a theory; it's a demonstrable truth. Man reads that truth. He thinks about it and does nothing and then says it doesn't work. How could it work? He never applied it. We can theorize for century after century after century. We have already theorized for many centuries. And the longer we continue to entertain these mental thoughts that have no act or deed, revealing their motives [are] not so pure, then we're not going to have the eternal fountain of youth. The fountain of youth is not something you're going to find in some distant universe. It is something that is ever present, but it's up to you, my friends. It has to mean enough to you.

The beauty parlors and cosmetic companies of your world, they will not give you this youth that you are seeking. They will not give you the spark of divinity. They will give you the cloak of creation, the mask to hide yourself behind. That's all they can grant to you. That's all man has to give.

When you permit your soul to express itself through the vehicle known as your own heart, when you stop looking at others and start looking at yourself, when you stop complaining about things in God's universes—for the moment you complain, you rise, with your great authority, greater than God. For you deny, when you complain and cry, you deny the immutability of

God's laws. You deny them because you never made the effort to understand them.

So let us think more deeply when we spend so much of the life-giving energy in crying and complaining and criticizing, for those very levels of consciousness rob you of your health, your wealth, and your happiness. They rob you of the peace that passeth all understanding. For to complain and to criticize is a revelation of how little effort, my friends, that we have made to understand the laws of life.

Thank you.

OCTOBER 5, 1975

Church Lecture 50

The Way We Are

Now this morning I am scheduled to speak, I believe, on, "The Way We Are." A most interesting question and a question, indeed, it should be to our own mind. The way we are. Now all philosophies have taught and continue to teach that it is truth that sets man free. They've also taught that man must know himself in order to find the truth so that he can be free. We understand in this philosophy that we're not about to know the truth because we're not yet ready to face ourselves. So we can't have truth and we can't have freedom until we're ready and willing and able to make that step to face ourselves. Now how does man face himself? He presents so many faces to so many different people, it is a wonder that man truly ever does find himself. For the mind conceives and conception guarantees, in a world of creation, its own deception.

We understand it is the soul, the divine, eternal Spirit expressing through the individualization of the soul, that perceives and that's known as perception. How does man reach that state of consciousness called perception? We don't reach anything inside, my good friends, until we're ready to face what is called personal responsibility. Now what do we mean by personal responsibility? We simply mean our ability to respond to the dictates of our own conscience. Now our conscience we understand to be a spiritual sensibility with a dual capacity that knows right from wrong, that it does not have to be told. And so it is when we accept that still, small voice within ourselves, called our conscience, and we do what that still, small voice dictates us to do, then we will face our personal responsibilities, the ability to respond to the laws that we alone have set into motion, by our own thinking, by our own acceptances in life, and by our own rejections.

As long as we, as individualized souls, continue to play the mental gymnastics of what is known as brain games, as long as we feel some type of satisfaction from the playing of those games, then we will continue to present a different face to different people under different circumstances so that we may have some degree of satisfaction in our lives.

Our philosophy teaches that satisfaction is a sleep of the eternal soul, that when man awakens by facing his responsibilities, that process of awakening is very irritating. It is not irritating to the eternal soul that is awakening. It is irritating to the restricted mind of man's own creations in his own life.

Happiness and joy is not something that man needs to chase outside in the universe to find. For the truth of the matter is that happiness and joy and the goodness of life does not exist out in the universe, unless it first is permitted to exist inside of our own self, for the law dictates that like attracts like and becomes the Law of Attachment. Now when we begin to grow up, to become mature adults, emotionally, when we face what we're really doing to ourselves, when we make the effort to trace every experience in life backward to the cause, when we look out into the universe at people and things and we take the reins on blaming others for our weak character and for our own frailties, when we stop doing that, we will start growing up. But we won't grow up until we make up our own minds, until we finally bow our own titanic egos to the greatest power there ever was or ever will be. As long as we continue these games of our brain, playing one against the other, we will be void, we will swim in the sea of loneliness, which is the direct effect of self-pity.

And so it is, my friends, in the teaching of this philosophy, we find no blame outside of our own universe. It is not the world and it is not God. When we become adult, we will not only know that eternal truth we will begin to apply it and become the living demonstration of this so-called heaven on earth in the here and the now. I admit that it takes a bit of effort to try to control one's own mind. The reason that it takes a bit of effort is because we've made no effort to control our emotions at all. Now our conscious mind thinks that we do. We go on our jobs and out into the world and we suppress these feelings. Someone says something to us and we don't like it; we suppress the feeling because it is our job, we are being paid for it, and if we don't suppress the feeling we may not have the job too long. That is not where truth lies. That is only where effect lies. The only value or benefit to any experience in all eternity is our own willingness to trace the experience, which is an effect of a law, in through the jungle of our own mind. And we will find that we set that law into motion, although our mind is not readily going to admit it.

And so it is, my good friends, that the truth in life is we are where we are because we have made our minds what they are. We alone have done that. We can change it at any moment or we can continue on the wheel of illusion and delusion that it's someone else's fault. We can continue to blame the employers and the friends, the husbands, the wives, the families, the ministers of the churches, and everyone else and we will sink deeper and deeper and deeper into what is known as the cesspool of self-pity, the epitome of illusion and delusion. No one, no soul, in truth, wants to remain on this so-called karmic wheel of delusion. The soul does not aspire to remain in such a disastrous condition, for the mind is the vehicle through which the soul expresses.

So, my friends, it is taught to "Suffer senses not in vain for freedom of thy soul is gain." But let us be, in our suffering, which is the effect of the games we are playing, let us be just a little bit considerate and not demand in our consciousness because we are suffering the victimization of our own ego games, let us be a bit considerate of another that we do not try to make such effort to pollute everyone around us and the whole universe. The world is very concerned about ecology. It is very concerned about the pollution of the air. It is well and nigh time that we be concerned, or at least interested, in the pollution of our own eternal soul, that we be a bit more concerned about the pollution that our mind is pouring out into the atmosphere. You see, my friends, self-pity demands company for its own survival. Let us not choose to be the victims and the support of people's own self-pity, for if we choose to be so, that is a choice we have made in consciousness and the self-pity that they pollute the atmosphere with rises within our own consciousness, for like attracts like and becomes the Law of Attachment.

And so, my friends, be on guard, for all souls express through a mind of eighty-one levels of consciousness. And if someone is near you, 'round you, about you polluting your aura with self-pity, that simply reveals that you are not standing firm with your divine spirit, with your eternal soul if you don't open your mouth and make some changes in the atmosphere around and about you. Do not blame the person that is around you that is polluting the atmosphere. You have the divine right of choice to rise in consciousness to clean air within your own mind. And if you are strong in your faith in God, you will not only breathe the clean air in the midst of the pollution, but your clean air will rid the atmosphere of this pollution of misery and pity, which is nothing more, as any psychiatrist would let you know, than a type of insanity, which means an imbalance of our own mind.

When we start to think a bit more of God and a bit less of self, we won't have to be so concerned about the pollution in the world. God is the only power that sustains all things in all dimensions. Man (his mind) is that force which has deluded itself that it is the king of the universe, and that delusion guarantees the suffering that man calls hell.

Our philosophy also teaches that man is freed in hell and saved in heaven. Now when you've had enough hell, when you have wallowed in the depths of this cesspool of self, when you have truly hit the bottom, you will be freed from it, for then you will surrender and let go to an authority greater than your created minds. When that happens, freedom for you, your soul, is assured. It is instantaneous.

Now some people think that once they've gained freedom, they have it. Oh, how I wish that could be true. But that, too, is another delusion. Man has the right of choice. And so when he hits the bottom, the suffering becomes so intense he chooses to surrender to a divine authority. In that moment, in that instant man is freed from his own delusions. However, the brain ego mechanism doesn't take long—sometimes a matter of seconds—to recognize it is no longer king and then it rises on its throne and that freedom, that peace, and that joy that you were experiencing becomes, instantaneously, the bondage of hell.

And so our teaching is, stand guardian at the portal of your thought that your eternal soul not descend into the depths of living hell, for that is not the destiny of your soul. It is only that God in his infinite mercy and kindness gave man the right of choice that he may choose consciously in the eternal moment between heaven and hell in the here and now.

So my students and friends and visitors to Serenity, don't be so concerned about where you're going after you leave your physical bodies. Don't waste your time and energy on such foolishness, because you already know where you're going because you already know your own mind. If your mind is disturbed and filled with pity, that's where you are in consciousness. The only change there's going to be, at so-called physical death, is you're going to take off a suit of clothes. You'll either burn it and purify it, or you'll bury it in some sod somewhere and let the worms have it. But you will be, your soul, in your mental body. So you already know your mental body. So you already know your heaven or your hell. Now some religions teach a purgatory, which is a wonderful teaching. It implies purification. Well, you've already lived enough years to know what purifies you. When the suffering's intense enough, you change your mind and you get out of it. Now that's called purgatory and it's process is purification. Well, we're already in hell, purgatory, or heaven right now. So don't be so concerned about tomorrow. Take care of today and you'll know right where you're going.

Thank you.

NOVEMBER 2, 1975

Church Lecture 51
Beginning Anew

I also am scheduled this morning for a lecture entitled, "Beginning Anew." And how appropriate that, indeed, as another link is added to the chain that leads ever upward to freedom and to the Divine, which is a consciousness that we are in, in this moment, that we start off seeing a new year—only a matter of days away—that we see, always hopefully, that it will be a little bit better than yesterday, that it will take the good of the moment and project it forward into the universe for our own benefit, which, in truth, is a benefit to this world.

My good friends, in this association, for many years, much has been spoken on the universal, infallible, divine laws of God, the laws of Divine Infinite Intelligence. We have also spoken on the laws that man establishes and we know that man's establishment of law is an obstruction, a temporary obstruction, to the laws of the Divine. For the divine laws of God are infallible, immutable laws. They are laws upon which all souls may rely. There and there alone lies the security in a world that is governed and controlled by the Law of Progression, which is a law of constant change.

What is it that changes for man, but his own mind? His soul, his divine, infinite, eternal spirit—it does not change. It is the way that it was, it is the way that it is, and it will always be that way. It is the divine law of God that all souls shall be free. It is the law of man that the soul shall be bound, that the soul shall suffer. It suffers from a lack of expressing its own divinity. And that divinity is the fullness and the freedom and the joy of life itself.

However, each moment, each day in all of our activities we continue to establish what is known as man's law. We rely upon the effect of our efforts. We rely upon those effects in keeping with what our minds have accepted from past experiences. And because our minds have accepted that this is possible and that is not, that this is probable and that is not, we limit the expression of our own fullness of life. It is because, in the relying upon the limited acceptances in our own mind, it is because of that, that we suffer. It is because of that reliance upon our mind that we have denied God.

We speak in words about God. We talk about it and ofttimes think we're doing something about it in our lives, but when it comes down to the application of what we say we believe, we run into great difficulty. We run into the difficulty of the reliance that we have upon the experiences in our mind that controlled our life in yesterday and yesteryear. And so it is, because of that reliance upon established mental patterns, because of that reliance, we deny our godhood and we pay the price of obstruction of standing in our own, eternal light.

We all want to be free. We especially want to be free when we are experiencing difficulties and suffering. When things are going the way that our mind says is pleasant to us, there is not much thought, let alone interest, in divine law. But things do not always go the way that our minds want them to go, because our minds have created those laws. Those are created laws. They are not infinite laws, but they are laws of mental, mind substance. And that that is of mental, mind substance is creation.

Now creation is a Law of Duality, a Law of Opposites, a law that dictates the positive and the negative in perfect rhythm and in perfect balance. And so it is that we can easily tell when we are relying upon mental, so-called intellectual laws, for the mind immediately dictates, according to its limitation, that it shall be a positive effect or it shall be a negative effect and those relying upon the mind will have the wonderful confusion and contradiction that the intellect guarantees, for that is the very nature of the intellect: to contradict (positive and negative) in order to maintain and to sustain its own mental balance. Now if the mind—if it was within the power of the mind to have balance without contradiction, then the minds of men would have balance without that Law of Duality. But because the minds of men are subservient to the infinite, intelligent Divine Consciousness, the minds of men contradict themselves and a house divided cannot long endure, nor stand.

And so it is in beginning anew that we make the effort to begin anew—a new attitude of mind, a new feeling about life, an effort of our own will not to dictate to ourselves, to our eternal, infinite, eternal spirit, how the effects of our efforts are going to be. When man is concerned, as men are with their minds, on the effect of expended energy, they establish a dual law. They establish that law and though the seeming effect may seem to be good, it only guarantees its opposite, for they have stepped in the way, with their self-importance, in the way of God's infinite, eternal laws. No matter what your thought of the moment may be, no matter what your chosen path may be, consider beginning anew, a new thought and a new attitude in reference to what it is you truly desire.

Now the mind or so-called brain, the vehicle through which it expresses, is controlled by what we call desire. And the minds of all men ever seek to balance—for that is the law that governs nature—ever seek to balance the multitude of desires of the mind, for the nature of the mind is desire. Without desire, our souls would not be incarnated into what we call the form of this earth realm. We understand that desire is the divine expression. Without it, man cannot express. But man must learn to choose wisely what he desires for the law is infallible and whatever it is you want in life, that very wanting is establishing that law. And believe me, my good friends, we always get what we really want.

Now ofttimes we don't think that we do, but we always do. We get the principle of the law which returns unto us. So it is if a person says, "I desire to be a successful person in life." That is an established law of the mind. Now the person *will* become a successful person. They may not become successful in the way that they think they are successful, but they will be successful according to the laws that their own minds have established. After all, a person cannot say that one who is a complete flop or failure in life is not successful, for they are successful in being a failure. And so let us consider wisely what it is that we are choosing to be.

This philosophy understands that we are, in truth, spirit, formless and free; whatever we think that and that alone we shall be. For that is our divinity. We have been given that divine, eternal choice. And so it is when you seek to gain understanding, you will indeed gain understanding. You will gain whatever it is that you seek to gain. But the payment, so-called, and the price for gaining it is not considered by the minds of men when they choose so many multitudes of desire.

A person may say, "Well, I just want to be happy." Now when you say you want to be happy, the question must rise in the mind, "How many levels of consciousness in my own mind,"—and there are eighty-one levels of consciousness—"have I considered when I decided that I wanted to be happy?" A person makes that statement and he goes through life and he finds certain times when he is happy. He finds other times when he is miserable, but that that he asked for, he has in truth received. He asked from a level of consciousness for happiness and whenever he is on that level of consciousness, he experiences happiness. But he did not consider the other eighty levels of consciousness. And so when he is not on those levels of consciousness, he is not happy; he is miserable.

And so this philosophy teaches total consideration is divine love. That's what divine love is. Total acceptance is divine will. That's what divine will is.

And so pause in consciousness in the eternal moment, the only moment that you have any power over in truth, the moment of now and ask yourself about your own life. For our life is the direct effect of the laws that we alone have established. God granted us this great freedom—this 10 percent choice—to choose our own desires ever in keeping with the eternal law of the soul that is destined to free itself while yet encased in flesh.

And so, my friends, beginning anew takes a perspective, an effort, an application of the Law of Personal Responsibility. To take unto yourselves this moment the personal responsibility, which is the infinite, divine law, to face ourselves, to be honest with ourselves. If you are not happy with the company you keep, it is only, of course, revealing the level of consciousness that you insist upon entertaining in thought. If you are not happy with your state in life, look within, for deep within your own consciousness lies the power to change your attitude of mind and the moment you truly change your attitude, you will change all things around and about you.

So, my friends, each experience in life is God's divine mercy, revealing to us alone the laws that we have established and that we insist upon the continuity of them. So look wisely at experience. Look at it straight in the face and accept, through the soul faculty of humility, that you alone have established that law.

Serenity and the philosophy of The Living Light knows beyond a shadow of any doubt that God is not a doer; God is Intelligence, infinitely expressing itself. We know beyond any shadow of doubt that there is one intelligence, and only one, expressing through everything; that so-called division and so-called separatism is an illusion created by our own minds that we may feel a self-importance. The need for feeling important is created by the mind as the soul strives to express itself fully, wholly, and completely through the form called the mental body. When man obstructs the freedom and the flow and the joy of his own evolving, eternal soul, then the soul, not having the fullness of its own divinity and being obstructed by the intellect of men's minds, causes a feeling of great need and inadequacy in the mental, emotional body. Man, at that time, starts to do whatever the mind thinks is necessary to fill that great void, that gap in his own consciousness. And so it is as little children, educated by a world called civilization [that] programmed the minds of children to limitation, to obstruction, to separatism in order that they may continue, by establishing mental law, this inadequacy called egoism, the soul suffers.

God is an infinite, intelligent Power called Divine Love, called impartial Energy. When man, through this inadequacy of egotism and egoism, causes these obstructions to that flow of God, then he pays a very dear and great price for he starts into what is called the games of life. As a little child he knows—his little mind, for it is programmed by civilization—he knows what will bring him attention. And attention is the vehicle through which God's love flows. All things that are obstructing the divine, eternal flow of God have a need for attention, for they have a need for energy.

And so it is we grow from childhood to so-called adulthood and we slowly, but surely, commit suicide. Each moment we try to kill ourselves by the games of our intellects. We destroy the peace of God and God's right to flow freely through our form. And so man in truth is his worst enemy. And man in truth can be his own best friend. It is time, my friends, in beginning anew, that we stop destroying the vehicle through which our eternal soul is expressing. The vehicle through which our soul is expressing is the house and the temple of God. And when we continue dictating to God how things shall be, we continue to destroy that temple of God. That is the payment that we are making in this moment. And so the time comes we cry like voices in the wilderness to whatever god we have conceived in our mind, totally disregarding the God of impartial, eternal truth that doesn't change to suit the whims of man. For the minds of men shall never know the God of Gods. The minds of men are only capable of knowing the false, conceived gods of authority that they have created by their own intellects.

And so all prophets have taught that it is easier for a child to enter the kingdom than a man of great knowledge and intellect. For the more we expand the intellect, the mental body, the less we express the simple, the humble expression of God. We cannot (our minds), and we will not, change infallible, immutable law. It is not only foolhardy to attempt to do so, it is a revelation of a type of insanity to insist upon trying to do so. We can do many things with our minds, but our minds are limited in respect to divine law. If we have difficulty in acceptance, then we know, to the degree of difficulty that we have in acceptance, we know how much we are relying upon our limited mind. If we are concerned over the effects of our efforts and, God forbid, if we dictate what those effects will be, it reveals to us what our true god is that controls our soul. If we dictate or are concerned over the effects that is telling us, in truth, that our god is an idol, a false god created by our own ego. If we do what we have to do because it is right to do it, because we know it in the depths of our being and are not concerned over the effects, then we are freed. For a man not concerned over the effects of his efforts is a wise man, who knows God's infallible law. And what need is there for concern, if you know the law of God? You have no interest and no concern over effects, for the law itself reveals the effects and you have nothing to be interested or concerned about.

We all know the law of gravity. We're not concerned nor interested in what the effect will be. We already know the law and, therefore, we already know the result. And when you begin anew and you change your attitudes, you will awaken to infallible law. And awakening to infallible law, you will flow with the it and you will have no need for self-concern. You will have no need to wonder when your life is going to change—it's in the process of changing all the time. You will have no need to wonder about wealth or health or poverty or sickness, for you will know the law and knowing the law, you will know your life. And knowing your life, you will be freed and you will be what God designed you, in truth, to be.

Thank you.

DECEMBER 7, 1975

Church Lecture 52

Forgiving, The Path of Freedom

Now this morning the lecture is entitled, "Forgiving, The Path of Freedom." And before going on with that lecture, I would like to give forth a clarification of the spiritual understanding of the word *forgiving*. We understand that word to mean to give forth that which binds our soul to the laws of duality called creation. And so in explaining the spiritual meaning of that word, the question must arise within our mind, "To give forth what and to give it to whom?"

Now we look at life and we know that it is not within our power to hold the stars in space. It is not within our power to change the immutable laws of gravity. Those things, of natural law, it is not within our power to change those divine principles. Now man thinks, because he can make so many things, that he can change everything. The only "everything" that man can change is in keeping with divine law. He can change all his attitudes, all his thoughts, and all his feelings. But he cannot change the divine laws which are the final and total authority of life itself.

And so it is that the ancient prophets, the Biblical prophets, taught that, "Vengeance is mine saith the Lord." And we know that word means the law. *Lord* means the law of God. When man does not give forth these so-called resentments that he entertains because someone else did not think or do the way that we decided they should do, then man takes or attempts to take the divine law from God unto himself. How does man do that? He does it by a lack of awareness of the Law of Universal Brotherhood. Now what is the Law of Brotherhood? It is the Law of Personal Responsibility. And the Law of Personal Responsibility demonstrably reveals to all people that we and we alone have established mental laws and transgressions of natural law; that all of the experiences in life are revelations of laws that we alone set into motion. When we accept that demonstrable truth that we alone are the cause and cure of all of our experiences in life, then we will begin to manifest in the universe the Law of Brotherhood. We will no longer take or attempt to take from divine law that which shall never be ours.

And so it is as we go off into the world and we feel slighted by what someone does or does not do, we feel resentment and anger [to] the way that they speak and the way that they act. We are transgressing that Law of Personal Responsibility and the effect of that transgression is known as the Law of Bondage. For in transgressing that Law of Personal Responsibility, we give power and authority to another individual. And when we do that, we haven't sold our soul, we have given it for naught. This is the great sadness when we do not make the effort to forgive, which means to free, to rise in consciousness to natural law, which says, in truth, an eye for an eye and a tooth for a tooth. That law may seem harsh to those of us who choose to be in what is commonly referred to as sentimental soup, but it is a just law for it is a demonstrable, divine law. And it dictates impartially whatever happens to us in life is caused alone by us. It is the delusion of what we call self-defense that causes the mind to entertain the possibility and probability that these causes are out there.

When we seemingly grow up on this Earth planet, especially in this seeming materialistic age, we lose our early, it seems, concepts of a God. And we go on and educate ourselves, seemingly, that that's the way life is. And when we do that we step back in consciousness with the well-known cop-out, "Well, it's the circumstances that I was born under. It's the breaks in life. Some people are lucky, but I just wasn't." What ridiculous thinking, to dictate to our mind that there is such chaotic laws in the universe that things just happen by chance. Nothing happens to us by chance. Nothing ever did and nothing ever will. The only reason that we tell ourselves that there are accidents in life and that things happen by chance is because we've never made the microscopic effort to find the causes of all things within us. It doesn't rain by chance. The sun does not shine by chance. We do not breathe by chance. We do not walk by chance. And we do not speak by chance. We establish laws. And those laws, demonstrable, return unto us. And so when you're having what you call the breaks in life, be not only grateful for them, for gratitude is another divine law that will increase those so-called breaks—and in gratitude will definitely make the change—but stop and think, when things are going well, how they got to be that way.

The true sadness on earth is that man does not want to bother when he's having the breaks of life, so-called, and things are going well, to make the effort to find out how it's happening. No, that's not how the mind works. It waits until all the breaks are gone, 'till we've run out of time, so-called, and money and everything else that seems to mean something to us and we're on the bottom of the pit, down in the dredges in our own emotions. And when we're down there we start to cry for a little light, for something to make us feel better. Usually, we are sufficiently strong enough to call a person that we think will listen to all of our emotional disturbances and we feel better for a short time. And then we go back down again.

I have spent a lifetime on earth in what they call mediumship. I grew up in a family where it was a day-to-day occurrence. And I have seen Spiritualism go through, as a movement, much trauma and disturbance. I have seen its expression in a world that does not understand it. But I am grateful that I have viewed that world and know it's not the world; it is the expression of those souls who claim to be Spiritualists that don't make sufficient effort to demonstrate the immutable laws that they have been privileged in this incarnation to know. And so I speak on this that we may greater understand what is in our world today, for when we gain understanding, we are then in a position to give forth the opinions and things that bind us.

Whenever any philosophical or religious movement transgresses the very laws that it teaches, it is destined to its own suicide and its own destruction. The Spiritualist movement knows the Law of Personal Responsibility. The Spiritualist movement knows that like attracts like and becomes the Law of

Attachment. The Spiritualist movement knows that we get out of a thing what we put into that thing and not one iota more.

Now, what are the transgressions of the many souls that compose the Spiritualist movement? When a movement brought to the world to awaken it to universal law, the only thing that can free the souls in any world in any dimension, having that valuable asset, emphasizes its science of communication far out of balance with the philosophy that reveals the laws that govern it, then you have transgression of natural law. And when that happens, when the science of this religion is so overbalanced with its philosophy, you no longer have the religion of Spiritualism, but you do have what the world calls spiritism.

It is not the fault of the public. If there is error—and error is evident and obvious—it is the mediums within its own movement. And when a person in the profession of mediumship, bearing such a grave responsibility not only to the world of earth, but to the world of spirit, abuses that great privilege to glorify their senses, to sacrifice the very principles of communication, to become degenerate, sidewalk fortune-tellers, then you have problems where problems should never be. The *only* purpose, the *only* worth to psychic, to mediumship, its only value and its only worth is to reveal to this earth world the laws of life and how, properly applied, they can free the human soul.

I sincerely mean to put in[to] the Serenity Association—and it was founded upon that very principle—a balance between the science of Spiritualism and its philosophy.

If you go to a doctor because you are ill and he gives you medication that numbs the effect, which you call illness, but he does nothing to remove the cause of that illness, then you can only be foolhardy to continue to go to that physician, if you could call him that. And so it is, my good friends, with mediumship, if it is the law that you have established, each time you turn around to go to a medium to help you out of the transgressions that you insist upon doing, then the medium themselves is doing you the gravest disservice they could possibly do to your eternal soul, for they have then become your crutch. And that is certainly not freedom.

I speak on this important subject on this lecture of forgiving that, perhaps, as the word goes forth into the universe, that you as the public may make a little effort in consciousness when you investigate the Spiritualist movement, to look beyond the seeming phenomena; that it is possible for someone to know something about you that your minds do not yet know themselves, but it comes to pass. What does that reveal? It only reveals that there are laws established. It only reveals that there is one God, that there is one consciousness. That's what it truly reveals. It did not come to your world to entertain the senses. It did not come to your world to glorify people. It came to your world as revelation. The first three hundred years of the Christian movement was the Spiritualist movement, for each of their temples had their mediums and their prophets. But you do not find the mediums nor the prophets in the Christianity of today. And we must ask our self the question, "Why?" Because of the abuses, not the uses, of the science of Spiritualism.

It has great value when it is placed in its proper perspective, for without it we would not have this philosophy of The Living Light today. Its value has been, and is, a living demonstration for those sincere students who have truly made the effort have had proven unto themselves, beyond a shadow of any doubt, that they and they alone are responsible and that they and they alone can change their lives. We do not understand that any prayer to any God changes our lives. That is not the teaching of The Living Light. However, if in your efforts to pray, you establish the Law of Total Acceptance, which is divine will, then that divine will flows through your life and the transformation of your life is the result.

Let us face this new year, hopefully—and hope's eternal, though truth is inevitable—hopefully with a new attitude towards life, hopefully with a gradual, but sure, recognition and acceptance that we are not alone no matter what we want to think about life. Let us awaken in consciousness that we are in truth, indeed, an inseparable part of one consciousness; that whatever we think and whatever we do is affecting another human soul, not only in the physical body, but in bodies ethereal.

Now every single person here, within the sound of my voice, knows, for they have had the living demonstration, that all is one in consciousness. Each person within the sound of my voice has had an experience, and continues to have, in life of a fondness for a particular individual, for another soul. And sometimes they have been amazed that the person they're in rapport with had the same thought that they did at the same time. Well, the principle of the law is revealing itself. You know how the person is feeling and how they are thinking and what they are doing, dependent upon your willingness to forgive, to give forth, to surrender your own opinions and all of those restricted thoughts that you think is you. When you're in what they call love, that begins to take place, and when that happens, you know what your husband, your wife, your girlfriend, or your boyfriend is feeling and thinking. Well, my friends, that takes place with you with whatever one person or two that you are in rapport with, because you say to yourself, "Well, I'm in love and that's what happens when you're in love." Friends, when you're in love with God, you will know what happens everywhere, at all times, and you will have the feeling for the souls that are struggling to be freed from the glory of their bloated nothingness.

Thank you.

JANUARY 4, 1976

Church Lecture 53
When It Means Enough

As our chairman has already stated, this morning's lecture is entitled, "When It Means Enough."

Now it seems that in life's experiences there are many things frequently presented to our mind and we have to make a decision and choice in those moments of what we call opportunity. But these decisions and these choices that we make are ever dependent upon our sense of values. And our sense of values in life are dependent upon the degree and the guidance of discipline that we have had at a very early age. Without discipline in life, our sense of values run far out of proportion and out of perspective. For the law states clearly that man does not value what he does not make effort to attain. So that which drifts easily into our life, as little children (that that we don't need to make great effort for) does not rise high on our list of values. The years pass and we grow up and become larger people, larger physically, but rarely larger emotionally and mentally. For our sense of values, dependent upon the guidance and discipline of early life, is not in perspective to the moment of adulthood in the life that we live here on earth.

And so it is that many things mean enough to desire them, but so very few things in life mean enough to work for them. To stick with something that we have chosen in life, regardless of the calling of many other desires, takes a bit of will power. But that will power, which is the right of all men, is used so little, until the day comes in our life that something means enough that we will work at it every day, in every way. We will not dictate to the divine intelligent law how much we have done to attain it. For when we entertain that type of thinking, then you may be rest assured we never really attained it in the first place. When the going gets rough, those who have been lacking in discipline are the first to quit, for they never strengthened their own will power. And before the victory, we turn our backs and then we wonder why success has not entered our lives. It has not entered our lives and cannot enter our lives until it means enough to give up all other values that in any way interfere with what we have chosen to do in life.

It has been stated in this association that the key to success is the principle of effort and that the principle of effort is the lack of concern. That simply means that we make a decision in life; we choose what it is we want to become; we place our attention upon the becoming, not upon the overcoming of other values in our life. And so it is, my friends, all souls whose destiny in truth is the fullness of life, to the mind is the success of life. And so we must learn in time that something—whatever it is that you choose to make it—but something must mean enough to you or you will look at life in regret, in discouragement, and in self-pity.

It is only the lack in our own minds of continuity of effort to that we have chosen to do in life, it is only that lack of directing the mind that causes us to entertain these thoughts of discouragement and of failure. We all know that life in truth is ever as we think it and it is ever as we alone take it. And when it means enough to think it in peace and success and joy and fullness, then that is the way that we will take it, regardless of what others think and regardless of what others say or do. They are not responsible for our life. They are only responsible for their own.

And so let us remember, our success in life is dependent upon how much it means to us. Not by what we tell our self it means to us and not by what we tell others how much something means to us, but how we demonstrate it. And we demonstrate our values each and every moment of our life. We demonstrate those values by our acts and deeds. We demonstrate to ourselves and to all those who have eyes to see and ears to hear what our values are, for we are the living demonstration of those values. And when the going gets the roughest, the true value that man has within in his own heart is the one that rises in the final analysis.

Know in life what it is you want to do. Just know what you want to do. For the easiest step there is, is to attain it. But you must know what you want to do on Monday as well as Sunday and it must be the same thing in the morning as it is in the evening. And no matter what other desires entertain your mind, that very thing you want to do must have, always and forever, the highest priority.

We delude ourselves by ourselves. No one does that to us. We delude ourselves by thinking that the way to attain something is to go outside and chase it in the universes. That is not what life is all about. Whatever we choose, when it means enough, will permeate our conscious and our subconscious mind. Those are the electro-magnetic fields of our universe. And it will broadcast out in invisible waves, in ways the minds cannot conceive. And like a great magnet in the universe, it shall gravitate to you, to the degree that you truly accept that is what you want. Our minds are like radio stations: they are broadcasting when we are awake and when we are asleep. And all things in the universe are receptive to this broadcasting when they tune in on that frequency band. And so, you see how simple the Law of Success truly is when it means enough to you. For you will rise in consciousness and steadily broadcast the very thing you so earnestly desire and in so doing the law fulfills itself and you become that which means enough to you.

Thank you.

FEBRUARY 1, 1976

Church Lecture 54

Our Brother's Keeper

When those words, *brother's keeper*, are mentioned, it calls forth from within the consciousness of man many different experiences of his own past. And the question does arise within the mind, "What does that statement mean in truth, 'our brother's keeper'?" Does it mean that we are responsible for the thoughts and the activities of another? Or does it mean that we are not responsible for the thoughts, acts, and activities of another? And in that question rises the answer from the depths of our own soul where demonstrable truth waits to express itself to our own conscious mind.

First, we must look within ourselves and ask the honest question, "Are we in truth a separate, independent unit in all of God's universes or are we an inseparable part of a whole, called Divine Infinite Intelligence?" If our answer is affirmative to the latter, which any reasonable, thinking person cannot help but answer affirmatively, then we know that we are personally responsible for our own thoughts, our own acts and activities. And in keeping with that personal responsibility we, indeed, become our brother's keeper. How does man in truth become his brother's keeper? By being the demonstration of honesty within himself. And then all of those people who are attracted into his universe, those mirrors remind man himself how he is thinking and is he being honest with himself.

The teaching of this philosophy is that total consideration is the expression of divine will. But it is not possible, it is not possible to consider the needs and efforts of another, when we in truth are not considering the fullness of our own life. That we limit ourselves to a particular desire that is constantly changing within our own mind, and while we are—our consciousness—in these many changing desires, we do not consider the whole of our own being. This is in keeping with the demonstrable law that man is his own worst enemy and that man alone may become his own best friend. For if we are not making the effort to become a friend to our self, then we cannot grant to the world or to another that friendship that we are not granting ourselves. For no man can grant to another what he has not first granted unto himself. And so it is that God, indeed, helps those who help themselves.

And so, my good friends, our brother's keeper reveals to us in the world in which we live how much housekeeping we are doing in our own minds. Are we in truth making the effort to become a free channel for our eternal being to express itself without the censorship and limitation of past experiences? The only beneficial purpose to a review in consciousness of any past experience is to bring it into the eternal moment, to view it for what it is in truth and, in so viewing it, to make the wise decision to no longer be controlled by it.

We must someday make the effort to become fully aware of our self. Sooner or later that dawns within our consciousness: our eternal right to happiness and to the joy of living. And as that right dawns within our own being, we begin to recognize and to realize that we indeed have been a great enemy to our self. But we do not have to remain that enemy. We do not have to continue to live in the limited censorship of our own limited mind. Limited by errors of ignorance. Limited because at the time we limited the expression of our eternal spirit, we didn't know any better, because we could not see. Man cannot see clearly the light of reason when man is in limited consideration of any particular mental pattern that he, his eternal soul, is striving to express through.

And so, my good friends, our brother's keeper must first be a keeper unto our own soul first. And in so doing to accept the eternal truth that we and we alone are personally responsible for every experience that we encounter in life, that every rejection that we encounter to our seeming efforts, we must face as our own responsibility. For if we continue to project the cause of our experiences onto other people outside, then we, indeed, are transgressing the very law of our brother's keeper. For we are granting, not only to our self, but to those with whom we come in contact, we are granting the greatest deception ever known by the human mind. And that great deception is to blame others for our own frailties or strengths. For if we blame someone for our own weaknesses, then we must, in keeping with that law, blame them for our strengths. And when we continue to do that we not only deny the law, the demonstrable Law of Personal Responsibility, but we give power to another human mind over our eternal soul, for we have given power to our own mind over our eternal soul. For we have permitted the delusion and deception of our mind to dictate that we and we alone are victims of mental patterns of other people. And so those who spend their time in blaming others for their frailties have already, within their own being, granted their created mind and its accepted, limited mental patterns authority over their eternal life.

We understand in this philosophy that God, the eternal, divine, infinite, intelligent Spirit, is equal to our understanding in the sense that we may have a bit of that Divine Intelligence expressing through us or we may have its fullness. That is dependent entirely upon our own efforts. It is dependent on putting the so-called uneducated ego in its proper perspective.

So many philosophies have taught, and continue to teach, the annihilation of the human ego; that is the farthest thing from the teachings of the philosophy of The Living Light. The ego is necessary to help us as an instrument through which our soul is expressing. It is the process of educating the human ego that is necessary. And how does man educate his so-called self-will and uneducated ego? First, we must understand what the uneducated ego truly is. It is dependent upon the limited acceptances, rejections, and experiences of yesterday projected into the eternal moment, censoring the infinite, eternal Spirit of Consciousness that is trying to flow through us, based upon the hopes and fears of yesterday. That, my good friends, is called the uneducated ego.

And how does that compare to an educated ego? Very simply. When we make the effort to educate it, we are aware at any moment what is motivating us to any thought, to any act, and to any deed. And being aware of what our true motivation is, we are freed in the eternal moment of now, for we now see our own motives in life, which are the causes of the laws that man establishes. And seeing his own motives, the very cause of his own laws, man then, and then only, is in a position to choose wisely what he wishes to think and do. For he knows—he does not have to have the outward experience—he knows his motives, the cause of the laws that he is, alone, establishing. He, therefore, knows its effect. He doesn't need to be psychic or mediumistic. All he needs to do is to make the effort to become aware of the mental patterns of yesterday that are controlling his moment of now. And [from] that effort, revealing the laws of life, man will then use reason. And using reason, he will be transfigured by the power of reason, which is a soul faculty, granting to mankind peace and harmony, for reason is a perfect balance and it sees very, very clearly.

That, my friends, is when we truly become our brother's keeper, for that is when we grow up as individuals and we become mature and adult and we face ourselves.

How can we be a friend to something we don't truly know? And when we truly do not know ourselves, we find that we're an enemy to ourselves. Every philosophy the world has ever known has stated, "O man, know thyself and ye shall know the truth and the truth shall set you free." Now we all accept that only the truth will set us free. But how many of us accept that truth is individually perceived, that truth is not something that is outside in some church or temple or philosophy. Truth is everywhere in the universes. It is within and without, and it is waiting to knock at the door of your conscience when you are ready and you are willing to let go of those things which disturb you.

Thank you.

MARCH 7, 1976

Church Lecture 55
The Fifth Anniversary of Serenity

As you all know a birthday only comes once a year and so it is this day that we celebrate the birthday of the Serenity Church. For it was five years ago this day, May 2, 1971, that Serenity Church held its first service here at the American Legion Log Cabin. I feel that it would be not only of interest, but of benefit, in keeping with the philosophy presented by this association to share with you the short, but very full five years of the Serenity Church.

As most of you, at least my students, are aware, I had somehow over the years gained an adversity in my consciousness to what we call, in this world, churches. Although I had been a member of a church in San Francisco for a number of years, I had convinced myself that that is the one thing that I would never want for myself. It is interesting in life how we view our experiences from such a limited perspective. And so it was in those years past that my view was quite limited in keeping with my own personal hopes and aspirations, as all views are limited by all of us. And so eight years ago, this August 20th, I was instrumental in founding the Serenity Spiritualist Camp Association. We purchased that year, in 1968, December, forty acres of land in the mountains of Mendocino County. And I was indeed very happy, for, to me at that time, forty acres was plenty of space for the varied personalities to express themselves. And therefore, no one would be congested in that large an area.

Only a few years were to pass when I was to meet my own adversity: a church. And so it was on February the 22nd of 1971 at the request of those souls, long ago passed to the higher life—[they] requested that a church be opened in order that they may present, through an organization, what we now have as the Living Light Philosophy.

There is a teaching in that philosophy that states the Law of Payment and Attainment. There is no such thing as a credit in spiritual awakening. We all pay in advance. Now, the reason that we pay in advance for any type of spiritual awakening is quite simple. We must ask our self, of course, "Oh, what is the payment?" The payment is to give up the obstructions in consciousness that stand before our eternal soul and the divine, eternal Intelligence called God. That means anything in our mind that we have convinced our self we cannot do without—that is the very thing we shall learn, in time, to do without in order to be free.

Now, I am very personally familiar with these things that we stop and we think, "Well, I can do without anything." But that's not the way it really works. We think we can do without things, until those very things are removed from us without our own conscious choice. At least we think we have not made a conscious choice, when they are taken from us, but the truth of the matter is somewhere in our evolution we did make a conscious choice and the law fulfills itself.

And so it is in the opening of this church five years ago today. As I stated, it had become my adversity—any church—just the thought of it. For to me in those years past, I saw what I believed was so much personality and dissension. Such a total waste of energy. Such a deprivation, to permit oneself not to enjoy the beauty and the love this earth has to offer. However, I bowed and surrendered to the request of the Spirit and these doors opened May 2, 1971. And all of the reasons that my mind had given me for never having a church, I learned to face. For like a great magnet, that that is entertained in mind goes out into the universe and it returns unto us. But through that, through facing those adversities, a great deal has been gained. For it is in the five years of this church that the Living Light Philosophy has truly come into its own and has brought to this world the simplicity of eternal truth.

No philosophy ever given to the world is readily appreciated, *if* it is a philosophy that is instrumental in causing man to face himself. If it is that type of a philosophy, then it is the last thing that man and his mind truly wants. "Why is it," we must ask our self the question, "that we do not in truth want to face ourselves?" We cannot face ourselves until we accept the divine truth of personal responsibility: that we and we alone are personally responsible for every experience in life that we encounter; that there is nothing outside—whether they call it the devil or God—that is responsible for what we do with our life. That type of a philosophy of simple truth presented to the mind causes the mind to back off and to go through an emotional type of trauma. For we know in the depths of our own being that our life and our world is the way we make it and it is the way that we take it.

And that our errors of yesterday, that have caused experiences that are not pleasing unto us, is something that has passed and gone, *if* we have learned the lesson that it had to offer to us. If we have not learned the lessons of yesterday's transgressions of natural law, then we continue to experience the effects of today's transgressions. It does not behoove man—in fact, it is the direct opposite: it is detrimental to man to think of yesterday and become discouraged. For discouragement is the path to hell. Yet, encouragement is the path to heaven. This and this moment alone is the only moment in which you have the choice of choosing a life of prosperity and happiness and health and joy. You cannot choose yesterday's moment, for yesterday's moment has gone and past. And as the Bible teaches us, let the things of the dead, bury the dead. Let us live in the moment in which we are consciously aware.

And so it is, today, that we look at this moment and we may review what has passed only in the sense that, hopefully, through personal analysis we have learned the lessons that have been offered to us. And if those lessons have not been well learned, then we will continue to stumble along the eternal path of evolution.

We all know that patterns of mind that we have attached our self to for a lifetime are not easy things to change. But there is a law greater than the laws created by the minds of men and that is the law, the divine Law of Evolution. Whether we like it or not, we are changing. Whether we want to let go of those patterns of yesterday, in truth, it does not matter, for those patterns are leaving us. For the divine eternal law of the evolving soul is greater than the created laws of the minds of men. Now we can make this evolutionary process a joyous one. Or we can make it the greatest struggle that we will ever know. We can do that by choosing wisely what thoughts and attitudes we will permit our minds to entertain at any moment.

The greatest delusion ever placed over the evolving soul is the delusion of the mind that gives credit and power to people and to things seemingly outside of its control. And so man in order that he may, once again, regain his own divinity learns—usually the hard way—that that delusion is his greatest so-called hell.

Everyone within the sound of my voice has spent enough years already on earth to know that all things come and all things go; that their passing or going can be a pleasing and gentle experience or it can be a great emotional grief and sadness. The passing and going in our life does not mean the passing and going to another dimension of consciousness. It means the passing and going of all things. The passing of a job and especially the passing of material substance, called money. We are rich or we are poor depending upon our choice in any moment whether to regain our divinity and declare our divine right within our own mind or to entertain the delusion of the mind that somebody or something or circumstance has power to bring us happiness or to bring us sadness. The mind that insists upon entertaining the delusion and granting of that power outside of its domain will never find the peace that passeth all understanding. They will ever be the victims and the puppets of mental, dual creation. One moment will be a moment of joy, only to guarantee the next moment of sadness, for creation is governed by a dual law, a demonstrable law of positive and negative.

The Living Light Philosophy does not view the Divine as a positive, or father image, as a negative, or mother image. Its understanding and acceptance is the neutrality of the Divinity. The Divinity, called God, sustains all things, *all* things. Its energy—its intelligent energy is ever available to all forms. It is through the process of surrender to that Divine Intelligence that man is freed, that man is successful, that man is healthy, that man is happy, that man is fulfilled. And ever to the degree and the willingness to surrender the patterns of mind, which we have relied upon for so many years, to the degree of surrendering those obstructions from our consciousness are we truly freed. For man's insistence upon the superiority of his intellect over the humble servant called Divine Intelligence is where man's problems begin. And it is, also, where they end, when he gives them to that Intelligence that knows and does not have to be told. The very essence of Divine Intelligence is the expression of joy, but we cannot touch that essence until we are willing to be receptive to it. And we cannot be willing to be receptive to it, until we give up all those things in our mind that block it from our own universe.

It is, indeed, interesting, perhaps, to note in working with the mind and the spirit, the soul and the form that man, his mind is well likened unto a programmed computer, for that is the way the mind truly works. And whatever is permitted to enter the computer of the mind, that and that alone is the laws that are established by the mind. It has been stated many times in this church that it is not what you need to put into the mind to free your soul, it's what you need to take out of it to free your soul. The mind is already filled with a multitude of things, and those things are what rob us from our happiness.

And so in facing my own adversities, I learned a law, through demonstration, a law revealed in this philosophy that states: "Our adversities become our attachments. It is a subtle law." For that, whatever it may be in life, that we find our self adverse to simply reveals we are entertaining that in consciousness. We are directing divine, neutral energy to that. And because we are doing that, we guarantee the experience in our own lives. For an adversity, in truth, is a fear. And fear, in truth, is negative faith. And so it is the things we fear the most in life befall us. But it is also true, the things in life in which we truly have faith uplift us in consciousness to planes supernal. But man cannot have positive faith in life as long as he permits his mind to be discouraged, as long as we insist on thinking of yesterday and not applying the lessons wisely.

It was only a few days ago that it was given to one of my students: reason, what the mind calls reason—our philosophy teaches to keep faith with reason for she will transfigure thee. And so one of my students said, "I see this as reason and that, to me, is reasonable." What the mind calls reason is dependent upon what the mind has already accepted. And so the reason of the mind, based upon the limited, accepted experiences in one's life, proves not to be reason, but the direct opposite of it, for each person has many varied experiences. And if we base reason upon the limited experiences of one person, then all of the other souls, they have to be out of reason. That's not where we find reason. We understand that reason is balance. And what is balance? Balance is the accepting of infinite truth: that man is a physical effect of a mental body, that the mental body is an effect of the soul body and that the soul body is an effect of the divine, Infinite Intelligence expressing, known as Spirit.

And so, if it is balance, reason, and truth that we are seeking, still the mind, for the mind is a dual instrument. It has a no for every yes. It has a doubt for every acceptance. And it has a fear for every faith. Therefore, within the confines of the human mind we cannot, in truth, find reason, balance, or freedom. So we must permit ourselves to go beyond the mind to what is known in this philosophy as the Divine Intelligence, the Spirit, formless and free.

On your programs it states that "I,"—that is the true I— there are two types of I's. There is the I that we think we are; that's known as the thought of I. And then there is the I that we truly are. And that I, we don't think about; we just are. And it states that "I am spirit formless and free,"—Think, my students, formless and free—"whatever I think that will I be." And so here we are this day, the effects of what *we* think. We are not the effects of what someone else thinks. We are only the effects of what we think. And if we will remember that, if we will truly bring it into our consciousness each and every moment, that we are the effect of what *we* think; we are not the effect of what everyone else thinks.

Thank you very much.

MAY 2, 1976

Church Lecture 56

Plants, Animals, and People

As our chairman has stated the lecture chosen for this evening's discussion is, "Plants, Animals, and People," a topic that should be of great interest to all of us, for without plants and animals, there would be no people on this earth realm, for they are indispensable to our very survival. And because that which is indispensable to the survival of any species is, in truth, an inseparable part thereof, so plants and animals, in truth, are an inseparable part of our self, as we, in truth, are an inseparable part of them.

Now many people have looked at those forms as though they were on a lower step of evolution in this great evolutionary plan. But looking at something as a step below is only an acceptance and a recognition that above our self, there is another step. So let us, in our consideration of this discussion this evening, let us entertain the thought and the possibility of this eternal and divine truth of the inseparableness of form, for that that is separated is the delusion created by our own mind. And when we spend some time in our thought and in our consideration of these other forms of life, when we truly take a bit of interest in what is inside expressing through the form, not just the outside covering that differs so drastically from our own, but what is motivating the form, [we will begin to consider] the intelligence that is expressing through the form.

Now, all people who have studied to any degree at all into spiritual matters are very well aware that love is the power of the Divine; that it is love which is, in truth, the communion with all forms, whether they are in the physical cloak or they are in the spiritual cloak. And so it is with plants and with animals. They respond to the only universal language the universe has ever known. The only language the universe will ever know, and that is the language of love.

It is my firm conviction, after many years of study into these various dimensions, that any sincere and honest, spiritually-minded person seeking to find the truth that frees their own being should make great effort to study and communicate with, on a daily basis, plants and animals. For in so doing, they begin to free themselves from their overidentification with themselves and their particular species, called humanity.

We all know that we cannot be free unless we make the effort to broaden our own horizons. And we cannot broaden our own horizons unless we make the effort to look beyond them. And we cannot make the effort to look beyond them unless we can accept, in our consciousness, the possibility of an equal intelligence expressing through forms that are different than our own.

Animals and plants, in their basic personalities, are no different, in truth, than the human being. They have likes and dislikes. They have fears and faith. They have acceptance and rejection. They have want, need, and desire. Not only do those simple, basic things apply to animals, but it also applies to the plant kingdom. In truth, it applies to all kingdoms everywhere there is form.

When we make the effort to communicate with these other forms in the simplicity of truth, these forms will respond, for they—that intelligence flowing through them is limited only by their form and it is limited by nothing else. An animal and a plant has a mind and that mind dictates to the form how much to eat and how much not to eat, when to eat, and so forth. That is a very basic thing to all form. The form of the animal has the need for attention. It has the need for what you call love. It has its own temper, depending on its varying personalities. And it has its own goodness, for it is a form through which God is expressing. When we make the effort to find that goodness inside of our self, we will then find that goodness inside of those other forms. And in so finding it, we establish a rapport, for the God within us is then expressing with the God that is expressing in the plant and the animal.

It is a known truth that anyone sincerely desiring to communicate with any form can do so, if they do not dictate the rules of communication. It is our minds and our limited so-called education that dictates how the form shall communicate, and in so doing we establish an obstruction between our self and the rest of God's creatures. We not only establish this obstruction with the animal and plant kingdom, we establish this obstruction with our own species. We establish it from our own error of ignorance and from our own delusion that we are a special, unique creation in the universe. That places us in a level of consciousness which, in time, we begin to experience the loneliness of so-called individualization and the freedom of universal consciousness. Man experiences loneliness and animals experience loneliness and plants experience loneliness. They experience it from an error of thought in their own minds. We look at the plant and animal kingdom and we do not consider, recognize, nor accept that each form has personality, for each form is, to some extent, just a little bit different. But we do not see that difference and therefore, we do not understand. And because we do not understand, we cannot in truth fully, freely, and wholly communicate with it.

It is known in this philosophy of The Living Light that the purpose, the *purpose* of our soul entering earth form is not only for our own soul evolution, but an instrument for the evolution of all forms in which it comes in contact. Now we all breathe, we all drink, and we all eat. And some of us have the thought to bless the food that we eat, but do we truly know why we do that, if we do it? I am sure that we will all agree that vibration is an effect of our own mental attitude. So when you touch a plant, become aware of what your attitude is. And when you touch an animal, become aware of what your attitude is. Because in becoming aware of your attitude, you will know in that moment whether you are harmonious with nature or you are discordant. And so there is a clear and just reason why some animals attack some people and those same animals do not attack other people. If you emanate a vibration of fear, which is a negative, discordant vibration, not only received by an animal, but also received by the plant kingdom and everything that is exposed to it, it puts the form into a self-defense state of consciousness. And in that state of consciousness, self-preservation demands that it attack.

As I stated earlier, I am firmly convinced of the absolute need of spiritually-minded people, sincerely seeking the truth, to make the effort to communicate with these other planes of consciousness. For you will find in the animal and plant kingdom a simplicity that has been long forgotten by the human species. But in that simplicity that you will find, you will gain, through your own efforts, a greater understanding than you have yet gained to this day. If we find, within our consciousness, an adversity to the acceptance of other planes of consciousness that we have considered beneath us, then it simply reveals unto us an error in our own thought and a denial of the expansion of our own mind.

We all know that the Earth is no longer flat, because we now know it never was. And now we are moving, in this Aquarian age, into an awakening of the possibility of communion with all forms in all dimensions. This does not mean that this possibility of communication has just now been invented. It only means that we have—most of us—just now become aware of the possibility. The telephone was not invented by Alexander Graham Bell. Electricity was not invented by Thomas Edison. It always was. And everything you see and everything that enters your consciousness is not something new. It always existed. The newness of it is that man just became aware of it. The scientific demonstration of the recent years that plants have feelings and emotions and personality does not mean the plants have just now evolved and developed that. It just means, in our errors of ignorance, we have finally begun to awaken to that demonstrable truth.

So let us take a different view of plants and animals. And let us consider, for we all spend much time in taking care of our inner being by the food and drink we take, let us consider entertaining a level of consciousness of gratitude and appreciation for the food that enters our human body. For when we entertain those levels of consciousness, that food passes through our system and is refined and is evolved as it returns to the source from whence it has come, and in that case the Earth planet. We are here, on Earth, responsible, personally and directly responsible, as instruments of the divine evolution not only of our own eternal, evolving soul, but of all forms, people, plants, and animals that we come in contact with. And the greatest service that you, as individualized souls, can do in helping this evolutionary plan to be fulfilled is to have greater consideration, interest, and thought when you eat and drink.

It was once stated in this philosophy in reference to a question on the killing of animals for food, What was man's responsibility? Man does not kill in the sense that the animal no longer exists and is annihilated. The only thing that man can take is the physical form. No one can take that which is not within their power to take. And so animals have been placed on earth, as well as the carrots and beets in the field, to be used. And remember, when in your experiences you find it necessary for you, in order that you, in your experience, may survive, take the life of a plant or animal, give some consideration and joy to the Divine Intelligence that is expressing through that form that when your day comes, there may be some higher intelligence, a form more evolved than your own, may give you some consideration and joy when your day comes.

It is in the best interests of our self and to our four-legged friends, for those who have earned the responsibility of having them in their care, to spend a few minutes daily in discussion with them. And the discussion is preferable in the early hours upon their awakening. We must learn to treat the four-legged friends much differently than we have been treating our two-legged friends, for the four-legged friends are simple, kind, and extremely sensitive. Therefore, we cannot use our blown-up nothingness called the human intellect to commune with them.

We must become the little children and sit down with them and talk to them. And not be so bloated in our nothingness of our own intellect to entertain the thought that they don't understand, for they do understand. They don't need to study English or any language to understand what you're feeling. They don't need dictionaries to understand what your thoughts truly mean. For they are receptive to your true self, not what you think you are, but what you really are at the moment that you're talking to them. You will learn, if you will make that effort each day, and you will see a greater God than you ever dreamed possible.

Thank you.

JUNE 6, 1976

Church Lecture 57

Accepting Our Birthright

Today's topic for discussion, entitled, "Accepting Our Birthright," means more to us than accepting life the way we think it is. Because life the way we think it is, is constantly changing, because we, in truth, are constantly changing. Our lives are not the way they were ten or twenty years ago. They will not be the same for us ten or twenty years from today.

Our soul entered this earth plane in keeping with the evolutionary laws of nature. When our soul, our true identity, our true being came to earth, it brought with it, in its memory par excellence, all of the experiences and the lessons to be learned and that had been learned on our evolutionary journey. Deep within our consciousness lies this memory par excellence. And it is through that memory par excellence that that inner something guides our lives into the experiences and the lessons that are necessary for our own eternal freedom, happiness, joy, and peace of mind.

And so it is that we look at life and we see so many experiences taking place within us, around us and about us. And often the question arises within our consciousness, "Why is this happening to me? Why am I experiencing this disaster in my life? I have tried to do what is right, and yet my experiences are not as pleasant as they should be." My good friends, because we have decided to do what is right, then we have judged what is right. And because we have judged what is right, we have established a law in our consciousness to bring to us all experiences necessary to free us from the bondage of our own judgments. For judgment is based solely, wholly, and completely upon the accepted experiences, upon the thinking that we will permit our minds to entertain. And the thinking that one mind permits itself to entertain is not always what other minds permit themselves to entertain. And so when it is that we view life from the seat of judgment, we guarantee those lessons and experiences necessary that we may surrender our thoughts and dictates of right and wrong for that that is taking place in Life herself.

This soul evolution, establishing laws of untold centuries ago, goes on regardless of what we choose to think or choose not to think. For the lessons that we are encountering are, in truth, what is absolutely and indispensably necessary for our own peace and freedom. And when we find these experiences in life that are so unpleasant, let us step back in consciousness and view their cause, not their effects, but their causes. We cannot view the cause of anything that we are involved in. We must step back in our mind and look from a vantage point of objectivity to see, in truth, where we really are, not where we think we are, but where we really are. We bear a great responsibility in entering this earth realm, for we have come to earth with untold centuries of experiences and lessons.

And so it's like walking on a treadmill. If we do not stop and pause to think, we will continue to revolve in the same level of consciousness century after century after century. For multitudes of souls on earth and those who have gone before us already know that a change is necessary within their own mind. For they know beyond a shadow of any doubt that they have a job to do. They also know that that job they have to do, they have not yet begun to do.

And so, my good souls, let us awaken within our own mind and let us face our personal responsibility for what we have to do in life. We did not come here to simply enjoy the pleasures that earth has to offer us. That is only a very minute part of the wholeness of our being. So often people think well what can they, as one soul, as one individual, do to improve life itself. Let us not forget that we are an inseparable part of a united consciousness, that whatever changes we make within our own mind has a direct and an indirect effect upon all minds. Although we cannot often consciously see this effect, we are indeed a part of the cause.

We look at life and rarely care to think about leaving this earth realm, but transition is no respecter of people or age. And so we must be prepared in our own thoughts, in our own mind of what we're going to do when we leave this physical body, for it will come to us much sooner than we care to think about it coming to us. And our mind will go with us. And we will experience all the things that our mind has and is creating. You have often heard the truth spoken that thoughts are more than things, that thoughts indeed are forms. So unless we make an effort to entertain thoughts that are harmonious and peaceful and in keeping with the laws of balance, called nature, then we will experience the distortion of those thoughts that are called distorted forms.

Life around us and about us is just the way that we accept it. It is no greater. It is no lesser. It is no more beautiful, nor is it anymore ugly than we alone permit our minds to accept. So let us accept our true birthright. Let us accept the lessons and the experiences that we encounter in life. For those lessons and those experiences are what we alone have earned and we alone have set into motion that we may grow through them, that we may graduate in this school of life from one grade to another and another and another. For that, my friends, in truth is what life is all about. It doesn't matter whether we like or dislike something. It does matter that we alone have established laws and brought the experience to us.

In the evolving and freedom of our own true being, called our soul, we face all of the attachments of yesterday and yesteryear. We face all of the judgments and we face all of the adversities. This philosophy teaches that our adversities become our attachments because we direct energy to anything we are adverse to. And by directing that energy to it, we create and attract it into our lives. We also, through our own attachments, become controlled by the things we are attached to, for we, and we alone, have directed this neutral energy to our own attachments. And so it behooves all of us to weigh out and balance in our lives, to weigh out our true purpose for being here, to recognize, to realize, and to finally accept that our life indeed is the way we make it, that our life is just exactly the way that we are taking it. So isn't it of more benefit to each and every one of us to take life and make life a pleasant and beautiful and harmonious place to be? Because we cannot run away from life, for we are an inseparable part of life. And that's just the way our lives will ever be: just the way we alone choose to make it. But that choosing is not something that you can think of on Monday and forget on Tuesday. That choosing is a moment-to-moment experience that is taking place within our mind. For each moment we choose which way to think. And each moment we choose which way to feel. Because we are not consciously aware of that moment-by-moment choosing process, it is taking place as if by habit. And so, because it is by taking place moment-by-moment life is no longer under our control because we no longer are making the effort to be consciously aware of that choosing process.

Thank you.

JULY 4, 1976

Church Lecture 58
Dynamic Perspectives

As our chairman has stated, this morning's lecture title [is], "Dynamic Perspectives."

We have a saying in this Living Light Philosophy which reveals the truth concerning the separation of truth from creation. And that saying, that little truth is, "We always get what we really want, while being deluded by what we think we want." Now that may seem to be a contradiction, and in truth it is the contradiction of creation and the divine eternal truth. Our minds entertain many thoughts of what we think we want, while our hearts, the vehicles through which our eternal soul is expressing, feel the contrary, the direct opposite. And so it is that the philosophers of old have given to us the teaching, "As a man thinketh in his heart, so shall he becometh." Those prophets did not leave us with a teaching that said, "As man thinketh in his mind." So we must learn, through dynamic perspectives of our eternal soul, to become aware of what are heart feels and what our mind dictates.

The seeming so-called struggle in life is because our mind refuses to accept the dictates of our eternal soul that has been evolving for untold centuries; that part of us that is the true being, that knows the lessons that we must have in life in order to free ourselves and enter the kingdom of heaven, which is a state of consciousness available to all souls in the eternal moment of now.

And so it is that experience upon experience enters our life in keeping with the laws that our mind insists upon establishing for us. The basic principle of this philosophy is the Law of Personal Responsibility. When that principle becomes a lighted torch for our path through creation, then we will see clearly that the lessons of life, in truth, are the blessings of life. For sooner or later, as one experience is compounded by a multitude of like-kind, we will finally become the vehicles through which the Divine Intelligence expresses in all its fullness. Our teachings are that divine will is total acceptance in consciousness, respecting and accepting the infinite divine right of God to express through all forms of creation.

When, because of our self-will, which is an expression of our acceptances and rejections in life, we dictate in our consciousness, we become the judges—the judges, my friends, not of something outside, the judges not of others, the judges of our self, for the judgment takes place in our mind. The payment takes place in our mind. We think, in our delusions in creation, that we are judging others. In truth we are not. We are judging our own perspective of things outside. The principle of personal responsibility does not affect that that is outside. It affects that which is inside. And so when we in our refusal to accept that this process, called life, is viewed individually by each and every form, that the laws are established by the individual, that sooner or later in evolution he will recognize and accept the divine Infinite Intelligence, which sole purpose is to serve. God demonstrates each and every moment that great law of service, for if that would not be true, all of creation would no longer exist.

The divine infinite Spirit, called God, sustains all of life. This intelligent Energy not only sustains heavenly paradises in consciousness, it also sustains the direct opposite, known as hell. If we do not see the truth in that statement, then it reveals to us that we are still a house divided.

The law clearly reveals that man's destinies are his denial. For when man denies the right of an intelligent Energy to express, then man, rising in the judgment within his own consciousness, superior and above that which sustains his very thought, then man and man alone must pay for his lesson that he has yet to learn. It was once stated that the steps to the depths of hell are the steps of judgment, that the rail upon which we lean as we descend is the rail of pride. For man takes pride in his denials, for man feels superior in his judgments. But to attempt to step to heavenly heights at the expense of other souls, regardless of their forms, is a payment that is indeed extracted from us seemingly against our own will. And so it has been taught, "an eye for an eye, and a tooth for a tooth." And it is taught that like attracts like and becomes the Law of Attachment.

What are the experiences of life? The reflections of inner attitudes of mind. We don't need to continue on the wheel of creation. We can make a choice and surrender to the divine expression called reason. For to keep faith with reason is to transfigure and to transform our very lives. There is no form, be it human, animal, plant, or mineral, that does not express belief and faith. For without belief, there is no identification. And without the Law of Identity, the Divine Intelligence does not sustain the form. So each thought that man entertains by the Law of Identity, by the Law of Faith, by the Law of Belief man creates the shape, the size, the beauty, or its opposite of that form, that man, through his thought—through the vehicle of thought—is creating.

You have heard much talk in this day and age—and in the movies and everywhere it seems to be present—concerning psychic matters, and obsession and possession. Any thought that controls the soul, that entertains the mind repeatedly, sooner or later becomes an obsession. Now usually we do not view obsession in people until it becomes so blatant and so obvious that the cure, seemingly, cannot be found. And so we take those people and we send them to our psychiatric clinics that they may receive some type of treatment to be able to once again function in society. My friends, there are many types of obsession. And if you sit peacefully and quietly each day, slowly, but surely, that which has possessed and now obsesses you will reveal itself to you. We prefer to think that we have no obsessions. We prefer to think that perhaps we have a few possessions. The truth is, we have neither. Only the minds of men have possessions, which guarantee obsessions.

Your soul is free. And it is free in this moment. Man is not aware of his freedom; man is not aware of his heaven; man is not aware of his paradise, because man is in the mind and not the soul. When we still this mind—and it takes a bit of daily effort—we become aware of heaven. We become aware of the joy of living. We become aware that indeed we are serving, for all things, all forms, all souls are serving, for God never stops serving. And God, that Divine Energy, is flowing through you constantly.

Now in dynamic perspectives let us view what we are serving, for no moment ever goes by that we are not diligently working and serving. The question must be asked honestly of ourselves, "Who or what am I serving? Am I serving a thought pattern that I have possessed, and because I have possessed that thought pattern, I am now obsessed by it?" Because the law, just, impartial, and beautiful, reveals, through our efforts of honesty, who and what we are really serving.

If in our sincere efforts to still our mind and be free, we become aware of the thought patterns that we have served seemingly for a lifetime, then it's time to view them in pure objectivity. And to ask our self the question, "Has this thought pattern served me well? Is this pattern of mind instrumental in bringing me peace and happiness?" And then go beyond that thought, that thought pattern. Go beyond it in consciousness, in peace, that you may view what it looks like. For by energy directed through the mind of mental substance, we have all created what is known as thought forms. Those forms are our children that we have created. And we, by entertaining that thought, the form grows from a little babe into a great giant. And the more we entertain the thought, the stronger the form becomes. Until one day, the form decides what it wants, when it wants it, and how it wants it. Then our little soul goes into bondage, into the victimization of the forms that we alone have created.

Now those are called the thought forms, and they live in our mind. And the day comes, we leave the physical world and we take nothing physical with us on our journey in evolution, but we take our thoughts. We take all the thought forms that we have created and we live with them. We hear them. We see them. For they are ours. Now the very nature of the mind is to preserve that which it entertains; that law we cannot escape as long as our soul is expressing through mental form. And because it is the nature of the mind to preserve that which it entertains, does it not behoove us to entertain thoughts of harmony that we may create in consciousness angelic forms which will be the instruments to free our eternal soul? The choice is up to man.

Our journey through this life, where, by the mercy of the Divine Intelligence, most of us do not view the forms of our own thoughts, is a short journey. The days go like seconds and the years like days. And all of us are facing each moment that day. We delude our self by saying, "I'm only so many years here on earth; I have much time to go." But as we view life and we become a bit realistic, we know that's far from true. Our moment waits for us. And when the law is fulfilled—and our mind cannot dictate that law—we shall leave this earthly form.

It would be much more satisfying for the ears of man to hear about the heavenly, beautiful heights, but would it be honest with oneself having viewed creation for what she really is, a dual law with the duality of form? Would one be honest with oneself knowing where we're all headed in this moment to speak of angelic, heavenly heights without revealing the truth to man: that his soul, our soul, is freed in hell and saved in heaven? But the hell and the heaven is not in the power of something outside of you. It never was. It's in your choice of each and every moment.

We all must pay in life for the lessons that are necessary for our eternal peace. Many of us have had moments of that peace. And we know how we got there. The teaching is that freedom is the direct effect, the effect of self-control. And because all minds know that truth and all souls expressing through the mind seek that freedom, which is its true home of the eternal being, that truth rises from the depths within us: control thy mind and be free. But when it reaches into the area of consciousness known as pride and the functions of the human-created body, it directs that need for the control of the self to the control of people and things outside of itself. And that, my friends, is when frustration really begins.

So you see, my good friends, we indeed always get what we really want, while being deluded by what we think we want.

Thank you.

SEPTEMBER 5, 1976

Church Lecture 59
Review and Renewal

This morning's topic for discussion, "Review and Renewal," is something that is taking place each and every moment of our life, for each and every moment of our life we are having experiences in consciousness, in mind. And we view each experience by a reference, through the Law of Association, to some experience of our own past. We do this in such an automatic way that we are no longer consciously aware that we face the multitude of experiences of our days controlled by those experiences that are similar in years that have passed and are in truth no longer serving a constructive or beneficial purpose in our lives. We are controlled by yesteryear until such time as we make the conscious daily effort to become aware of our own true self, to become aware of our mind and that eternal part of us, that true being, known as our Divine Spirit encased in individuality called soul. If we take the moment each day to review consciously the experiences that we encounter, then we shall renew ourselves by an awakening known as objectivity. We will no longer become the puppets of yesteryear's experiences. We will no longer be controlled by that which has already passed.

I know it is not a pleasing thought to any mind to think that it is not thinking in the moment that it is experiencing, but we know that we react in certain ways to certain things. But we must make that effort to find out why we react to experiences in life the way that we do react. And when we start that inward journey, we will find that it will not only take us, in time, back to our early childhood, but it will take us beyond the veil to the experiences in evolution before we ever entered this old earth realm. For these lessons of life—and many indeed there are—continue to repeat themselves again and again, year after year, and century after century, until such time as we change our attitude of mind, our level of consciousness in reference to the lesson to be learned.

Someone once said that the only benefit to experience is that it continues to repeat itself. It only continues, my friends, until we accept what the experience truly has to offer us. As long as we refuse to accept the experiences in life that we encounter, that simply reveals that we have not yet learned the lesson that the experience is offering to us.

Everyone entertains the thought and the possibility of the fullness of life. We all desire to be happy and we all desire to be successful. The truth of the matter is we are indeed all successful in what we alone have chosen to do in life. It was once said that a failure is the greatest success, for it is success in a negative, but it is indeed success. So as you look at life, you can honestly perceive that we are all indeed successful. We are successful in being unhappy because we have decided what happiness is. We are successful in being a failure in business because we have decided what success is.

Now, my friends, stop and think. The human mind views life in a duality. It views life in opposites, in the positive and the negative. And so, as long as we insist upon viewing life by the created mind, then we are going to have this continuous positive and negative experience in our consciousness. We are blinded in our own path in life because we stand in our own light in life.

Man and his eternal being, known as spirit, being an inseparable part of a divine, eternal Intelligence that had no beginning and has no ending, is designed by the Great Architect to be a joyous servant of that Intelligence of which we, in truth, are an inseparable part.

Now any man of common sense, viewing the universe and all the things around and about him, cannot help but in time to accept that the Intelligence that holds the universes in space is certainly far superior than the limited intelligence of our limited minds, which are but the effect of many experiences in life itself. And so we must ask our self the question in review, "What in truth am I relying upon? Am I relying upon an Intelligence that demonstrates its superiority in the universe or am I relying upon the limited experiences and acceptances of this short earth life?" When man decides that he is a separate, unique entity in creation, when man decides that his only source of supply, that his only source of good is what his limited mind can create, then man has placed himself, through the error of ignorance, into the bondage of so-called hell, for man has separated himself from truth. He has separated himself from the only intelligence that can free him from his own errors in life. But how does man get to rely upon this great, demonstrable

Infinite Intelligence? He slowly, but surely, through the process of reason, begins to awaken himself.

Man knows that many things he can accomplish, but he cannot, when he truly views life, he cannot create life. That is not within the domain nor the power of the individual man. He may bring together the poles of opposites in creation, but it is the Divine Intelligence, and the Divine Intelligence alone, that brings life. And it is the Divine Intelligence alone that takes life.

Man, in all of creation, is the greatest borrower ever known in the universe, for man borrows even the thought he entertains from something that has gone before. There is no such thing as an original thought in the minds of men. They simply become receptive to that which has gone before them. By not viewing that which has already been in the universe outside of our limited mind, man is deluded in his beliefs and he believes that *he* is doing this or *he* is doing that. It is the same thing as your automobile. How do you know that your automobile does not believe that it's driving you where *it* wants to go? We believe, of course, that we are driving the automobile. But how are we sure that that is true? Are we sure because we're the one that turns the key? But are we sure that we are the one that turns the key in the ignition? Or is it something else that is moving through us that is turning the key that moves the automobile? How can we be sure? How can we be sure of that that is controlling our mind?

Ofttimes in life we say we forget. But why do we forget? What causes that to take place in our mind? We justify it with many excuses, of course, for we have our self-image at stake. There are many things that we all have done in life that we choose to say, "circumstances caused me to do that." Now do we mean by that statement that we are not in control of our thoughts, acts, and activities, that circumstances are in control of our life? My good friends, if circumstances are in control of our life, then who is the cause of circumstances?

This philosophy teaches the Law of Personal Responsibility, the ability to respond to the true being, the individualized consciousness. If we are not responding to that, then it is evident and obvious we are responding to something else. And that something else we like to call, in life, circumstances. That is something that is outside, that some intelligence somewhere has sent to us. Now that kind of a god is not what this association and this philosophy believes in. Because if we believe in some kind of an intelligence that sends us circumstances that does not make us happy, then we've got some kind of a god that we believe in that we would be best doing without.

Let us think about the demonstrable laws of life, the laws of life that you can personally demonstrate unto yourself, that you are already demonstrating unto yourself; it's a matter of viewing them. Now the law says that like attracts like and becomes the Law of Attachment. Therefore, man must view his attachments and accept that whatever his attachments are, they are in keeping with his own desires. But the trouble with desire, my friends, is it changes so often. It changes from moment to moment. The moment you fulfill it, it demands more. It's kind of like a cup with a hole in the bottom: you keep pouring water in, but you never have any to drink. That's what desire is in the minds of men. It is never enough. Now it certainly isn't reason, nor common sense, to desire that which is never fulfilling.

How does man free himself from desire, when desire, in truth, is the divine right and the expression of the Divinity? Man frees himself from desire by giving back to the Divine the desire that his mind entertains. And when you give back to the true source that which your mind has stolen, then the Divine will fill your life and you won't have to live in the unquenchable thirst of so-called desire. Now which, in truth, is the most reasonable? Which makes the most common sense? But to give back to the Divine that which the mind has stolen takes an acceptance, first, that there is a Divine.

You see, my friends, when things go the way that our little minds would like to have them go—and our little minds change all the time— but in those moments when things are going very nicely, according to the dictates of our own mind, then there is a possibility, and a good possibility, that man can say, "Yes. Oh, yes, there's God. Of course there's God. I feel great. God means good. And I certainly feel good." Then our faith is directed to something greater in that moment. "There must be something that brought me all this good because I know myself better than anyone else and I know I haven't made that much effort."

But then there's the other side of the coin. Then there's that side that we entertain so frequently—things aren't going the way that we would like. We don't have enough money we decide. We don't have enough happiness. We don't have enough of anything. And our friends and our relatives and our husbands and wives, they're not doing what they should do. And how do we know they're not doing what they should do? Because we have decided what they should be doing. And because they are not doing what we have decided they should be doing, then they are not doing what they should be doing. So let us give that some thought. Those are the moments that all of a sudden there can't possibly be a God. Usually, you know, man thinks that he turns his sight to God when things are totally falling apart. But we must ask our self the question, Does man feel good when everything in his life is falling apart? No. I haven't yet met a man that feels good while his whole life is in a disaster. Man feels good when things are going the way that he would like to have them go. That's when he feels good. Now good means God, so that's when he's found God. So let's give that some deep thought this day, my friends.

And let us review the experiences, which, in truth, are lessons of the past, and in reviewing those lessons of yesterday let us make greater effort. Let us renew our effort by changing our mental attitude to the experiences that we encounter in life, because only by changing our mental attitude toward those experiences will we be freed from them and will we make another step ever upward in evolution. There's one thing about the Law of Evolution: in spite of the dictates of our mind, we are in truth evolving. Whether we like it or not, we are not so great in our consciousness that we can change the infinite Law of Evolution.

It is stated here that through repetition change is made possible. And so let us look at our lives and let us see the many repetitions of lessons that we have already encountered. But let us be of good cheer and let us be encouraged, for through that repetition, my friends, you are establishing the law, the infallible Law of Change.

Do not hold to things. Do not hold, my friends, for that which you hold destroys you, and that which you free unfolds you. Look at the many thoughts in life and things that we have already held to. It is not the things that you garner up that frees you and brings you happiness. It is the things that you give in life that bring you the joy of life. It is in the giving that we are eternally blessed in this moment. Not in the receiving, but in the giving. For as you give you become a clearer channel for that great, divine, eternal Intelligence to flow through you unobstructed. It is the givers in life who are never without. It is the givers in life who are freed from want, need, and desire. It is the givers in life that have the abundant, divine, eternal flow of God. It is the givers in life who are never concerned with money, for they have no lack thereof, for they have become the channels through which the greatest power of all time, beyond time, flows through them. My friends, in your giving will you find joy. And in your giving will you free yourself from the things that bind your being. It's in your giving through your heart, not your head.

Thank you.

OCTOBER 3, 1976

Church Lecture 60
The Lessons of Life

Today's topic of discussion: "The Lessons of Life," reveal, through honest analysis, the evolutionary process of our eternal being, known as the human soul. Each moment of each and every day we attract from the cosmos all of the lessons, known as experiences, that are necessary to free us from the bondage and error of ignorance. Experiences or lessons that continue to repeat themselves in our consciousness reveal to us the need to make greater effort to free ourselves from entertaining in consciousness those patterns of mind, like great magnets, that attract from the universe the repetition of certain lessons or experiences.

This philosophy teaches that change is made possible through the Law of Repetition. And so it is that man may find a greater peace and purpose in life by accepting, with a joyous heart and an honest mind, these many lessons and experiences in his day-to-day activities.

The greatest cloud or delusion created by the human mind is the delusion that the cause of any experience is outside and, therefore, beyond the power or the control to change it by our own efforts. And because we entertain so frequently that delusion of "blame outside," we become ever-increasingly controlled by the fluctuating changes of creation itself. We all know that creation offers to all of us a duality of experiences and as long as we permit our minds to entertain a need for creation, then, as long as we do that, we shall continue to experience this so-called good and so-called bad, this so-called fullness and this so-called lack.

Wise is he who seeks not the things of creation. Wise indeed is he who seeks that substance, that essence, that Intelligence that brings the good things of creation, for he who seeks the things and not the cause of things is ever controlled by the fluctuating desires of the human mind.

It is not easy until we are willing to make the effort to find our true purpose on this earth realm, for the lessons that continue to repeat themselves in our lives are the very things that are necessary for us to make the changes in consciousness that will bring us this goodness, which, in truth, is our divine right. Now divine right is not dependent upon people, places, or things. Divine right is dependent upon divine acceptance. Now we all use this divine acceptance, which in this philosophy is known as divine will. We use it in many limited ways. And because we limit in our mind this use of divine will, we alone suffer the consequences. For the limitation of divine will in consciousness is the transgression against universal, demonstrable law itself. Each and every rejection that we entertain in our minds binds us to the dual Law of Creation. And each and every acceptance we entertain in our mind frees us in the divine flow of God itself.

This philosophy teaches that our adversities become our attachments; it is a subtle law. My good friends, our adversities in life are, in truth, attachments waiting to be recognized. The life that we are already aware of, this limited earth life, has revealed to us that yesterday's attachments are often today's adversities and vice versa. And so who would hitch their wagon, so to speak, to such a star, that would bring us to heights and drop us to depths? That is not where a wise man places his reliance, for to do so is not only foolhardy and detrimental to the peace and the mental balance through which our soul is striving to express, but it is a living of suffering, of limitation, of lack, and frequent disaster. That is not what life is all about. Life is not only the lessons yet to be learned, but life is that great beauty, that truth, that joy, that peace, that happiness, that is in the very moment of our own acceptance.

God cannot—for God does not work that way—God cannot change your thought, for the divine law of God is to sustain. God is the greatest servant ever known or ever shall be known. Therefore, God sustains whatever thought, whatever pattern of mind, whatever attitude you choose to make. And the choice is ever up to us. If we choose thoughts in mind that do not bring joy and happiness and fulfillment, this great God sustains that thought that you alone have chosen to entertain.

And there is no prayer that will free you from the thought that you alone choose to entertain in mind. The only thing that will free us from the thoughts that we are thinking is the choice that we alone, in any moment, have to make. We may choose the thoughts that bring us that which our mind is dictating that it needs. That thought is then sustained by the very power that holds all of the planets in space. That is the Intelligence to rely on, for it is the only reliable Intelligence that we shall ever know or that we have ever known. It seems the frequent frailty of the human mind is to attempt, to *attempt* to rely upon that Intelligence and then, after a short period of time, to dictate that in certain areas that Intelligence is not at home. The reason that we think that way is because the thought and the dictate of our mind has not yet permitted that Divine Intelligence to bring us that which we are so dearly seeking in life.

This philosophy teaches to put God in it or forget it. Now we must all awaken, someday, to that great truth: that it is human to forgive, but that it is Divine to forget. And so when the statement is made to put God in it or forget it, we must become divine in that moment in that effort to forget. Now we know that it takes will to forget anything. It takes the will of the Divine within us to change our own thinking. And that will of the Divine is known as total acceptance.

Let us pause for a moment and take stock of the things that we accept in life. Let us be honest with our self in that analysis and we will become aware, to our great surprise, of how little we accept of the abundance of Life herself. We think we accept so much, but when we take stock of what we really do accept, we find we are extremely limited in our lives. Therefore, that demonstration of honesty with ourselves reveals to us how small our

God truly is, for our God is no greater and our God is no smaller than our willingness and our demonstration of acceptance.

It was stated once in our class that when man says, "O God, that's all I got," that God answers, "O man, if you're so smart, that's all you'll get." So when we dictate to the Divine, we are, in that moment, becoming greater than the Divine. Now we all know that we are not capable of doing the job of Infinite Intelligence. If we were capable, we would certainly be doing it. It is not within our power to create a life. It is within our power to abide by the divine, natural law through which life may come to earth. But we, as individuals, are not yet great enough to create life. But we are great enough to change a thought and change a life—our life. No man can change the thought of another, but every man can change the thought of himself. Philosopher upon philosopher has stated throughout the ages, "As you believeth in your heart shall you becometh," for the heart is the expression of the eternal soul, your true being.

Remember, my good friends, you are not the experiences of yesterday. You are not the experiences of today. You will not be the experiences of tomorrow. You are that Intelligence which is behind those experiences. It is your mental body that is being refined that it may become a pure instrument for the expression of your true being. You are not the things that you entertain in thought. You are the cause that is behind them. Do not be deluded by the changing thoughts of your mind, for they change moment by moment. For if you permit yourselves to be deluded by them, you will rob yourself of your divine right of peace, for they are the expression of creation and they are governed and controlled by dual law.

It is stated that energy follows attention. And so demonstrably true it is. Choose more wisely your thoughts, for they are the magnets that are pulling you to your own waiting experiences. There is nothing that can pull you anywhere that you alone do not set into motion. There is no God and no angel that controls your mind. You are the one that uses it for the good or abuses it through errors of ignorance. We are more than what we think we are, because we are thinking so very limited in our lives.

We did not begin our journey on this, the earth realm. We will not end our journey on this, the earth realm. And when we accept that demonstrable truth, we will free ourselves from ourselves. And it is the freeing ourselves from ourselves that is the true joy of Life herself.

Thank you.

DECEMBER 5, 1976

Church Lecture 61
The Fullness of Life

This part of the year, traditionally, for all of us, is a most important part of the year, for it is a time when we take a view of our past experiences and in so doing, at least in thought, we make decisions in hopes that our future will be better, at least in some ways, than our past has already been. In speaking this morning on, "The Fullness of Life," this philosophy, so demonstrable in its revelation of what is known as the divine will. We understand that divine will is total acceptance. We also understand that divine love is total consideration, and desire is divine expression. And yet, especially with the expression of the divine, called desire, we seem to stumble so frequently in the darkness of the seeming nights of satisfaction.

Why is it that all philosophers for untold centuries have taught, when man is freed from desire, then man is freed from his problems? There seems to be a contradiction in that type of teaching, if, in truth, desire is the expression of the Divinity. When our minds record in our consciousness a desire for anything, we make a decision and in that decision we establish for ourselves the law of judgment, for the decisions that we make are dependent upon the limited acceptances of our past experiences. And because our reliance, in that moment, is not upon God, from whence the desire is truly emanating, but it is relying upon what we have accepted and rejected in our life's experiences. The moment that our mind makes the judgment, the desire of God becomes, for us, the possession of man. It is in an error in our thinking that we experience what we call need. The need is an error in our thinking created by our own judgments, for by relying upon past experiences we judge the ways in which our desires can be fulfilled. And in that dictate, we are no longer in the divine flow of God's expression, but we are, in that moment, the victim of our own rejections and our own acceptances. We come in that moment under the law, the dual law, of the mind. For every day, there is a night, to the mind. For every right, there is a wrong. For every good, there is a bad. For every yes, there is a no.

We all can readily accept that the Divine Intelligence, known as God, denies the infinite life to no form. And so, when we, in our judgments, deny in our consciousness, then we have fallen, so to speak, from the grace of God, for we have become a judge in consciousness greater than the infinite, intelligent Power that is sustaining our very thought.

The fullness of life is the acceptance of life, but man dictates to God how life shall be. That, known as judgment, is the greatest cross we have to bear as we slowly, but surely, evolve throughout the planets and the universes that are beyond the counted hairs upon our head. So let us pause more frequently and let us first become aware of what we are rejecting in life. For it is those rejections in our mental attitudes of life that bring to us the necessary experiences and lessons of life that our soul may rise to higher planes of consciousness in the here and the now.

Man's need is life's denial, for his need is his own judgment and that judgment keeps him from the very thing he knows he should be doing. We all know what it is that we have come to earth for, but we so frequently forget our purpose of being here. Many are the centuries that have already passed and untold millions of experiences we have already grown through. Let us begin this new year as a new life by taking an honest view of what we have done with what we already have.

The fullness of life is like the raindrops that fall in this very moment of our experience. They do not fall in one place and deny the sustenance to another. They fall in keeping with immutable law and that law is governed by an Intelligence greater than all human minds. It shares its blessings and its goodness with all who are ready to accept it, but the readiness of acceptance does not come until we take an honest look at ourselves. To give thought to things outside our control is to enter the veil of illusion, for it, in the moment that we enter this veil of illusion by giving thought and power over us to things outside, that is the moment that we lose in consciousness the power of goodness that is our eternal right.

Many students over these years of teaching have stated what a struggle they have with tolerance. But what is intolerance? Intolerance is a judgment and a denial of the right, the eternal right, of God's expression. Because we do not agree with those with whom we associate, we believe that we are, then, intolerant. My good friends, it is the steps of awakening that we are in such judgment. Let us pause for a moment and let us listen to the voice that spoke so many years ago, when it stated so simply, "I am only a witness of time passing on. A witness of things that have come and gone. Never the jury or judge will I be, for I am the witness, the life and the tree." So let us, from this moment on, be the witness of life and then we will know. We will not have to seek. And we will not have to search. We will not have to ask where God is, for we will know God in our own acceptance.

Thank you.

JANUARY 2, 1977

Church Lecture 62
The Awakened Soul

In speaking on the lecture title this evening, "The Awakened Soul," the title implies the possibility of a soul asleep. And in a sense that is true, for we understand the soul to be an eternal, an inseparable part of the Divine Allsoul, known as God. We understand that, that that has no beginning has no ending. Therefore, our true being, the soul, has always been and, therefore, will always be. It is only the mind, the created substance, that comes and goes. And it is that created substance, known as the human mind, that is the veil between our eternal soul and the view that is our divine right of eternity itself.

So many people, in investigating this understanding and philosophy, come to investigate it not from a realm of investigation, but from a realm of judgment. The decision has already been made before they come to investigate. You cannot be objective with anything as long as you entertain thoughts and dictates of the human mind concerning it.

And so it is with the awakened soul. As we accept God's right of expression in all things, our soul awakens accordingly. To believe in a dual power of God and its opposite, called the devil, is to accept the duality of creation. But there is something above and beyond all creation, for there is something that sustains creation.

And so it is well mentioned in the Bible, so long ago, that God knows our thought before we think it. But how does God know our thought before we think it, unless God, the divine, infinite, eternal Intelligence, sustains the thought that we think? We know in this philosophy from the living, personal demonstration that man has been granted by the grace of Infinite Intelligence the right of choice. But what ever man chooses is man's right. And it is also God's right to sustain the thought, the act, and the deed that he chooses.

And so it is that our life and our earthly experiences are so filled with what we call needs. But when we view what needs truly are, from a realm of reason and objectivity, we see that they are merely the effects of neglect. Whatever man neglects is destined to cry for attention and energy. And so it is the business of life to be awakened that we may view clearly our own neglects. If we work, which is our right to do so, then we are not in the needs of the many things that we desire, for those needs are filled for we no longer neglect the very process necessary to bring unto us that which is rightfully ours.

And so the question arises within the mind, "What is rightfully mine?" And when that question rises, we forget what has already been. Man's right is the right of the Divine to the goodness that life has to offer. To the awakened soul, man experiences that goodness, for man no longer judges and dictates to God how it shall be.

This philosophy teaches that total acceptance is God's will or divine will, that total consideration is God's love, the love of the Divine. And each and every moment of our life we are using total consideration and total acceptance because we are demonstrating unto our self the total acceptance and total consideration of any level of consciousness that we are choosing in the moment of our own experience.

The suffering of life is the neglect of life. We neglect so much in our life and that is the reason that we suffer. Why does man neglect? Because man has risen in his self-importance and is dictating to divine Infinite Intelligence how all of his life shall be. He no longer flows in the stream of harmonious consciousness. He tries to stop along the shore. And in that effort, he suffers because he denies the right, God's right to all experience and all expression. And that that we deny in life becomes our own destiny.

Man says it's difficult to accept the authority of God. But it is not difficult in truth, for man is already accepting authority:

the authority of the dictates of his own mind that are based upon yesterday's experiences, denying the demonstrable truth of evolution. Without change, there is no evolution. And therefore, if man refuses to accept the possibility of constant change, then he becomes an obstruction to the divine, eternal right of God.

Many times we have spoken in this philosophy that man is the greatest borrower in the universe, for all that man thinks he has is only loaned for a time. And man does not know how long that time shall be. When we accept that truth, then we will no longer suffer the pains of need, for we will no longer neglect the demonstrable truth of evolution. We have entered this earth realm not as something new, as a divine principle. The only newness is the slumber that lies between us and the great eternity. For man to entertain the belief that he entered earth as a new beginning is to accept an ending, for all of life demonstrates that truth. So man's thoughts, garnered here on earth, have beginnings and man's thoughts, garnered here on earth, have endings. When we accept that truth, when we view our lives and we know inside of ourselves that we're not thinking exactly the same as we did those years past, then we know we must learn to let go. For whatever man lets go of, God takes control of.

And so it is the goodness in life that we know deep inside of us is our true home. And because we know that and our minds dictate how it shall be, we suffer the pain and the loss. Again and again the truth is revealed to those who are ready, willing, and able to accept it. But we cannot experience in life what we are not willing to accept. All of our experiences reveal our own acceptances. Remember, my friends, you have been granted by divine grace the right of choice. All you need to do is to pause and think.

This philosophy teaches the Law of Personal Responsibility, that you and you alone, as an eternal soul, are responsible to God. You are not responsible to man. You are responsible to God.

And remember that God knows our thoughts before we think them. And that responsibility is very clear. When you experience things that are distasteful to you, remember it was your choice. God simply sustains that choice. It is his love and his will of total consideration and total acceptance, but you alone have made the choice. And only you alone can accept something better. Nothing in life will ever be better until you first accept. It is through your own acceptance that change is made possible for you, the gracious, harmonious, and joyous way. If we refuse to accept the right, the infinite right of evolution, known as change, then we're swimming against the tide of life. And the tide of life is greater than the thoughts of man. We are the ones, and we alone, who will sink. But be not discouraged, we shall rise again.

All of us here know that there is something better than what we have already experienced. But let us not fall into the judgment of how to attain it. Let us graciously accept all that life has to offer and in that acceptance know we are moving along the stream of consciousness to a heaven that waits us, not in some distant century, not in some guarantee from so-called death. For our mind goes with us and all of those thoughts and attitudes, for we are the fathers of those emotions and the mothers. They belong to us, for we have created them. It is God's love and consideration that sustains them.

And so remember, my good friends, when you view the sawdust in another's eye and you act accordingly, you are blinded by the plank that is in your own. But when you view the sawdust in another's eye and you accept God's right of it being there, you are free to enter the gates of understanding beyond which lies the peaceful, eternal shores of joy and bliss.

Thank you.

FEBRUARY 6, 1977

Church Lecture 63
Harmony, The Law of Health

This morning's topic for discussion is, "Harmony, The Law of Health." And it will behoove us to first consider the untold eons of time that our soul has already been evolving, through many lives and in many, many different planets and levels of consciousness. The eternal soul is the witness in so-called time, designed to be ever the observer and not the observed. But as man observes the objects of creation or form, the tendency of the human mind is to identify with that that it views. And it is through this process of identification with the objects that we observe that we become bound by so-called limit or form or creation. For as we, in our observations, identify through the vehicles known as the human mind, we believe that we are the object of our view. And it is in that believing or bondage of identification that man experiences what is known as discord or disease. For in the viewing and identification processes man sees a great variety of manifestation. Man sees and views contradictions and identifies with the dual law, known as creation or limit or form.

How does man free himself from that limited process of his human mind? Through an education of his mind. An education is something that takes place when man makes the effort, the daily, moment-by-moment effort to accept the infinite, divine right of God to express through a variety of levels of consciousness. For he who believes, which is identification with the authority of man—whoever believes in the authority of man is controlled by the authority of man. But he who accepts the divine, infinite right of God to express through all levels of consciousness, whoever accepts that and makes the effort to understand the level that is being expressed, is freed to live in peace and harmony. Now this identification or bondage is what is taking place at all times whenever we are controlled by our limited human mind.

It has been stated in this philosophy, and many that have preceded it, that peace and peace alone is the power, that peace, in truth, is God. To bring peace into our lives is not what we should be seeking. To permit the peace that exists already within us to express itself should be our constant effort. For we, in truth, are an infinite, eternal, intelligent energy, called by many soul. Beyond soul is a formless, free spirit. As it expresses through the Law of Identification, it individualizes and gathers unto itself an untold multitude of experiences.

The teaching in this philosophy is that like attracts like and becomes the Law of Attachment, the Law of Personal Responsibility. Again and again, the teaching goes that all of life is the mirror, the mirror reflecting our own thoughts, our own attitudes. Because we are the fathers and mothers of our thoughts, we can change all experience in our lives. The experience being the effect of those thoughts. And so through this struggle of creation and through the bondage of identification the good, in truth, is rising. For sooner or later, we begin to think more deeply about our lives. We begin to see that we are not the limited thoughts that we used to think we are. We are more than what we believe, for we are the cause beyond the belief. We are more than what we see, for we are that that causes the seeing. So let us awaken our consciousness in this the moment of which we are truly aware. Let us truly become the observers for we are, our eternal life, expressing through this limited form. This body that we have now is known as the temple of God. Everything that happens to it reveals what our attitudes and thoughts truly are. The particular bodies that we have earned in our evolution here on earth reveal to us our attitudes of mind, our rejections and acceptances of times long past.

So many people in this day and age are interested in these dimensions in which we truly are expressing. They want to see them and they want to hear them. They want to have the personal experience. I assure you, my good friends, the personal experience of anything, be it an experience of material, physical substance or mental or spiritual substance, is ever dependent upon the Law of Identification. You cannot experience anything that you do not first identify with. If you identify wholly and completely with a physical dimension, then that is the only thing that you will be consciously aware of experiencing. If you identify only with your limited mental acceptances, then that's all you will ever be aware of experiencing.

We are an eternal soul, expressing through a mental and physical body. Our levels of consciousness are numbered by eighty-one. And those numbers multiply in consciousness through your own acceptances. Let us broaden our horizons in this the moment of which we are consciously aware. Let us broaden them by our own acceptance.

Acceptance in this philosophy is known as the divine will, the will of God, the power that sustains us. If we insist upon identifying with poverty, then we will never experience wealth. If we insist upon identifying with poor health, then we will never experience good health. It's all in our hands. The Infinite has given us charge over all creation, but the creation we must first work upon is the creation of our own being. From the elements of nature it has been refined, only to return, this physical body, to the elements of nature ever in keeping with the eternal Law of Evolution. For all that is form is in an eternal process of change and our body is in form and so is our mind.

This teaching reveals that negative faith is known by man as fear, the authority of the limited mind over your eternal life. Why does man fear and rise his intellect in his mind superior in his life over his eternal being? He does it in keeping with the very law of creation and it is known as the Law of Self-Preservation. So whatever you identify with, you put yourself in and you become the very object of your identity. And you strive, through that process of the mind, to preserve what you have identified with. And that preservation process is known in this philosophy as fear. But let us use reason and awaken wisdom from within our soul and ask ourselves the honest question, "What I have identified with in yesteryear has served its purpose in my evolution. It was necessary in keeping with the laws that I alone had established and it served its purpose." You no longer need to be bound by the attitudes and beliefs of yesteryear, for you are moving ever forward. Move graciously through the process known as evolution, the constant process of change. For the human mind cannot stem the tide of change, for change is the divine right of the Infinite Intelligence. The blade of grass does not remain the same year after year. A petrified opinion never freed a human soul.

And so, my friends, as you face each day, as you face each moment, accept the new experience that you and you alone are personally responsible for. Accept the experience, not with an attitude of mind that it will last for how long, not with an attitude of mind that you will be bound in your poverty and destitution or poor health. Accept the experience as the effect of an error of ignorance that takes place within the human mind, for it is an error of the human mind that we believe and do not observe. For when man believes and identifies, he is no longer the observer. He loses the soul faculty of perspective. He loses his own perception for it is blinded, that soul faculty from where wisdom rises supreme in time, it is blinded by the judgment of the human mind.

So let us live the peace that is our divine, eternal right. Let us live it this moment in all things and in all ways. For that is why we have evolved to earth, that is the true purpose of our soul's journey: to bring peace and harmony over all creation. That is what the Bible meant when it stated, "I have given you charge over all creation," for you have charge over all thoughts and all things.

Declare the right, your divine right. Let those express through the levels that they so choose. Let us remember the right of the Intelligence that is the cause behind it. Let us free ourselves from the judgments, the errors of ignorance. Let us lift our hearts to something that is greater than what our minds can possibly conceive, for that that is conceived is destined to its own death. And because man has identified with conception man has destined himself to identify with death. There is no difference between birth and death. It is, in truth, one and the same thing. It is merely a process of change. We conceive and die each moment to thoughts. And so it is that they reveal the forms they truly are. If you want the evidence that your minds dictate, then take control of your mind and your soul will view the eternal life and the eons of time that you have already expressed.

Thank you.

MARCH 6, 1977

Church Lecture 64
Promise, The Destiny of Life

[*The recording of this lecture began moments after Mr. Goodwin began speaking.*]

—to choose between his own thoughts or to choose from the inspiration that rises from his eternal soul, God's promise is indeed fulfilled. It's like a man that entertains the thought of being tired; to entertain that type of thinking takes more energy, utilizes more energy than the thought of being filled with energy. The reason that it takes more energy to entertain thoughts of tiredness is because the thought of being tired is dependent upon the judgments of the human mind. And the judgments of the human mind are always dual or contradicting, for the human mind, being a mental substance of creation, is a positive and a negative instrument. So when man entertains thoughts of tiredness, he is entertaining thoughts of self and, in so doing, is becoming a law unto himself. By that I mean to say that the promise of God, which is the fullness of the divine law, is to be receptive to the whole, to be an open channel or vehicle of acceptance through which the divine, infinite Energy that sustains all of life may flow without the obstructions created by the human mind.

And so it is that man in his many life experiences slowly, but surely, is going through the process necessary for him to, in time, accept the personal responsibility of his own experiences and his own life. The sustaining of life is the law of God, and all around and about us we see that demonstration.

This philosophy teaches to love all life and know the Light, for to love all life is to rise in consciousness to the godhood that is, in truth, our real home. For God demonstrates his love for all of life, for it is God that sustains all of life. Now God has been called many things. And of those many things man must realize that he and he alone expresses God in the ways that he and he alone chooses.

Each and every day of our life we are experiencing the dictates of our own mind. And those experiences continue on through evolution, through incarnation upon incarnation, until man learns the true lesson that life has to offer. And that lesson is the lesson of God's will, the divine will; it's known as total acceptance. Whenever the limited will of the human mind rises to dictate in any experience, in *any* experience its authority over the right of divine will, then man suffers. Man suffers not from his acceptance in life; man suffers from his denials in life. And so this philosophy teaches that our destiny—our denials, in truth, are our destinies. So when we wonder what we're going to do or where we're going to be, then all we need to do is to become aware of our own denials. For each denial that we have in consciousness is a rising of the self-will of man over the divine right of God. We all know—and our experiences in life [reveal it]—when we accept the right of the experience to express itself, we become free from the payment of the experience. Because in that moment, through our own acceptance, does the will of God flow through our consciousness, for we have accepted and that acceptance is that moment of divine will. But man slowly, but surely, in this life and lives yet to come and lives that have already been, is gradually learning that great lesson.

And so when you have something that you desire to accomplish, remember, in those efforts to accomplish you must pay the price of the control of the human mind, for without the control of your mind, the limited laws of the mind become established.

For many centuries our individual souls have been evolving. And there are many, many centuries that yet face us in our evolution until there is a total acceptance within us of all experiences that our minds encounter. Illumination is directly dependent upon our willingness to accept. Without that willingness, there is no illumination. Without that acceptance, there is no fullness of God's love. So let us think now in this moment in this experience, what is it within us that is dictating? Is it our eternal soul or is it the limited experiences that this short earth life has already given to us? My good friends, lessons are given in many different ways that hopefully, in some day, we will in truth accept the cause of them.

The greatest failing known to man is the failing of placing the blame and responsibility in life's experiences outside onto someone else or something else. This is one of the greatest delusions ever created by the human mind, but this delusion does, in truth, serve a good purpose: it serves the purpose of preserving the rigidity of our own will. It is that rigidity that slowly, but surely, is being broken. It is that rigidity that is man's true suffering. For a wise man long ago stated that a petrified opinion never saved a human soul. So it is our opinions that we have become addicted to. It is our opinions that, in truth, are causing our lack of goodness in our life, but those opinions, created by our minds, can be changed. They're changed through the power of prayer. For the mind to try to change an opinion that it has already accepted is only a battle and a house divided. It is through honest prayer that we are freed from these dictates of yesterday. It is through our own constant effort of prayer in all of our endeavors, in all of our thoughts, place God, that Divine Principle, in your thought and God will move whatever mountain your minds may have already created as your obstruction. If you will remember that in each and every moment of your life, you will live to see, through experience, that there is a power and an intelligence that is totally neutral, totally impartial that brings the promise of your own soul's aspiration.

In reviewing the experiences of our lives, we can see, so clearly, how many times we have thought one thing and manifested the direct opposite. To think one thing and demonstrate the direct opposite is the law of failure. That law, so often, so many of us in our short earth life have already demonstrated. Why does man think one thing and manifest the direct opposite? We must ask our self that honest question.

In this philosophy, which teaches that there are eighty-one levels of consciousness, that the eternal soul is in a constant process of moving through those levels of consciousness, that it is through honest prayer that man is able to sustain the soul in one level of consciousness to accomplish and fulfill the law established on that level of consciousness. If that is difficult for you to understand, then stop and think of the many, many things you cannot remember. Think of how faulty the human memory seems to be. It's not really faulty at all. It simply reveals that man, experiencing a certain experience on level twenty and moving to level six at another moment, does not, on level six, know what took place on level twenty, unless he has gained, through total acceptance, some degree of illumination.

And so it is that man thinks one thing on one level of consciousness, moves in a moment to another level of consciousness and demonstrates the direct opposite. Because man, through a lack of awareness, has become a house divided. And the Bible teaches us, long ago, that a house divided cannot stand. So let us, my good friends, no longer be a house divided. Let us awaken within ourselves to these many levels of consciousness and when we say something and establish that law, let us unite that we may be aware of the law that we established yesterday. And no matter what we think it takes, let us fulfill those dictates until we have the sufficient experience to know beyond a shadow of any doubt that whatever happens to us in life eternal we are the only and direct cause thereof.

Think of all the things that you have thought that you would like to do, and think of the many excuses that rise within your mind that says, "That was the reason I did not accomplish it." I assure you, my good friends, the easiest thing in the world is to accomplish what you desire. The difficulty is in knowing what you desire and sustaining the effort necessary to do it. The law is most impartial. The law works for everyone. But it does not work for us unless we work with it.

This philosophy reveals these simple laws of God. They are available to all of God's children. But unless we are willing, through the Law of Continuity, to sustain what, in truth, we desire in life, then it shall not come into our being, but we shall continue to be successful in our failures in life. A man must say, "Well, I don't choose this and I don't choose that." And in the next moment, he says the direct opposite. Don't you understand? My good friends, when we face ourselves, when we become honest with ourselves, we know where we are and we also know why we are where we are. So if you are not fulfilled in where you believe that you are, then that is opportunity knocking at your door telling you, very simply, make a decision in your consciousness in this moment in the now. And make that decision with sincere prayer and you will have the help that is needed to fulfill it.

Man's fears plague him each day, every day. They plague the mind because they have been sustained by the mind for so very long. They don't need to do that if we make the effort to change our thinking. Life, the effect of our thought, changes when we change our thought. And so, many people come to this philosophy in the hopes of a better life. That better life is waiting for everyone, but it is directly dependent upon their willingness to change.

Thank you.

APRIL 3, 1977

Church Lecture 65
Six Years of Serenity

I'm sure that those of you who have been with us since the beginnings of this church, perhaps, have noted on this our sixth anniversary that whenever we induct new members we no longer read the words that have been set down in our manual by our National Association verbatim. And we have found it's no longer necessary to ask new members in this church to promise to support financially, as well as spiritually, the efforts of this church, for by accepting the Law of Personal Responsibility, it is not necessary to make such other promises.

My good friends, it was on May the second of 1971 that these church doors were opened. It was on August the twentieth of 1968 that, with a group of four people and myself, the Serenity Spiritualist Association was founded. It had been my hopes and desires at that time in '68 to found a spiritual retreat. The thought of a church was certainly the lowest on my priority list of values, that is, for myself. I had experienced the so-called good and the so-called opposite by being a member of another church for over ten years, namely the Golden Gate Church in San Francisco. And at that time of my evolution and growth, seeing so much personality and seeming conflict of interest, I had made a decision—and whenever man makes a decision it's known as a judgment—that that is not what I would be interested in being involved in, namely a church. Because a church represents a group of people.

And so I had decided I did want to carry on with my spiritual endeavors. But a nice, spiritual retreat with forty acres of land, if two people couldn't get along there was plenty of space to walk and be at peace. And so it was that in February of 1971, February the twenty-second to be exact, I received what I can look back at, perhaps, as the heaviest birthday gift I have ever received: it was a request from the world of spirit to open a church. To me that looked like a great burden from the experiences of the years preceding that request by the Spirit. However, being assured by those angels that any and all decisions governing the church organization, all its rules and regulations and any choice that had to be made would be made by them, I then agreed to open a church in order that this philosophy may be presented to a much larger group of people than it was being presented to in my home at that time. And so I look over these six long, but short, years and I view the growth and the evolution of this association. On the dedication of this church six years ago, the Spirit informed us that many would come through these doors, that they would never be denied the divine right or choice: to go or to grow.

Now what do we mean about growing and or going? All of us in our evolution must face the effects, which are known as experiences, of our own judgments. Whenever we decide what is right and what is wrong, whenever we decide what we shall do and what we won't do, we establish the dual Law of Creation. And so it is that we are constantly faced with the effects or experiences of our own judgments.

This church was founded on the basic principle of personal responsibility, founded upon the total acceptance, which we understand today to be divine or God will; that life, in truth, is the way that we alone are making it; that life, in truth, is indeed the way that we are taking it. Therefore, we do have at any moment in consciousness the divine right to accept the peace, the harmony, the promise of God, the fulfillment and the joy of life.

It is in our mind that our peace or our wars are waged. The greatest deception ever created by the human mind is to look outside of itself and judge its own personal life, for to so do is to guarantee the fulfillment of the Law of Comparison. We live in a world of creation. A world that demonstrates its manifestation of variety. Our soul is constantly in a process of movement, moving within our consciousness through eighty-one levels of expression. At any moment that we decide that a certain attitude, a certain thought is truly us, then we are controlled, in that moment, by experiences that are, in truth, founded in our yesteryears. And so it is the very purpose of this organization to bring this simple, demonstrable truth to the world that is seeking it.

Our life can be what we so desire it to be. But in order for that to take place, we must learn to accept. It is the denials in life that are our own destinies. For each time we deny the divine right, God's right of expression—and our denials are effects of judgment—so each time that we permit our minds to judge, we establish the Law of Denial and, in so doing, are destined to experience all that is necessary to free us from judging. For our understanding of God is a God of divine, neutral Infinite Intelligence. All things in creation are sustained by this neutral, infinite Divine Love. This Intelligence does not in any way demonstrate what we know as the Law of Denial. For if it did, it would no longer be a neutral, impartial, intelligent Energy. Man, when he is in a state of peace, is receptive to this Intelligence, and, being receptive to it, becomes it in the moment of his own total acceptance.

We look around and are quickly deluded by the variety of expression. We do not often spend the time to investigate. This philosophy teaches that presumption is the Law of Descent. It also teaches to investigate everything and to presume nothing. We understand that judgment is the steps down to hell, that we lean upon the rail of pride; for in truth, it is our pride that makes our judgments. And so as all philosophies have taught: humbleness is the path of peace; acceptance is the door through which we enter into paradise. Let us enter into that heavenly consciousness by making the daily, moment-by-moment effort to free our self from the judgment throne that is crowned by pride.

All of the disturbances that enter our lives are the effects of these judgments. They are the laws of denial. For there is a part of us, known as the human mind, that has been designed by an Infinite Intelligence, sustained by an Infinite Intelligence, and that part of us, known as the human mind, is designed to preserve whatever has been fed into it. And so we must, from our own efforts, separate truth from creation: our eternal life, known as our soul, from our temporal life, known as our human mind. For this eternal part of us has always been and therefore, it shall always be. Our soul has experienced untold numbers of experiences. It has recorded much and has entered this earth in order to continue on with its own unfoldment.

Many people have come, and continue to come, to this school and to this church seeking something better. This philosophy offers a demonstrable way to something better, but only through the efforts of the seeker can they find it. So often when we think that we want something better in our lives, we do not consider what we must give up to gain that something better. Usually there are certain disturbing experiences that we no longer want in our lives, but there are a few pleasurable ones that we want to keep. I can assure you, my good friends, the disturbing experiences within your lives are inseparably related to the pleasurable experiences in your lives. And so if it is the path of peace and happiness that you are seeking, then you must be willing, through study and application and through daily effort, to give it all to what is called God: to give the good as well as the seeming bad. In spiritual unfoldment you cannot be a miser. You must give it all or nothing at all. For in keeping with the Law of Divine Will, known as total acceptance, you cannot give with reservation. For each time you give with reservation you are standing outside of the divine flow. You cannot give with judgment. You cannot give with dictate of what you will receive. For giving from those levels of consciousness are dual experiences yet to return unto you.

This philosophy, as many philosophies preceding it, teaches the greatest gift that you may give in life is the gift of self. But what is the gift of self? It is the gift of what you believe is you. Now each moment, each day, each year, we believe differing things are us. Whenever we are entertaining a desire and awaiting its fulfillment within our lives, at those times we believe that that is us. But desires, like days, they quickly change. And so yesterday's desire is not today's desire. And today's desire is not tomorrow's desire. So whenever we permit ourselves to believe that we are the desire that we are entertaining at any moment, then we have deluded ourselves. For we, the eternal us, is formless, changeless, whole, complete, and free.

Think, my good students, of what it is you want in life. And whatever it is you want in life, whatever is your number one priority, give that, your greatest desire, to God. For that, then, is your total self, for the mind believes that it is the desire that it entertains. And so the greatest gift you have to give is the gift of your own totality. And when you give that, you become, in that moment, an inseparable part of a united Whole, called God. And when you unite with that great Intelligence of the universes, to you, in that moment, all things are. You longer have want, need, and desire, for you have once again gone home. And being home, you awaken in consciousness to your true divinity. No longer do you race and search. No longer are you the victims of fluctuating desires. You are the united Whole in the moment of your own total acceptance.

Thank you.

MAY 1, 1977

Church Lecture 66
Inspiration

In this morning's topic for discussion, "Inspiration," we must view this soul faculty known as inspiration as an inseparable part of a trinity, for inspiration flows through the soul faculty of reason and consideration. In this association it was long ago established as a principle and a policy for all of our speakers and all of our students to come before you without thought of what they are to speak about. For to give thought on what you are to say is to rely upon the human mind that is limited by the experiences that have already been recorded in it. That is not what we understand to be inspiration. For inspiration, flowing through the soul faculty of reason and consideration, must be free to consider all. And the human mind is not designed to consider all, for what the human mind considers is ever dependent upon what it is willing to accept and to reject.

And so it is, my friends, that when we rely upon our minds to be inspired or to find the way through any seeming obstruction, we are depending and relying upon a vehicle that guarantees a duality; it guarantees a yes for every no. And so we must consider something that is greater than the limited vehicle of form to inspire us. I am sure that we will all agree that this life, as we view it, cannot possibly be the wholeness of truth, for if it was, then truth would not free us. And so we must consider something that is greater than the experiences in life that we have already encountered.

As we make the effort in our ever-growing and expanding evolution, we soon discover that there is something that the mind cannot grasp. There is something that comes from somewhere that the mind cannot control. So often we take so much in our life's experiences for granted, for the law clearly states that man values only that which he makes an effort to attain. And so it is the mind not being capable, not being capable of creating life does not have the true value for what is known as life. The mind is designed to accomplish many things, but it was never designed to accomplish life itself, the spark of divinity. For the mind is a vehicle of expression, which is the effect of a higher vehicle of expression. And above and beyond all the vehicles through which intelligence expresses, there is the formless and there is the free.

The formless and the free spirit, which we truly are, is not something that you are going to find in some future century in some future realm of existence. It is something that is in the very moment of your acceptance. But if you make a judgment of what it is and how you will attain it, then you are far from experiencing it. For that judgment and dictate is a revelation that we are yet in the mental vehicle of expression and far from our formless, free spirit.

So let us, in our considerations, let us first think, and think more deeply about what we really are and what we are really doing. The law clearly states and demonstrates that man is a law unto himself. And so often have you heard that the wheels of God grind slow, but sure. Whatever it is that you are presently experiencing, you may be rest assured that it is in the process of passing. It is when things within our mind are in the process of passing from our consciousness that we experience the great struggle and the suffering. The reason that we experience the suffering and struggle as experiences are passing through our consciousness is because, through our errors of ignorance, we believe that we are those experiences. It is our belief in creation that is our conscious awareness of creation. It is our belief in the experiences that we encounter that makes us, through the Law of Identity, an inseparable part of those experiences.

It has been known by many philosophers for many ages that the greatest difficulty of all difficulties is to help man to change his beliefs. It has taken untold centuries for the planet Earth, the people upon it, to evolve to the present state of evolution. And it will take centuries yet to be for man to accept the freedom that his very soul is crying out for. It will take centuries for the masses because beliefs are rigidly held to. We hold to our beliefs so tenaciously because we believe that we are them. And through that belief do we have our ups and downs and are we robbed of the peace that passeth all understanding. Take hold of your thought. Awaken yourself consciously to what your beliefs really are. For as man has stated long ago, "As you believeth in your heart, so shall you becometh." For it is the Law of Identity and you have, through that belief, identified with and become a part of the experiences of your life.

It may seem to be a very simple thing to sit and say, "I shall change my beliefs. I no longer believe in illness. I no longer believe in poverty. I no longer believe in suffering. I no longer believe in the struggles of life." But there is one soul faculty that must be awakened to its fullness before the transformation can take place. And that soul faculty is known as the soul faculty of inspiration, reason, and consideration. When you awaken within your conscious mind the fullness of that triune soul faculty, then you will have qualified yourself to flood your consciousness with the infinite, demonstrable truth that you are formless and you are free.

You drive your cars along the highway, but you know you are not your automobiles. You wear your suits of clothes, but you know you are not the things you wear. And yet in the greatest of all illusions, the illusion of time and experience, you wear your physical suits, your human bodies, and believe that you are them. It is because, my good friends, you have identified with the limitation of form. You have identified and because of that overidentification you believe and, therefore, you become.

Surely it is reasonable, and common sense and practical to believe in the goodness of life, which is in truth your own divinity. But to believe in the goodness of life, you must identify with the goodness of life. How does man identify when he has lost control of his mind and thoughts fly, seemingly, free through his mind? Man must first learn the simple lesson of life: the lesson of control of the self; the control of the thoughts that pass through the minds of self. For the greatest gift to God is the gift of self and you cannot give to God what is not within your possession to give to God. So first, we must consider control.

And when thoughts pass through our mind that are not harmony—for harmony is the Law of Health, and the Law of Health is also inseparable to the Law of Wealth. For that that is healthy is abundant, harmonious, and good. And so to believe in the opposite, to believe in lack and limitation, to believe in poverty is to be a demonstration of ignorance. For then we are demonstrating discord and denial. And in demonstrating denial and discord, we are becoming, in our human throne, greater than the God of Gods that frees us.

So think, my good friends, think what a thought passing through your mind does not only to you, the recipient of it, but what it does to the world, as you, by receiving, send it forth into the universe to make a deposit in universal consciousness of discord and denial. Each and every form has the infinite, divine right of its expression. And in that infinite, divine right of expression it has the infinite, eternal Law of Personal Responsibility. We are responsible to all creation. And every philosophy ever brought to your world has taught that eternal truth. You are responsible for the thoughts that you permit to pass through your mind. Be they thoughts of harmony and peace, then you will be the living demonstration of health, wealth, and happiness. Be they thoughts of discord and denial, then ye shall reap the effects of the transgression of God's immutable, divine law.

Let us not be discouraged for what has gone yesterday. Let us remember that eternity is the moment of which we are consciously aware. So let us work with the eternal moment and let us let yesterday go. Let us accept, consider, reason, and believe our right to a God of peace and harmony flowing through our consciousness. And as we accept and believe that demonstrable truth, life's experiences will be more pleasing, harmonious, and we will live a fuller life, a more abundant life. And we will, in that living, grant the right to all creation. We will then become an instrument of the Divine, to serve our true purpose in life: to assist all of creation to awaken to their divine right of joy and happiness on this earthly realm.

To those of us who have, in the present or in the past, looked forward to a heaven that takes place for us after we leave the earth realm, consider something a little different, my friends. Heaven is what you yourself have accepted and are demonstrating. If your thoughts are those of peace and harmony, then your life is abundant, good, and full. But if it is the opposite, it will not change when you leave your physical bodies, for you take with you your mental bodies, for they are composed of mental substance.

Thought is not composed of physical substance. Mind is not composed of physical substance. It is composed of mental substance and it expresses through a physical body, here, in this earth realm. When you, in your evolution, awaken to these mental realms, then you will see the thoughts of men. But first you will see the thoughts of your own mind. They will not all be pleasant, for not all your feelings or decisions or judgments are pleasant. But they are yours. That is the house in which you are living. You are living, my good friends, in that house this moment. But you can clean up that house; you can change it. And one of our basic teachings is very simple: put your house in order each and every morning before confusion sets in. So let's clean up our house and then we can move to clean up our own backyards. Those houses are built by your thoughts and your attitudes. They are the mansions, the palaces, or the hovels in which you live. Because we are not, perhaps, yet awakened to those homes that we have built does not exempt us from the law nor from the home we must enter.

In my thirty-seven years in serving on this Earth planet, I have yet to find a heaven where harps play eternally beautiful music. I do not believe that it is because I have an adversity to harp music. I do not believe that it is because I have an adversity to any music. But in all of my years of experiences in these other dimensions, I have yet to find a heaven of that description. And I remember many years ago, when I was very young, and I asked that question about heaven. The answer came very clearly: "The workers win." You see, my friends, our heaven is within our consciousness. It is dependent upon your acceptance and your beliefs, for those are the laws that you have demonstrated. Do not sit back on your haunches and believe that heaven is awaiting you and, therefore, it shall be, for you must demonstrate the law for yourself.

So think, my students, and think again, more deeply than ever before. All of life is the effect. All the outward manifestations are the direct revelations of inner attitudes of mind. How many times in the course of a day do we ask the question, "What is my attitude of mind this moment?" It has become such a habitual thing—our attitudes of mind—that we are rarely conscious of them. We are very conscious of the effects of our attitudes of mind, but so rarely aware of the attitude itself.

You have seen in your experiences in life, and often questioned, how adults could, under certain circumstances, act like immature, little children. The teaching of this philosophy is simple and clear: desire has no light. And so man must first work on the control of his own desires, the control of his own thoughts that he may, through the faculty of reason, the light that transfigures us, educate the desires that he entertains in consciousness. And in that education of those desires shall the veil of darkness disappear before his eyes and he will see beyond the physical substance that he has viewed in these earthly realms. He will see beyond, to the forms that thoughts take. If they are ever in good, then they are in God and they are harmonious and that that is harmonious is beautiful. And that that is discordant is its opposite.

So let us, my friends, become more aware of our thoughts, more aware of our attitudes that we may grow up here and now. Grow up and face the ability to respond to our own acts and deeds—not to put the blame outside, not to put the blame on others and, surely, not to put the blame on God.

As I stated in the beginning of this discussion, it's our beliefs. Let us believe in a God that is good, in a God that is abundant. And ever dependent upon your belief and the laws that you demonstrate, will God express through you his goodness, his abundance, his health, his wealth, and his happiness. Let us discard the false gods that we so tenaciously hold to in our judgments, that we so tenaciously hold to in our dictates. Let us move on from those false gods of creation and move to the one infinite, divine God that sustains all things in the universes. And in moving to that acceptance and belief, we will no longer be so concerned about pieces of green paper; we will no longer be so concerned about what others are thinking or doing; we will no longer be so concerned about what yet is to happen, for we will know. For we believe and God demonstrates.

Thank you.

JUNE 5, 1977

Church Lecture 67
Man's Law

This topic for today, so appropriate in the celebration of freedom in our country, is entitled, "Man's Law." It would behoove us first to consider the soul faculties, which are, in truth, the attributes or expressions of our eternal being, in comparison with what is known as the sense functions of the mental body that our soul is presently expressing through. So often in philosophies there seems such a contradiction to give up one thing to gain another, instead of considering a harmonious blending or balancing of both. We all understand, I am sure, that man, in truth, is a triune expression, for he is spirit, expressing through a mental and physical body.

Now whereas the body that we are now aware of is composed of the elements of this particular planet, it returns to this planet. And so it is that we must consider, in our consciousness, this eternal stream of evolution of which we are, in truth, an inseparable part.

So often in our mundane, earthly experiences we wait, so to speak, for so many, many things of creation. And little do we know that waiting is a function of the human mind, compared to patience, a faculty of our eternal soul. And so we are considering at this moment the difference between the faculties of the soul and the functions of the mental body. When man is patient, a soul faculty, then man has the support and the understanding of all the soul faculties. He has faith, poise, and humility. And he has the very power that will transfigure him, known as the faculty of reason. For, you see, my friends, when we express our soul, uncluttered by the sense functions, then we do not have to question, we do not have to wonder, and we do not have to wait. For we are in the eternal consciousness in our soul faculties and we know in that moment. Therefore, patience loses the pain of waiting. Bringing about a balance between our eternal being, called soul, and our temporary body, known here, in this earthly realm, as mental and physical substance, takes a bit of effort on a constant, daily program.

So often in these spiritual paths in life man rushes in where angels fear to tread because he views the possibility of attaining the many things that he has desired for so long by making some effort to understand any philosophy or any particular teaching. But he does not view the time that it is going to take before he, as a student—or she—will accept the necessary steps to their own attainment. In keeping with this understanding of a triune expression, we can awaken that truth within us when we still the functions of our being, when we still the human mind.

It is stated that destiny in life is the effect of our denials. And so it is that denial or rejection is the principle of the law established by man or by the human mind. When man, viewing creation, makes a choice, which is his divine right, he does not stop with choosing. He moves from choice to justification and to judgment. Those are the very three expressions of the sense functions of the human mind that establish the Law of Destiny. It is not in choosing that the law is established, but it is in the need of the human mind to support, to protect its choice. That is what establishes the Law of Destiny.

For the human mind is commonly referred to as the throne of negative faith. For whenever we rely upon our mind for anything we establish the Law of Mind and that law fears. It fears because, in its illusion, it believes that it owns or possesses. And it is in that illusion that we justify and we judge. Because of that, man is faced with a constant panorama of so-called loss and gain. Man is filled, in his days, with fears that he is not even consciously aware of. It is stated that man fears the unknown, but the unknown exists only to the human mind. The unknown is not unknown to your true being, for it cannot be, for you are, in truth, an inseparable part of that whole. And so we find that when man makes his choice and justifies and judges, that man closes himself off, so to speak, from the universal goodness which he is, in truth, an inseparable part thereof.

We must ask our self the question, "What is, in truth, our need to be different?" Is this something that rises from our eternal being? And the answer quickly comes, "How can you, in truth, be different from what you truly are?" What is this need? Then the need, we must see clearly, rises from the human mind, for the human mind views variety. The human mind, being a part of creation, sees creation. But the eternal being sees it as a passing scene, for in truth it is but a dream.

All of experience and all of life is taking place within our being. That is, in truth, the only place that it is taking place. And so with that acceptance of simple truth, life can be what you choose to make it if you do not fear to possess it. It is in the effort of the human mind to possess that man finds the true struggle in life. He who does not seek to possess has all that he could possibly use wisely. And let us look at our life and see how much we have gathered up, how much we have garnered unto our self.

We must view our mental realms as an abode, a home, in which we are, in truth, living. For we are the ones, in truth, that are living with our thoughts and that are living with our feelings. Now we, we alone have created those thoughts and we alone have created and sustained those feelings. So in understanding that mental home in which we are residing, we can begin to clean house. For we live in a mental home that is so filled with so many things that it's difficult for us to find peace within it. We must awaken within ourselves; as we open our physical eyes in the morning, we must look within, become aware that it is within—what we are, in truth, experiencing. It is our view. And our view in life is directly dependent upon the judgments that we have made.

And so in your daily activities when you go out into the world of creation and you experience so many different things, remember, your refusal to accept the demonstrable, harmonious laws of life is your fear to protect what you think you possess. And the things that we think we possess, by that very attitude of mind, are in the very process of leaving us. Look at your life to this day. See the many things that you have garnered and gathered up unto yourselves. Much of it has gone, but we keep adding more. We add and add until the mountain before us becomes such an obstruction that the light barely shines at all.

Let us think each day. Let us truly make the effort to think what we are doing that we may free ourselves from what is known as the robotical level of consciousness; to free our self from the level of consciousness that reacts without the pause and the moment which is necessary for our eternal, true self to rise up and view and whisper softly in our ear, "That is not the way." For centuries that have already gone past have taught you that. We must awaken within ourselves the untold centuries that we have already expressed. It is the illusion created by an identity with a limited body that blocks our view from the multitudes of experiences of centuries long, long past.

Look at the newborn child. They are not all the same. Their minds are not all the same, nor are their bodies, for their bodies are the effects of their minds. And the minds are the effects of their evolving souls. And so it is that as we study nature—and the human body is an inseparable part of nature—we can begin to see why our hair is blonde or black, why our eyes are blue or green. There is a reason why the temple, God's temple, known as the human body, why that temple has been created the way that it has. It is a constant revelation to you of the lessons that have been learned, of the laws that have been transgressed, and of the lessons you should be about learning this moment. We must not look at this temple, called the human body, in sadness or despair, but we must view it objectively with the light of reason. For it offers to you, the evolving individual, it offers to you all that is necessary to express your eternal soul and to have the fullness of life. It did not create itself by chance, but it was gathered up in keeping with the laws that you established before entering this earthly realm.

So whatever it is you like or don't like about what you call yourself, remember, it is exactly what you yourself established. Your next body will be in keeping with what you are doing now, for it is the law; that *is* the Law of Destiny. You change your clothes daily and sometimes more frequently. When you look at the great, eternal stream of consciousness, you change your bodies just as often. For your bodies are in a constant process of movement and change and they are being directed by your attitudes, by your rejections, by your denials, or by your acceptances.

This philosophy teaches that acceptance is the will of God. And if it is, in truth, goodness and the abundant life that you are seeking, then you must demonstrate God's will. And God's will demonstrates all over the universes and reveals that it is, in truth, acceptance, for there is nothing in all of the universes that God denies, for God is the Intelligent Energy that sustains everything. So think, my good friends, your tomorrows are the effects of today. And your temple, the human body, will be exactly as you and you alone are creating it. Does it not then behoove us, in seeing that simple truth, to let an intelligence, that is certainly more capable and qualified than our limited mind, govern and guide that temple, that house in which we are residing? The moment, whatever your problem may seem to be, the moment you give it up, it rises into a realm of consciousness within you where all things good are not only possible, but constantly being demonstrated.

Thank you.

JULY 3, 1977

Church Lecture 68
The Fullness of Life

In speaking today on "The Fullness of Life," let us first come to the understanding on what the fullness of life truly is. We understand in this philosophy that the fullness of life is an effect of an ever-expanding consciousness. The expansion or broadening of our horizons in life is dependent upon the faculty of acceptance. The fullness of life is not something that someday we will suddenly acquire. It is a process that is taking place this very moment. We become aware of a fullness in our life when we experience that which we have desired. And so it is that in the desiring is an expanding of our consciousness.

This philosophy teaches that desire is the divine expression. It is not the principle of desire that is the problem of man. It is his unwillingness to accept the necessary steps to attain whatever it is that he does desire. No form on the Earth planet or in the mental or astral realms of consciousness is freed from the divine expression, known as desire. The freedom from the bondage of desire is directly dependent upon the education, not the annihilation, of desire. The minds of men cannot annihilate or end what is the right of the Divine.

And so we see here, in our earthly view, that all forms, all creatures, including man, are experiencing what is known as divine expression or desire. How does man educate desire in order that he may consciously become aware of the fullness of life? The education of desire is when it is united with the soul faculty of reason. For it is in the light of reason that man knows beyond a shadow of any doubt the law that clearly demonstrates, moment-by-moment to us, whatever we are seeking is also seeking us. For man is a law unto himself. And so man needs not to be worried and to be impatient with his desires. Man simply needs the common sense to pause and to place it under the light of eternal reason, for all of life has been given to man in keeping with man's own evolution.

We cannot stop evolving. We cannot stop what our mind calls changing, for change is inevitable to evolution. But what, in truth, is change? Change is an expansion of our consciousness. For the things that took place yesterday, and we think we have changed from, in truth still exist in consciousness. We have only broadened our horizons and in that broadening or expansion of our consciousness, we no longer identify with those particular experiences except through the soul faculty of recall.

Now we all have what is known as a memory par excellence. All that has been, all that is, and all that will ever be, man in truth is inseparably united to. The division (that man thinks he is a separate and eternal entity) is a division created by the function known as identity. We identify with a country. We identify with a group and we identify with a philosophy and we identify with churches and we identify with a multitude of things. It is in that identification that we become controlled.

Man can soon see, at any moment he chooses to see, whether or not he has a desire or a desire has him. Now this is a very important thing to view. If man has desire—and we all know we do—then we are able to control that desire in our own minds. But if the desire, the created form, created by mind-substance, has man, then man is plagued by that so-called form or desire that he alone has created. So let us pause more often in our daily activities that we may become aware whether or not we are remaining the master of our ship of destiny and experiencing the fullness of life or whether we have become the victim of our own uncontrolled thought pattern.

Man, in his experiencing, first forms or controls a thought from mental substance. And in that forming, creating, and controlling, unless man awakens within himself the corresponding soul faculty to that function that he is entertaining, then man becomes controlled by that which he has created. But it is a divine and most just law in order that man may someday accept the simple, eternal truth that he is not the king of the universe, that what we believe God to be is not what God truly is demonstrating. When we create this so-called god in our mind, then that creation is dependent upon our limited acceptances in life and our own rejections or destinies in life. Therefore, our god, being created by our minds, is in a constant process of changing, as our own minds are in a constant process of changing, whether we like it or not. The created or false gods in our minds slowly, but surely, begin to disintegrate as we begin to awaken within ourselves that this divine, intelligent Energy is a servant to all, that it is impartial, that it is unlimited, and that it is, in truth, what man knows as peace.

It is when we, as individualized souls, make the daily, moment-by-moment effort to place the principle of peace firmly and fixedly in our consciousness that we begin to view life as a constant, passing panorama of events.

There is no security, there is no true peace, there is no true love in what is known as creation for the mind is perfectly balanced between the finite and the infinite. And it is when man, no longer realizing that delicate, but perfect balance, begins to tip the scales [that he] capsizes his own boat or ship of destiny. For every so-called good that the minds create, that delicate balance in mental substance creates its opposite. Without that principle and balance, identity would not be possible. And so it is as man, in his efforts, is unfolding on what is known as the spiritual paths of life, [he] must be ever aware and ever conscious of this delicate balance. Many philosophies have taught that as man believeth in his heart so he becometh. We understand in this philosophy that the heart is an instrument of the expression of the divine spirit, that the mind is the great censor, for the mind does not permit any inspiration or idea to pass through it that it is not already in keeping with what it has prior acceptance to.

And so man's so-called struggle in life is what he calls preservation: the preservation of what is known as self. For man has identified with what his limited experiences on earth already are and in that identification, man calls that "self."

[In] the ancient philosophies, the first and very basic teaching was in all your giving, to give the gift of self. For in the giving of what you call the gift of self, you are freed from the limited and restricted laws that have been established by your own minds. And so on the spiritual path of illumination and awakening, there is no illumining, there is no awakening without the gift of self. There is no true realization of the fullness of life or the universal consciousness until man is ready, willing, and able to give the greatest gift that he has to the Divine, and that, my friends, is the gift of self. For without that gift, without a giving of it, a wall stands between man—within his own being—and his freedom, his abundant living. And when that disappears, man will have the realization of the true purpose for his experience here on earth.

Thank you.

AUGUST 7, 1977

Church Lecture 69

Harmony, The Law of Health

In speaking to you once again on "Harmony, The Law of Health," we must first view life, the effects and the experiences that we encounter in our daily activities, when, through an awakening within us, we finally accept that all forms and all experiences in life are, indeed and in truth, sustained by an impartial, a neutral, intelligent Energy. And so it is that soon we shall discover to work upon the effects is not to free us from the cause. We must, in time, go beyond these effects that we encounter and that going beyond takes place within our own consciousness. This philosophy has taught, since its inception, that peace is the only power that sustains all form. What man does with that great, intelligent power, known to us as peace, is the choice of each and every man.

In our eternal soul evolution we establish, through what is known as our errors of ignorance, certain mental laws that we must fulfill in mental realms. It is these experiences of fulfillment of these transgressions that man is often blinded by. Instead of accepting these experiences as necessary lessons through which the soul may unfold and continue to evolve, man is deluded by the belief that he is the experience. Man is not the experiences of what this earth has to offer. Man is not, in truth, the experiences of what heaven has to offer. For man and man alone is the creator of all of his experiences. And because man and man alone is the creator, man and man alone can change those experiences. But we must, through the Law of Disassociation, slowly, but surely, become objective. Many philosophies have taught, and continue to teach, the Law of Detachment: to be in this world and not a part of this world, to ever be with a thing and never to be a part of the thing.

This philosophy teaches that that which controls us has power over us. And so it is in our mental worlds that we create a vast number of forms or so-called mental attitudes and patterns of mind. In time, through a directing of this neutral, intelligent energy to certain patterns of mind, these forms in mental realms are created by us. It is these forms, through the directing of energy by us, that in time become the masters of our mental world. Now many of you are a bit familiar with what is called thought forms. But, you see, a form is more than just a form. It has intelligent movement. It has want, need, and desire. And we, being the creator of these thought forms by directing intelligent, neutral energy to certain patterns of mind, those forms have all that we have in our mind except one very important principle: and that is an eternal spirit. For we can create many things, and many things in truth we do create in mental realms. But we, as mental beings, cannot sustain the forms we create, for we are not the source itself—that is, our minds. We are the vehicle or instrument through which the Divine Source of intelligent energy is flowing, but we are not, our forms, the source itself.

And so it is in this teaching of harmony, the Law of Health, that we must view in these realms the many forms that we have created. And we must take an honest appraisal, an honest stock of what we have already created and view whether or not the forms we have already created are harmonious and in accord with each other. If they are not, we can very soon realize, for they are discordant. And discord is the birth of disease.

Now I know that many of you, perhaps, will not agree, for you view the world of creation and you view the souls entering many forms. And some of the forms, from their expression, appear to be harmonious or healthy. And many of the forms appear to be discordant or diseased. But you cannot view life's experience as the beginning in all of eternity, for each soul has established its own laws in mental realms and the physical body is a direct effect of the mental form created by the minds of men. Whether that form was created prior to this earth experience or is one of recent creation is demonstrable by an honest view of oneself.

Philosophers for untold time have taught, "O man, know thyself and ye shall know the truth, and the truth shall set you free." To know oneself is to go beyond what the limited experiences of the human mind have to offer. Man cannot make the judgment of what he will find, for in so doing, he establishes a mental law and is on a mental level of consciousness and can only experience what the mental level of consciousness has to offer.

Our teaching is that acceptance is the divine will or the will of infinite, intelligent Energy. Now all of us have acceptance. It is not something that we need to study to gain. It is a broadening of our acceptance that helps to free us. For, you see, acceptance being the will of God, the divine will, when it is limited in its expression, it becomes out of balance in these many levels of consciousness. So it is a broadening of our horizon, it is an opening of our minds that our heart, the vehicle of our eternal soul, may fully express. We need not be concerned about our heart for our heart is the vehicle of our soul. The obstruction to the feelings that rise from our soul and are experienced in our heart, the obstruction is the human mind, because its acceptance is out of balance and in discord with the will of the Divine.

In viewing so-called poor health or good health, we must honestly look at the human body as what it truly is: the temple of God through which this divine, intelligent Energy may express through what is known as the human form here on this earthly realm. And because man in his evolution has merited that vehicle, in that meriting comes, hand-in-hand, the responsibility to care for the vehicle he is driving. For if we do not care for the automobile we drive, we soon experience the day when it no longer functions harmoniously.

And so these tools—and one of them being the human body—are designed to serve a harmonious and just and good purpose. If we do not take care of the tools that our eternal soul has earned, then we will soon find the day when we will have to serve the tools, for the tools are no longer in condition to serve us well, as they have been designed by a great architect to do so.

So man's responsibility in the experiencing of good health, which is his true wealth—for when man has good health he has no need, no want, and no desire to seek the wealth of an earthly realm, for that wealth he is already experiencing in what is known as good health. For the law clearly demonstrates that like attracts like and becomes the Law of Attachment. So whenever we, through our own endeavors and efforts in life, attain this good health, there is no thought, there is no concern about the wealth of the world, for we have everything. And having everything is indeed a great responsibility. But the weight of responsibility must never exceed our love of God. For should the weight of responsibility in life exceed our love of God, then we shall be burdened by what we have desired.

We also understand in this Living Light Philosophy that desire is the divine expression. And so it is not the principle of desire that causes man his problems and his struggles. It is the direction of it, limited by the human mind, that causes man his difficulties. For it has not been placed under the faculty of reason, for it is the light of reason that transfigures us and lifts us to heavenly heights of consciousness, to peace and harmony, to joy, that makes this life worthwhile. My good friends, make the effort this moment to make your life worthwhile through a broadening of the divine will that is flowing through you, known as total acceptance. For unless you make this moment good and worthwhile for you, then tomorrow's moments will not be what you truly desire. It is indeed the divine right of man to desire the good of life, for man's true being is the good of life. And as water ever seeks its own level by its own weight, so the eternal soul ever seeks the goodness that it truly is.

There is no such thing as a lost soul. There is no such thing as a bad soul. For all souls are a part of an infinite, intelligent Goodness, known as the Allsoul. It is the vehicles and the forms through which the soul is ever striving to express its fullness that are ofttimes contaminated and polluted.

We look at our earth realm today and we see and we question and we wonder about what we say is so much pollution of our atmosphere, so much pollution of the waters of the planet. But who did the polluting? Not the animals in the forest, nor the birds in the sky. No, it took some animal with a much higher expression of intelligence to do such a thorough job. Now think, my good friends, if like attracts like and becomes the Law of Attachment, and that is a demonstrable law that you experience each and every moment of life, then the pollution of our planet, of which we are presently the inhabitants, is a revelation of the pollution within our consciousness. So if we want a change outside, then we must first make the effort to do the changing inside.

We all know that joy is an inside job and we all know that health, wealth, and happiness is ever dependent upon our own efforts to bring the light of reason into our mind. As long as we permit our minds to dictate and to judge that the cause of our problems is in the power of someone else, then we shall continue to serve the false gods created by our human mind that place the cause of things outside of our self. When we begin to accept, in all areas of our life, personal responsibility, then we are on the path to being free from the victimization and the control of people and forces outside of our zone of action.

We and we alone choose our thought. We and we alone are responsible for the feelings and the experiences that it offers to us. We do not, unfortunately, often accept that it began within us. But, my good friends, the cause of all things is within. Though at times it is painful, there are indeed times when it is pleasurable. And so that's just the way the duality of creation really is. But let us, in our acceptance—for all of us are accepting something—let's add to the list of our acceptances our right, our divine eternal right to the wealth, the health, and the happiness that is, in truth, the goodness that God has given to us.

Thank you.

SEPTEMBER 4, 1977

Church Lecture 70
Life's Purpose

Speaking today on the topic of "Life's Purpose," we may well consider the demonstration of life as we know it this moment. We look around and about us and we see that all things in form—all these things of creation and of nature—are in a constant process of change. And so, by watching that demonstrable principle, we cannot help but in time to consider that life may flow more harmoniously for us, dependent upon our acceptance of the willingness to change and to flow in harmony with all of life, of which we are, in truth, an inseparable part.

In this day and age, here on earth, there is much investigation and scientific study into life, its purpose and its continuity. I am sure that most of you present are aware of the so-called Kirlian photography, where the scientists have been enabled to photograph what some call the aura of all forms. This so-called aura of form, be it a plant, animal, or human, is simply the vital body of the form itself. We are all aware that at times we feel filled with the vitality or we have the opposite feelings, the lack thereof. It has been scientifically demonstrated in our day and age that this energy field expands or contracts ever in keeping with the attitude of mind of the individual.

So often in life we question the experiences that we encounter. We only question them from a level of consciousness that is not yet aware of the law the we established by our own mental body. This school, here at Serenity, teaches the various levels of consciousness. It teaches the nine bodies that our eternal soul is at present inhabiting. Now we all seem to be aware of our physical body; that is only the grosser body of the other eight. Some of us are aware of our mental body; at least we are somewhat aware of our thoughts that emanate therefrom. We are also aware, some of us, of our astral body, from the experiences that we have had in reference to what is called astral flight. All of us, at sometime, are aware of our vital or energy body. Whenever we direct thought, we create form. This divine, intelligent Energy is passing through us constantly. When we leave this physical body, this intelligent Energy continues to pass through and to permeate these other bodies, which we are presently inhabiting.

We have, in this great, evolutionary journey, lived many, many experiences before ever coming to this Earth planet. Now for us to personally experience [those experiences] once again, we must awaken within our conscious mind what is known as the memory par excellence. We did not enter Earth as a new form. We have entered Earth with untold centuries of evolution and experience. When we leave the physical bodies, regardless of what planet we are on, we must pass through these other remaining eight spheres and the nine planes of consciousness to each sphere. We do not have to wait for this day when we leave this physical body to become aware of these different spheres and planes. It is simply a matter of acceptance within our own mind. The moment that we accept the possibility of all things, then all things are demonstrated for us by us. For we all, I am sure, will agree that to God, the Divine Intelligence, all things are possible. It is the awakening within our self of this God-consciousness by the daily and constant effort of broadening our own horizons. We look at nature and we see this constant process of change, without which evolution would not be possible.

When we, through our own identity, identify with a thought and believe that we are the thought with which we have identified, then we become that thought, that form. We become it by consciously directing energy to it. We have all had the experiences and the difficulties of trying to remove a certain thought that seems to plague our mind. The reason that it is difficult to remove a thought from our mind is because by directing energy to it, the thought form has, at that moment, become greater than our self. It is only a temporary thing. It is through an error of our own ignorance that we have narrowed our horizons and have overidentified with a created thought form. These experiences in evolution are necessary for us. They are necessary because we alone, in our evolutionary path, have chosen them to be so.

In this materialistic age that is in a process of changing, there are many, many things that seem to amaze the human mind. You hear about the possibility of science creating life.

Science and no mind will create life. They will simply be the instruments through which these positive and negative poles of nature may be brought together in a laboratory, and that is as far as the mental world can bring life. But there is an intelligent Energy that must enter that form and if that intelligent Energy does not enter that form, then there is not life as we presently know life. This life principle, this intelligent Energy is everywhere present; it is never absent or away.

So often in communication with these other dimensions that are here with us every moment, there are times when the Spirit will reveal the birth of a child ofttimes years before it takes place. We must ask our self this question "Well, how is that possible? How is it possible to know beyond a shadow of any doubt events that are yet to take place?" Because, you see, my friends, time and space is an illusion created by our own mind. We can go beyond all illusions; therefore, it is possible for us to go beyond the illusion of time and space. But as long as we insist upon holding on to thoughts and attitudes of yesteryear that are no longer serving a beneficial and useful purpose in our life, then we cannot broaden our acceptance and our horizons and we cannot experience that which is waiting for us to experience.

These energy fields—that are everywhere—are either in harmony with other forms and energy fields or they are in discord. One moves harmoniously forward on the stream of consciousness through the divine will, known as acceptance. The moment that we accept, we no longer become or are the obstruction in our own path. It is known by other philosophies as standing in one's own light. Let us think and let us consider that we are, in truth, an all-encompassing Intelligence that is presently, seemingly limited by the form through which the Intelligence is flowing.

In this day, they speak of plants; that they have feelings, that they have, therefore, thoughts. For you cannot have a feeling, no matter what the form, without a mental body to register and experience what is called thought. For many years this philosophy, The Living Light, has taught that this Intelligence is merely limited by the form through which it is expressing. If man, within his own being, makes the effort to go beyond the judgments of the human mind to accept the possibility, the possibility of experiencing the allness and the goodness that life has to offer, then man indeed will understand, for he will indeed communicate. He will communicate with all of life, not on the levels of consciousness that he dictates that communication must be made, but in a level of total acceptance. Therefore, the demonstration in this scientific, so-called, age is that plants indeed have thoughts, indeed have feelings, indeed have personality and respond and react to the thoughts and feelings of the human mind.

Now, my good friends, the plant, having those feelings and experiences, is certainly no different than the animal. Supposedly the animal is of a higher evolved form. And in the animal kingdom, man, the human, is of, yea, even a higher evolved form. I tell you in truth the only difference is in the refinement and complexities, through refinement, of the form itself. There is no difference to a hurt feeling that a plant experiences than a hurt feeling that a human experiences, except the human, through its evolution, has much, much more complexity.

We have earned or merited the experiences that are before us, here, on this the earth realm, and so has all other form. However, by having merited forms that are more evolved in the sense of their complexities and abilities, man has responsibility over all creation. That is, indeed, a heavy responsibility until such time as we accept the inseparability of truth. There is only the error of ignorance that separates us from the goodness of all life.

When we leave this physical body, our mental body takes us onward, evolving to astral realms and finally into what man calls spiritual realms. We come from what is known as an Allsoul, an infinite, intelligent Consciousness. We come from it not in distance, nor in time; we come from it in our own acceptance of life itself. We are as far from heaven as our denials and rejections have made it so. We are as close to God, the goodness, the abundance, and the fullness of life, as our own acceptance will permit us to be. Man has landed on the moon, but he could have landed there untold centuries ago. But the acceptance of that possibility had not yet been fully registered in the human mind.

Whenever we permit our minds to entertain the need of anything, we set into motion the Law of Denial, for we have limited our minds to view and, by that viewing, to dictate that there are things that we desire that we have not. We have made that decision. We have made that judgment. We have not only done that, but we have decided, in mental realms, that certain steps are necessary, that certain laws must be fulfilled in order for us to experience what we choose to desire. The divine Infinite Intelligence does not do that. It simply sustains whatever judgment that we choose to make.

Many philosophies teach the way of positive thought. But, my good students, we must go beyond positive thought. We must go to the source, that which sustains not only positive, but negative thought. Let us go beyond these mental images and thoughts that we permit our mind to create. Let us go to that light that is available to us this very moment. There we can view the great panorama of creation, not only in a physical realm, nor a mental, but in universal realms that are here, that are, in truth, within.

I know that most all of you are aware that man is the microcosm of the macrocosm. But his mind does not relate to what that truly means. You are not only the Sun and the Moon and the Earth, but the universes, not the limited universe that surrounds this earthly planet. All places you have been, for all places you are, all places you will be. It is dependent upon your own acceptance. You cannot experience what is not accepted.

And so, my good friends, to be dissatisfied can serve a very good purpose, for it can be, and usually is, instrumental in us making the effort to change in our own mind. This philosophy teaches that irritation wakes the soul and satisfaction lets it sleep. So when we find our self irritated, we also find changes taking place within our own mind. Those changes, all changes, serve a good purpose.

Now, we call the day "light" and we call the night "dark." But I tell you, my friends, on these poles of opposite in so-called creation, it's all a matter of degree. The night is the lesser light and the day, the brighter. And so we find ourselves in all types of thoughts and we say that this thought is good and we say that that thought is bad. But in order to have that experience we must be in a mental realm, for it is in a mental realm that you have the duality of creation; you have the peace and the war, the so-called goodness and the so-called bad.

This philosophy is based upon the demonstrable principle that acceptance is the will of God. There is no need to experience lack when plenty surrounds us. There is no need to be poor, for in so dictating that need do we deny the goodness of God. We have the right, the eternal, divine right to choose the abundant good or to deny it. There are no circumstances or forces outside of our self that are doing it to us. For the demonstrable truth is very clear: that man is the cause and the cure of all of his experiences. God cannot move through man to help him sustain a way to greater goodness unless man first accepts that possibility. God is not a doer and God is not a giver. God is a sustaining, intelligent Energy and all of life teaches us that simple truth. We alone are choosing what we will permit to be sustained in our life. To make the changes that we desire, we must be willing to direct this intelligent Energy to the goodness that is our right. But as man begins to make that effort, the patterns of old do not quickly change.

I am sure that we will all agree that it is indeed quite frequent [that] we put the blame outside. Have we ever stopped to consider, when we are not happy with the government under which we live, how many times we have blamed the government for the conditions of the country in which we live? By so doing we become the instruments to direct this intelligent Energy to negative thought forms concerning our own government. [If] we want changes in that that is around us, we must make first the effort to change that which is within us, for that which is around and about us is ever in keeping with a level of consciousness that we insist upon expressing. How many philosophies have taught that life is a mirror reflecting back to you what you send into it? It is because we have yet to make the effort to become consciously aware of our thoughts, to become consciously aware of our feelings—not spasmodically, now and then. Let us choose this moment. Let us choose our right to the goodness of life. And in so choosing, be rest assured, my friends, the goodness of life will manifest itself for you, for like attracts like and becomes the Law of Attachment. So whatever it is that you are seeking, first become it—you must first be aware of it, then become it by believing it.

All of life is ever dependent upon our belief. But we have not used that wonderful faculty to its fullness consciously. We have heard many times that we become what we believe, because that is true. So when you stop to think and you look at life and you are not happy with the way things are, then it's simply a matter of changing your belief. And by belief, I don't mean religion. I don't even mean, necessarily, philosophy. Life is dependent upon your belief. If you do not believe, then you do not become, and then for you life is nonexistent. It's like the agnostic or the atheist. They say they don't believe, but in their very statement they do believe, for they believe in their thought form that they have created, and they have a right to do so.

Does the atheist experience the continuity of life beyond this earthly experience? Oh, they certainly do, but they experience ever in keeping with their belief. As long as man believes that there is no existence beyond earth, then when he leaves this earthly realm, that belief exists in a mental body in which his eternal soul is encased. But there's one thing about belief: belief takes form from created substance and it must be sustained. In other words, we must continue to believe in order to experience. We cannot experience without belief, so we are all believing something. And the truth is we're believing so many different things. So the atheist leaves the earth realm believing in the total annihilation of the personality and the being itself and lives in a mental body of that creation. But the day comes—rather quickly to many—where there is great difficulty in sustaining that belief by directing the divine Energy to it. I assure you, my good friends, there are few, if any, people who believe in total nonexistence when they find themselves alone. The one thing that is not considered in total annihilation is the gnawing suffering of loneliness, for that is something that is deep within all of us when we close all doors to life. And because we can only create an illusion of closing doors, the illusion does not last forever and ever.

Let us, then, as we face a new year, very soon, let us take stock of what we really believe. Let us view our short earth span. Through recall, we will see that many of our beliefs have already changed. Through making the effort to become aware of our present situation, we will see that many of our present beliefs are in process of being changed. And when we, in our daily activities, communicate with people, let us become more aware of our own feelings, because we cannot grant to another what we have not first granted unto our self. So let us become more aware of our thoughts and feelings that, in so doing, we may become an instrument of awareness of the thoughts and feelings of the people with whom we work and communicate. Then we will know what it's like, we will really know what it's like, when our cherished thoughts and beliefs are being threatened.

Thank you.

OCTOBER 2, 1977

Church Lecture 71
The Joy of Teaching

In viewing this topic for this morning, "The Joy of Teaching," we must take a good look at that subject matter and not be restricted in our thinking to understand that teaching is limited to any particular profession. For example, we look at life and we view, in truth, that all of life is teaching us something, whether we are speaking with another of our own species or some of the so-called lower forms of life on the planet, for there is an exchange whenever we come into contact with any of life's forms. And in that exchange and action and reaction, this flow of energy that is passing through us from the Divine Source is, in truth, the experience, once we have awakened to it, that is known as the joy of teaching. For we are all teachers and we are all students. For we are, in truth, all giving and all receiving.

When we awaken our sight to these dimensions in which we truly live, then we can see what is truly going on as we speak forth our word, as we move, as we breathe, and as we expose our universe to the universes around and about us.

It is in the purpose of our eternal being's evolution to share all that it has gathered unto itself, for it is in that unobstructed flow that the light of reason dawns within us. When we permit, by limited thought, judgment to rise, what is good and what is bad, when we spend our lives living in those levels of consciousness, then we limit ourselves and retard our own progression. We all know that the laws of evolution are greater than the thoughts of men, for the divine law of constant evolving is the very power that sustains the thoughts of men.

So when we, in our activities, in our daily jobs and experiences, take the moment to pause and to think beyond the experience of the moment, then we will slowly, but surely, begin to see the lesson that is contained within the experience. For there is no experience that man can encounter in life that does not contain a lesson that he and he alone has personally earned. This philosophy has taught for some time the laws of personal responsibility. But until we make that daily effort to become aware of whether or not we are accepting this personal responsibility, whether or not we are denying that right of growth within ourselves, for within us lies the power to change all things within our lives. We need have no concern for what is outside, for that which is the manifestation is but the effect of the causes that we, in truth, have the power within us to change.

So let us look at life this moment. Let us view objectively, with the light of reason, the things that we desire within our lives to change. You see, my students, whenever the mind permits the illusion, the dictate that anything is outside of the power that lies within us, then we are the victims of so-called circumstances.

We have the right of choice. And each and every moment of our life we are, in truth, exercising that right of choice. We have the choice to stay in any situation that we have already chosen, for if we have not chosen a situation or an experience, it cannot be recorded within our own minds. So we are constantly choosing these experiences and, like great magnets, we are pulling them out of the universe into our lives. Think of that great ability that we have within us. Just stop for a moment and think: that each moment you in truth are choosing. You are choosing the moment the way you want the moment to be. If you have not yet awakened to that power within you, then you cannot yet accept it. And it cannot be awakened within you, until you first accept the demonstrable truth that everything that is taking place in your life is an effect of the attitudes of mind, the levels of consciousness that you are choosing.

You can change this moment. You cannot, of course, change that which has passed in the great illusion of time. But you can change this moment. Our soul, certainly, has entered the earth realm in one of its grades of school with many tendencies and laws that have been established by prior evolutionary experiences. But we need not be bound by those laws for the power within us can establish, this moment, new laws; that these other laws that have already been established can be neutralized. And so we are never left without the right of choice. But we cannot exercise that right until we accept that we have it, and we cannot accept that we have it until we free our self from the delusion of our mind that places the power and the blame to things outside of our own self.

It is the very purpose of this Living Light Philosophy to show you many paths that lead to one, eternal light of reason. And so it is when you study and apply what is given forth, then you become a teacher, an awakened teacher to yourself. You don't have to speak it out to those who are not interested, for unsolicited help is ever, ever to no benefit. You cannot help a person until they open the door through the Law of Solicitation. And it is the Law of Presence which is the Law of Solicitation. But let us not be deceived in this Law of Presence to limit it to the physical body. For of what benefit is the physical body if the attention of the mind is not where the body is?

So many people are concerned that their bodies don't do what their minds would like them to do, and that happens to so many people. But, you see, my good students, a house divided cannot stand. And so we must unite our mind with our body, but we cannot unite our mind with our body until we permit the balancing power of the divine Spirit within us. You may question or be a bit surprised that your body does not react exactly to the dictates of your conscious mind, but all you have to do for that demonstrable proof is to look at the world in which we live: that the pharmaceutical houses are selling by the untold trillions of dollars so-called diet pills and diet fads; that everyone, with rare exceptions, that you talk to is on some type of a diet to get their physical body to respond to the conscious dictates of their own mind. I can assure you, my good students, you don't need to go to a drug store and buy pills in order for you to help your body to respond to the sincere desires of your mind. All you need to do is to unite your thoughts.

We are aware that there are eighty-one levels of consciousness through which the eternal soul is expressing. But we must unite those levels of consciousness and not be a Dr. Jekyll in the morning and a Mr. Hyde at night, for that is not a house united. Let us take stock of our thought. Let us take stock of our wishes and our desires. And let's be reasonable bookkeepers of life. For you've got to be a good accountant to live a life of peace and harmony. You've got to take stock of your desires and place them in the proper priorities in your life.

You see, everyone knows that we cannot have our cake and eat it, too; that we must pay for every attainment in life. And it is these little payments that we cry so much about. I've never in my life witnessed anyone crying about some attainment of good that they are experiencing in their life. It is the tears for what we judge to be the payment of life. But we must all pay our dues. The seed planted in the ground has the painful experience of growth. So if you feel that your struggle is great, then take another look at your struggle, for your growth is ever in keeping. And so the teaching has been given long ago: the greater the reward, the greater the effort. For in truth, we get out of anything what we alone are putting into it. We don't get something out that we're not putting in. However, if our total attention is upon what we're putting in, then there is no attention left for what we are getting out. Now think about that and think about life. If we become less attentive to what we think we are doing, we will be more attentive to what is really taking place in our life.

It's like the man who is running a race. And in the midst of a race he becomes aware of how many times he's been breathing in that running. In that moment of awareness, he slows down in order to direct some of the energy to the thought of self, of what he is doing. Now think, my good friends, how many times in the course of a day do you ever think about your breathing? How many times in the course of a day do you ever think about how many miles you may be walking? How many times in the course of a day do you stop and become aware of the color of your skin? Is it getting lighter or is it getting darker? How many times do you look at the pupils of your eyes? I would say it cannot be too many times in the course of a day. But think of the multitudes of times that you think about things not going your way. Think about that. Don't you realize, my good friends, if you didn't have a physical body, you would not be experiencing a physical world? And so, doesn't it behoove us to become a little bit more aware of what we're doing to this body, this vehicle that we're driving around? Is it in good working order? Are we keeping it harmonious? And are we enjoying the ride that it's taking us on? Is the body taking us where we want to go or is it going in a contrary direction? That question must be asked.

How many people, they stop and they think, "Well, the years have passed and I have not accomplished what I decided, when I was younger, that I would accomplish." But the problem is, when we were younger we were so interested in so many distractions of our mind that the energy never got directed to our goal. If you want something out of life—and it is our very nature to want something out of life, for into life we put something.

But, perhaps, you want a little bit more and surely that is the right of all form. For life has so much, it has so much to offer to everyone that is in it. And we're all in it or we're not aware of it. It has so much to offer. As you give more, you will get back more. But you cannot dictate to the Divine what you're going to get back for what you think you're giving. It's when we think we're giving so much that we get so little. Because, you see, the energy necessary to return so much to us is all being directed to the thought form of self, of how much we're giving to life. And so, we're not only a house divided, but we cut off our nose to spite our face. Surely that is not what life has to offer.

Oh no, my friends, all of the abundance that you view in life, the only separation between you and experiencing that abundance of life is the dictates, through errors of ignorance, of our own mind. If we have established laws that it's going to take X number of years to experience what we want to experience, the law is impartial; it certainly will abide by your dictates. For it is the power of the universe, known as God, that is sustaining your very thought. And if you choose to dictate when the goodness you are seeking will be experienced in your life, the Divine, the greatest servant of all servants, called God, will abide by your very judgments. And in time you will see: "It's no longer beneficial for me or for anyone to spend so much energy dictating to the Divine Source."

The animals in the field and the birds, they don't spend their time dictating to the Divine Source where their next morsel is coming from. No, through a humble acceptance, the something within them does everything that is necessary. If you have a dog or a cat and you don't feed them, you may be rest assured they will get fed, for they have that humble acceptance. They don't dictate that they must go to their next door neighbor of where they live to eat, though they may readily go there. But if the door is closed, they'll go on and on and on and on. But you may be rest assured, they will not die from starvation. Now think. That's a four-legged form on this planet.

What are all of these fears that we entertain? That we will not have a roof over us. We will not have food in our stomach. We will not have this and we will not have that. Let us take a lesson from the so-called lower species. They have their coats to keep them warm and they find their shade in the summer to keep them cool. And they do not concern themselves over all these petty things. Let us look at the human species as a bird or a cat or a dog or a lion or a tiger or a bear would look at us. In a state of total shock that we should worry, that we should entertain the thoughts of where our next morsel is going to come from. The squirrel is aware that winter comes and the snow falls. And he does what is necessary. And he knows that it's sure to come and so he works like a little beaver to put away sufficient unto the need of the winter. Enough morsels to carry him through 'til the summer. For he knows and has learned those great lessons in life that everything has a season. And so he abides by those simple laws.

Let us abide by the simplicity of life and leave the complexities to those who enjoy them so much. Let us look and see how beautiful everything flows. We're concerned about the water, we're concerned about this, and we're concerned about that. Our concern is a dictate of our own mind. And mental substance, disturbed in the universe and the atmosphere, has an effect upon the peace and the harmonious flow of Nature herself. It has an effect because we are part of nature. And that which is a part of anything has an effect upon the whole. So the more we worry about anything, the more we demand to control it. You see, my friends, the demonstrable truth is very clear: we worry about what we insist upon controlling. When we stop insisting upon controlling things, we will stop worrying about things. Then we will not only be a teacher, but we will be a good student. For you cannot be a good teacher unless you are, at the same time, a good student. For a good teacher never stops learning, and a good student never stops asking.

Thank you.

NOVEMBER 6, 1977

Church Lecture 72

The Source

This topic, "The Source," is something that we consider in all of our thoughts and activities, for our mind is ever questioning, "What is the cause of this and what is the cause of that?" And so it is with all of our experiences each and every moment, we are ever seeking to find the source or the cause of these experiences.

The other day one of the ladies of this association had what is commonly referred to as an accident. An accident implies something that just happens without known cause or responsibility. This philosophy teaches and demonstrates that there are no accidents in the universe. There are experiences. We don't have car accidents or any other types of accidents. We have, if we choose to say, car experiences. For if we will take the time and make the effort, we can, in a moment of pause of our thought, awaken within our self the soul faculty of reason. And reason will cast light upon the shadows of the mind and it will reveal that we, in truth, set ourselves up for all of our experiences.

Everything that we encounter in life, every experience, is in truth premeditated. Because we are not fully aware of the levels of our own consciousness, we immediately deny that simple truth. But we meet the people that we establish laws in consciousness that we should meet in order to fulfill the very things in life that we truly want. You see, the truth is, my good friends, we always get what we really want. Whether we call that an accident or we call it having a new car or a home—it doesn't matter what we call it. Life is the mirror of reflection. The experiences of life are the illusion of the karmic wheel of repetition.

Now many of you, I know, have studied the varying philosophies offered in this world and you are well aware of this so-called karmic wheel. That that turns repeats itself ever in keeping with the cycle for which it has been designed. And so it is that man experiences in keeping with the cycle that he, in his own evolution, has established.

So how do we find the true, simple source of life? We find it when we pause to think. We find it in our pausing, in the moment that we accept, when we accept that we are vehicles through which intelligent Energy is expressing itself. This intelligent Energy, called by most people God—its very nature is to express itself and anything that stands in the way of the full and free expression of this intelligent Energy, anything that stands in the way, known as an obstruction, is going to be refined. Now that that is refined is changed. Our struggles in life are nothing more and nothing less than our unwillingness to accept change. And yet change is inevitable. We look all around at life and we see everything in a process of change, but when it comes for us to change, we're only willing to make the changes that we have already dictated, decided, and judged is in our own best interests. And those other changes, that we have also judged are not in our best interests, we are not only unwilling to change them, but we are fierce in our tenacity that we shall not. That's known as standing in one's own light.

My good students, after thirty-seven years of this work, I can assure you, whatever in life you judge you shall not do, you establish the very laws necessary in consciousness that you shall have to do. You see, it is our denials that are our destinies. Look at your lives already and I'm sure you will agree, of the many things that you judged you should never do and look at you today, many of them you are already doing. For that's the way evolution is. You cannot stop it. And when you face something that your authority and your mind and your ego cannot stop, then common sense and reason speak softly and say "Move aside; otherwise, you'll be moved right over."

So that's the way it is with our thoughts. Don't hold to them so tenaciously. They build walls and obstructions between you and the goodness and supply of life. For each dictate that the mind makes, for each judgment shall fall. For the divine, intelligent Energy sustains all thoughts, all life, all forms. And when you, in mental worlds of consciousness, judge what is right and judge what is wrong, you live to see the day there is a neutral path of peace and harmony that grants and accepts the right of all expression. And without that simple, neutral path, man continues to build and man continues to destroy. And surely it is foolhardy to build something and then destroy it. Only to build it again and to destroy it again.

Those lessons, we are here on earth, this time, to learn. Let us learn those simple lessons that we may not have to continue century, after century, after century to repeat them. And if we do learn them now, if we make that effort this moment and each day, then we will rise from the levels of consciousness called duality. We will no longer be controlled by the karmic wheel of illusion. We will view experience. As a captain takes control of his ship, we will take control of our destiny, for we will awaken within ourselves that faculty of reason. We shall grant the right of expression and in so doing, we shall become aware of the source of all of life. And in that awareness, apply the laws that demonstrate the abundant good and divine right of all.

Thank you.

DECEMBER 4, 1977

Church Lecture 73

New Experiences and New Attitudes

How appropriate, on this the first day of a new year, to consider "New Experiences and New Attitudes," as most of us are well aware, that all experience is directly related to an attitude of mind. And so it is in life that we are constantly encountering new experiences as we are constantly changing our attitudes of mind.

And so it is that man, in truth, is at the helm of his ship, the master of his destiny, though he may not yet know that simple truth. For he and he alone is encountering all of the experiences that he has set into motion by his own attitudes in life. And so the first step in becoming consciously aware that we are, in truth, getting exactly what we want from life is to awaken within our self by first pausing to think and redirecting this infinite, divine Energy from responsibility that we seem to choose to push outside of our sphere and our zones of action. Once we accept, consciously, that we are indeed responsible for all of the experiences that we have, we start on the conscious effort to reach the cause of all things in our life.

When we look outside and we see, so often, how successful someone else is and we quickly make the judgment of what caused their success and we try to apply those judgments to our self, they frequently do not work for us. For our judgments in life do not see clearly. They have total consideration of themselves. They are limited by what our few years on earth has offered to us by our own acceptance. And so we must go beyond the limited judgment of past experiences and start anew in this moment to awaken within us the possibility of all the good that life has to offer.

This philosophy does not teach, nor does it believe, that God is a limited God, that God is a personal god in the sense of giving to one and taking from another. Man gives to himself and man takes from himself ever in keeping with his limited judgments, which are known as his errors of ignorance. And it is these errors of ignorance that cause our struggles in life.

Let us, in beginning anew or beginning again, begin with an attitude of mind of our divine, eternal right to all of the goodness that life has to offer. As we believeth within us, so we becometh. But we must remember, my friends, from a lack of control of our own mind we believe many things one day only to disbelieve them the next. We do not give our self that opportunity to cherish our belief, to feed the necessary energy to it for a sufficient length of time for its goodness to return to us.

We are what we think. I have seen it said often in these latter years, especially with such diet consciousness in our country, that we are what we eat. We are only what we eat because we are what we think. We must first think before we eat, and we all think before we act. Ofttimes we do not think that we have thought before we have acted, but no act is possible without a thought to precede it. We do not often appreciate the reactions to our actions and we simply say, in order to justify them, that we did not give that thought or we did not think about it. I assure you, my friends, on some level of consciousness we think about everything that we do and we also think about everything that we do not do. We are indeed aware the moment we make the effort to pause. We are aware of what we are doing and we most certainly are aware of what we are not doing. For our experiences each and every day are revealing to us constantly what we are doing with our life.

God, this divine, intelligent, impartial Energy, that sustains all things in life, that accepts everything, is sustaining each and every thought that you choose to entertain in mind. The demonstration of nature reveals to us that the will of God is total acceptance, for there is nothing your eyes can view, nor your ears can hear, that the infinite, impartial, divine, intelligent

Energy, known as God, is not sustaining. So if we wish to be more godly, if we wish more good in our life, then we must first make the effort to express the will of the Divine. And to express the God will or the good will, then we must, through an effort of tolerance that brings understanding, accept the right of all expression—to accept the right of expression that we judge to be bad as well as we accept the right of expression that we judge to be good. For, in truth, nothing is either good or bad, but our thinking makes it so. And so our thoughts have created many things.

This philosophy does not teach that God is a judge. And so when man chooses to judge, then man is placing himself superior to the humble, divine, intelligent Being, called God. When man rises in his superiority, as he sits on a throne of judgment, placing himself above and beyond in consciousness the divine intelligent Being or Energy, known as God or Good, then man suffers the consequences of his own transgressions. For each and every judgment that we hold so tenaciously and so dearly to establishes the Law of Destiny within our life. And once that law is established, we must follow it where it is destined to lead.

And so we find, before judgment comes desire. And it is the unfulfillment of our desires that cause us to entertain so much judgment in life. So let us view what our desires are that we may be freed from these limited paths of destiny, the effects of judgment. Let us view desire in the light of reason. Let us accept the demonstrable truth: that desire is indeed the divine expression.

When we have these desires—and none of us are free from desire while yet in flesh—when we have these desires that plague our mind, we must pause in reason and in total consideration, for we must make decisions. And these decisions must be based upon what is in the best interest and the good of the whole of my life. For it is natural to desire, but it is detrimental to judge how the desires that we entertain in our minds shall be fulfilled. It is the judgment of the fulfillment of desire that limits man and causes man so much lack in life, so much struggle, and so much discord, which is the true cause of all disease.

No mind balanced in the realms of harmony experiences discord or disease. The students of this philosophy are well aware of the causes of discord or disease. Being aware, they have the great privilege of choosing the path of harmony, called peace, or the path of discord and disturbance in their lives. But the path of peace and the path of harmony is not possible, it is not possible without tolerance, without understanding, without reason, and without the application of the soul faculties.

Our life is designed by the great Architect to be a life of fulfillment, of enjoyment, and of constructive good. If you are not experiencing the fulfillment of life and the constructive good that life has to offer, then you must, for your own sake, make the effort to become consciously aware of your attitudes of mind. For it is only your attitudes that are depriving you of the goodness and the abundance of life itself.

We live or experience this earthly life for a very, very short time in this great sea of eternity. Our mental body is not something that can be physically detected. It is composed of a mental substance from a mental world. And that mental body will carry you, your consciousness, into another world when you leave the physical, which returns to the source from whence it came. It is this mental body that it behooves you to become aware of while yet on this Earth planet, to become aware of the many levels that exist in your mental body. Because, my friends, you cannot control, nor educate, that that you are not yet aware of. And freedom is the effect of control. Without the effort to control the contradictory thoughts that exist within the mental body— your mental body, my mental body—you are not free. Unless we become aware of the promptings of those levels of consciousness, unless we become aware of those dictates within our mind, we cannot control them. And without the control of them, we become the victims of them.

The experiences of unfulfilled desire are common to all species, not only the human race, for all form desires, for it is the very law of expression. The suppression of desire is very detrimental to the health and the welfare of any form. For in suppressing infinite, divine, Energy, or God energy, it disturbs the mental equilibrium of our mental body. We find, then, ourselves frustrated, filled with obstructions and life loses the beauty and the goodness and the purpose for which it has been designed. This philosophy teaches clearly to educate or to fulfill all desires within your mind. To educate a desire is to cast the light of reason upon it, for we find so many things that we want and so much we would like to do.

God has granted unto all of us the ability to accomplish anything that we choose to accomplish. It is possible for all people to have whatever they choose to have. The problem lies in the lack of effort to choose and, once having chosen, to pay the price of attainment or fulfillment. So often before the victories of accomplishments in life, we quit, only to go upon another path of desire to try another way. We quit because we judge that there's too much effort and it is too much of a struggle. I can assure you, my friends, that once you knock upon the door of opportunity, the path is as easy, as clear, and as simple as you choose to make it by the control of your own judgments.

All of the goodness in life that we all are seeking is waiting in front of us. All we need to do is accept that possibility. Through that Law of Acceptance, the will of God moves and brings unto you your heart's desire. If it is in the school of your own evolution to learn the benefit and wisdom of patience, then you shall wait for the fulfillment of your desires in keeping with the laws that you alone have established in this evolution long before you entered this earth realm. But do not look backward to blame the errors of the past for the trials of the present; look to the moment of the now for in this moment you have the power within you to accomplish whatever you choose to accomplish.

Learn to encourage yourselves, my friends, for there are few on this earthly realm who are willing to encourage you for any length of time. For we can only grant to another what we are granting to ourselves and so few of us have learned to encourage our self.

This year, as was forecast last Sunday [*Fifteenth Annual World Forecast*], offers to you one of the finest years that there has been in many. It is a year of opportunity as never before experienced for many, many, many years. If you are willing to make the changes necessary in your attitudes towards life, then you will experience the goodness that this year of '78 has to offer. I personally firmly intend to accept the goodness that is waiting for me. For my God is not a small God and my God is not a stingy God. When we free ourselves from telling God what kind of God that he is, when we accept that it is a God of goodness, then will we experience that type of God in our life. It is our mental world, created by the dictates of our mind, that stand between us and all of the goodness and fulfillment of life that is our divine, eternal right to experience.

Remember, my friends, stop blaming outside and you will find out very quickly what is going on inside. Remember that the human mind, by its very nature, is very tenacious. It strives to defend whatever it has accepted. And so if we want to free our self and if we truly want truth, then we must accept the right of all, of all expression in all of life, because truth needs no defense and we cannot experience that fullness, that freedom and that truth as long as we limit the experiences of life, as long as we dictate how things shall be. Let us free ourselves today from the dictates of what tomorrow is going to be. And let us make tomorrow by becoming consciously aware of our attitudes towards today.

It is this moment that this philosophy is basically interested in, for we know if you change this moment for the better, you will never again be concerned about your tomorrows. You will never have to worry about entering heaven or hell, for this moment you will rise in consciousness, through a little effort, to enter the gates of heaven, which is a state of consciousness that all of us are growing to. It is not a place, my friends, that any of us are going to go to. If we do not have heaven in our consciousness and in our heart today, we cannot enter it tomorrow. Free yourselves from the fear of hell by changing your attitude this moment. Then you won't have to worry whether the angels and their harps will be there to play your tunes. You will know where you are because you will know yourself. And when you know yourself, you will be free. You will be filled with the joy of life, which is, indeed, the demonstrable will of God.

Thank you.

JANUARY 1, 1978

Church Lecture 74

The Continuity of Change

As our chairman has stated, our topic for this morning is, "The Continuity of Change." And so it is as we view our lives and we view the world, we see that change is an inevitable law that nothing in form escapes. Each and every moment there are changes taking place within our mind and within our body. And within the minds and bodies of all forms of life is this Law of Evolution, ever-expanding, through the process of change. It is our difficulties, our refusals to accept the changes in our life that cause so many problems and so much struggle for us.

We cannot hold to the forms of creation for they are in that constant process of evolving. And so it is that the thoughts that we form in our mind, we should not attempt to hold to them, for in so doing, we are bucking the tides of life, so to speak. That does not mean that we should not make the effort to direct our energy to that which is beneficial and constructive and for our own good. It does mean that we cannot experience freedom if we insist upon our attachment to our fruits of action. Now what are our fruits of action? Usually we think of the things that we have garnered unto our self, we consider those things of creation our fruits of action. But rarely do we consider the thoughts that we create in our mind as our fruits of action. And it is our attachment to these attitudes of mind, it is our attachment to the decisions we have made in our life that stand as great obstructions in our path to our eternal, evolving being, known as the eternal soul.

Something cannot come out of nothing. And so the individualization of the human soul did not come from nothing. But whatever we come from, we are destined by the very law to return to. So let us consider the truth that all things come from something. Therefore, all things must return to the source that gave them birth. As Mother Earth has given birth to our physical bodies, so Mother Earth is destined to reclaim that which is hers. And so it is with the attitudes of mind, they are formed of mental substance from a mental world and they are reclaimed by the world that gave them birth, as our soul is reclaimed by the Allsoul, as our spirit is ever returning to the Spirit from whence it came. So, my good friends, change, the continuity of change is something that it would behoove us to consider more often in our daily activities.

In this philosophy we have tried, and continue to try, to teach to those who are seeking the benefit of the divine will, known as total acceptance. For whatever you accept in life, you free from controlling your life. For example, we make our judgments concerning too much rain or not enough rain and because we do not accept the right of the rain or the right of its lack, we are affected by it. I assure you whenever you flood your consciousness with the right of expression of all things in all universes, you free yourself from being controlled by those things. That does not mean that you should do all things. But it does mean that we should not rise up in our superiority over divine law and judge what is to be and what is not to be. For that is not the type of God that is the living, constant demonstration to the minds of men.

For the intelligent Energy sustains whatever you choose to think. It is the same Energy that holds the stars in space. It is totally, wholly, and completely impartial. Remember, friends, our God is personal only to us when we judge our God to be so. For the God of the Spiritualist is a God of Infinite Intelligence. A God that just *is*. It doesn't change. It did not come from something and shall not return to something. It *is*. It is like truth. It needs no defense. It sustains all things. It sustains all forms. It sustains all thoughts.

And so in your life experiences, if you are not pleased with what you do experience, remember, there is an intelligent Energy that will sustain and support your right of choice. And once you make that choice to change your life for the better, that you consider you have a right to be—and indeed is that a right of all form—when you make that choice, remember, it is the same intelligent Energy that supported the levels of consciousness you had before you made the change. It is up to man to choose in life how he wishes his life to be.

But we cannot intelligently choose how we wish our life to be unless we know the laws that govern our life. And the very simple law, clearly demonstrated, is life shall ever be the way you take it, for life is always the way we make it. And we can make our life whichever way we want it to be, for we have already made our life the way it is this moment.

Let us not give this great power of the Divine to things outside of our self. Let us not look outside for the cause of our happiness, for the cause of our goodness, for the cause of our abundance, for it does not exist outside for us until it first exists inside. So whatever you are seeking in life, if you have not yet found it inside, you cannot find it outside. How does man find what he is seeking inside? By first accepting the demonstrable Law of Personal Responsibility: that he alone has the ability to respond to all things within his own being, within his own sphere of action. And when we face that demonstrable Law of Personal Responsibility, we will start on the path to changing our lives the way we want them to be.

The Living Light Philosophy teaches that there are eighty-one levels of consciousness: that there are forty sense functions and forty soul faculties; that there is one Divine Intelligence supporting all of them. The soul faculties, the attributes of our soul, are expressed through our conscious mind. The functions of our being are expressed through our subconscious mind. But, remember, my good friends, nothing gets into our subconscious until it has first gone through our conscious mind. But once having entered into our subconscious mind and established itself firmly as a pattern or attitude of mind, it is not easily, nor readily, changed, if we do not make the effort each day to know our self. For you cannot change what you are not aware of. You can only change within or without, for all changes that you experience without have first taken place within.

So, through acceptance, the immutable Law of Evolution, the continuity of change, which is the refining process of all form, we move with that harmoniously, joyously, and experience the abundance and the good in our life that is truly our divine right.

There is no intelligent power, God or otherwise, that I have ever believed in that dictates that what one shall have, another shall not. Everything is possible to all people. The obstruction and only obstruction to the possibility of something greater than what we have yet experienced is the judgments that we alone make. For we establish the Law of Judgment, the Law of Denial, and that becomes our destiny in life. The moment that we judge how we shall gain anything, we establish a mental law, and all mental laws are dual laws. They are not only positive, but they are also negative. We can rise above those mental realms of consciousness by giving up what we know as judgment. When we are seeking something, if we will experience the divine law, which is known as total acceptance, then we will not have to travel along the mental laws of creation and experience the loss and gain. For there is no loss and there is no gain to divine neutrality. There is no loss and there is no gain to the spirit. There is no loss and there is no gain to truth. There is no duality.

So it is within our power to make whatever changes are necessary in this moment that we may be in the world of creation, that we may be with the things of creation and never be a part of them. When we learn to separate truth from creation, when we learn to awaken within our self to the infinite possibility of a greater life—not sometime after we've left a physical body. Life does not become greater then, unless we make it greater now. My students, do not look to so-called death as an open door to heaven. For heaven and hell are a state of mind that we are in a constant process of growing to. It is not some place that we are going to; we are in it now, this moment. When we lose a physical body, there is no dramatic and drastic change that takes place automatically in our mind. Our mind takes us to a mental world. Our spirit evolves us on to a spiritual world. We cannot experience spiritual worlds after we leave the physical body, unless we make the effort to still our mind and experience those so-called spiritual worlds in the here and the now, this moment.

It all depends on our willingness to accept the possibility of something greater regardless what our judgments have dictated in the past. I assure you, if you let your judgments go, the gates of heaven and all of the goodness that is waiting for you will open. For each time you bow a judgment, which is a superiority over the Divine Intelligence, an illusion created by mental substance, each time you bow a judgment, you open a door to the fullness of life.

Thank you.

FEBRUARY 5, 1978

Church Lecture 75
Our Changing Attachments

In speaking today on "Our Changing Attachments," when we think of attachments, that usually brings to mind the seeming possessions that we have in this material world. But we do not often consider that they are the effects of our various levels of mind, of our attitudes. And so it is that we become, soon, aware of the attachments that we have when they start to change. Now this changing process is ever in keeping with the Law of Evolution, for each and every moment we are in a process of change. And so it is that we can accept these changes graciously and ever look for the good that lies within them or we can hold tenaciously to our attachments in our own mind and, of course, suffer the experience of them going anyway.

A wise man looks at earth and creation around and about him and he knows that by the law of anything coming to him, it is indeed the same law that it shall pass from him. So whether or not in our attachments we judge that it is good or we judge that it is bad, remember, it is ever from the same essence. It is our thoughts that make things in life right or wrong and, of course, it is our right to our thoughts.

But what does all of this have to do with life eternal? I assure, my good friends, that is life eternal for we have a mind. Without a mind, we cannot experience. The purpose of the soul's incarnation is to cast the light of reason, a soul faculty, upon the vehicle called the mind. And so it is as we, with a bit of reason, look at life with our mind, then we can understand that change is something that we are in a constant process of.

Whenever you experience the loss of anything in your life—and the truth of the matter is you are experiencing the loss of something each and every moment—pause in those moments that you think you are experiencing loss. For if you will pause, you will see the birth of gain—not the gain of what you already seem to have, but the gain of something ever greater. For our horizons, our minds, are ever opening and broadening to new thoughts, to new ideas. And that is, indeed, the purpose of life, that we may in time consider the right of all expression and in considering the right of all expression, choose that which we wish to identify with. For as you consider the right of all expression, unless you choose what you will identify with, then you soon find that you, as an individual, are in a state of confusion, confusing what you think is right and confusing what you think is wrong.

I know that it is difficult for the human mind to accept all things, for the human mind is an instrument designed to attach to whatever it accepts. And the human mind is an instrument that uses what is known as fear to protect what it thinks that it has. And so our philosophy teaches that the human mind, with its instrument called fear, holds tenaciously, for it does not yet accept the divine, infinite truth that all things, in truth, originate from one infinite, divine, intelligent Source, that we are, in truth, an inseparable part of that intelligent, infinite, eternal Source, that we have, in our journey in evolution, wandered from it—not that we are separate from it, for we cannot be separate. We can only, in our mental delusion, believe that we are separate from God. We shall all return to that Source. It is not a matter of centuries or years or even days ahead. It is a matter of a moment of choice in this moment. We may choose in this moment to once again reunite in consciousness with the divine, abundant good, which is our true being, or we may choose to remain separate from the good, which is, in truth, ourselves.

So let us, this moment, let us pause to think. Let us not be so confused and distracted by the passing panorama of creation. For if we do, then we are in a constant process of indecision. A wise man makes his decisions and accepts everything necessary to attain it. But so often in life we make a decision and we choose something without a full consideration of the payment; we can only see the possibility of the attainment. And it is when we are close to the victories in life that our minds rise up in their superiority and they look at the payments and they say they did not choose those payments. They did not choose those payments because they did not consider the possibility of those payments, for they only looked at the possibility of their attainments.

My friends, every loss is a gain, and every gain is a loss. To accept what creation really has to offer is to understand it. And to understand anything is to place you, your consciousness, in a position to work harmoniously through it. So if we start from the very basis of understanding, that what all of nature is demonstrating to us, the Law of Duality, when we understand that our mind is a vehicle of duality, then we can work with it in an intelligent and reasonable way.

Let us cast the light of common sense upon our attachments in life, but let us never forget that those attachments exist in mental substance, that what you view outside of your life is only an effect of your attitude towards it. Let us never lose sight of that light of reason. And let us ever remember that we can change our attitude for we and we alone gave birth to our attitude. And when we change our attitude concerning anything, that thing changes in our consciousness. To do otherwise is to be but the victim of so-called circumstances. We become the victims of circumstances through an error of ignorance. When we awaken to what that error is, then we can make the necessary changes in our own mind.

I assure you that life is ever as great, as good, as wonderful, and as joyous as you alone choose to accept it. You have that right of choice. That is your divine birthright: to choose the freedom, the beauty, the goodness, and the joy of your eternal being, known as your soul, or to choose the constantly changing panorama of the vehicle known as your mind.

My good students, your mind has recorded what your short, earthly experiences have been. Therefore, it can offer to you nothing more than those experiences. But your eternal being, your soul, has experienced untold numbers of vehicles of mind. It didn't come to earth brand new, from nothing. And it shan't return to nothing because it didn't come from nothing. Your parents were chosen in keeping with the law that you alone set into motion. Your mind, which has recorded only your earthly experience, it cannot reveal that to you. But in a moment of peace, when your mind is still, your soul can reveal the cause of all of your experiences. And without an awareness of the cause of your experiences, you cannot reasonably make the necessary changes in your mind.

So does it not behoove us to be at peace and to permit our soul to speak to us? For it speaks in a still, small voice, and that soul knows all things that it has experienced in all lives. It will guide you on the path of reason. It will guide you and is ever attempting and working to guide you, that you may experience the good in your life. But if you permit your mind to reject that inner knowing from your soul, then your limited earth mind, with its limited experiences, will continue to control your earthly life.

When you leave this physical body—and we are all leaving it more often than we consciously know. We are leaving it when we sleep, and we are leaving it many times when we are inspired— what you call inspiration. That is what's really happening, but it takes a reeducation of the senses of the mind to view that simple truth. We leave our body many times during the course of a short twenty-four hours, but we are not fully aware of what is taking place. Sometimes we call that daydreaming and sometimes we call it just dreaming. That does not mean to imply that whenever we dream we are leaving our physical body, for that is not true. There are ofttimes when we do and there are ofttimes when we do not.

But we have this mental body that has experiences in a mental world. Now this mental world, that you have created, is limited to your own creations. And that limit of your mind is the same limit that other minds have created. For example, if you believe in your mind that in certain areas of your life the world is indeed miserable, then everyone who believes that way in their mind, you are inseparably united to. Whether or not you consciously know them has nothing to do with the demonstrable law that like attracts like and becomes the Law of Attachment. Now the Christian Bible revealed that truth clearly when it said, "Where one or more are gathered in my name, there shall I be." So, where you, in your decisions and beliefs, are strong and firm, be rest assured that your beliefs, your judgments, are supported by untold thousands of minds. Not only minds that are still expressing through a physical body, but minds that are expressing in a mental world that have left the earthly flesh long, long ago.

So many people, especially interested in the religion of Spiritualism, are first concerned about what types of spirits may get a hold of them. The only type of spirit that has a hold of anyone is ever in keeping with like attracts like and becomes the Law of Attachment. If you express an uncontrollable temper, I can assure you there are untold billions of people who have passed on who still express an uncontrollable temper. Now, when you express that in keeping with that law of like, thousands of them flock to your rescue. [*Many members of the congregation laugh.*] How often a person in expressing their temper is, for a moment, aware that they should take control of themselves, but find it so very difficult. Now let us not, in that understanding, blame everything onto some discarnate spirit, for we and we alone made the first step.

But as you look at life and you see how simple and how quickly the divine laws of life work, isn't it only reasonable, my good friends, that you direct energy to the positive in your life, to the good? And because the nature of the human mind is to constantly expect something, why not direct it to expect something greater than you already think that you have. Now we are all expecting. We expect when we wake up and we expect when we go to sleep. There is never a moment when the human mind is not expecting something. But in that expectation, what is it that rises up from the depths of our subconscious? Are we consciously making the effort to be aware of what the effect of our expectations in life truly is?

We have the right to use this vehicle called the human mind to bring the good into our lives. For if we cannot bring the good into our lives, then we surely cannot be the instrument to bring the good into anyone else's life. And as the Bible clearly states, "O physician, heal thyself." If we cannot become the living demonstration of goodness in our personal life, we certainly are in no position to dictate or try to counsel another how to bring the good into their lives. So let us look at life's demonstration and let us never forget that the demonstration in our life is the revelation of what we alone are doing.

Thank you.

MARCH 5, 1978

Church Lecture 76

Attaining Universal Consciousness

In speaking to you this morning on the subject of "Attaining Universal Consciousness," we must understand that we are all in the process of that attainment. The human mind is designed to store information and to create, from that information that it has stored, experiences in our life. We know that we are not the mind, that the mind is a vehicle or instrument that our true being, known to us as the eternal soul, uses to express on this planet.

Now we are all faced, each and every day of our lives, with new experiences. And when we face these new experiences, our mind, which has stored all of the information it has gathered from the past, having no reference to the new experience, reacts in keeping with its design to protect the information that has already been fed into it. And so we find, in our lives, continuing experiences repeating themselves over and over again and again and again. That process, sooner or later, helps us to awaken within ourselves the separation of truth from creation; the separation of our eternal being, the soul, from the vehicle of the mind that it is using.

Now, we all know, as a personal demonstration in our lives, that we are not the mind. We are not the experiences of the mind, for we are all aware that we are, in truth, in a constant process of changing. When we, in a moment of peace and stillness within us, view the experiences that we are encountering in life, we quickly see the cause that has been, and continues to be, within our own mind. To free our self from the limitations of this computer called the human mind takes a daily and constant effort. It is not a matter of spending many hours in a meditation each day. It is a matter of being alert and being awake within that we may see clearly what we are heading into.

When we make that effort we slowly, but surely, begin to broaden our horizons, to become aware of the world around and about us, for our world is not limited to this physical and mental world. It is not so limited. We are experiencing many dimensions of consciousness. But because we have permitted our minds to overidentify with this limited Earth planet, we cannot see clearly. We do not hear clearly because all things that we see and hear are censored by the limited experiences that we have already accepted in our lives.

We are destined to attain this universal consciousness, and we are indeed in process of doing so this moment. Now that process for us can either be a great and miserable struggle or it can be one of peace and joy. That is ever dependent upon our daily effort to separate eternal truth from limited creation, to separate this true being that has experienced many lives, many bodies in many, many, many centuries. That part of us that is our true being, without a beginning, knows no ending. It is our mind that fears, not our soul. For our soul knows that the experiences that we are encountering, they have come by laws created by our mind, that they will pass ever in keeping with our own effort.

In this philosophy it is clearly stated, whatever we place our attention upon, we have a tendency to become. So our lives this moment are the revelation and the demonstration of what we have been placing our attention upon. Now we have, of course, the choice. We and we alone may choose what we will place our attention upon. You see, my good friends, divine, infinite, neutral Energy follows the direction of our mind. We channel this energy through our thought, through our attitude. And we and we alone create the experiences that we have in life. But because we alone are the creators of those experiences, then we must encourage our self for we alone can change them.

Now if, in our efforts to make these changes, our faith, which is in truth a positive attitude of mind, if our faith is strengthened, if our faith is encouraged by certain thoughts and beliefs, then it is only in our best interest to use those thoughts and beliefs to strengthen our faith that we may be freed from this instrument of the human mind called fear. We understand that fear is negative use of this intelligent, infinite, divine Energy. Let us begin this moment by first becoming aware of our thoughts, becoming aware of our attitudes, for in order to change anything in our life, we must first become aware of it.

And in making this daily effort to become aware of our attitudes of mind, to become aware of the thoughts of our mind, then let us pray for the light of reason that we may set into motion new thoughts and new attitudes, that we may have the courage and the endurance to sustain, on a daily basis, the Law of Continuity. So often in life we quit just before the victory. But we must ask ourselves why do we quit before the victories in our lives? Let us look through our life. Let us see what we did when we were young, when we were little children. Did we establish that pattern, that attitude of mind, to quit before the victories? If we did, then we must pour equal energy, equal effort into changing those established patterns that indeed are not serving us well.

I have stated many times, and state again, beyond a shadow of any doubt life is ever as great, ever as good, ever as abundant as we alone choose to accept it. That is the way our lives really are. Now we can make that choice, but in order to do so, we must give up some cherished opinions that we have entertained for some time. We must give up the thoughts and the attitudes that tell us that life is so bad. We must give those up in order that we may gain this great and good life that we all indeed are seeking. For we cannot be a house divided and be a success in anything. We must first know within our self, in the depths of our very being, that there is no power, there is no force outside of our own personal universe that can bring us anything good or so-called bad. It is within us. It is our effort to become receptive to a level of consciousness in order that we may experience that that we are desiring in our life. But, in so doing, my good friends, in making that effort to rise in consciousness to that level, we must let go of everything that stands in the way. So when we make the choice to have a better life today, we must, in making that choice, be willing, be ready, and be able to pay the price, whatever it may be. So, in doing so, in making that choice, consider all of those factors and consider that the eternal law, known as evolution, is indeed the demonstrable Law of Change.

We are changing each and every moment. Indeed, we are changing. Slowly, but surely, our horizons, our experiences are becoming broadened. We are indeed becoming aware that whatever experiences we have in life, there are others who also have those experiences. They have survived and moved on from that level of consciousness. That we should view with great encouragement for ourselves, for what is possible for one is indeed possible for everyone.

In the broadening of our horizons, in the attaining of universal consciousness, remember that that attainment is an effect of a broadening of your consideration. As you gradually begin to consider the things around and about you, to consider the trials and tribulations of another, you slowly, but surely, begin to free yourselves from the limited experiences of your past.

God, it is taught in this philosophy, helps those who help themselves. But how does man help himself? We help our self by helping another, for God, this Divine Infinite Intelligence, works through man, not directly to man. I know of no God that manifests all of the desires that my mind entertains, but I am aware of a God, impartial, intelligent, and neutral that works in keeping with infinite, divine laws that are infallible. We can choose to flow with those infinite, divine laws, if that is what we wish to do. As you make an effort in your lives, as we all make an effort in our lives to help another soul along the path, we rise up in our own consciousness in order that we may be instrumental for this intelligent Energy to flow through us unobstructed to help another. And so, you see, as that effort is made, indeed we are the ones who are benefited, as well as the one we are trying to be instruments of the Divine to benefit.

We are an inseparable part, my good friends, of one intelligent Consciousness. We may think what we choose to think, but we cannot separate our being from the universal whole. We can only delude ourselves for a time, but even in that delusion, we have not separated our true being from what we call God.

And so it is in this universal consciousness that we are all moving towards, let us not view the steps of payment, for energy follows attention and the steps of payment become more than we are willing to bear. Our responsibilities in life, we must never allow to exceed our love of God. And so we must, for our sake, remove our thought, our attention from these little payments of evolving. For whether we like it or not, we are evolving. We will continue to do so. So let us accept the inevitable Law of Evolution. Let us accept it graciously that we may flow with it harmoniously. Let us let go of that [which], by the very laws of change, is leaving our universe. Let us take hold of our mind, through some effort of self-control, that we may not experience this negative faith called fear, that we may be assured within our very being that our life is ever-expanding, is ever-serving the purpose for which it has been designed.

The good that we see is the good that we experience. So let us look in all things for the good that is in them. For all things, we understand, are sustained by intelligent Energy. And that intelligent Energy, to us, is known as God. So if we look for the good in all experience, then the good, or godness, that is in us is what we will experience. And in so doing, our lives shall be fulfilled with a more positive attitude. Our health, our wealth, and our happiness is in our hands, my friends. For the divine Energy is already within us. It is not something we need to go somewhere to get. It is never away. It is ever present. But it is dependent, *it is dependent* upon our acceptance.

I know that it is difficult for any mind to accept the fullness of life when the thoughts of the mind are dictating to us the opposite. I know it is difficult, but I also know it is not impossible. And because it is not impossible, we can experience what we choose. If we will only make that little effort each day to remember that, that we may, in life, become the actors instead of the reactors. None of us want to be the reactor to anything, not in truth.

We cherish in our mind that we are unique, but as we broaden our horizons, we find that our uniqueness is indeed very general. But in so awakening to that simple truth, we no longer feel that we are alone. For I assure you, my good friends, no matter what attitude of mind you entertain, no matter what level of consciousness you experience, you are never alone. There are untold millions of people yet on earth and many billions more in other dimensions who are right there beside you. Whether that is a level that is negative or positive, good or bad in keeping with your personal preference, you are never alone. There are many at your side, ever in keeping with the infinite, divine law that like attracts like and becomes the Law of Attachment.

How many, many married people I have counseled in this past thirty-seven years. How many times has it been pointed out to them, in their trials and tribulations: by the Law of Attraction you have merited the mirror of yourself. Look in the mirror and make the changes in *your* consciousness and you will no longer have to be concerned about your husband or your wife. For that that is around and about us, my friends, is, in truth, our mirror. We can try to smash the mirror, but there will always be the pieces in which we can see the reflection.

So in this life and all those lives yet to be experienced, remember, you are captain of your ship, you are master of your destiny, whenever you personally choose to be so. Yesterday may not have been the way we wanted it to be. Our fears that tomorrow will be the same is the very law that creates the continuity of our yesterdays. We must, in order to have a more abundant life, we must remove those fears. And if it is necessary for you to exercise greater determination within you, then do so that you may have what is rightfully yours. No one denies us but our self. And when we accept that truth, we begin to make the necessary changes in our mind and we have a new life to experience. If you decide it will take you years, then you have established the mental law of judgment, and you must follow the law that you alone establish. But if you release that thought and if you, in truth, accept a greater Intelligence, to whom all things are possible, then for you the time may indeed be very short.

Thank you.

APRIL 2, 1978

Church Lecture 77
Seven Years of Serenity

Friends, on this, as I have mentioned earlier, this very special occasion for this association, to one part of my mind seven years has passed very quickly, but to another attitude of my mind it seems to me that it's been over seven centuries, for so much has happened in these seven years to this very day. I have witnessed many changes since the founding of this church. I have seen hundreds and hundreds of people come, and I have seen hundreds and hundreds go. But I have always been assured that if man presents to the world that which he truly believes and makes the effort in his life to demonstrate that it is not important whether or not people stay or people go. But it is important that they have been the witness. For in truth we all are the witness. We are the witness of passing events. We are the witness of the illusion of time. We are the witness of varying thoughts and feelings, the witness of emotions. We are ofttimes, so ofttimes, the witness of our own judgments in life.

And so it is in the growth of this church and this association, there have been those who have been pleased with the work that it has tried to do and continues to do, and there have been those who are not pleased. But only a fool would believe that he could please everyone all the time. It is not the purpose of Serenity to please the world. It is the purpose of this organization to stand upon the rock of principle to bring forth to the world the understanding that it continues to receive concerning the purpose of life.

This philosophy is not a stagnant philosophy. It is a philosophy that is in a constant process of change and growth. Its principle has never changed, for you do not change truth and still have truth. But the expression of truth ever varies as our mind becomes more receptive to more thoughts and ideas that we find beneficial in our life. No philosophy in this world today will be popular that not only teaches, but demonstrates, the Law of Personal Responsibility. This church was founded upon that principle and its teachings are very simple: whatever in life that we experience we are directly responsible for. It is difficult in our experiences in life, it is ofttimes difficult to accept that weight of responsibility. But once having accepted that, that principle, we begin to grow. We begin to grow inside, for there are many experiences in our life that we are not pleased, nor happy with. And when you accept the principle of personal responsibility, you begin to face yourself, where the changes must, someday, be made.

All of creation demonstrates and teaches us the Law of Evolution, the process of constant change. If we are not flexible in a world of creation, then, like the tree that refuses to bend, we shall break. Let us not hold to any set attitude of mind, for in so doing we guarantee the law to change it. Let us ever be receptive in a broadening of our horizons that we may, in so doing, truly accept the right of all expression. He who accepts the right, the right of the Divine Intelligence to express in any way that it sees fit without the detriment and hurt to another is accepting in truth the love of God.

This church does not believe, nor has it ever believed, that there is any God that judges and dictates to his children that you must live this way or that way, for to believe in that type of God is to establish limits to the growth and expansion of our own consciousness. History repeatedly teaches us that organizations and societies in our world that refuse to change with the changing times did not endure.

Religion has gone through a multitude of changes since man first placed his feet upon this planet. Religion has risen in popularity and it has descended in popularity. But it has survived. It has survived, ever in changing form, because that spiritual principle expressed in a world of creation is ever adaptable to the needs of the people of the time. One might say, when they study religions, that there are certain principles that have never changed. It is not the principle of things that change. It is the form or expression through which it is flowing that changes.

Our world still has the basic elements from the birth of the creation of this planet. The expression of those elements has changed, but not the elements themselves. You, your true being, views an ever-changing world around and about you, but your true being does not change. That eternal part of you, that has always been and, therefore, will always be, that is changeless because, my good friends, it is formless. In order to have change in anything, you must have form, you must have limit. But your spirit is not form; your spirit is not limit. It is our mind, the vehicle through which our true spirit is expressing, that is limited and, therefore, in need, of course, of changes, expansion, and growth.

Those who enter these doors each Sunday come for varying reasons. Ofttimes they are brought by someone who has visited before. And indeed my heart is grateful whenever I view these people come to this church, for regardless of their motive, regardless whether or not they return, they have had an experience. Whether it is consciously accepted or rejected is not important, for it is recorded in memory par excellence. When we leave this earthly realm permanently, when our physical body returns to the elements from whence it was garnered, our mental body continues to grow and to expand.

It is perhaps, to some, sad that they are not yet aware that they are moving in and out of their physical body, but they are not aware, yet, of the reality, the conscious realization of that process taking place. They may recall a vivid dream or they may think that they are daydreaming, but worlds that are around and about us, of which we are an inseparable part, are here and now this moment. So often I have heard the Spirit say, "We are only a thought away." But how often do we in this physical, material world, how often do we think about this life eternal?

Have we, because of our own decisions and judgments, closed the door to the demonstrable truth of life eternal? If we have, it simply reveals, of course, to us that in our investigation in life we were never satisfied with the answers that we had received concerning life eternal.

But where does that leave the Law of Personal Responsibility? Is someone else responsible for our lack of intelligent investigation into the most important subject that we could possibly consider? The subject of eternal life. Someone else is not responsible for our investigation, for our effort to learn about life. That is our personal responsibility. If we have decided, after perhaps a few years or even months of investigation, that the subject is not worthy of thorough investigation, then we are yet to live. We are yet to awaken to our own responsibility and the abundant good that is in this moment, the eternal moment of now.

I have heard in these thirty-seven years of this work, I have heard from many that they will think about this spirit world or this other world when they get there. Well, the surprises that await them may not be as pleasant as they would like to think. For when you are going somewhere, no matter where you decide to go—and, you see, whether we like it or not, we all decided to leave this physical world. I don't think there is anyone within the sound of my voice who will say they've decided not to go, for the law is inevitable. We cannot escape that. So somewhere along the line in our evolution, we decided and we merited to enter earth into a physical body, to stay in that physical body X number of years, and to move out of it and move on. Because we do not recall that we alone made that decision does not exempt us from the responsibility that we have, each and every one of us, incurred.

We understand that heaven is a state of consciousness that we are in a process of growing to. It is not some specific place that we are going to by our wishes and by our prayers. It's a state of mind, my friends. You and I are all in a process of growing to that state of mind. If we make the daily effort to make our life more complete in this moment, today and each and every day, we will not have to be so concerned about these heaven and hells. For they are all, I assure you, self-created. They are mental realms. No one with any common sense would call a so-called hell a spiritual realm, for there's nothing spiritual about hell except the escape therefrom.

So let us think today about what we're doing with our life today, for then our tomorrows will be filled with the spirit and the joy of living. Let us not be so concerned about what tomorrow brings. This is the moment that we can do something with. It is the only moment that is within our grasp. We can do something with our attitude towards life. Now we can do something. We can do something about the way we really want to live. That is truly the great blessing: the blessing of moment-by-moment choice. Whenever we begin to feel, as we all do at times, a bit discouraged or despondent, or we start to view the past, our past, in regret because we didn't do things yesterday that prove today it would've been best for us to do—you can't make changes intelligently that way. For the past is gone. You can do a lot about today.

This is indeed, I assure you, a beautiful world. It is a wonderful world. We can choose this moment to see that world, for that's the way it really is. But to see that world of beauty and harmony, in which we truly live this moment, we must make the effort to free our mind from so many judgments. It is not God or some power outside our self that tells us it's a terrible day. It is not someone else that is establishing a law that we are suffering in illness and misery, in shortage. No, my friends, it isn't someone else that's doing it to us. It's our mind. It's our choice. It is our right. To get along with another, we must first get along with our self, for we cannot grant unto another what we have not granted to our self. If we grant to our mind the right of difference, if we grant to our mind the freedom from judgment, then that qualifies us to grant that to another mind. And then, my friends, we begin, through that process, to find out who we really are.

We all know how fallible our mind is. We can look past, if we wish, and see how many judgments and decisions that we made yesterday and years ago and we can see so often we were in error. That same process takes place this moment. Whether we like it or not, we are on a realm of consciousness that involves people. We communicate with people. Sometimes we don't want to and the jobs in life that we have we are forced to, if we want to keep our job. And ofttimes we find so much difficulty with other people. The ones that we're forced to work with or to communicate with. I assure you, my friends, it's not those other people, but it is other levels of our mind that yet are in need of the light of reason. For when we cast the light of reason over any thought in our mind, we open the door to consider more than the thought is dictating to us.

Our world has gone through many changes. It is constantly in the process of those changes. Tomorrow will not be exactly the way it is today. There will be something new that is added to your life and something old that has been taken away. Now that is happening all the time. Sometimes you are aware of it and sometimes you are not aware of it, but it is taking place. So what does reason and common sense dictate? Let us not hold to the form of thought, for it came to us and it must go. If we hold not to it, then we shall not be controlled by it and not being controlled by it, we shall experience the freedom, for we have demonstrated the truth; we have awakened within our self.

The Living Light Philosophy teaches that freedom is the direct effect of self-control. Now let us pause a moment and view that. What does that really mean? The control of self grants the freedom of our true being. But then man asks the question, "What do I need to control?" And the answer comes very simply: that that you need to control is what is presently controlling you. For if you have something controlling you, then you are not free, but you are bound. And it is our thoughts, it is our judgments that control us. But we can free our self by the very simple principle of discipline.

When you choose to experience a happy moment, you immediately set into motion within your consciousness all of the experiences that are recorded under the department of happiness. You cannot have the experience of that happiness unless you have some degree of control of your mind. I know you will all agree that when you think of anything, your mind immediately rises with the direct opposite, for all minds work that way in a world of creation, which is duality. So, my friends, when your mind thinks of peace, your little computer rises up with war. And when it thinks of abundance, your mind dictates lack. And when it thinks of happiness, your mind rises up with its direct opposite. Without controlling our mind, there is no freedom that we can experience in our mind. Now some people believe that when they do what they want to do, they are experiencing freedom. But if you would trace the cause and the motive of that, I don't think that you would long call that freedom.

To awaken within is the teaching of all philosophies, for without knowing our self we cannot know the truth, the truth which sets us free. Truth is individually perceived. This church and this association and this philosophy and religion cannot give you truth. No one, no study can give you truth. It can show you the varying ways that many people have found truth for themselves. Truth is individually perceived. Whichever path in life that you are on, if it is doing something for you, then you can be rest assured, my good friends, you are doing something for it. For we get out of anything in life—we get out of life what we put into life. And if we feel we are not getting enough out of life, then pause and think. It only reveals we are not yet putting enough into life. If we think that yesterday had so much greatness and goodness and happiness and joy for us, then all we have to do is pause and ask our self, "What did I do yesterday that I had such wonderful experiences?" For we all know the way, but it's a matter of taking those moments each day to think where we're going, to think and think more deeply.

When these doors opened seven years ago, I stated at that time, "These doors are open for all God's children, that includes everyone." Whether we believe in God or we don't believe in God, that doesn't change the infinite, divine, intelligent Energy. It does not change it one iota. It does change us, but it does not change the very Source that sustains us, for that is not within the power of man. I stated on the day of dedicating this church that many souls would come and many would go. This church offers the opportunity to everyone who is interested to grow or to go. For the light in life, the light of reason is never brighter than the night of ignorance. For that's the way it is in creation. That's the way it is in this old, physical world.

But let us never be without hope. So often man despairs in life. Just before the gates of victory he quits, he despairs. Why does man become so discouraged and why does man despair, when the effort to be successful, when the effort to truly experience the fullness and the divine right of your life is not really that great an effort? It's just a constant effort. It's a little bit every day, instead of a lot now and then. Usually we wait until so-called disaster strikes and we run out either to the psychologists, the psychiatrists, or to the churches, to the priests and to the ministers to bring about a miraculous transformation from the emotional disaster that we find our self in. There is no miraculous cure. There is no so-called quick cure to anything. If it took a hundred pounds of energy to put you in the depths of despair, well it's going to take a hundred pounds of positive acceptance of something greater to lift you back up again.

So let us not, each day, think so much about this world that we're trying to race through and keep our bills paid. Let's take a few moments of those twenty-four hours every day and consider the possibility of something better. For I assure you in the midst of the Philistines God does deliver us. Every knock in your life is a boost. And I have not been without my knocks, but I never fail to speak to my mind when things seem adverse; I never fail to tell it that divine truth: Every knock is a boost. And before the gates of victory come the hissing hounds of hell.

So you see, my friends, I am not perfect and I never found anyone on earth or even in the spirit world that says they're perfect. Not being perfect, I have a mind that I must work with and I tell you from personal experiences our minds are programmed, just like a computer. If you make the effort each day, it will work for you, because I make the effort each day and it does work for me. To first become aware, when you are in these varying levels of consciousness, that it is an attitude of mind that you are expressing at the moment. It is not you, but it is an attitude of mind that you have created. You are not free from the responsibility of that level of consciousness, but you are free to choose something better. So no matter what you have or have not in life, remember, there is something better waiting for you. But it's up to you to open the door of reason and accept it.

Thank you.

MAY 7, 1978

Church Lecture 78

Our Invisible Friends

In speaking on the topic of, "Our Invisible Friends," as we view recorded history we see from the Oracles of Delphi to the present day and in all religions of the world, there never was a time when man did not speak of these so-called invisible friends.

As a thought in the mind releases intelligent energy into the atmosphere around and about us creating the very form of the thought that we think, so it is that these dimensions that we are moving through, we fail to see and we fail to hear simply because our minds are so active creating the forms of our own mind that they build a shield or a wall, so to speak, between us and these many dimensions in which we truly live. For man to personally experience these worlds around and about us, he must first make the effort to control his own mind, that it may be in a state of peace, not releasing this intelligent energy and creating these multitudes of forms. For unless he does, he can see or hear only the reflections that rise up from within himself.

All religions are founded upon words and teachings that have been brought to our earth realm from other dimensions. But we soon forget the source. We soon forget our humble beginnings as we become so active in this mundane and material world.

The basic teaching of this philosophy is the teaching of personal responsibility and following that teaching is the demonstrable truth that like attracts like and becomes the Law of Attachment. And so it is as man, through an error of ignorance permits his mind to be overactive with this mundane and material world, he can only attract back into his life like kind.

This journey in this earth realm is a very short journey for all of us. The years, they go very, very quickly. And yet, it seems we give so little thought and so little consideration to this great eternity, to these dimensions that we are destined to experience—and sooner than most of us think. My good friends, [when] we came here to earth, we came with an awakened spirit. But that awakened spirit slowly, but surely, early in our earth years was dimmed. Dimmed by an overactivity of our mental body. Because of that, we wander in the darkness of this earthly realm. We doubt and we fear. Both doubt and fear, a function of the human mind, does only one thing to our life: it brings to us a repetition of the experiences that we fear, a repetition of the things that we doubt. It is when we direct this intelligent energy to the Source that sustains our very life that we begin to awaken from within once again. And we begin to see a bit more clearly not only where we are going, but where we have been.

Ever since the beginning of man, these intelligent, so-called invisible friends—invisible to our physical sight, but surely not invisible to our eternal sight. It is the divine birthright of each and every soul on this planet to know where they have been before they came, to know where they are in evolution this very moment and to know beyond a shadow of any doubt where they are going. That—your birthright and mine—is ever available to us, but it takes a little effort on our part. It takes a little effort each and every moment to remember the world on this earth that we are presently experiencing is a mirror revealing our own mental world.

But there is something greater than the thought of man. There is something far greater than the mind of man. There is the intelligent Energy that sustains it all. This intelligent Energy is what we really are. We are not the flesh. We are not the form. Those things of creation are born and those are the things that die. So it would be indeed most foolhardy to attach our self, by the Law of Identity, to things which are destined to return to their source. It is through our attention that the Law of Identity is established. And once we establish this Law of Identity, we cannot help but follow the path of attachment. It is our attachments in life that bring us our suffering and our pain. And so all philosophies throughout our world have taught to free our self from our attachments, for they have been given birth by us and they shall die by our own hand.

My good friends, there cannot be peace, there cannot be harmony, there surely cannot be freedom, until we make the effort to gain a level of consciousness of objectivity to the experiences of life itself. Most of us, unfortunately, somehow believe that life is experience, but I assure you that life is the very essence of joy itself. But to experience that essence, that joy, that so-called heaven, is to be free from the forms created by our own mind.

It is through this help that we receive from those who have experienced this earthly life and who have gone on to other dimensions to other levels of consciousness, it is through their assistance, for they are indeed with us daily, that we are inspired and encouraged to make, yea, even greater effort.

So often in this religion I have heard Spiritualists, some, say that their guides and teachers, they've gone on; they're no longer with them. They no longer have these invisible helpers. It is sad to hear a statement of that type, for it reveals by its own demonstration that these so-called angels, these helpers from these other worlds, they haven't gone anywhere; we have just lowered our level of consciousness. We have become so overactive with our material, mundane world that we can no longer see, we can no longer hear, we can no longer sense.

There is never a gain in life without a loss, and there is never a loss without a gain. And so it is up to us to choose wisely, this moment, what it is we wish to gain, for that is the nature of the being. It is the nature to experience in this earthly world. It is our nature to evolve, to grow, and to expand. But for each expansion, there is a contraction. For every gain is a guaranteed loss. So when we choose, let us pause before we choose and let us accept the personal law of responsibility and be willing to lose whatever it is we must lose to gain whatever it is we choose to gain. For if we look at life in that way, we will begin to see life in a more balanced and more objective way. We will begin to grow up emotionally.

Fear, which is the mind's control over the eternal soul, is something that each of us experience each and every day. We experience it because we haven't yet learned, perhaps, how to free our self from this temporal, mental body. This mind that we have is in a constant process of evolving and changing. Because it is in a constant process of evolving and changing and expanding, we experience in our life each day what we call fear. We fear for our jobs. We fear for our homes. We fear for our material supply. We fear for our health. We fear for so many things each and every day. I am aware that some of us, perhaps, are not willing to admit to ourselves that we are filled with so much fear. But all we have to do is take an inventory of our daily experiences and then we will become quickly aware of how much fear we are experiencing. The reason that we look in this physical world and see so very much negativity is because it is the expression of fear.

As long as we permit our minds to believe that we and we alone are life itself, that there is no intelligence outside of us, personally, that is sustaining and supporting us, then we can be rest assured we shall pay the price of Lucifer. It's called the price of pride. For if you will recall, Lucifer rose in his great pride to be equal with the intelligent Energy that was sustaining him, called God.

These invisible friends that are around and about us each and every moment, ever in keeping with the Law of Attraction, we shall meet someday. If we do not meet them while yet in the physical flesh, we are guaranteed to meet them when we leave this physical world. For the physical body, garnered up from the physical substance of earth, is destined by the Law of Return to go back to this physical earth. And our mental body, which we have identified with, is destined to return to the substance from whence it was garnered.

My friends, there is no lasting security in identifying with the things that come and are guaranteed to go. The only thing that we will ever or have ever had or will ever have is the possibility of awakening to our great, eternal life, to a stream of consciousness that is far beyond the limited forms created by our human mind. For in truth, we are this essence of life. We are a stream of consciousness that ever moves through untold multitudes of so-called experience.

But we must remember, we are not the experience. We are not the thought. We are the intelligent energy that has created the thought, but we are not the thought itself. It is when we believe we are the thought that our problems start to rise. It is when we believe we are the fear and the experience—that is our struggle. For it, in truth, is revealing to us that we have identified with the duality of creation and through that identity, we have attached our self to that vibratory wave. All of life is vibration. And we *are* the vibration that we alone, through identity, have chosen. But we can choose a new vibration. To us, it's called an attitude. We can choose that new vibration and we can, then, free our self from that which we have chosen to free our self from.

We cannot see and we cannot hear what we do not accept the possibility of. We could not have landed on the moon or gone into outer space until someone on this earth realm had accepted the possibility. We cannot experience these invisible friends in our conscious mind until we first accept the possibility. To infinite, intelligent Energy all things are possible. To deny that there is something that is not possible to infinite, intelligent Energy is to rise as Lucifer rose in his pride and, therefore, suffer the consequences. When you accept the possibility of all things, when you accept the possibility of all good in your life, you will set into motion the Law of Identity upon which you may experience what you are choosing to experience. But you cannot experience until you first accept the possibility.

Why has it been for untold eons of time so difficult for the masses to accept the possibility of life eternal, to accept the possibility of communication with other dimensions that their physical senses cannot experience? Why is it so difficult? It is difficult because of fear. Man fears what he judges he cannot control. That's the way all minds work. So when you encounter an experience that your mind says it cannot control, you may be rest assured you will immediately experience fear. But, my friends, whether or not we accept the possibility of all things today, we can be encouraged for we are destined by the very Law of Evolution to accept the possibility of all things someday.

We are, in truth, an ever-expanding consciousness. We are not as limited today as we were yesterday. And indeed in keeping with the very Law of Evolution, we will not be as limited tomorrow as we are today. So does it not behoove us, in viewing the demonstrable laws of life, does it not behoove us to expand our consciousness through a little more personal effort? Why leave it to so-called circumstance, which is nothing more than a lack of understanding the laws that we have set into motion? Why leave it to so-called accident, which is, again, an error of not understanding what laws we alone are setting into motion? Is it not a better way to be aware of what we are doing with our mind and with our life? Is it not better to take a hold of the reins and look our destiny square in the face, knowing that we and we alone are making the choice? For that, in truth, is really the way that it is.

Those invisible friends that are in our universe are ever in keeping with the laws that we alone have established. They are, in truth, no better and no worse than what we, in truth, really are. But who is to judge who is better and worse?

Man himself is his own best friend. And man himself is his own worst enemy. For it is man's personal thoughts and personal acts that lift him to heavenly heights or take him in the opposite direction. There's nothing outside that can ever affect our life, unless you have something inside that is setting that law into motion. For all experience in all of life is ever within us. Remember, my good friends, whatever it is in life you want, whatever it is in life you don't want, it's within your hands, for it's within your head. It's never out there. It is a delusion of the mind that dictates to us that it's outside. That is not where it exists. It's inside our self. All our health and all our wealth and all our happiness is inside. That's the great treasure that, in truth, is ours.

If you have difficulty in finding that great treasure of life, then you may be rest assured you have some denial. And it is that denial that is your destiny that's keeping you from finding your true wealth. Everything you could possibly desire you already have. Because your physical senses do not yet experience it, simply reveals that you have not yet truly accepted it.

We understand in this Living Light Philosophy that acceptance is the will of God. It is the divine will. For there is nothing in all of the universes that is denied by the intelligent Energy. When we permit our minds to deny, we rise as a judge, superior to the God that sustains us. And it is those denials in our consciousness that keep us from experiencing the health, wealth, and happiness that already exists within us.

So I assure you, my friends, if you are having those experiences and your life is not complete and fulfilled, pause each day for a few moments, look honestly within, permit your judgments and denials to rise up in your consciousness that you may work with them through the great power of forgiveness. For to forgive is to give forth and that that you give forth is then in the hands of a great and higher law.

There is no reason for anyone to be without their share of the goodness of life. And the goodness of life is everywhere present. I sincerely hope that it may be in keeping with your soul's evolution to make that daily effort to accept the possibility of something greater. For if you will truly do that and you will flood your consciousness daily with that demonstrable truth, you will soon in life experience that something greater, that something better than you already have.

Thank you.

JUNE 4, 1978

Church Lecture 79
The Power of Acceptance

In keeping with the basic teachings of this philosophy—"The Power of Acceptance"—we understand that the will of God, the divine will, is total acceptance, for we look about life and we see that there is an intelligent Energy that is sustaining and supporting all forms of life. Therefore, that demonstration is indeed the revelation that God, or the divine will, is a total acceptance. We also understand that divine love is a total consideration— that nothing to God, the Divine, is left out. And so it follows that we put God into all of our endeavors or experiences and by that I mean we put into our consciousness a total acceptance and a total consideration.

Our struggles in life are not the effects of what we accept in life. Our struggles in life are the effects of what we reject. For each thing that we deny the right of expression to, we establish the law that rises supreme over the divine, intelligent Energy, called God. And from that error of ignorance, we experience the struggles of life.

Now many philosophies have taught throughout the ages that this God, this intelligent Energy, takes care of the lilies of the field and the insects that crawl the ground. And our life and experiences reveal that this is indeed demonstrably true. And so it is a simple process of reeducating our mind to accept the right of all expression that we may move through our experiences with the divine will and, in so doing, be freed from the trials and tribulations and struggles created by our minds that reject and deny the many experiences of life.

When we raise our levels of consciousness to a realm of reason and common sense, we free our self from this illusion that we are the experience. We are experiencing many things in our life, but we never are those experiences unless we permit our minds to delude us into the false belief that we are the experience. We are no more the experience than we are the physical body through which we are presently expressing. The experience contains within it the lessons that are necessary for the evolution and the freedom of our eternal being. But we cannot see those lessons that are there for us if we do not accept the right of the experience to express. Therefore, man in his daily activities becomes a house divided, establishing laws and rejecting the effects of the laws he establishes. But a house divided cannot long endure.

And so as time marches on, as man continues to evolve, he slowly, but surely, begins to accept and move in the divine flow and experience the divine freedom. For it is a perfect balance between divine will and divine love that brings to man what is known as divine peace, that which passeth—for it is beyond—all understanding. This great peace, the effect of the balance of total acceptance and total consideration, is something that we are all striving for. It is not something that we attain in some future heaven, but it is something that is attainable in this the moment of our choice.

The greatest blessing that man has ever had or will ever have is what is known as the divine right of choice. But when man chooses by dictating within his consciousness that other or opposing experiences have no right to existence, then he is going against the will, the divine will of God. That is when man pays the price of struggle. That is when man pays the price of suffering. For we cannot consider the whole without accepting the whole. And in everything there is God. There is good in everything, for that good or God is the intelligent Energy that is sustaining it.

Now if we pause and take the time to accept all of the experience, then we will be in a position in consciousness to consider all of the experience. But so often in our daily lives we only look at a very small fraction of our experiences. We look at the ones that control us, the ones that we judge—that portion of the experience that we judge is controlling us—in the sense that it is an obstruction to what we judge and decide we wish to accomplish. We do that because that that disturbs us is what controls us. And so we look at the experience, what we judge is the disturbing part of the experience, and are controlled by it. We cannot see the whole. We cannot see the good or God that is in it and because we cannot see it, we cannot make the necessary changes with it.

Man, having the divine, eternal birthright of choice, has the choice to do what he wishes to do in his life. That choice is not the choice to deny the right of everything that he judges he doesn't want, to deny the right to everything else its own existence in life. That, my friends, is man's true problem and struggle, because he denies the will of God. He not only denies the will of God, but he denies the love of God. When you do not consider in total, then you are not in the divine love of God. When you do not accept in total the right of all things, you are not in the divine will of God. And that which goes against the Infinite, the Infallible is destined to fall. It is the experiences that we have within our self of the falling that we call the struggles of life.

There is indeed a better path. There is the path of harmonious evolution. Change is inevitable. We cannot deny it. We cannot stop it. We cannot reject it. Whether we like it or not, all things in form—be they thoughts or humans—are in a process, the forms, of changing. Our thoughts, their forms, are constantly changing. By a total acceptance of that divine right, we move harmonious in evolution. We no longer, so to speak, beat our heads against the wall. We no longer constantly direct the impartial, intelligent, infinite Energy to the obstructions of life.

We all know, I am sure, that whatever in life we place our attention upon, we have a tendency to become, for we establish that Law of Attachment. And it is that Law of Attachment that blinds us into the false belief that that is us, the real person.

When we totally accept and totally consider all of these experiences, they come and they go, but we, the eternal being, ride upon that ship of destiny to the harbor of peace and harmony, for that is the ship of reason. Man cannot experience what is known as reason until man has total consideration and total acceptance in his life. It is when we move in the realms of judgment, rejection, and denial that we experience all the traumas and the storms of life.

In these coming days we celebrate the freedom of a country, but more important than the freedom of a country is the freedom of the people who compose the country, those who live within it and are affected by it. We have a great responsibility in our life to stand upon the rock of principle, to accept the right of all and not, in that acceptance, sell out our own right. There is enough room in God's infinite universes for the right of all things to live and express.

There is only the great error of our mind; when it rises to control, we experience fear. For man cannot possibly experience fear until man has made his judgments of denial. It is when man rises superior to the Infinite and establishes the mental laws of judgment that man fears, for then man now lives in the blindness of a restricted mental realm. That is not the way the Infinite Intelligence has designed life for all of its children. It has been designed in order that we may live and enjoy life and experience the fullness and the goodness that is our birthright.

We have spent untold centuries in evolution before coming to this Earth planet. Our responsibility in life is indeed very great, for we are, by the right of our evolution, the examples to all of life. We cannot take those responsibilities lightly, for each harmonious thought that we have in our mind sends a healing balm out into the universe and has a direct effect upon all of nature, from the blade of grass to the human being. And not only does it go out across the earth realm, but out into outer space affecting untold multitudes of intelligent beings.

So when you find yourself limited, restricted, in what is known as self-thought, remember that your world is shrinking and someday it will shrink, by that law of self-thought, to the point where you will give it up. And when you reach that so-called bottom, you will begin the path of rising again to broaden not only your horizons, but the goodness of your life.

Whatever it is that you have or have not, remember, your thought concerning it is sustained and supported by the same intelligent Energy that will bring you something better. But that can only happen when you open the door of opportunity, and the door of opportunity is opened by your own choice, by your own acceptance. For each denial that you set into consciousness closes the doors of opportunity that are waiting to open. It is our dictates that send us on our destiny, through the path of denial.

Whatever you want or whatever you are experiencing that you don't want, remember, you have choice. You can change it. You may change it not by rejection and denial, that will only keep it in your universe, year after year and century after century. You can change it by first accepting its right of existence and, in so accepting, accept the right of something better and something greater. And I can assure you, my friends, if you will do that, if you will do that each and every day, that infinite, intelligent Energy called God will support your new choice. And you will indeed experience the goodness, the success, the abundance of a joyous life.

Thank you.

JULY 2, 1978

Church Lecture 80
Survival, The Miracle of Life

In speaking on the subject of "Survival, The Miracle of Life," we all, of course, personally relate to that topic. In the many experiences that we encounter in this earth realm, we always and shall forever survive them. There are still some people in the earth realm here with us who are under the illusion and the false belief that to leave this earth realm is to finish or to end any and all experiences and to end life, because life itself and all of nature is a living demonstration that the minds of men can change many things, but they cannot change the very principle of life itself. We cannot, in and of ourselves, begin life and that that we cannot begin, we certainly do not end.

When we leave this earth realm, in this seeming miracle of survival, we take with us all our thoughts, all our emotions, and all our attitudes, all of our feelings and all of our experiences. Whether or not we continue to live with those experiences—the ones we enjoy and the ones we do not—is ever dependent upon the control that we have gained of our own mind.

As freedom is an effect—not a cause—of the control of the distractions of the human mind, so it is ever dependent upon man himself in his choice and in his efforts whether or not he will enjoy the peace and the harmony, the abundance and the good that life has to offer. For if he does not enjoy it this moment, then he's not going to enjoy it the next moment unless a change within the consciousness takes place. Because we have, by our own divine evolution, earned or merited what is called free choice, we alone set our destiny into motion.

No one and nothing can change our life but our self. But because we do have that choice, we can do that at any moment that we so choose. But we must first learn to accept that we are, in truth, the masters of our ship, that we are, in truth, the captains of our destiny. Once we have accepted that, we start upon the path of freeing our self. For in the experiences that we encounter in life, the ones we like and the ones we don't like, we personally relate to the responsibility of them. Whenever we permit our mind to dictate the illusion that the cause of anything is outside of our own thought and our own mind, then we cannot have the peace, the abundant goodness that life, in truth, is offering to all creation.

So it comes down to the same teaching that has been given to this earth realm for untold centuries: again and again the spirit tells us—and has through all philosophies—for man to know himself. Are we, the question must be asked by ourselves, are we making that effort on a day-to-day basis? Are we truly making the honest effort to know our self? Because we cannot change what we do not know; therefore, we must begin with the effort to know our self: to know why we feel rejected, to know why we are not healthy, wealthy, and wise. For there is always a reason, and that reason exists within us.

Why should we suffer through life when life was not designed to be suffered through? It is not our purpose, in coming to earth, to struggle and to suffer. The struggling and the suffering is an error in our thinking. And when we correct that error, the suffering and the struggle will no longer be existent for us.

Many, many people have tried and have taken away their physical life by self-infliction, called suicide, but that's all they have removed—is a physical body. They have not removed the cause. They have not removed the thoughts in their mental body. For the mental body is composed of mental substance and they cannot destroy it.

So we must look at this beautiful, seeming miracle of life. No matter what we do and no matter what we don't do, we will continue on in the stream of consciousness, called life eternal, for that's what life truly is.

If, in your thinking, you say to yourselves, "Well, I do not recall any experience prior to earth,"—How much of experience do you recall when you were two or five years old? But those experiences, they exist. They exist within consciousness—in your consciousness, in my consciousness. To become aware of them, we must first free our self from the limited thinking of identifying with this limited earth experience. We must first accept the possibility of a broader horizon. It is in the acceptance of anything that the law is established to experience it. So remember, when we accept the right of everything, we move in consciousness to a divine realm of neutrality. For infinite, divine Intelligence, or God, accepts the right of everything. And therefore, everything exists. It is when we accept the right of anything that we become freed from the control of it.

For example, if we have, in our thinking, disturbances, and we permit our minds to dictate that we are not happy because of a job, because of a wife or a husband or a person, then we establish the law through which the thoughts, acts, and activities of that person control our life, because we, in our thinking, have established the delusion, for us, that this or that job or person or thing is the true cause of our experiences in life. Those delusions, indeed, are plentiful in the errors of our ignorance. Indeed, they are the true and only cause of our problems and our struggles in life. For when we permit that type of thinking, we deny the right of expression of one of God's children. And in that denial is the Law of Bondage, for us, established. We lose our peace of mind. We lose our joy and happiness. Those are the things that we must sacrifice—a few of the things—for rising with such authority to deny the right of Infinite Intelligence to express in any way that it so chooses.

However, if we look at those around and about us, at those people with whom we are personally involved and related, and we ask our self the question, "This experience I am finding not to my benefit. The cause, I know, is deep within my own consciousness. It is, in truth, a judgment that I have made in my life. The judgment may have served me well, when I was six or seven." We must first find, within our memory par excellence, when the judgment was made and why it was made. Then we will realize, beyond a shadow of any doubt, that that judgment, in truth, did not serve us well and certainly is not serving a good purpose for us today.

For all feelings of suffering, for all feelings of rejection, all feelings of limitation, all feelings of lack, all discordant thoughts and feelings are the children of denial because we have denied, in our own mind, the right to the abundant good of life. We have denied the right of abundant good for us through an error in our thought by believing that we may attain the fullness of life in keeping with rigid, set judgments that we have accepted in our life.

To God, or the Divine Intelligence which exists within, around, and about us, all things are possible. Man's only limit or struggle is what his mind dictates. There is enough for everyone. If we believe there is not enough for everyone, then that very belief is a denial of the abundant goodness of God. And we must pay the price of our judgments; we must pay the price of our denials. It is in the payment that we suffer. But we must all pay, and we all are paying. There is no credit in the evolutionary process of life. Each step along the way we are paying for, but we can, in making these payments, make them in a harmonious way by accepting—perhaps, for many, for the first time in their earth experience—by accepting the very cornerstone upon which this religion is founded: the cornerstone of personal responsibility; that each and every soul has the ability to respond to all of the laws that it establishes.

For man, we our self are a law unto ourselves. Let us use those laws in our life; let us use them wisely, for they were intended by divine design to be guidelines along the way that we may know beyond a shadow of any doubt that our heaven exists within us, that we do not need to wait for who knows how long for Gabriel to blow his trumpet. The only trumpet you will ever hear is the sound of the echoes of your own unfulfilled desires.

This philosophy very clearly states never suppress desire, for to do so, leaves it unfulfilled and, like a plague, it grows within your consciousness. Educate it or fulfill it. How does man educate his desire? We have stated many times: by casting the light of common sense upon it, the light of reason that has total consideration. Stop and think. In the course of one day, untold thousands of desires speak within your mind. Some of them you are consciously aware of; most of them, you are not because there are so many that are calling and demanding energy, attention from you. That's known as the experience of time pressure: there's not enough time for this and there's not enough time for that because this great hailstorm of unfulfilled desires keeps raining upon our peace and our harmony.

No one person in any universe can do everything. But we can do some things. And the some things that we choose to do, let us do them well or not at all. For to do that that we choose to do and to do it well is a demonstration and a revelation of consideration. When you have total consideration, then you have the love of God flowing in any of your endeavors.

Let us reassess our lives today. Let us choose wisely our priorities. And then, I can assure you, we will find time and energy for all of the things that are truly worthwhile to bring us this goodness of life. But, friends, we all know what it is like to blame another for our frailties and for our unwillingness to make the changes we know we must make.

It is such a waste of effort. It is such a waste of time and energy. It is truly such a waste of life to blame another person because we feel miserable. To blame another person because our unfulfilled desires are not being fulfilled, it's certainly a long ways from growing up emotionally. Let us pause when the thoughts of blame enter our minds. And let us put the light of common sense upon it and then sincerely make the effort to bring about the changes within our own thoughts that will grant us, in life, what we are truly seeking.

To those many souls who yet remain in those astral realms, who, having faced disturbing experiences here on the earth realm, they live with the many forms created by their mind. Because those forms were not harmonious or pleasant, they are discordant and disfigured. But they are only the effects of their own disturbing thoughts. You see, there's no escape from our self. So let's first learn to know our self. We can't escape from our self, but we can change any part of our self that we are not happy with. That that is inevitable a wise man faces fully in the here and now. He doesn't wait until he leaves this physical body and then sees, in astral mental substance, the distorted forms of his distorted thoughts. When we bring unity to our mind, we bring success to our life. And we are here in evolution to succeed. It has taken many, many centuries for our soul, which is our true being, to evolve and come to this earth realm.

There is an insatiable part that keeps speaking to us to move ever onward. We know, we know deep within our self that all of the goodness in life we are entitled to. And when we do not experience that goodness of life, we become frustrated; we become a house divided, for we know what our divine right is. We know it deep within. And because we do not often experience the fullness of that divine right, the frustration, the discord, and disturbance takes control of our life.

But I assure you, the cause of the discord, the lack of not experiencing the fullness of life is only thoughts, created by our mind, that are not in harmony with each other. And so, the war within continues on. And then slowly, but surely, usually, our health begins to go. We begin to experience not only in the mental world discord, but the physical body, chemically, begins to war against itself. Each thought of harmony and peace and goodness that flows through your mental body affects the chemistry of your physical body.

This philosophy clearly reveals that each and every part of your human body is directly related to an attitude of mind existing on a level of consciousness. Many students have experienced the demonstration and have been freed from an untold number of so-called diseases. Because when you find the cause, the cure is ever evident.

So, my friends, in survival, the miracle of life, in spite of our discordant thoughts, in spite of our errors of ignorance, we do survive. We not only survive here, but we survive *here*after. And why do you think they call it *hereafter* and not *somewhere-else-after*? Because it's not somewhere-else-after, a million miles in the sky, called heaven. We go only from this physical body to whatever body we have completed that our soul can express through. And usually that's a mental body and it's quite well completed. How harmonious it is, is dependent, of course, upon our self. So when we leave here, we're still here, whether we like it or not. And we are still *here*after, until we decide we've had enough of this realm and we start to make the decisions within our own mind to get out of it. You can't just say, "I want to go someplace else." Because when you do that, all of the obstructions that keep you where you are, they rise up. And those obstructions, they have to be worked with. Because you are the fathers and mothers of them, only you—the fathers and mothers—can send them back into the seeming nothingness from which they have risen.

Make your heaven here and now. Then you will not have to be concerned about those astral realms and those mental realms. You will not have to be concerned about the summerlands of life; you will not have to be concerned about Gabriel or meeting some great divinity when you leave this earth realm, for you will have, through your efforts, risen in your consciousness and, experiencing this great peace that passeth all understanding, you will have entered through the gates of heaven here and now.

But remember, my friends, before the gates of heaven, stand all the hissing hounds of hell. For before any victory in life, be it in the material or spiritual realms, the dues you have incurred, they must be paid. But they are never—never is the cross, *never* is it heavier than the so-called crown, for they are, in truth, one and the same thing.

Life, of course, is dependent upon our view. And our view, of course, is dependent upon our attitude. It is our attitudes that change our life. It's such a simple thing, in truth, to do. We can choose to be miserable and say it's too hot or we can choose to say how beautiful it is and experience that cool breeze passing in the atmosphere. Now how does man experience a cool breeze that his mind says doesn't exist? He experiences it because his mind says it doesn't exist, his mind can say it does exist. Stop and think, my friends, that's how you take control of your life. It doesn't exist because it's what your mind says. It does exist if *you* permit your mind to cause it to exist.

It is much easier to get support of the negative than it is the positive. And why is it easier? And why do people support the negative? The complaints and the gripes and the matrimonial struggles. Why do people so easily relate to the discord in life? Because it takes a little effort to make some change. They're already in the negative in some area, so they relate very quickly to the struggles of life and how miserable everything is. Because to do otherwise, they would have to make the effort and make some change.

Well, my good friends, we are here today and we are gone tomorrow. And we never know what moment that tomorrow is going to be. Some people—some of my students have said that some, they carry minimum insurance in this church, in this association. And I learned it—that word—from some of my students. And I felt it quite interesting. Because we look at religions, and we have to ask our self the question, "Am I involved in that religion because through it, as an instrument, I may meet people who are trying to make changes and better themselves. And I myself need a little bit of moral support in making efforts to make these changes?" Or do we involve our self in religions of this world because of the possibility, of the slightest possibility "they may know something about where I'm going. And I would like to know a little something just in case it's not too pleasant a place." Well, we have got to think about that a little bit.

I assure you, you don't have to worry about the place you're going being pleasant or the opposite if you make the effort *now* to make your life pleasant. And you can make your life pleasant by stop denying the right of God and taking the power and giving it to another human being. Each time you permit a human being to disturb your peace and goodness of life, you have denied your God, and, in so doing, you shall pay the price. And we do it all the time. We blame outside rather than face inside. And it is the insistence of the uneducated ego to blame outside for what is going on inside that denies them the great abundant goodness of life.

Thank you.

AUGUST 6, 1978

Church Lecture 81

New Attitudes and New Experiences

In speaking with you today on, "New Attitudes and New Experiences," in accepting the demonstrable Law of Personal Responsibility, then we can understand that we always in life get what we really want. When we hear that truth, our mind rises up to contradict it and to deny it because we have yet to spend the time in honest self-analysis and thought that we may awaken to that demonstrable truth that our desires are in a constant process of change. The desires of yesteryear, many of them, are no longer the desires of today. We establish these laws in life, as man is a law unto himself, so whatever that we permit our minds to entertain, we establish the law and must follow it until we make the changes within our self.

So when we say that we always get what we really want in life, as we look at our lives we see that indeed is very true.

It does not mean that we already have what we've wanted for so long, but we are in the very process of attaining it. It is the necessary things, for us in life that we have set into motion that we must grow through, for having so many desires, they are not all harmonious with each other. And so a wise man early learns in his life to choose wisely his goal. For everything that is necessary for us to attain the things that we choose and desire, we already have. We have been given, by the very laws of our own evolution, all of the things we could possibly desire. But we must remember that life and all of its experiences is dependent upon our attitude of mind.

What is it that causes us to think that some people in life we like and some we do not? When the truth is that everyone in life, we love. This seeming contradiction in our mind is ever dependent upon our attitude of the moment. And so we find our self in our communication with people; one moment we think we like them, and the next moment we think we do not like them, when in truth we love them all the time. For each of us loves our self. Now if that was not true, we would not be expressing on this planet the way that we are. For without love, which is the intelligent Divine Energy, known by man as God, nothing would exist, nor would there be any experiences to encounter.

It is when people that we view from a different attitude are not harmonious with our expectations and with our judgments concerning how they should think and act—that is when we make the judgment within our self that we do not like that person anymore.

That is not where the change shall take place. The change, my friends, takes place in our own mind. Everything that we experience in life is going on within our self. Because we have yet to fully accept the Law of Personal Responsibility, we are deluded by the belief that the experience is taking place outside. Nothing, my friends, takes place outside. Everything for us takes place within us. These heavens and these hells are the effects of our own attitude of mind. They do not change by some magic wand or a spontaneous change of thought. They are dependent upon our own effort. If we do not find here, on this earth that offers us all of the opportunity that is necessary for us to reach these heavenly states of consciousness, then we will not find those heavenly states of consciousness hereafter.

The word *hereafter* is such an important word because so few people truly understand what it means. To most of us *hereafter* means some dimension somewhere out in space, not related to the earth, mundane world. But *hereafter* means exactly what it says: *here*, after we leave a physical body. For the mind, composed of mental substance, is not subject to the physical laws of this the Earth planet. And so that that is important to us and that that we find filling our minds each day with is what exists in our mental body. And that is the body that we express through when we leave this physical body. It does not change because of the transition from this physical world. It remains the same the moment after that it was the moment before. So let us in this life find the peace and the heaven, the happiness, the abundance, and the goodness that is waiting for us to experience. We have this so-called magic key in our hands this moment. It is dependent if we are willing to turn that key in the door of reason.

We can change our attitude in this moment by changing our thought, by becoming aware of that that controls us, the attitudes and patterns of mind of yesterday, by first becoming aware that we are, through our own errors of ignorance, we are the victims of those patterns of mind. By first becoming aware, we start on the first step to control them through a daily effort of disciplining our own mind. When we awaken in the morning, when we become consciously aware of this mundane, earthly world, we have a choice. We have that golden opportunity to choose which direction we will take for the day. We can choose to make it the most important day of our life. We can choose to be objective and not become emotionally involved in the various acts and activities and attitudes of others or we can swim in that tide of duality and contradiction, in that tide of discord. But we alone make that choice when we awaken. Let us awaken not only in the morning of our daily life, let us awaken in each and every moment of our life.

To keep faith with reason is an absolute, demonstrable guarantee of the transfiguration of our life in this, the eternal moment. This, my good friends, *is* your eternity. The moment of which you are consciously aware *is* your eternal life. Yesterday has passed and tomorrow is yet to be. Grasp hold of the power of the universe in this moment of which you are consciously aware.

For wherever you go and whatever you do, you will always be at home with you. So unless you make the effort to be a good friend to yourself, then you cannot experience a friendly world or friendly experiences in life.

When we accept our divine birthright, which is the right of choice, and we use that right wisely for our own good, then we become the living demonstration and qualified to share that good with another. But if you are not good to yourself, you cannot be good to another. And we understand, of course, here, that good and goodness is God and godliness. So whatever you expect from another, let you first expect it from yourself, because, in so doing, like attracts like and becomes the Law of Attachment. So whatever you are seeking, seek it inside first and you will not have to concern yourself with why you don't have it because of someone else. That is the great delusion, my friends. We judge how we're going to get where we want to get and each of those judgments, we must follow. God, the Infinite Intelligence, did not establish those mental judgments. Man established those mental laws. God impartially sustains them.

Whatever your thought, it is sustained by the power that sustains all life. You have the right of choice. God does not interfere. The Infinite Intelligence is a neutral, eternal, intelligent Energy. Whatever you choose to do with it, you, by your very birth, were granted that right. You and you alone will pay the price. You will enjoy or not enjoy the fruits of your harvest. But I assure you whatever has already passed has passed. If you accept it as necessary steps in your evolution, which, in truth, it really is, then your change for the better moment of now, guaranteeing your better tomorrows, is within your grasp this instant.

There is no law that says you must suffer. There is no law of the universe that dictates you must do without the goodness of life. It is man's mental law that man is following. Here, in this the Living Light Philosophy we strive to accept a greater God, not one created by the minds of men. For anything created by the minds of men is limited by the minds of men. Let us, in this moment, expand our consciousness and accept our right to all the goodness that is here for us. We cannot experience it, my friends, until we accept it.

What happens when your minds think of the possibility of accepting something greater? In the same moment of that thought rises the thought of judgment and all of the experiences of yesterday—how it's to come about. When we question how and when we question why, we must then listen to the voice of the human mind. We must hear the echoes of our own uneducated ego with all of the dictates of the limited experiences not only of our present earth life, but of all of those lives of evolution throughout the untold centuries.

This is the moment in which we can make the change that will affect for the greater good of our life everything that lies ahead. When we take control of our mind, when we are at perfect peace in the dual tides of creation, when we accept that this too shall pass—for all things that are created, all things that are formed have birth; all things that are form have death. And so our thoughts have form and so they are born and they die. If they are born graciously and harmoniously, then they will die the same way. But if they are born in pain and struggle, then their death is guaranteed the same way. If you accept all experience in life with an attitude of mind that "It has come to me in keeping with laws I have set into motion and by laws I am continuing to set into motion shall it pass from me."—hold not to form, my friends, for form shall pass. It is our attachment, our mental attachment to the forms of creation that is our true suffering.

Whatever it is that you have, remember, it has come to you to serve a purpose. If it is not serving a good purpose in your life, then it is time that you let it go. If you hold on to it, then you suffer with its passing, for the Law of Change is the demonstrable Law of Evolution. And it is through repetition that change is made possible. Look at your life's experiences and you will see the repetition of certain attitudes of mind. You will see the repetition of certain experiences. But in that repetition the change is being made possible for you. For sooner or later, when we have the repeated experiences that we find not to be pleasant or beneficial to us, sooner or later we get weary of them. And whenever we get weary of anything—be it a thought or anything else—we begin to make the change for it to go. So when we've had enough of what we don't like, we will begin to accept what we do like, no matter what it takes.

Thank you.

SEPTEMBER 3, 1978

Special Memorial Service

For Bernie Pratz, Member and Friend of Serenity

A memorial service at the Serenity Church is a very special occasion, for to us there is only one life, and that life does not have a beginning and, therefore, does not have an ending. That is the life of the eternal spirit of which we, in truth, are. Bernie Pratz is a student and a member of this church, for Bernie Pratz, who has taken his flight to a higher level of consciousness known as heaven, is still a person.

It is not something that has been or used to be. When we understand that there is one consciousness, one infinite and divine Intelligence, of which we are, in truth, an inseparable part, when we look at life as life truly is, we know that if we lose an arm or a leg that we still are, that we still exist, for we still have a mind. We also know that this mind substance is not composed of the physical elements of our Earth planet. And so it is, we all face this eternal doorway called death, but we must realize in consciousness that so-called death, in truth, is birth, for when our soul entered this earthly realm, we died to another awareness and we were born to this awareness. And so it is that the cycle ever completes itself, for that that comes from a thing, by the very law of coming from it, is destined, in time, to return to it.

In this philosophy we know beyond a shadow of any doubt that those who have left this physical world are aware, awake, alert, that they are conscious, not asleep, that they are, in truth, aware of our every thought, our every act, our every deed, for they are aware ever in keeping with the Law of Rapport that we have established with them. And so it is, if you take a journey and you go to Europe or to the Orient, what peace or joy can there be for you if your family and your friends, whom you have left temporarily behind, they mourn in sadness and emotion for you? You could not very well enjoy your trip, your journey.

And so that is the way, in truth, that it really is. There are many who have gone before us. There are many who will go after we have left this earthly realm. So let us, in our efforts, remove the fear, which is only an error of ignorance in our mind, the fear and the superstition concerning life eternal. We are this moment consciously aware, hopefully, of where we are sitting and what is transpiring. We are aware, ever in keeping with the Law of Attention, for the Law of Attention declares that that which you place the attention upon, you, in truth, become. So if we place our attention upon the dark side of life, we place our attention upon the struggles of life, then we are never going to find the way.

We have a very simple affirmation in Serenity. It was brought forth for the children of our philosophy class, for all the small ones and the big ones, and the affirmation is something that had a very deep meaning, and still does, to Bernie Pratz. That affirmation is, "Thank you, God, I am at peace." For that's the only place that peace comes from. Peace does not come from the thought of man, for the thought of man is an expression, and that that is expressed, by the Law of Expression, is dual in its very nature of expression. And so we understand that peace and peace alone is the power.

And so it is that the effort was made in study and application of the simple demonstrable laws of life. There is a difference between a law that is demonstrable and a law that is the theory, or facts, of men's minds, for a law that is demonstrable is a personal revelation unto our self. That means that it is possible for us, personally, as individuals, to demonstrate for our self the eternal truth, that our soul has entered here, this earth realm, to enjoy what this realm has to offer. If we do not enjoy what earth has to offer us, then we and we alone, from a lack of understanding, are transgressing the demonstrable, divine natural laws of life itself.

There is, indeed, and has been, much misunderstanding in the world concerning the philosophy of Spiritualism. The misunderstanding is from the lack of sincere investigation. I can assure you when I first met Bernie—and many of you present are his friends—when I first met him, he was not, and is not, the type of an individual that is credulous, to accept anything without a thorough investigation and a proof unto himself, for that, as his wife well knows, is his very nature. And so it is that he made the effort and he spent the time to investigate what the philosophy was all about. For he did not take and does not take something on someone else's word, for if he was that type of a person, then he could not possibly have had the work that he had to do while on this earth realm.

We understand, for it is demonstrable, that emotion emanates from our very aura, from our being, a magnetic impulse; that this magnetic impulse attracts unto us whatever it is we direct it to. And so it is in so-called death, that we make great effort not to direct the emotions of sadness to those who have gone to higher levels of consciousness, for in so doing, like a rope pulling upon a person's neck, we pull them—we make great effort through our ignorance to pull them—back to an earth realm of consciousness. The ancient primitive religions of the world and many of the Eastern philosophies know that great truth. Therefore, there is always a rejoicing and a celebration when a soul leaves this earthly flesh.

Let us look at the human body as we look at our automobile. The automobile has been designed by man to do what man chooses to have it do for him. It's not the other way around. I don't know of any person of common sense that would have in their possession an automobile that dictated where we were going to go when it decided to do so. No, we have designed the automobile as a vehicle of transport, to be instrumental in helping us to express ourselves and fulfill our desires. Now that's what the human body is like. It is a vehicle designed by the infinite laws of nature to transport our eternal soul on this earth realm, that our eternal soul may express itself and fulfill many of the desires of our own mind. And so would we, in truth, grieve for an automobile when it no longer serves its purpose of harmonious and peaceful transport here on the earth realm? No one, no one would keep that type of car—not, surely, by conscious choice.

And so it is that Bernie Pratz was ready, willing, and able to go into his new vehicle, which is a level of consciousness, and leave the old clay behind here to return to the elements from which it was composed. Many people, over these thirty-five years of serving the spirit, have asked me what is the best thing that they can do to help someone that they love so dearly who has passed into another dimension. The best possible thing I know that any soul could ever do, in simple kindness, for anyone who has gone to the other world is to be happy, to do the things they know they should, and to enjoy doing those things while they are doing them. For to grieve for those who have been freed from the earthly clay is, in truth, the epitome of selfishness and the denial of God's divine right to take the soul, ever in keeping with the Divine's own laws.

I know I will not view, in my lifetime on earth, the abolishment of pagan ceremonies and funerals, but I also know that there is slowly, but surely, an awakening within the consciousness of mankind. What is it, in truth, that causes this great fear when we face this journey that we all, this moment, are facing? For it is not within the power of our conscious mind to decide when we will leave the earthly realm. That is not within the power of our conscious mind. So, in truth, we are each moment and each second facing what we call death. The question must arise within our consciousness, "Are we prepared for the inevitable, or are we, from an error of ignorance called fear, procrastinating?" Because if we are, then for us, I can assure you, it will be much more difficult when it comes.

What is the true cause of this fear? Where is the error of this ignorance? We look at a physical world and we have many physical things. And when we are faced with leaving those physical things and people, then fear arises in our mind. But, you see, the truth of it all is we do take it with us. The world is brainwashed to facts, and the facts look at the physical things and people we are attached to, and they see others who have passed on, and we say we don't take it with us. But the truth of the matter is we do take it with us. We take with us our mind, and everything that exists outside is an effect of what our mind is entertaining inside. All of life is a reflection, a mirror of what we, and we alone, entertain in thought.

Heaven is not a place that we are going to. It is a state of consciousness that we are growing to in this the eternal moment. So when we find that heaven, that peace that passeth all understanding in the here and the now, then when we leave the physical world, that is what we enter.

And I am so very grateful to know beyond a shadow of any doubt that Bernie Pratz, within three hours of leaving this physical world, entered what we know in our understanding as the Halls of Repose. He spoke to my mother in that dimension, who has been over there for sometime, and he had one request: that he may somehow get a message back to this earth realm what his journey was all about. He was prepared about the mind and how the mind works—that when we go through this so-called transition, that there are many thoughts that rise from the depths of our own subconscious, that there are many distractions to our mind as this transition process is taking place, but if we will keep our eye upon the light—for a light appears before us as our time nears. Untold millions of souls have seen it. They call the light an angel. It doesn't matter what you call it, it is a light to light your path. And if you keep your eye single upon the eternal light, you will arrive at your final destination. If you do not keep your eye upon that light that appears in your consciousness, then you will be distracted and pulled into realms which, in truth, are the effects of our own subconscious mind.

The day will soon dawn here on earth when the actual processes of transition will be detailed for all to study and to apply.

And so, my mother put into a few words Bernie's experiences when he left earth:

With the Light of God to guide me
I passed through the portal of death
Freed from the fear of dying
My mind at last came to rest.
As angels of love stood beside me
Their songs of joy in my heart
Peace, the heaven I longed for
Was mine at last, never to part.

Thank you.

APRIL 4, 1976

Special Discourse 1
Soul to Soul

Good evening, students.

In response to your soul's request, we have come to, once again, share with you our understanding on "Soul to Soul," why man has need. The human mind, as a vehicle through which the pure divine, infinite, intelligent Energy is expressing, is designed by the Great Architect to identify in order that it may be an instrument of creating, as it is, in truth, an inseparable part—the human mind—of creation. Because man, in the use of this vehicle known as mind, has overidentified beyond the balance of reason, man has and does continue to entertain thoughts of need. As the needs of man's mind continue to expand, man's eternal soul sinks ever deeper into self. This identification process of the human mind, designed to be an instrument of constructive good, has become, because of man's imbalance and lack of reason—this instrument has become—his own destruction. As man continues to entertain thoughts of self, man's needs continue to increase.

In communing soul to soul, man must first become aware and then free from this identification process. He must make the effort to be free from the bondage of his own mind. In communicating with others of his own species or with those souls in vehicles of other species, man, speaking to others, receives from others their needs and therefore, there is a total lack of understanding, for man speaks from a level of consciousness of his needs. And as the law is clearly stated—that like attracts like and becomes the Law of Attachment—as man speaks from the levels of his needs, he receives from the levels of others' needs. And the soul waits to be served.

We must be honest with ourselves for only in being honest with ourselves can we free our true being from this enslavement of the dual, mental law. In this honesty with our own motives and this awareness of our needs, we slowly, but surely, begin to let go and to surrender these self-related thoughts which we have, in truth, overidentified with. The soul, ever-striving to rise in the consciousness of man, becomes again and again the victim of the deception of the mind as the mind strives to fulfill the desires that it has attached itself to. In time these desires and these thoughts of needs become so momentous and such a great mountain before us that we finally begin to let go. As that process begins to take place, this faith and belief that we have had for so very long, this faith that has been directed to the mind and has become dependent upon the mind to fulfill its many needs, this faith begins to move into other levels of consciousness and that light slowly, but surely, begins to dawn.

When we begin to accept that we have no need, when we accept that all of the good is waiting to flow through us, we will no longer hold, for there will no longer be the thought of need. In that dawning in consciousness, we begin to rise to the heaven that waits in the moment of the now. We know for we have accepted the divine will that never faileth. We must make great effort—great effort each moment—to accept the divine right of all expression, for to deny the Divine's right of expression is to deny that goodness that waits to flow through our consciousness.

So many words flow in the universe and they flow in a stream of consciousness of divine will, total acceptance, of divine love, total consideration. The soul faculties begin to open like an unfolding rose as you make that moment-by-moment effort to identify with the stream of life itself. Then these thoughts of need will begin to leave your universe and you will begin to enter the consciousness of the whole. Each moment that you entertain a thought of self, a thousand thoughts of need rise in your consciousness, for you have identified with separatism. You have, in that moment, removed yourself from the stream of life, and because you have done that, you experience need.

My good students, because it is the very nature of the vehicle known as mind to identify, identify with the wholeness that is your true being. And when you identify with that wholeness, which is possible for all souls through the soul faculties of expression, want, need, and desire shall melt in that stream of consciousness, for you will return home on your little ship, and returning home is this moment. Go home, my good friends; the path has been clearly revealed to you. Permit yourself to flow through the soul faculties of consciousness, move in the gentle breezes of divine will with the clear and beautiful horizon of divine love, for then you will know the true purpose of life; you will no longer be concerned with the many things you think you need, for there will no longer be need. Man cannot need what he already has, and you already have truth and freedom. Joy and happiness, love and plenty you already have. It is only a matter of remembering each moment what you already are.

Lift the veil of delusion that the thoughts of need has dropped before your vision. Lift it in this eternal moment and go home to the whole of which you are, in truth, an inseparable part. For you have seen a world—and many worlds—for so many, very many centuries, and it has revealed unto you again and again your happiness is not in what you are garnering, your happiness is in what you are giving. And the greatest gift is the gift of the Divine. It's known as total consideration and it's called divine love. No greater gift can be given to the world than the gift of God. And you, my children, are instruments through which that great gift—the greatest of all gifts—can be given to the world.

You also know the law that you cannot grant to another what you are not granting unto yourself. And until such time as you grant the fullness of divine love to yourself—total consideration of all of you—then you cannot grant that to another, and instead, you become the obstructions to the greatest gift that is given to the world, the gift of divine love. And what is it that stops this gift from being given? It is the thoughts of self; it is the thoughts of need. And each moment that you entertain a thought of need, the obstruction of self becomes greater.

Consideration, my students, takes such little effort—consideration of your eternal being, consideration of principle. Value that precious gift more than all your seeming possessions and as you give the greatest gift of all gifts, you will receive so much, and yet more.

Become aware, more aware of what you are doing. Think of the many souls striving to rise through the obstructions of over-identification with self. Think of eternities, think of the many centuries it has already taken to bring you here this moment. Think of the many steps you've had to climb. This is not the time to fall back, for like the ball of snow, it goes quickly down the mountainside.

Reconsider, my students, your values in eternal life. You have earned a great responsibility. You have not earned that in one short earth life. You have earned a responsibility to the Eternal Light. You have received much in these latter incarnations and, yea, even more is waiting for you to demonstrate the Law of Application.

Do not be discouraged as you stumble on your mountain climb, but never forget you could, you can, and you will try a little bit more to surrender these thoughts of need, to surrender these thoughts of self that have bound you for so many centuries.

The time in your evolution is now; it is not tomorrow. Much good has been accomplished, but the job is far from completed. When you no longer have things to do, then you will know you've slipped to the bottom once again. When you think you're weary and when you think you've done so much, you have slipped back into the depths of self. There will always be the strength, the energy, and all that is necessary to do the work for God that you have to do.

And as you work without ceasing to serve that eternal Life, you will be healed of the things that are obstructions in your way, for you have all of the universes working with you to serve the Divine. Therefore, you are a part in consciousness, in truth, of that wholeness and that Divine Light ever rises ever higher as you become the instruments of the fullness of eternal Life.

And though your feet stumble many times in the darkness—and the darkness, you know, is only the thoughts of self—forget the self and find the Light, for in forgetting the self, you will find your true being.

It is such a foolhardy thing to believe that you are the experiences of yesterday. My dear students, you are not the experiences you have. You are greater than experiences. You are greater than the things you think you need. You are greater than the suit you wear this day. You are greater than all the forms of creation. You are that part of pure divine Light that is the true Life itself. Become aware of that truth. Become aware as you make the little effort to total consideration. Total consideration and then, total acceptance will follow and grant you the understanding that will permit you to be the instruments of giving the wisdom that heals the soul.

Good night.

AUGUST 1, 1976

APPENDIX

The Divine Healing Prayer

I accept that the Divine Healing Power
Is removing all obstructions
From my mind and body
And is restoring me
To perfect health, wealth, and happiness.
My heart is filled with gratitude
For the Divine Law of Acceptance
That is healing both present and absent ones
Who are in need of help.
Peace, the power that healeth,
Is guiding my thoughts, acts, and deeds
As God and I go hand in hand
Living a life of joyful abundance.

The Total Consideration Affirmation

I am the manifestation of Divine Intelligence. Formless and free. Whole and complete. Peace, Poise, and Power are my birthright.

The Law of Harmony is my thought and guarantees Unity in all my acts and activities, expressing perfect Rhythm and limitless flow throughout my entire being.

Without beginning or ending, eternity is my true awareness and sees the tides of creation, as a captain sees his ship.

As the Light of Truth is sustained by the faculty of Reason, I pause to think and claim my Divine right.

    Right Thought. Right Action. Total Consideration.

        Amen. Amen. Amen.

Divine Abundance

Thank
(Gratitude)

You
(Principle)

God
(Divine Intelligence)

I'm
(Individualizing)

Moving
(Rhythm)

In
(Unity)

Your
(Realization)

Divine
(Total)

Flow
(Consideration)

[The poem below is referred to by Mr. Goodwin in Church Lecture 32 and was transcribed from *The Serenity Sentinel* of May 1974.]

It Isn't the Church—It's You

If you want to have the kind of a church
   Like the kind of a church you like,
You needn't slip your clothes in a grip
   And start on a long, long hike.
You'll only find what you left behind,
   For there's nothing really new.
It's a knock at yourself when you knock your church;
   It isn't the church—it's you.
It's really strange sometimes, don't you know,
   That things go as well as they do,
When we think of the little—the very small mite—
   We add to the work of the few.
We sit, and stand round, and complain of what's done,
   And do very little but fuss.
Are we bearing our share of the burdens to bear?
   It isn't the church—it's *us*.
So, if you want to have the kind of a church
   Like the kind of a church you like,
Put off your guile, and put on your best smile,
   And hike, my brother, just hike,
To the work in hand that has to be done—
   The work of saving a few.
It isn't the church that is wrong, my boy;
   It isn't the church—it's *you*.

www.ingramcontent.com/pod-product-compliance
Lightning Source LLC
Chambersburg PA
CBHW020635300426
44112CB00007B/121